American Language Hub

LEVEL 3
Student's Book

JEREMY DAY
GARETH REES

macmillan education

Contents

Welcome

GRAMMAR

Verb tenses and structures

A **Choose the correct verb forms to complete the conversation.**

A: Excuse me. I [1]*look* / *'m looking* for room 14. I have an English class today, but I [2]*don't know* / *'m not knowing* where to go.

B: Room 14? It's right here. It looks like we're [3]*being* / *going to be* in the same group. My name's Diego, by the way.

A: Hi, Diego. I'm Yulia. So [4]*did* / *have* you studied at this school before?

B: Yes. I [5]*was* / *'ve been* in the same group last year. The teacher, Helena, is really nice. [6]*You* / *You'll* like her, I'm sure. So … why [7]*did you decide* / *were you deciding* to join this school, Yulia?

A: Well, about two weeks ago, I [8]*'ve tried* / *was trying* to help my son with his English homework, but I couldn't remember anything! So I decided to come back to school, after all these years!

B **Find and correct the mistakes in the sentences or questions.The first one has been completed as an example.**

1 How ~~many~~ *much* time do you spend doing homework every day?

2 It's an online course, so all the answers are check by a computer.

3 Everybody make mistakes when they speak English – even English speakers!

4 It's important to learn a lot of new words, but I don't really enjoy to study vocabulary.

C **SPEAK** **Work in pairs and discuss the questions.**

1 Why did you decide to join this class? Use the ideas from the conversation in Exercise A to help you.

2 What is the best way to learn English? Use the ideas in Exercise B to help you.

VOCABULARY

Describing places, illnesses and transportation

A **Complete the table with the words in the box.**

attractive bus ~~cold~~ ~~dirty~~ headache helicopter modern noisy ~~plane~~ temperature toothache trolley

Describing places	Illnesses	Transportation
dirty	a *cold*	a *plane*
	a	a
	a	a
	a	a

Collocations

B **Choose the correct words to complete the collocations.**

1 Is it better if somebody helps you *by* / *for* / *to* / *with* your homework, or should you always work alone?

2 When was the last time you *did* / *made* / *took* / *went* a day off from school or work?

3 Are you good *at* / *in* / *from* / *on* cooking?

4 Is it better to *borrow* / *earn* / *lend* / *pay* money from your friends or from the bank?

5 Is it possible to *have* / *stay* / *make* / *play* in shape without spending a lot of time or money?

6 Do you prefer to pay *by* / *on* / *for* / *with* your shopping by card or in cash?

7 What is the best way to *fall* / *get* / *meet* / *win* a good job in your country?

C **SPEAK** **Work in pairs. Ask and answer the questions in Exercise B. Ask your partner to explain his/her answers.**

A: I think it's better to do your homework with someone.

B: Really? Why do you think so?

PRONUNCIATION

0.1 **Listen and choose the words you hear.**

1 *where* / *were*
2 *can* / *can't*
3 *work* / *walk*
4 *mouth* / *mouse*
5 *have* / *of*
6 *this* / *these*
7 *cap* / *cup*

FUNCTIONAL LANGUAGE

Match the sentences (1–9) with the responses (a–i).

1 My name's Adam, by the way.
2 What a nice surprise. Long time, no see!
3 What do you think I should do?
4 Would you like me to check it for you?
5 Are you doing anything this evening?
6 Do you feel like watching a movie this weekend?
7 I feel really sick today … and I have an exam later.
8 In my opinion, young people these days are incredibly rude.
9 It was really nice to see you again.

a Why don't you try to find a new job?
b Sounds great. I'll just check that I'm free.
c You, too. See you later. Take care.
d Nice to meet you.
e Some are, but then some adults are, too.
f No. Why? Should we go out?
g Oh, no! Poor you! That sounds terrible.
h Yeah, I know! What are you doing these days?
i Yes, please. That would be really helpful.

1 COMMUNICATION

Wise men speak because they have something to say; fools because they have to say something.

Plato

A young woman enjoys her walk outdoors.

OBJECTIVES

- update your status on social media
- make a short podcast
- plan and conduct an interview
- use rhetorical questions in a presentation
- ask for, offer and respond to help
- write a report about trends

Work with a partner. Discuss the questions.

1 How does 21st century technology make it easier or harder to communicate with other people?

2 Read the quote. To what extent do you agree with Plato?

3 Which forms of communication do you use most often: face-to-face or electronic; written or spoken communication? Which do you prefer and why?

1.1 Communication today

- Update your status on social media
- Make a short podcast

G simple present and present progressive **V** seeing and hearing **P** schwa /ə/ **S** listening to check predictions

READING

A SPEAK Work in groups and discuss the questions.

1. Do you ever use social media sites? Which ones?
2. What sort of information do people usually post on social media?

B PREDICT Match the pictures (1–3) with the social media status updates (a–c). How do you think the people in the pictures are feeling? What can you guess about their lives?

a. On my way to the top! Looking forward to an amazing view!
b. Can't believe we're on vacation again! We're having a wonderful time!
c. Our beautiful new kitchen! Looks good, doesn't it?

C READ FOR GIST Read the social media posts quickly to check your predictions from Exercise B. Write about the true stories behind the pictures.

D READ FOR DETAIL Read again and answer the questions.

1. How do Katia and Elisa know each other?
2. Why was Katia confused?
3. When did Katia go to the top of the mountain?
4. How does Katia feel about her new kitchen?
5. How does Katia feel about her 'boring' life?
6. Why doesn't Elisa post pictures when she isn't on vacation?

My ***perfect*** *online life*

@Katia … is feeling confused
6 hours ago

Had a very strange experience today. I met my old school friend **@Elisa** for the first time in eight years. 'You're so lucky!' she said. 'You have such a perfect life! I'm so jealous!'

A perfect life? Me? I have a very normal life: I get up early every day, take the bus to work, watch TV … and that's all. In fact, Elisa seems to have a perfect life: her pictures always show her wonderful family relaxing in the sunshine on a beautiful beach.

But now that I'm writing this post, I think I understand what happened: on social media, our lives look perfect, but the reality is very different.

For example, last week I posted a selfie from the top of a mountain. In the picture, you can see I'm smiling. But in fact, I felt absolutely exhausted and just wanted to go home as quickly as possible! But you can't see that in the picture!

And did you see the picture of our new kitchen a few weeks ago? Well, yes, it's beautiful, but I didn't mention that it took six months to finish. Six months without a kitchen! And it cost us twice as much as we expected, so now we're getting worried about money. But no one ever talks about money problems on social media, do they?

I'm not complaining, though. I'm very happy with my life! I love being normal … and I don't mind that my life is becoming a little boring! In fact, I'm thinking of staying at home this evening – just me, my husband and a takeout pizza! Perfect!

Reply from **@Elisa**
4 hours ago

Hey, **@Katia**! Great to see you this morning. I know what you mean about our 'perfect lives'. I guess I need to explain about all those beach pictures. You see, I work really hard all year, and the only time I use social media is when I'm on vacation. That's why I'm sitting on the beach in all my pictures! It usually rains for most of the week we're on vacation, but of course we only take pictures when the sun's shining!

Glossary

jealous (adj) unhappy because someone has something that you would like or can do something that you would like to do

E SPEAK Work in pairs and discuss the questions.

1 Does your life look perfect on social media? What about your friends' lives?

2 Do you ever feel jealous when you see other people's status updates?

GRAMMAR

Simple present and present progressive

A Look at the underlined verbs in the social media posts. Which verbs are in the simple present? Which are in the present progressive?

B WORK IT OUT Match the sentences (a–f) with the rules (2–5).

a In the picture, you can see I'm smiling.

b I know what you mean about our 'perfect lives'.

c But now I'm writing this post, …

d You have such a perfect life!

e I get up early every day.

f So now we're getting worried about money.

Simple present and present progressive

1 Dynamic verbs (*talk*, *go*) usually describe actions.

2 We use the simple present with dynamic verbs to talk about actions that always, usually or never happen.

3 We use the present progressive with dynamic verbs:

  a to talk about actions that are in progress at the moment of speaking or writing.

  b to describe actions in a picture, video, etc.

  c to describe trends (e.g. something is happening more and more these days).

4 Stative verbs (*want*, *seem*) frequently describe feelings and ideas. We use the simple present with stative verbs.

5 A few verbs (*have*, *look*, *speak*, *think*) have two or more meanings. They are sometimes dynamic verbs and sometimes stative verbs.

C Find at least one more example of each rule (2–5) in the posts.

D Go to the **Grammar Hub** on **page 122**.

E Are the verbs stative verbs (S) or dynamic verbs (D)?

1 contain	S	7 include	____
2 cost	____	8 mean	____
3 depend	____	9 own	____
4 deserve	____	10 relax	____
5 enjoy	____	11 seem	____
6 happen	____	12 shine	____

F SPEAK Work in groups and discuss the questions.

1 Why are you studying English? Why do you need English?

2 How is this week different from your normal weekly routine? What are you doing differently this week? What do you normally do?

3 What are people doing more and more these days? What are some trends in your own life?

SPEAKING

A Work in groups. If you have some pictures on your phone, choose two or three to discuss with your group. If you do not, think about some of your favorite pictures of you and your friends or family.

B Tell your group:

- What's happening in the pictures?
- Does your life seem perfect or exciting in the pictures? What's the real story behind the pictures?
- Do you have any pictures of you doing normal things, e.g. watching TV? Why/Why not?

C Write a short social media status update for one or two of your pictures. Decide whether to make your life seem perfect or normal.

Writing a status

We frequently leave out the subject and *be* from the beginning of status updates when it's easy for the reader to guess the missing words.

- *(It) Looks good, doesn't it?*
- *(I) Had a very strange experience today.*
- *(It was) Great to see you this morning.*

D Read some of your classmates' social media status updates. Do their lives look perfect or normal?

LISTENING

A SPEAK Work in pairs and discuss the questions.

1 What do you use your cell phone for?
2 How did people do those things before they had cell phones? What problems did they have?

B PREDICT Work in pairs. You are going to listen to *A week without phones!* Look at the pictures and discuss the questions. Use the strategies in the box to help you.

> **Listening to check predictions**
>
> Before you listen to something in English, it's always a good idea to predict what you will hear.
>
> If there's a title and pictures, you can try to predict the connection between them. Then you can listen to check your predictions.

1 Who are the people in picture a? What are they doing?
2 What is the device in picture b?
3 What does the title mean? What's the connection with the people and the device?

1.1 **C LISTEN FOR GIST** Listen to Part 1 of the podcast and check your answers to Exercise B.

1.2 **D PREDICT** Work in pairs and discuss the questions. Then listen to Part 2 and check your answers.

1 What went wrong when Olivia and Jackson tried to meet up on Monday?
2 How did they solve the problem?

1.3 **E PREDICT** Work in pairs and discuss what you think Olivia and Jackson did differently on Tuesday when they met. Then listen to Part 3 and check your answer.

1.4 **F PREDICT** Work in pairs and discuss the questions. Then listen to Part 4 and check your answers.

1 Do you think Olivia and Jackson are enjoying the experiment?
2 What do you think they're doing more or less of than usual?

1.5 **G LISTEN FOR DETAIL** Listen again. Choose the correct answers, a, b or c.

1 When is the last day of the experiment?
   a Tuesday
   b Thursday
   c Sunday
2 Why does Olivia decide to stop waiting outside on Monday?
   a She doesn't want to get wet.
   b She thinks Jackson isn't coming.
   c She knows the university closes at four o'clock.
3 How does Sebastian know Jackson and Olivia?
   a They study together at the university.
   b Olivia met Sebastian outside the bakery.
   c Sebastian has seen them before in pictures and videos.
4 Why is Olivia enjoying the concert more than usual on Tuesday?
   a She isn't recording it on her phone.
   b The audience isn't having as much fun.
   c Jackson isn't there with her.
5 On Thursday, why is Olivia surprised at the end of the podcast?
   a The university buildings are amazing.
   b Jackson doesn't usually talk so much.
   c She can't believe Jackson forgot his camera.

H SPEAK Work in groups and discuss the questions.

1 What problems did Olivia and Jackson have during the experiment?
2 What good things happened as a result?
3 Do you think Olivia and Jackson's experiment was a good idea?
4 Would you like to try a similar experiment? Why/Why not?

VOCABULARY
Seeing and hearing

1.6 **A** Choose the correct verbs to complete the sentences from *A week without phones!* Then listen again and check your answers.

1. In this week's podcast, we're *looking at* / *seeing* / *watching* phones.
2. It *looks* / *sees* / *watches* like he isn't coming, and I'm not sure what to do.
3. I'm *looking* / *seeing* / *watching* for Olivia, but I can't *look at* / *see* / *watch* her.
4. I *hear* / *listen to* / *sound* your podcast every week, and I *look at* / *see* / *watch* all your videos.
5. Yeah, that *hears* / *listens* / *sounds* like a great idea. Thanks a lot.
6. Maybe you can *hear* / *listen to* / *sound* the music in the background.
7. He plays the guitar in the band, and he *hears* / *listens* / *sounds* really good.
8. It doesn't *look* / *see* / *watch* great, but it's good for telling the time!

B **WORK IT OUT** Complete the rules with the correct form of *hear*, *listen*, *look*, *see*, *sound* or *watch*.

hear, listen, look, see, sound and watch

1. When you ______see______ or ____________ something, it just happens, not because you're trying to do it.
2. When you ____________ *at* or ____________ *to* something, you do it because you decide to do it.
3. When you ____________ something, you look at it for a period of time, perhaps because it's moving.
4. When something ____________ good or ____________ good, it probably is good, but you aren't sure.
5. When it ____________ like or ____________ like something is happening, it probably is happening, but you aren't sure.

C Go to the **Vocabulary Hub** on **page 142**.

D Complete the questions with the verbs in the box. There are two extra verbs.

notice observe recognize spot stare

1. Do you ever sit in a café and ____________ the people through the window? Why do people enjoy doing this?
2. Are you good at remembering people's faces? Do you always ____________ people when you meet them the second time?
3. When you're traveling around (e.g. by bus), do you usually ____________ the buildings around you?

E **SPEAK** Work in groups. Ask and answer the questions in Exercise D.

PRONUNCIATION
Schwa /ə/

Schwa /ə/

Schwa is the most common sound in English. We use it for most unstressed vowel sounds, especially in words like *a*, *the*, *of*, *to*, *and* and *but*.

1.7 **A** Listen to the sentences from *A week without phones!* Underline all schwas. The numbers in parentheses tell you how many schwas to find. The first one has been done for you.

1. We're not looking at our phones for a whole week! (3)
2. We arranged to meet here, outside the university, at four o'clock. (5)
3. It's Monday afternoon and I'm late meeting Olivia. (3)
4. I'll buy you a cupcake to say thank you, and you can tell us what you think of our podcasts. (7)
5. Yes, I'm wearing a watch today – an old one from when I was a teenager. (7)

B **SPEAK** Work in pairs. Practice saying the sentences. Listen and check your partner's pronunciation.

SPEAKING HUB

A Work in groups. You are going to make a short podcast about an experiment. Choose one of the ideas in the box or use your own ideas.

a week of doing something completely new every day
a week speaking only English
a week without complaining
a week without the internet/TV, etc.
a week without spending any money
a week of helping as many people as possible

B **PLAN** Plan a short podcast (about two minutes). Imagine you are in the middle of your experiment. Write notes on:

- what you can see and hear during your podcast.
- what's going well and/or badly with your experiment.
- what you're doing more or less as a result of your experiment.

C **SPEAK** Record your podcast and present it to the class.

D **SHARE** After listening to the podcasts, discuss the questions.

- Which group's experiment worked well?
- Which podcast did you enjoy most?

E **REFLECT** Work in new groups and discuss the questions.

- Will you try any of the experiments in real life? Why/Why not?
- Would you like to make a real podcast? What would your podcast be about?

Update your status on social media
Make a short podcast

1.2 Who owns English?

- Plan and conduct an interview
- Use rhetorical questions in a presentation

G – subject and object questions P – pronouncing questions V – languages S – rhetorical questions

TOP 10 ENGLISH SPEAKING COUNTRIES

1. US 251,388,301
95.81% of population

2. India 125,226,449
11.38% of population

3. Philippines 89,800,000
92.58% of population

4. Nigeria 79,000,000
53.34% of population

5. UK 59,600,000
97.74% of population

6. Germany 46,272,000
56% of population

7. Canada 25,246,220
85.18% of population

8. France 23,000,000
36% of population

9. Australia 17,357,800
97.03% of population

10. Italy 17,000,000
29% of population

*The most amazing fact is that **only 11.38% of India's population** speaks English and yet it is the second largest English speaking nation in the world.*

USVisaTalk.com

LISTENING

A SPEAK Work in groups and discuss the questions.

1 Look at the infographic. What does it show? What do you know about the countries and the languages that people in those countries speak? Are you surprised by any of the numbers?

2 Who owns English? Who has the power to decide what's good and bad English?

1.8 **B LISTEN FOR MAIN IDEA** Listen to an interview about different types of English and answer the questions.

1 Why does Mona want to interview Juan?

2 Why did Juan enjoy his journey?

3 Where did Juan have problems with English?

4 How is Multicultural London English (MLE) different from the English we learn at school?

5 What's the connection between 'Standard English' and 'standard class' on a train?

6 Why is Standard English useful?

1.8 **C LISTEN FOR DETAIL** Listen again. Which person (Juan, Mona or Both) thinks …

1 traveling is a good way to practice your English? ________

2 it's difficult to understand people in England? ________

3 MLE grammar contains mistakes? ________

4 Standard English is boring but useful? ________

5 it's sometimes better when you don't sound like a native speaker? ________

D SPEAK Work in groups. Look at the sentences from the interview. For each one, discuss what Juan and Mona were talking about. Do you agree with their opinions?

1 'Millions of people speak like that, so how can it be wrong?'

2 'There are hundreds of other forms of English all over the world … They're all different, but I think that's really cool!'

3 'Surely Standard English is better, isn't it?'

4 'We don't need to speak like native speakers. In fact … it's usually better when we don't speak like native speakers.'

GRAMMAR

Subject and object questions

A Put the words in the correct order to make questions. Then listen to the interview again and check your answers.

1.9

1 you / I / a / questions / ask / can / few / ?

____

2 countries / did / which / visit / you / ?

____

3 England / happened / what / in / ?

____

4 changing / English / is / how / ?

____

5 MLE / uses / who / ?

____

6 mean / do / 'Standard English' / by / you / what / ?

____

7 to / you / need / non-standard English / saying / are / learn / we / so / ?

____

B WORK IT OUT Match the questions (1–7) in Exercise A with the rules (a–c).

Subject and object questions

a When we make questions in English, we usually put the auxiliary verb (*be*, *have*, *can*) before the subject. 1, ___, ___

b In sentences with no auxiliary verb, we add *do*, *does*, or *did* when we make a question. ___, ___

c When the question is about the subject, we use the same word order as in sentences. We don't add *do*, *does* or *did*. ___, ___

C PRACTICE Make questions about the missing information.

1 (Somebody) writes a blog for a website.
Who *writes a blog for a website*?

2 Juan visited (a number of countries).
How many _______________?

3 You (can/can't) give me an example.
_______________?

4 (A form of English) is becoming popular in London.
Which _______________?

5 (A number of people) speak non-standard English.
How many _______________?

6 Most native speakers (speak/don't speak) Standard English.
_______________?

D Go to the **Grammar Hub** on **page 122**.

E SPEAK Work in pairs. Student A – go to the **Communication Hub** on **page 149**. Student B – go to the **Communication Hub** on **page 150**.

PRONUNCIATION

Pronouncing questions

A Listen to two people asking questions from the interview. What differences do you notice in the way they speak? Who is easier to understand?

1.10

1 *Why do you want to talk to me?*

2 *What do you want to talk about?*

a Which speaker joined the words together?

b Which speaker is easier to understand?

B SPEAK Work in pairs. Read the information in the box. Then practice saying the questions. First, try to say them by joining the words together. Then try to say them as clearly as possible.

- What do you think?
- Where did you go?
- Do you want to talk about it?
- Why did you say that?

Pronouncing questions

Many English speakers join words together when they speak quickly. In questions with *do/did* + *you*, it can be difficult to hear whether the speaker is saying *do* or *did*.

- *What do you want to do?* /wɒʤə wɒnə duː/
- *How did you travel?* /haʊʤə trævəl/

C SPEAK Work in pairs. Listen to two people asking the questions in Exercise B. Which version is better for you to use, the first or the second speaker? Why? Tell your partner.

1.11

SPEAKING

A Work in pairs. You are going to interview another student about their experiences of using English and communicating with English speakers. Write five questions. Use the prompts to help you. You can also use your own ideas.

- frequently communicate / English speakers?
- using English in the classroom / in real life?
- for work / while traveling?
- problems: speaking/understanding?
- Standard/non-standard English?
- advice for others?

B Work in new pairs. Use your questions to interview your partner. Listen carefully and ask follow-up questions.

Follow-up questions

Really? Why?
What happened? What went wrong?
Can you give me an example?

C Work in groups and discuss the questions.

1 What was the most interesting thing you learned from your interview?

2 What advice can you give to other people about using English in real life?

READING

A SPEAK Work in pairs and discuss the questions.

1 Look at the title of the magazine article. What do you think it means?

2 Think of some examples where you can lose something if you stop using it. Have you ever lost a skill or an ability because you didn't use it?

B READ FOR GIST Read *Use it or lose it?* quickly and answer the questions.

1 Is the writer generally positive or negative about learning languages?

2 What's the connection between the pictures, the word cloud and language learning?

Use it *or* lose it?

1 What's the worst thing about learning a language? Is it the hundreds of hours you need to spend studying and practicing? No, although that's bad enough. In fact, the worst thing is how easy it is to forget everything!

2 How do I know? From bitter experience! Many years ago, I lived in Spain for a year and studied Spanish for hours every day. By the end of that year, I spoke Spanish fluently (but not very accurately). But now, 20 years later, it's all gone. My only evidence that I ever spoke Spanish is an old certificate.

3 So is there any hope for me and my Spanish? Recent research suggests that there is. Imagine your brain is like a big library. As you keep adding new information to that library, the old information doesn't disappear; it just gets harder to find.

4 How does this work in practice? When I see a dog, my English-speaking brain thinks of the word *dog*. But when I lived in Spain, my brain had two words to choose from, *dog* and *perro* (and yes, that's *dog* in Spanish!). My brain learned to block the wrong word: it blocked *dog* when I was speaking Spanish and *perro* when I was speaking English. Over time, my brain got very good at blocking words.

5 And what happened when I left Spain? The word *perro* stayed blocked. And, like a door that's been closed for years is harder to open, it became harder to unblock the word! Now, 20 years later, all those Spanish words are still in my brain. But they're blocked behind heavy old doors.

6 How can I open those doors? Two things: I need to make an effort to push the doors open again; and I need to keep the doors open by practicing regularly.

7 Is there anything good to say about this 'blocking' process? In fact, there's lots of evidence that it makes your brain work better. For example, look at the words in the box. As quickly as possible, say what color they're written in. Try it now. Did you notice how hard it was to say the color when the word itself was a color? That's because 'bad information' (the word on the page) blocked the 'good information' (the color of the word).

8 What's the connection with language learning? It turns out that bilingual people are much better at activities like this than monolingual people, because their brains are trained to block 'bad information' quickly and accurately. And in the modern world, where we have to deal with too much information all the time, the ability to block 'bad information' is the key to success.

9 What's the best thing about learning a language? Is it the ability to communicate with different people around the world? No, although that's amazing enough. In fact, the best thing is that it makes our brains more powerful.

C SCAN Read again. How many rhetorical questions are there? Use the information in the box to help you.

Rhetorical questions

A rhetorical question is a question that you ask when you don't expect other people to answer it. You usually answer the question yourself. It's a useful way of presenting information because it makes the reader or listener think about the answer.

When you read a rhetorical question at the beginning of a paragraph, always pause to predict the answer first. Then read the rest of the paragraph to check.

D Work in pairs. Look at the rhetorical questions at the start of each paragraph. Discuss the answers. Then read the paragraph again to check.

E SPEAK Work in pairs and discuss the questions.

What does the writer mean by 'we have to deal with too much information all the time'? Can you think of any examples from your own life?

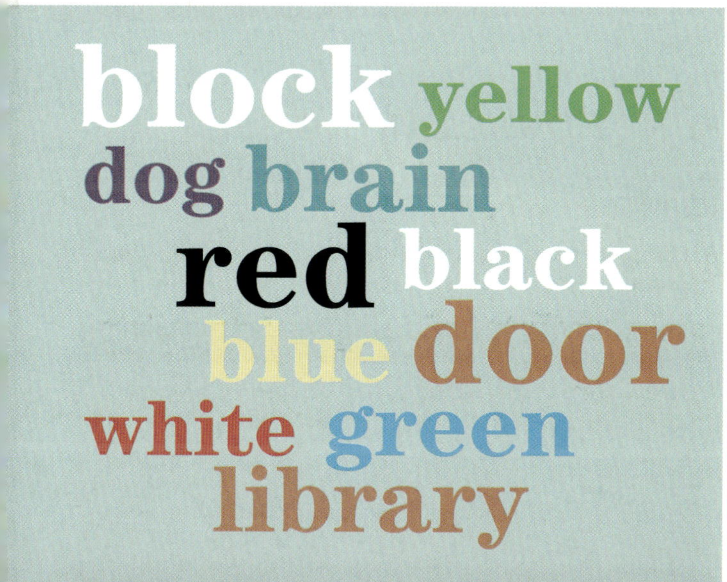

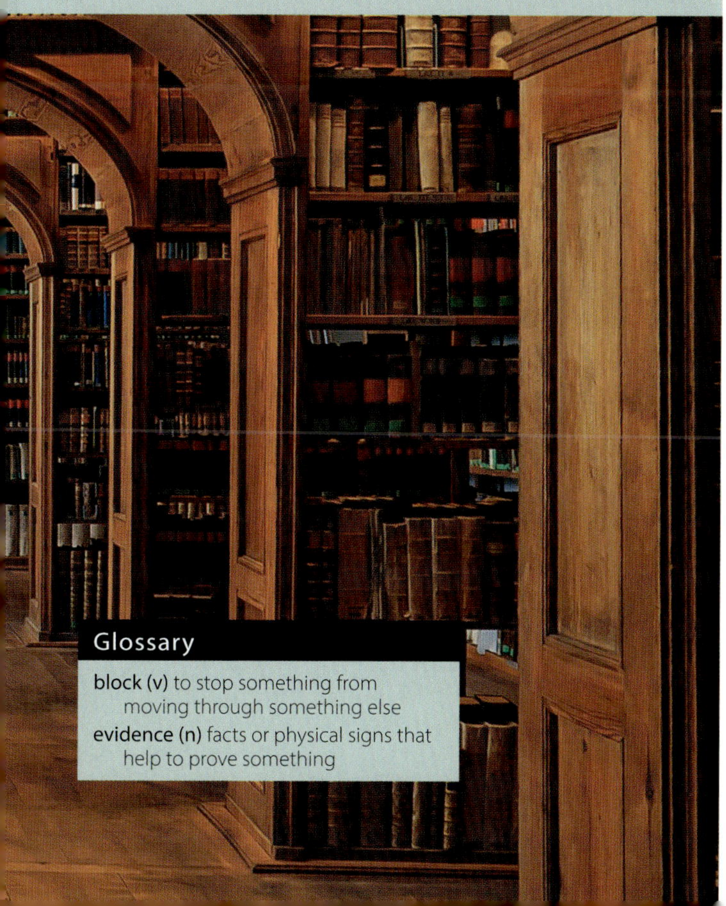

Glossary

block (v) to stop something from moving through something else

evidence (n) facts or physical signs that help to prove something

VOCABULARY
Languages

A WORK IT OUT Look at the sentences from the interview between Mona and Juan and from *Use it or lose it?* Then use the correct form of the underlined words to complete the definitions (1–5).

They used really strange words and phrases – lots of idioms that I've never heard before.

Plus, the people had very strong accents, so I couldn't understand very much at all!

By the end of that year, I spoke Spanish fluently (but not very accurately).

It turns out that bilingual people are much better at activities like this than monolingual people.

1 If you're ________, you only speak one language; if you're ________, you speak two languages.

2 A(n) ________ is a group of two or more words that go together as a unit (e.g. heavy old doors).

3 Your ________ is the way you pronounce words. It sometimes shows which part of a country you are from.

4 A(n) ________ has its own meaning (e.g. 'Use it or lose it'). It's usually hard to figure out the meaning just by looking at the words.

5 If you speak ________, you don't pause to think in the middle of sentences. If you speak ________, you don't make mistakes.

B Go to the **Vocabulary Hub** on **page 142**.

SPEAKING HUB

A Work in groups. You are going to give a short presentation about learning and using languages. Choose a topic from the list or use your own ideas. You can talk about English, your own language or both.

- accents
- standard and non-standard varieties
- advice on fluency and accuracy
- advice on how to practice
- how the language is changing
- why it's good to be bilingual

B PLAN Write three or four rhetorical questions about your topic. Then plan how you can answer those questions in a presentation. Write notes but do not write the answers down.

C PRESENT Give your presentation to the class. While you are listening to the other presentations, listen carefully and be ready to ask questions.

D REFLECT Work in groups and discuss the questions.

1 What did you learn from the presentations? What surprised you?

2 Will you use rhetorical questions again in your presentations or writing?

Plan and conduct an interview

Use rhetorical questions in a presentation

Café Hub

1.3 Welcome back

F – ask for, offer and respond to help **P** – intonation and stress

COMPREHENSION

A Watch the video. Complete the sentences with the names in the box.

Gaby Milly Neena Sam Zac

1 ________ owns a café.
2 ________ runs a vintage clothing shop.
3 ________ is Sam's best friend.
4 ________ lives with Gaby and Zac.
5 ________ is meeting Milly's mum tomorrow.
6 ________ agrees to lend Zac some clothes.
7 ________ falls over and hurts her arm.

B Work in pairs and discuss the questions.

1 Why is Gaby taking pictures?
2 Why does Sam say 'Oh no Zac, I'm so sorry …'?
3 Why does Zac need to borrow some clothes?
4 Why is Sam surprised when Zac asks for pants?
5 Why is Gaby worried about tomorrow?

C Imagine you wanted to borrow the items in the box. Who would you ask and why? Tell your partner.

$10 $500 a belt a book a ladder a scarf a suitcase or backpack some shoes or boots

Glossary

flat **(n) (British)** = apartment **(n) (American)**
mum **(n) (British)** = mom **(n) (American)**
trousers **(n) (British)** = pants **(n) (American)**

FUNCTIONAL LANGUAGE

Asking for, offering and responding to help

A Complete the phrases with the correct form of *give*, *help* or *need*.

Asking for help

Could you [1] ________ me out?
Would you mind [2] ________ me a hand?
Do you think you could [3] ________ me out?
I [4] ________ a favor. Can you lend me some clothes?
Please? ☐

Offering to help

I can [5] ________ you a hand with that. ☐
I'd be happy to [6] ________ you with that.
Can I [7] ________ you with that?
Shall I bring some stuff round to the flat later? ☐
Do you [8] ________ a hand? ☐
Do you need any [9] ________?

Responding to help

Thank you so much, that would be great. ☐
That would be awesome. ☐
If you wouldn't mind.
I can manage. I'm OK. ☐
It's OK – I can do it myself.
Listen, let me [10] ________ you. ☐

B 01:01–03:40 Watch the last part of the video. Mark the eight phrases you hear in the order in which you hear them.

MILLY

SAM

NEENA

ZAC

GABY

USEFUL PHRASES

A Match the useful phrases (1–6) with the phrases which show the meaning (a–f).

1 I'm really busy at the moment.
2 I don't know how to say this.
3 Good luck with that!
4 You're a legend!
5 I owe you one.
6 There you go.

a That isn't going to be easy.
b You are amazing!
c I must return the favor.
d I can't talk to you at the moment.
e I've finished.
f This is difficult for me to talk about.

B How do you say these useful phrases in your language?

PRONUNCIATION

Intonation and stress

1.12 **A** Listen and repeat the two questions in the table. Complete the headings with *falls* or *rises*.

1 Asking for help: intonation ____________.	2 Offering help: intonation ____________.
Can you lend me some clothes?	Can I help you with that?

1.13 **B** Listen, repeat and write down each question in the correct column. Practice the stress and intonation.

SPEAKING

A Work in pairs. You are going to write and perform a conversation where you ask a friend for help. Think about the following things:

- What sort of help do you need?
- Why do you need help?
- When do you need help?
- Who do you ask?

B PRESENT Write and practice your conversation. Then perform it for the rest of the class.

Ask for, offer and respond to help

➤ Turn to page 156 to learn how to write a report about trends.

GRAMMAR

A Complete the social media update with the simple present or present progressive form of the verbs in parentheses.

I'm in Moscow! As you can see in the picture,
I [1] *'m having* ________ (*have*)
coffee with some of my new friends.
I [2] ________ (*study*)
here on a two-week intensive language course.
I [3] ________ (*really enjoy*)
it so far.
I [4] ________ (*not speak*)
very much Russian at all, so it was
really difficult on the first day, but now it
[5] ________ (*get*)
easier every day, and my teachers are excellent.
Why Russian? Well, first, I
[6] ________ (*think*)
it's a beautiful language, and second,
I [7] ________ (*consider*)
studying at the university here next year.

B Read part of a report about social media trends. Then write questions about the underlined information in the report. Use the prompts to help you.

These days, more and more people [1]<u>are choosing to stop using social media completely</u>. I asked [2]<u>twelve people</u> about the way they use social media. [3]<u>Three people</u> said they never use social media, and [4]<u>two</u> are using it less and less. One student, Franek, believes social media is dangerous [5]<u>because it makes us feel jealous of other people's 'perfect' lives</u>. Another student, [6]<u>Lin</u>, thinks social media is useful for his work, but he never uses it with his real friends. He says his friends can speak to him face-to-face to find out his news!

1 What / more and more people / do / these days?
What are more and more people doing these days?

2 How many people / the writer / ask / about the way they use social media?
____

3 How many people / say / they never use social media?
____

4 How many people / use / social media less and less?
____

5 Why / Franek / believe / social media is dangerous?
____

6 Who / think / social media is useful for work?
____

VOCABULARY

A Complete the sentences with the correct form of the verbs in the box.

hear listen look see sound watch

1 **A:** 'I think we should go soon.'
B: 'Yes, that ________ like a good idea.'

2 I prefer normal phone calls to video calls – it's better when the other person can ________ you, but they can't ________ you!

3 Excuse me. I ________ for my dog. I can't find him anywhere. Have you seen him?

4 I usually ________ to podcasts while I'm traveling to work.

5 Can I call you back later? I ________ a TV show and I don't want to miss the end.

B Choose the correct words to complete the conversation.

A: Oh, this is nice, just sitting outside a café and relaxing. I think it's really interesting to [1]***observe* / *recognize* / *stare*** all the people on the street.

B: Yes, but be careful. It looks like you're [2]***noticing* / *spotting* / *staring*** at other people a little too much. It's pretty rude.

A: Don't worry! They're too busy to [3]***notice* / *observe* / *recognize*** me! They're all looking at their phones, anyway!

C Read about five English-speaking friends. Then answer the questions.

Angela only speaks English and no other languages.

You can hear that **Brian** is from New Zealand because of the way he pronounces *ed*.

When **Eryk** is speaking English, he doesn't make many mistakes.

Francesca speaks English as well as Italian.

George loves using phrases like 'use it or lose it' and 'plan B'.

1 Who speaks accurately? ________
2 Who's monolingual? ________
3 Who likes idioms? ________
4 Who's bilingual? ________
5 Who has a strong accent? ________

FUNCTIONAL LANGUAGE

Complete the dialogues with the words in the box.

busy could favor hand help mind want

1 **A:** Hey, Gary, I need a ________. Do you have a few minutes?
B: Sorry, Paul, I'm really ________ right now.

2 **A:** Do you think you ________ help me write this?
B: Sure, I can give you a ________ with that.

3 **A:** Do you ________ me to take a look at that?
B: If you wouldn't ________.

4 **A:** Hi, Sam. If you aren't busy, I could use your ________ with my application letter.
B: Sure.

2 EXPERIENCES

Nothing is a waste of time if you use the experience wisely.

Auguste Rodin

Skydiver in mid-air over Southern Australia.

OBJECTIVES

- talk about past experiences and things you want to do
- talk about a life-changing decision
- talk about an inspirational person
- talk about solving a problem
- ask for, give and refuse permission
- write an informal email

Work with a partner. Discuss the questions.

1 Look at the picture. What do you think of the activity the person is doing?

2 Read the quote. What do you think it means?

3 Tell your partner about experiences you have had that were:

- incredible
- unusual
- risky
- memorable
- eye-opening
- thrilling

2.1 Important decisions

- Talk about past experiences and things you want to do
- Talk about a life-changing decision

G– present perfect and simple past P– 's and 've V– collocations: making big decisions
S– listening for the main idea

READING

A Match the different types of lists (1–5) with the examples (a–e).

1 list of favorite things, e.g. movies, songs
2 shopping list
3 everyday to-do list
4 list of pros and cons
5 bucket list

a
- bananas
- cheese
- yogurt

b
1 Call Mom
2 Email the bank
3 Pay rent

c
1 Toy Story
2 X-Men
3 Beauty and the Beast

d
1 Swim with dolphins
2 Learn to surf
3 Do a parachute jump

e
For: cheaper / easy to find
Against: poor quality / ordinary

B SPEAK Work in pairs. How often do you make lists? What types of lists do you make? Why?

C READ FOR GIST Read *Not yet? No more!* and answer the questions.

1 Which sentence summarizes the blogger's opinion?
  a A bucket list is a great idea, but remember that you probably can't do all those things in your lifetime.
  b Make a list of things that are possible to do, rather than a list of dreams.
  c People write bucket lists just for fun and to dream a little, not in order to actually do those things.
2 How many of the people commenting on the blog agree with the writer?

Not yet? No more!

About me | Recent posts | Archive

posted by Julia
November 16 | Leave a comment

Have you ever written a bucket list? If so, have you done many of those incredible things on your list? I certainly haven't.

I wrote mine on New Year's Day five years ago, and I chose 50 things, like swimming with dolphins and climbing Mount Everest. However, after all these years, I've only done one thing on that list. Last year, I watched the sun rise and set on the same day. I still haven't swum with dolphins. I still haven't climbed Everest. And, I think I never will!

The problem is that you need an infinite amount of time and money to do all those incredible things or to learn those skills. I've simply never had that time and money. What is the point in making an unachievable list? How does that improve your life?

So, this is my achievable bucket list blog. The aim is still to do unusual things that are positive and life-enhancing, but without needing to be a millionaire or to have all the time in the world to achieve these goals.

Here's the start of my list. I haven't done any of these things yet, but I think I can in the future. What do you think? Achievable? Life-enhancing?

- Plant a tree.
- Do a charity walk or run.
- Write a poem.
- Learn how to make a fire in the wild.
- Ride a horse.
- Eat nothing but fresh food for a week.
- Stop using social media for two weeks.
- Learn and perform a magic trick.

Comments:

Yuka W: Thanks! Before I read this, my bucket list was only expensive travel ideas. I just wrote a new list of interesting but doable things!

dream_catcher77: Actually, I think a bucket list should be about amazing things. I wrote mine last year and I've done half of it already. This year, I've seen lions in the wild and I've done a parachute jump. Next month, the Pyramids! All because they're on my list.

Robin Stannard: Also, sometimes those incredible things are not so great. I've swum with dolphins. It was garbage! I'd rather swim with my friends. Keep it simple – it's still special ;-)

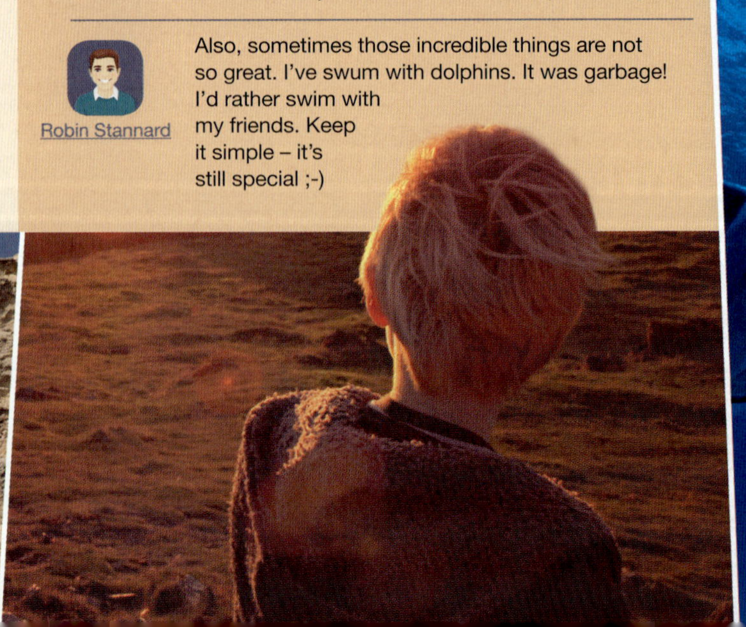

D READ FOR DETAIL Read again. Answer the questions.

1 How many things on her first bucket list has the writer not done?
2 Why is it not possible to do all the things on a typical bucket list?
3 How is her new list similar to her original list?
4 How many outdoor activities are there on her new list?

E SPEAK Work in pairs. Read again and discuss the questions.

1 Are the writer's choices good ideas for an achievable bucket list?
2 Which choices do you like most and why?

GRAMMAR

Present perfect and simple past

A WORK IT OUT Look at the sentences (1–4) from *Not yet? No more!* Underline the verbs in the simple past and circle the verbs in the present perfect. Then match each sentence with a diagram (a–d).

1 I wrote mine on New Year's Day five years ago.
2 I've only done one thing on that list.
3 This year, I've seen lions in the wild.
4 Last year, I watched the sun rise and set on the same day.

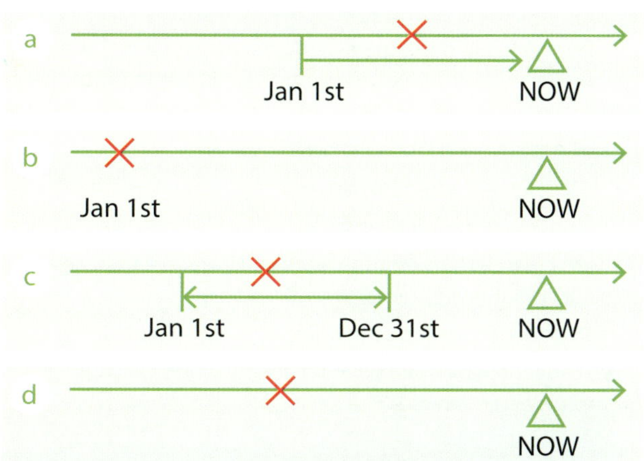

B Look at the adverbs of time in the box. Can you find them in the blog? Match the adverbs with the definitions (1–5).

already	just	never	not yet	still

1 at no time in the past ______
2 a short time ago ______
3 a situation has not changed or not completely ended ______
4 not happened before now, but will probably happen ______
5 happened before a point in time, perhaps sooner than expected ______

C Complete the rules with *present perfect* or *simple past*.

Present perfect and simple past

For actions that we completed:

during a finished period of time, we use the
1 ______.

during a period of time that continues to now, we use the
2 ______.

at a specific time in the past, we use the
3 ______.

before now, but we do not say exactly when, we use the
4 ______.

We frequently use adverbs of time with these tenses, but we do not use *yet* and *already* with actions in the
5 ______.

D Go to the **Grammar Hub** on **page 124**.

PRONUNCIATION

's and *'ve*

2.1 Listen to the pairs of sentences (1–6). Which sentence (*a* or *b*) is in the present perfect?

1 ___ 3 ___ 5 ___
2 ___ 4 ___ 6 ___

SPEAKING

A Work in pairs. You are going to write an achievable bucket list. Student A – read the bucket list on **page 148**. Student B – read the list on **page 153**. Has your partner done any of the things on your list? If they have, find out more details.

B Work in pairs. Choose eight things to put on your achievable bucket list. Use the ideas on the lists and your own ideas. They should be positive, life-enhancing and achievable.

C Work in groups. Compare your lists and choose ten things for a group bucket list.

D Compare your list with another group. Are their ideas the same or different?

a

b

LISTENING

A Match the words and phrases in the box with the pictures (a–b).

cross oceans	cruise along canals		
freshwater	houseboat	saltwater	yacht

B SPEAK Work in pairs and discuss the questions.

1 Have you ever been on a boat? If so, what kind?

2 Which of the two boats in the pictures would you prefer to travel on?

2.2 **C LISTEN FOR GIST** Look at the pictures (a and b) and listen to a podcast interview with Emma. Complete the sentences with *a* or *b*.

1 Picture ___ shows Emma's ultimate dream.

2 Picture ___ shows Emma's current reality.

2.2 **D** Listen again. Which of the phrases (1–8) from the podcast are the main ideas of Emma's story? Use the strategies in the box to help you.

1 I love swimming

2 yachts are very expensive

3 to make a decision to put a plan into action

4 it won't take me around the world

5 to stay motivated and not lose heart

6 learning to live in a small space

7 doing something similar to my dream, it's a start

8 the hardest part of any journey is the first step

Listening for the main idea

To help you catch the main ideas of a conversation, listen carefully for common expressions that we use to introduce a main idea.

- *The most important thing here …*
- *Well, it is important to note …*
- *And I stress the importance of …*

Listen carefully for common words and phrases that we use to talk about things generally.

- *in general, overall, on the whole*

We usually speak more slowly or loudly when we want to emphasize a main idea.

2.2 **E LISTEN FOR DETAIL** Listen again. Find and correct six mistakes in the summary of Emma's story.

Emma is 33 and she works in the sailing industry. She loves swimming and fishing. For the last few years, she's been learning how to sail. Her dream is to live on a yacht and sail around the world. She hasn't bought a yacht yet because she can't find one that she likes. She sold her house and bought a houseboat. The houseboat is an opportunity for Emma to learn to live on the sea and move from place to place. She is happy with her decision to buy a houseboat because it means that she has 'made the break' from the water to the land.

F SPEAK Work in groups and discuss the questions.

1 Do you agree that living on a houseboat will help Emma to achieve her ultimate dream? Give reasons.

2 What are the pros and cons of living on a houseboat compared to living on land?

VOCABULARY

Collocations: making big decisions

A Match the verbs (1–8) with the phrases (a–i) to make collocations that Emma used in her interview. One verb can be used twice. Use the audio script on page 167 to help you.

1 lose	**a** a decision
2 make	**b** a plan into action
3 put	**c** short-term and long-term goals
4 set	**d** toward a goal
5 stay	**e** a dream into reality
6 take	**f** motivated
7 turn	**g** the break/change
8 work	**h** the next step
	i heart

B Read the information from the people (1–3) about a life-changing decision. Fill in the blanks with collocations from Exercise A in the correct form.

2.3 **C** Listen and check your answers.

D **SPEAK** Work in pairs. Which decision in Exercise C do you think is the most achievable? Which is the least achievable? Give reasons.

SPEAKING HUB

A Think about a life-changing decision that you have made. Use the ideas below to help you.

- moving (changing cities/countries)
- studying (a new course, retraining, learning a new skill)
- a lifestyle change (becoming healthier, in better shape, more relaxed)
- turning a dream into reality

B **PLAN** Write notes about your decision. Think about:

- why you made the decision.
- how you put it into action.
- short-term/long-term goals.
- how you feel about the decision now.
- any advice you can give related to your decision.

C **SPEAK** Work in pairs. Interview your partner about his/her life-changing decision. Use your ideas in Exercise B to help you. Take turns.

D **REFLECT** Work in groups. Tell the group about your partner's decision. Then discuss all of the decisions. Whose decision was the most life-changing?

1

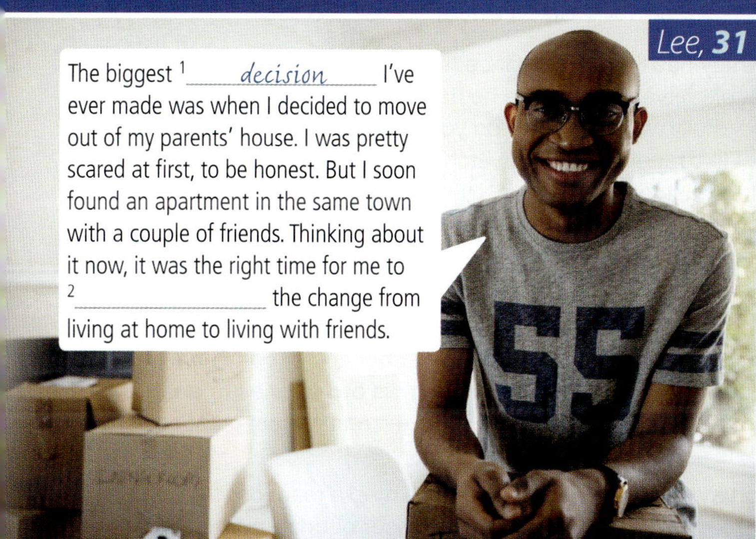

Lee, 31

The biggest [1] *decision* I've ever made was when I decided to move out of my parents' house. I was pretty scared at first, to be honest. But I soon found an apartment in the same town with a couple of friends. Thinking about it now, it was the right time for me to [2] ______ the change from living at home to living with friends.

2

Three years ago, I decided to climb El Capitan in Yosemite National Park. It was always one of those things on my bucket list. Since I started to put the [3] ______ into action, I've learned a lot about climbing and myself. My advice? Never [4] ______ heart! If you are [5] ______ toward a goal, you'll achieve it in the end. I haven't gone to Yosemite yet, but I know I will!

Maki, 25

3

Alessandra, 35

When I was a teenager, I wanted to be a famous movie star. But it didn't happen. My dream now is to be a chef. I've learned that the best way to [6] ______ a dream into reality is to be realistic. Set short-term [7] ______ to help you [8] ______ motivated. Becoming a chef is going to be difficult, but I've already started a course and cook regularly for friends and family.

- Talk about past experiences and things you want to do
- Talk about a life-changing decision

2.2 You can do it!

- Talk about an inspirational person
- Talk about solving a problem

V – dependent prepositions; problems and solutions
G – present and past ability
P – word stress: verbs with two syllables
S – deducing the meaning of unknown words from context

READING

A SPEAK Work in pairs and discuss the question.

How do retired people typically spend their time in your country?

B Read the ad taken from a local newspaper. Then answer the questions.

1 What is unusual about the ad?
2 Why do you think he has written the advertisement?
3 How do you think people reacted to the ad?

C READ FOR GIST Read *89-year-old seeks job* and check your answers to Exercise B.

D Look at the words in bold in the article. What do you think they mean? Use the strategies in the box to help you. Then work in pairs and compare your ideas.

1 seeks	3 spotted	5 role
2 snaps him up	4 enable him to	6 taking on

89-year-old **seeks** job: café **snaps him up**

An 89-year-old has found a job after putting an ad in his local paper asking for part-time work to stop him from 'dying of boredom'. Joe Bartley, from Paignton, south Devon, is due to start working in a café next week in the town after the owners of the family-run business **spotted** his ad.

'Whatever your age or your background, you deserve a chance,' said Cantina Bar and Kitchen's co-owner Sarah Martin. 'Most people have something to offer, and Joe is someone who is eager, who is putting himself out there. What is not to like about that? A lot of people who come here don't just come for coffee – they come for a chat – so Joe is perfect.'

Bartley has lived alone since his wife, Cassandra, died a couple of years ago, and he has been lonely. 'I miss my wife dreadfully, when you live on your own there is no one to speak to. I like reading, and I'll watch a little television, but there's a lot of trash on these days. I just got bored stiff with nothing to do. I thought even though I am 89, I can still work. I can clean tables, do some gardening – anything really.'

Bartley put his advertisement in the *Herald Express* last month. 'The owner called me and she asked me to come in. So I arrived at the café, we had a little chat and shook hands.' He is now looking forward to earning his own money to **enable him to** pay his rent. 'I can't believe it really. I feel great about it,' he said.

Bartley told *The Guardian* that the media reaction has been incredible, adding that he is in danger of becoming a celebrity. 'When I first put in the ad, I thought it was just an old guy looking for work – I don't really see what is strange about that,' he said. 'But have I now reached celebrity status? That might worry some people, but it doesn't worry me.'

His new **role** in the café was not the only job offer he got. Glenn Rodgers, an independent baker in Barnstaple, north Devon, offered him a job, but the bakery was too far away for Bartley to travel.

Rodgers wanted to offer the senior citizen a job to put a 'smile on his face'. 'More employers should think about **taking on** older staff,' he added. 'Why not give him a chance? Also, it works both ways: employers are getting experienced reliable staff who really want to work.'

Bartley will get a ride to work with his new employer on Sundays, but will take a bus the rest of the week. 'He is delighted and we are looking forward to it,' said Martin. 'We think about these things all the time. We are never going to be rich, but we like to give something back to society.'

Deducing the meaning of unknown words from context

When you do not know the meaning of words and phrases, you can use their context to help you understand them.

Think about:

- What type of word or phrase is it (noun, adjective or verb)?
- Does it have a prefix (*un-*, *im-*) or suffix (*-ment*, *-ion*)?
- Where is it in the sentence and what other words are near it?
- How does the word relate to the paragraph?
- What possible meanings of the word suit the topic of the sentence, paragraph and text?

E SPEAK Work in pairs. Look at the readers' comments on the article. Do you agree or disagree with them? Why?

Comments

Smart1

Joe is an inspiration to us all! He should be very proud of himself for getting a job that some would say is more suitable for a younger person.

ID2

If no one had replied to the ad, Joe could have thought about volunteering. Mind you, even those roles are hard to find these days!

Jan1003

The government should be more aware of this problem and work with communities to help people like Joe. Loneliness is a big problem nowadays.

4Kent

Though fairly typical of this newspaper, it's great that this issue is in the news. We need to prepare for our retirement now, so we can retire comfortably, not serve coffee in our old age.

VOCABULARY

Dependent prepositions (verb/adjective + *for/of*)

A Look at the phrases from *89-year-old seeks job* and from the comments. Are the words in bold verbs or adjectives? Complete each phrase with *for* or *of*.

1 look ________ work
2 prepare ________ retirement
3 typical ________ this newspaper
4 suitable ________ a younger person
5 proud ________ himself
6 aware ________ this problem
7 work ________ a café
8 ask ________ part-time work

B Complete the questions with a verb or adjective from Exercise A.

1 What do you ________________ for in an ideal job?
2 Do you think age ever makes people more or less ________________ for some jobs?
3 Which of your achievements are you most ________________ of?
4 What big changes in your life are coming soon? How can you ________________ for them?

C SPEAK Work in pairs. Ask and answer the questions in Exercise B.

SPEAKING

A Think of three people who should receive an award for inspiring others because of their special or unusual achievements.

B Work in pairs. Discuss your choices and choose the most inspirational person. Write down some of your reasons for choosing that person.

C Work in groups. In pairs, give a short presentation about your inspirational person, explaining why the person should win the award. As a group, vote for who should win the award.

D Tell the class about your group's choice. Why did the group feel the person was special? Did everyone in the group agree with the vote?

1

2

3

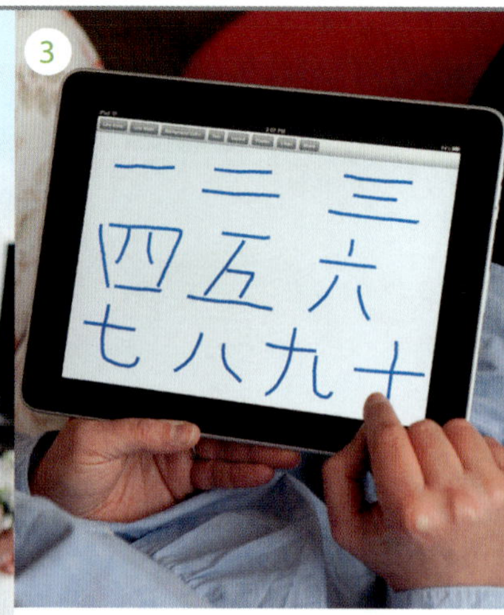

4

LISTENING

A SPEAK Work in pairs. Look at the pictures (1–4). What are the people doing? What problems could they have when they do these things?

2.4 **B LISTEN FOR MAIN IDEA** You are going to listen to four people talking about a challenge or problem. Complete the sentences (1–4) with the phrases in the box. There are four extra phrases.

> by pretending to be a different person
> by spending a lot of money   by taking classes
> by using a different skill   by using books   during a vacation
> on his/her own   with the help of his/her family

1 Matt solved a problem ______________.
2 Suzanna solved a problem ______________.
3 Nancy solved a problem ______________.
4 Roberto solved a problem ______________.

2.4 **C LISTEN FOR DETAIL** Listen again. Choose the correct words to complete the sentences.

1 Matt *knew* / *didn't know* how to cook simple hot food.
2 He found useful advice on *the internet* / *TV*.
3 Suzanna needed to give a speech at *work* / *a family event*.
4 She *read* / *didn't read* her speech aloud from a script.
5 Nancy *knew a little* / *didn't know any* Chinese.
6 She *made several* / *didn't make any* mistakes when she first sang to the children.
7 When Roberto was a child, he *tried* / *didn't try* to learn to swim.
8 He *has* / *still hasn't* swum in the ocean.

D SPEAK Work in pairs and discuss the questions.

1 Which of the four challenges do you think is the hardest?
2 What advice could you give to someone who can't do those things well?
3 Have you had any of these challenges yourself? What did you do to deal with them?
4 Is it more important to solve problems yourself or ask for help?

PRONUNCIATION

Word stress: verbs with two syllables

A Work in pairs. Look at the verbs from the listening below. Take turns saying the verbs and marking the stress.

1 achieve	3 complete	5 regret
2 arrive	4 create	6 study

B Does the stress normally come on the first or second syllable?

2.5 **C** Now listen to the verbs. Check and repeat.

GRAMMAR

Present and past ability

A WORK IT OUT Look at the sentences (1–9). Write *a* if they are about having (or not having) a general ability or skill in the past. Write *b* if they are about doing something (or not doing something) on a particular occasion in the past.

1 I was able to speak very basic Chinese. a
2 I managed to cook them a very tasty meal. b
3 I was able to complete the speech. ____
4 I couldn't boil an egg. ____
5 I could make a salad. ____
6 The first time, I didn't manage to make anything. ____
7 I wasn't able to swim. ____
8 I wasn't able to stop my hands shaking. ____
9 I couldn't say no to him. ____

B Choose the correct words to complete the rules.

Present and past ability

1 When we talk about ability or skills in general in the present, we *use* / *do not use* *can/can't* or *(not) be able to*.
2 When we talk about ability or skills in general in the past, we *use* / *do not use* *could, couldn't* or *(not) be able to*.
3 When we talk about ability to do a specific task on a particular occasion in the past, we *use* / *do not use* *(not) manage to, (not) be able to* or *couldn't*. We do not usually use *could*.

C Go to the Grammar Hub on page 124.

D SPEAK Work in pairs. Play *True or false?* Follow the instructions.

1 Write two sentences for each idea (a–c). One sentence should be true and one should be false.

  a something you can do now, but which you couldn't do five or ten years ago

  b a problem you had because you weren't able to do something

  c a particular time that you managed to do something that was difficult

2 Listen to your partner's sentences. Ask questions to find out more information, then guess which sentences are true. Take turns.

VOCABULARY

Problems and solutions

A SPEAK Work in pairs. How good are you at solving problems? Give yourself a score out of five. Explain your score to your partner.

B Look at the personality test. Complete the sentences with *problem(s)* or *solution(s)*.

How do you feel about difficult situations and problems?

Use this personality test to find out. How true are the following statements for you on a scale of 1–5?

1 = False
2 = Mostly false
3 = Sometimes true / Sometimes false
4 = Mostly true
5 = True

1 If I can't **solve** a difficult ______________, I don't give up. I keep trying until I find a ______________
1 2 3 4 5

2 I always try to **deal with** ______________ because ignoring them only **causes** more ______________.
1 2 3 4 5

3 When working in groups, I **suggest** a lot of ______________ to any ______________.
1 2 3 4 5

4 When I have a ______________, I look at it from different angles to **come up with** the best ______________.
1 2 3 4 5

5 When I deal with a complicated ______________, I **analyze** the possible ______________ with lists of their pros and cons.
1 2 3 4 5

6 I prefer to discuss a ______________ with other people. Then we can **agree on** a ______________ together.
1 2 3 4 5

C WORK IT OUT Match the verbs in bold in the personality test with the definitions (1–7).

1 to think of something such as an idea or a plan
2 to study or examine something in detail in order to understand or explain it
3 to decide together what will be done and how it will be done
4 to offer an idea or plan for someone to consider
5 to take action to do something
6 to find a solution to something that is causing difficulties
7 to make something happen, usually something bad

D Go to the **Vocabulary Hub** on **page 142**.

E SPEAK Take the personality test. Go to the **Communication Hub** on **page 148** to see what your answers may show about you. Then work in pairs and discuss your answers.

SPEAKING HUB

A You are going to answer a question that employers frequently ask in job interviews to find out about problem-solving skills.

> Can you tell us about a time when you faced a challenge or a difficult problem that you successfully dealt with?

B PLAN Write notes about:

- the situation.
- what action you took to deal with the situation.
- what you learned from trying to deal with the situation.

C SPEAK Work in pairs. Ask and answer the question. Write notes about your partner's answer.

D REFLECT Tell a classmate what your partner said. Think about what you both heard. Whose answer was best?

- Talk about an inspirational person
- Talk about solving a problem

Café Hub

2.3 Picture this

F – ask for, give and refuse permission
P – intonation and stress in questions

COMPREHENSION

A ▶ 00:00–00:50 Watch the first part of the video. What wakes Gaby up?

B Work in pairs. The actual photo shoot is not successful. Look at the stills and predict the difficulties that Gaby has.

1

2

3

4

C ▶ 00:51–04:00 Watch the second part of the video and check your ideas. Then complete the sentences with *Gaby* or *Eric*.

1 ________ gets ________'s name wrong.
2 ________ is in a hurry.
3 ________ can't set up the tripod.
4 ________ gets ________'s name wrong again.
5 ________ drops the camera.
6 ________ fixes the camera onto the tripod.
7 ________ suggests more light on the bowl.
8 ________ suggests putting fruit in the bowl.

FUNCTIONAL LANGUAGE

Asking for, giving and refusing permission

A Eric was in a hurry and wanted to start the photo shoot right away. Check (✓) the phrase he used.

Asking for permission		
		Least formal
Can we start …	☐	↑
Could we start … right away?	☐	
May we start …	☐	
Is it all right if we start …	☐	
Would it be OK to …	☐	
Would you mind if we started …	☐	↓
		Most formal

Giving and refusing permission	
Sure, I don't see why not.	I'm sorry, but …
No problem.	I'd like to help, but …
Yes, of course.	I'm afraid that isn't possible.

MILLY

SAM

NEENA

ZAC

GABY

B Write down phrases asking for permission in the following situations. Choose an appropriate level of formality.

1 It's very hot in the classroom. You want to open a window. Ask your classmates.

2 You have a dental appointment tomorrow. You want to leave work early. Ask your boss.

3 You are chairing a business meeting. You want to start. Ask everyone in the meeting.

4 It's a beautiful day and you're in a park. You want to sit on the grass. Ask the park ranger.

5 You're in front of somebody's house. You want to park your car there. Ask the home owner.

6 You're in a lecture with 200 other people. You want to ask a question. Ask the lecturer.

USEFUL PHRASES

A Choose the correct alternatives to complete the useful phrases. Watch the video again if necessary.

1 *Call / Name* me Gaby. = Please use the name 'Gaby' when you talk to me.

2 I can't thank you *enough / at all*. = I am very grateful to you.

3 You *must / should* be Derek. = I am sure your name is Derek.

4 I don't have *this / that* long. = I have very little time.

5 We're *almost / fairly* there. = We have nearly finished.

B How do you say these useful phrases in your language?

PRONUNCIATION

Intonation and stress in questions

2.6 **A** Listen and repeat the questions. Does the intonation rise or fall after the main stress in the sentence?

1 Could I open the window?

2 Can I leave work early?

3 Is it all right if we start now?

4 Would it be OK to sit on the armchair?

5 Would you mind if I parked my car here?

6 May I ask you a question?

B Practice the stress and intonation in the questions in Exercise A.

SPEAKING

A Work in pairs. You are going to write a conversation in which you ask permission for something.

- Decide on the situation: why do you need permission and who from?
- Decide on the level of formality.
- Write your conversation.

B PRESENT Practice your conversation. Then act out your conversation for the class.

Ask for, give and refuse permission

➤ Turn to page 157 to learn how to write an informal email.

Unit 2 Review

GRAMMAR

A Complete the comments (1–2) about achievable bucket lists with the correct form of the verbs in parentheses.

Comments

1 Maybe the best bucket list is a mixture of easy and hard to achieve . I [1] ________ (*do*) both simple activities and bigger adventures. Both [2] ________ (*give*) me great memories. I once [3] ________ (*learn*) to bake a cake in the morning, and then [4] ________ (*do*) my first bungee jump in the afternoon. The cake [5] ________ (*taste*) great after that! I [6] ________ (*do*) a bungee jump since, but I [7] ________ (*made*) plenty of cakes!

2 How about awesome adventures that also benefit other people or society? A few years ago, I [1] ________ (*want*) to ride an elephant, so I [2] ________ (*find*) a position as an international volunteer at an elephant conservation park. I [3] ________ (*stay*) there for two months. It [4] ________ (*be*) great to help a charity and do something on my bucket list. Since then, I [5] ________ (*do*) loads of similar things.

B Find and correct the mistakes in five of the sentences.

1. When I was a kid, I could to swim. I learned as a baby.
2. They wasn't able to score a goal. What a boring game.
3. I managed to finish everything.
4. I couldn't to ride a bike until I was 19.
5. I am able dance fairly well.
6. I'm afraid you didn't managed to pass. You'll have to retake it.

VOCABULARY

A Match the sentence beginnings (1–5) and endings (a–e).

1. I don't believe in setting ___
2. It's easy to stay ___
3. I'm sorry you didn't get the job, but don't lose ___
4. When I moved to the countryside, I ___
5. I was nervous about taking ___

a. the next step, but I knew it was the right time to make the change.
b. motivated when you really enjoy what you do.
c. turned my dream into reality!
d. long-terms goals – I prefer to focus on my weekly plans.
e. heart – there will be other opportunities.

B Complete the sentences with the correct form of the words in the box and *for* or *of*.

ask aware look prepare
proud suitable typical work

1. We're lost. We need to ________ help and get directions.
2. I ________ a new job. I check a few online agencies each week.
3. This behavior is ________ Jane. She has always been difficult.
4. She's giving a presentation tomorrow. She needs to ________ that tonight.
5. Is this movie ________ young children? I'd like to watch it with my niece.
6. We have both ________ the same company all our lives. That's very unusual.
7. Is your boss ________ all the problems with the project?
8. I'm very ________ my achievements. It's never too late to learn something new.

C Choose the correct words to complete the results of a personality quiz about problem solving.

The results show that when you try and [1]***deal / solve*** a problem, you like to make quick decisions. This can be helpful, but sometimes you should take more time to [2]***analyze / come up with*** the problem first. This will help when you have to [3]***deal with / suggest*** complicated situations and need to [4]***come up with / cause*** many different solutions.

The results also show that when you work on a team, you expect to [5]***solve / agree on*** solutions quickly, and if you don't, you usually lose interest. However, if you don't take the time to look at the pros and cons of your solutions, this might [6]***cause / suggest*** more problems.

FUNCTIONAL LANGUAGE

Put the dialogue in the correct order.

A: Alright, no problem. In that case could you lend me your phone? ___
A: Hey there, Pete. Would you mind if I borrowed your laptop? ___
B: I'm afraid I can't do that either – I'm expecting an important call. ___
B: I'm not sure to be honest – I have a lot of work to do today and I need it. ___
A: Yes, Arsenal is playing and I want to check the score! ___
A: OK, never mind. ___
B: Is it for something urgent? ___

3 ON THE MOVE

View from Nelson's Column in Trafalgar Square towards Westminster, England.

> I never travel without my diary. One should always have something sensational to read in the train.
>
> Oscar Wilde

OBJECTIVES

- talk about a difficult trip or travel experience
- talk about behavior on public transportation
- evaluate suggestions and justify a choice
- talk about why a plan didn't work
- tell a story
- write an email of complaint

Work with a partner. Discuss the questions.

1 Look at the picture. What different types of transportation can you see? How does the city's transportation compare to that in your own city?

2 Read the quote. How do you pass the time on public transportation?

3 Which types of transportation would you describe with the adjectives in the box?

convenient	dangerous	essential	exciting	expensive	free	fun	noisy	relaxing	safe	stressful	tiring

3.1 Travel experiences

- Talk about a difficult trip or travel experience
- Talk about behavior on public transportation

G – narrative tenses
P – word stress in nouns ending in *-ion*
V – collocations: travel information; nouns ending in *-ion*
S – skim-reading to build a map of a text

LISTENING

A SPEAK Work in pairs and discuss the questions.

1 What types of transportation do you use? How often do you use them?
2 Which do you prefer and why? Which is your least favorite?
3 What problems might there be for each one?

3.1 **B LISTEN FOR GIST** Listen to a call-in radio show. What is the topic of today's discussion?

a bad or unusual trips to work
b bad or unusual trips in general
c bad or unusual trips on national holidays

3.1 **C LISTEN FOR DETAIL** Are the sentences true (T) or false (F)? Correct the false sentences. Then listen again and check your answers.

Junko's experience

1 There were no trains because of the bad weather. ___
2 She didn't sit at the bus stop for a long time. ___
3 She stopped a police car to ask for help. ___
4 The police found a taxi for her. ___
5 She arrived at her friend's house in time for dinner. ___

Alan's experience

6 He missed the first train because the taxi was slow. ___
7 The second train stopped moving after half an hour. ___
8 When the train reached its destination, he was already two hours late for the interview. ___
9 Because the traffic was heavy, he walked from the station to the office. ___
10 Another job candidate was late because of the train problems. ___

D SPEAK Work in pairs and discuss the questions.

1 What mistakes did Junko and Alan make? Who made the worst ones?
2 Who had the worst or most unusual trip? Why?

GRAMMAR

Narrative tenses

A Look at the pairs of sentences from the call-in radio show. In each pair, who is the speaker? Write J (Junko) or A (Alan). What tenses are the underlined verbs?

1 **A:** It was raining when I left. ___
B: It was snowing. ___
2 **A:** I took the next train, but after about 30 minutes, that train broke down. ___
B: I found a bus stop and sat down. ___
3 **A:** A police car was driving by, when it suddenly stopped. ___
B: We were still not moving, so I got out and walked. ___
4 **A:** We arrived about two hours late, and that meant I'd already missed the interview. ___
B: I'd arranged to go to a classmate's house for dinner. ___

B WORK IT OUT Complete the rules with *simple past, past progressive* or *past perfect.*

Narrative tenses

When we tell a story, we use a range of past tenses.

1 We use the ______________ to describe the main events in a story, in the order that they happened.
2 We use the ______________ to describe a longer action that is interrupted by a shorter event. We also use it to describe a longer action that is not a main event in the story, such as the weather.
3 We use the ______________ to describe an event that happened before the main events in the story.

C Match the timelines (a–d) with the rules (1–3) in Exercise B.

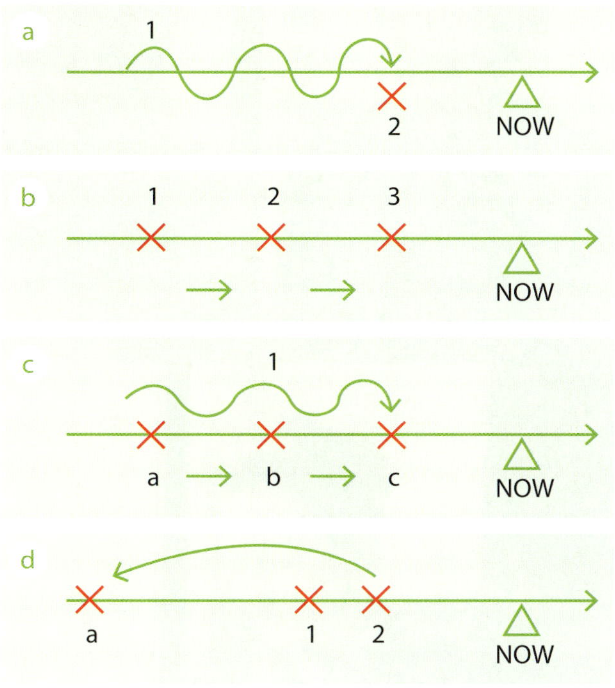

D **PRACTICE** Complete the stories with the correct form of the verbs in parentheses.

It [1] ______________ (*rain*), and I [2] ______________ (*drive*) at night in the countryside when a wild animal suddenly [3] ______________ (*jump*) in front of me. I [4] ______________ (*manage*) to avoid hitting the animal, but I [5] ______________ (*go*) off the road into a field and I couldn't move the car. Unfortunately, I [6] ______________ (*forget*) to charge my phone, so I couldn't call for help. That was a long walk home!

I [7] ______________ (*travel*) to work on the train when a ticket inspector [8] ______________ (*ask*) to see my ticket. I [9] ______________ (*look*) everywhere, but I had no idea where I [10] ______________ (*put*) it. I emptied out my pockets but it [11] ______________ (*disappear*) completely. There were two kids across from me, and while I [12] ______________ (*pay*) the inspector, I [13] ______________ (*notice*) they [14] ______________ (*smile and laugh*). They got off at the next station, and my ticket [15] ______________ (*be*) on their seat. They [16] ______________ (*find and hide*) it.

E Go to the **Grammar Hub** on **page 126**.

F Work in pairs. Go to the **Communication Hub** on **page 149**.

VOCABULARY

Collocations: travel information

3.2 **A** Listen to a traffic news and travel update on a radio show. Answer the questions.

1. How many types of transportation do they mention?
2. Which has the fewest problems?

3.2 **B** **LISTEN FOR KEY WORDS** Listen again. Choose the correct words to make the collocations used in the travel update.

1. rush *hour* / *job*
2. traffic *lights* / *jam*
3. road *sign* / *work*
4. severe *delay* / *problem*
5. slight *delay* / *interest*
6. good *conditions* / *service*
7. subway *station* / *line*
8. cancel *a train* / *an event*
9. heavy *rain* / *traffic*
10. overcrowded *trains* / *buses*

C Go to the **Vocabulary Hub** on **page 142**.

D **SPEAK** Work in pairs and discuss the questions.

1. When was the last time you were stuck in heavy traffic?
2. What do you think about traveling during rush hour?
3. Which is worse: being on an overcrowded train or in a traffic jam?

SPEAKING

A You are going to tell a story for a radio show. Think of either an interesting or a difficult trip that you have made. Write notes to help you plan your story. Think about:

- Background information (When? Where? Why?)
- What was the weather like?
- What happened on the trip?
- How did it finish?

B Work in groups. Share your stories. Ask and answer questions about the stories.

C Which story do you think would be best for the radio show? Which was the most interesting, unusual or difficult trip? Which was the funniest story?

READING

A SPEAK Work in pairs. Look at the pictures (a–c) and discuss the questions.

1 What are the people doing?

2 Which activities do you like / not like doing when you are traveling?

B SKIM Read the article quickly and answer the questions. Use the strategies in the box to help you build a map of the text.

Skim-reading to build a map of a text

You can build a map of a text by identifying the main topic and the paragraph topics.

Read the title and the first paragraph to find out what the main topic is.

Read the first sentence of each paragraph to find out what the paragraph's topic is. Make a note of the paragraph topics.

1 What is the main topic or idea in this text?

2 Match the headings (a–f) with the paragraphs (1–6).

a The details of what the research discovered

b Epley's conclusions regarding the research

c How the research changed Epley's life

d Avoiding conversations and reasons not to

e How the research was carried out

f The reason why Epley and Schroeder did the research

a

b

DAY2DAY SCIENCE Your source of science news

Is it time to start talking to strangers?

1 Using your cell phone. Putting on your headphones. Staring out of the window. Those are all classic ways to avoid talking to strangers on public transportation. However, this may not be the best thing to do for your well-being. Recent research by Nicholas Epley, a professor of behavioral science at the University of Chicago, and Juliana Schroeder, a PhD student, reveals that people are happier when they talk with other passengers rather than ignoring them.

2 The inspiration for the research came from Epley's own daily commute. Humans are, by nature, social animals, and being social is key to our happiness. However, the commuters that Epley saw every day were behaving in very antisocial ways, avoiding all communication as if they were sitting next to a rock. He wondered why nearly everyone acted against their social nature in this situation. Is talking to a stranger on a train truly less pleasant than sitting in silence? Or is everybody wrong?

3 To find out, Epley and Schroeder designed two experiments. In the first, Epley simply asked people to imagine starting a conversation with another passenger. Would it be a pleasant thing to do? Would they feel happy afterward? In the second study, they asked commuters to actually start conversations with strangers on their trip, and then to complete a survey about the experience.

4 His studies revealed a difference between people's expectations of talking to strangers and the reality. In the first study, people generally said it would neither be a pleasant thing to do nor increase their happiness. In addition, they felt that most strangers would not want to talk.
In contrast, the second experiment showed that people enjoyed their commute more when they talked to a stranger and their general level of happiness increased. It also revealed that the reaction was positive because they all took part in the conversations, even though they were not aware it was an experiment.

5 Based on the findings, Epley feels that passenger cars filled with silence, blank expressions and little eye contact are the result of basic misunderstandings and false expectations. Despite what everyone thinks, strangers are happy to talk and talking makes you happier. Once people make the decision to start a conversation, they find this connection to others improves their own lives.

6 Since publishing the research, Epley has put his findings into action and changed his own commuting behavior. He no longer uses his cell phone and he starts conversations with opening lines as simple as 'I like your hat'. He regularly finds himself sitting next to someone he has talked to before, which 'just makes it more pleasant'.'

C Work in pairs. Compare your answers to Exercise B. What other information can you remember from your skim-reading?

D **SPEAK** Work in groups. What do you think of the results of the research?

VOCABULARY

Nouns ending in *-ion*

A **WORK IT OUT** Look at *Is it time to start talking to strangers?* again. Find and underline nouns that end with *-ion*.

B Complete the definitions with nouns from Exercise A.

1 to have an ________________: to have a belief about what something will be like or what will happen

2 to have a positive ________________: to feel good as a result of something that happens

3 to make a ________________: to choose something after thinking carefully

4 to have a ________________: to have a relationship to something

5 to have a confused ________________: to look like you don't understand something

6 to be in a difficult ________________: to be doing something that is not easy

7 to be in ________________: to be sharing information, ideas and feelings

8 to be an ________________: to give you new ideas or the enthusiasm to create something with them

C Go to the **Vocabulary Hub** on **page 143**.

D **SPEAK** Work in pairs. Do you agree or disagree with the statements below. If you disagree with them, change them so they are true for you.

1 Communication with other passengers is a waste of time. I don't know them and I might never see them again.

2 How far you choose to live from work is a very important decision. There is a connection between everyday happiness and the length of your commute.

PRONUNCIATION

Word stress in nouns ending in *-ion*

3.3 **A** Listen to the pronunciation of the nouns ending in *-ion* and underline the stressed syllables. Some words may have two stressed syllables.

1 action 2 connection 3 communication

3.3 **B** Listen again and repeat the words. How is the stress pattern similar?

3.4 **C** Underline the stressed syllables of the nouns ending in *-ion*. Then listen and check your answers. Repeat the words.

1 decision
2 expectation
3 expression
4 inspiration
5 reaction
6 situation

D **SPEAK** Work in pairs. Practice saying the words. Listen and check your partner's pronunciation.

SPEAKING HUB

A Go to the **Communication Hub** on **page 154**.

B **SPEAK** Work in groups. Compare your lists and explain your reasons to each other.

C **DISCUSS** Decide on the top three most annoying things. Discuss ways of stopping that behavior. Compare your ideas with another group.

Talk about a difficult trip or travel experience

Talk about behavior on public transportation

3.2 Travel smart

- Evaluate suggestions and justify a choice
- Talk about why a plan didn't work

G articles and quantifiers **P** sentence stress: quantifiers **V** gradable and ungradable adjectives
S listening for signposting

READING

A SPEAK Work in pairs and discuss the question. Do you think there are too many cars on the road where you live or study?

B READ FOR MAIN IDEA Read *Whatever happened to Helsinki's Kutsuplus transportation service?* Match the headings (a–e) with the paragraphs (1–5).

a The advantages of Kutsuplus
b The disadvantages of Kutsuplus
c How Kutsuplus worked
d Was Kutsuplus a success?
e What was Kutsuplus?

Whatever happened to Helsinki's *Kutsuplus* transportation service?

1 ___

A few years ago, Helsinki, Finland, decided it had a problem: there were **too many** cars. So the Helsinki Regional Transportation Authority decided to hold a three-year trial of an on-demand minibus service designed to reduce the number of cars on the road. It was called *Kutsuplus* and it allowed passengers to choose where they wanted to go.

2 ___

Passengers went online and selected a start and end point for their trip. They then paid online and went to their nearest bus stop. **A minibus** arrived and took them to the chosen end point. If other **people** wanted to go to the same area at the same time, no problem: there was **plenty of** space and they could share **the minibus**! Even if people wanted to go to different places in the same area, **the online service** was able to choose the best route available, so everybody was happy!

3 ___

For passengers, the key benefits of *Kutsuplus* were convenience and cost. They could choose where they wanted to go and they didn't have to wait long for the bus to arrive. During the time of the trial, the average *Kutsuplus* trip cost $5. In comparison, the average cost of a taxi ride started at $6, but could be much more expensive for longer trips. Surely this would make *Kutsuplus* a great success! Well, not really …

4 ___

Although it was more convenient than a normal bus or the subway, unlike a taxi, the minibus wasn't able to take people exactly where they wanted to go. Passengers had to use the nearest bus stops as the start and end points of their trip. Another major problem was that there were very **few** buses in operation. By the end of the trial, *Kutsuplus* had 21,000 registered users, but only 15 buses. This would have a big effect on the result of the trial.

5 ___

In general, Helsinki residents had positive feelings about the service. **A lot of** them felt that it was convenient, especially for people who lived in areas where there wasn't **enough** public transportation. However, with **not enough** buses in operation, it wasn't convenient for everybody. In the end, city officials decided not to continue the service.

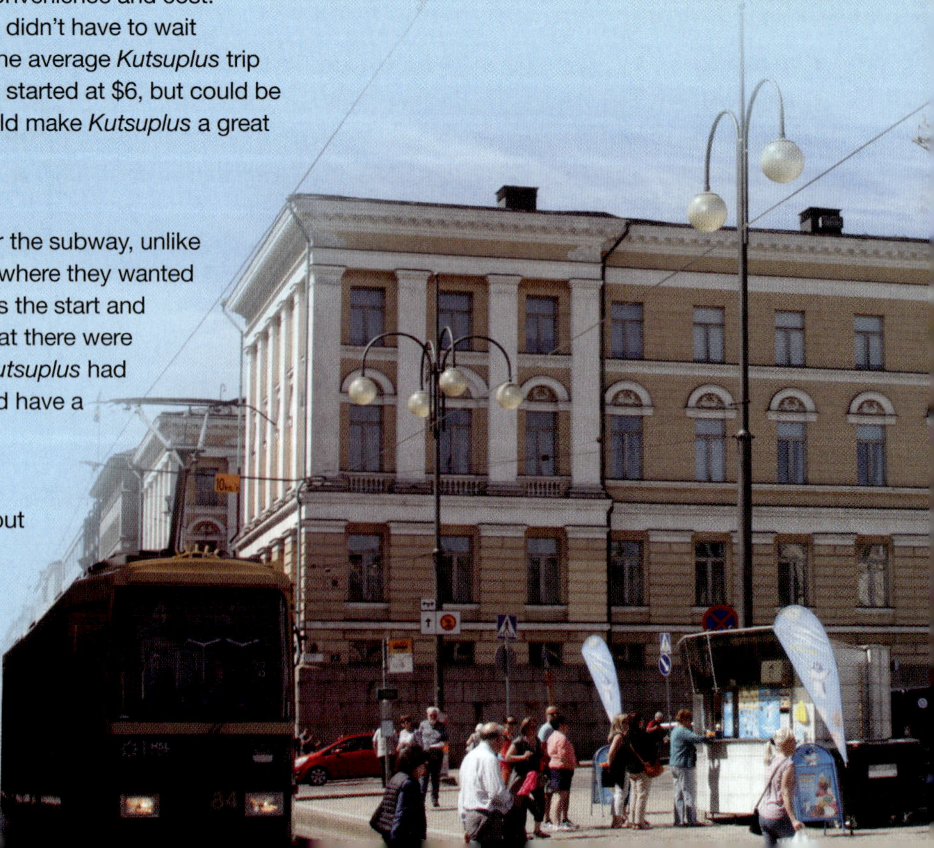

C READ FOR DETAIL Read again. Complete the sentences by choosing a, b or c.

1 The long-term goal of *Kutsuplus* was to encourage people to stop …
 a driving cars. b using the subway. c hiring minibuses.

2 Passengers could choose the start and end point of their trips by …
 a asking at the bus stop. b calling the driver. c using the internet.

3 There were … registered users by the end of the trial.
 a a small number of b not enough c a lot of

4 Overall, people who lived in Helsinki thought the service was …
 a useful. b expensive. c unfair.

5 The local … stopped the service.
 a businesses b government c residents

D SPEAK Work in pairs. Do you think the *Kutsuplus* service was a good idea? Why/Why not?

GRAMMAR
Articles and quantifiers

A WORK IT OUT Look at the words in bold in paragraph 2 of *Whatever happened to Helsinki's Kutsuplus transportation service?* Then complete the rules with *a/an, the* or – (no article).

Articles

1 We use ______ the first time we mention a person or thing.
2 We use ______ the second time we mention the person or thing.
3 We use ______ when it is clear who or what we are talking about.
4 We use ______ when we talk generally about people or things.

B Find and underline other uses of *a/an, the* or – (no article) in the same paragraph and match them with the rules (1–4) in Exercise A.

C Go to the Grammar Hub on page 126.

D PRACTICE Choose *a, the* or – (no article) to complete the questions.

1 How long does ***a*** / ***the*** / – trip from where you live (or are staying) to where you study usually take?
2 Would you like to go by ***a*** / ***the*** / – different type of ***a*** / ***the*** / – transportation? If so, which one?

E SPEAK Work in pairs. Ask and answer the questions in Exercise D.

F WORK IT OUT Look at the quantifiers in **red** in the text. Then choose the correct words to complete the rules.

Quantifiers

1 We use quantifiers to talk about ***amounts*** / ***qualities***.
2 Quantifiers go ***before*** / ***after*** nouns.

G Go to the Grammar Hub on page 126.

H SPEAK Work in pairs. What is the public transportation system like in your town? Does your town need more or fewer buses, trains or taxis? Why? Tell your partner.

PRONUNCIATION
Sentence stress: quantifiers

3.5 **A** Listen to the sentences from the article. Check (✓) the sentences you hear. Which words are stressed?

1 a <u>A lot</u> of them felt that it was convenient. ☐
 b A lot of <u>them</u> felt that it was convenient. ☐
2 a There were very few <u>buses</u> in operation. ☐
 b There were very <u>few</u> buses in operation. ☐

3.5 **B WORK IT OUT** Listen again and repeat the sentences. Do we usually stress the main noun or the quantifier?

C SPEAK Work in pairs. Practice saying the sentences. Listen and check your partner's pronunciation.

SPEAKING

3.6 **A** Listen to an expert explaining why the *Kutsuplus* service was canceled. What reasons does the expert give?

B Work in pairs and discuss the reasons. Do you think the local officials were right to stop the service? Why/Why not?

C Work in groups. Summarize your discussion. Explain your opinions and listen to the opinions of others.

D Work in groups. Plan how you could continue the service or do it differently.

LISTENING

A SPEAK Work in pairs. Look at the poster and discuss the questions.

1 What event is the poster advertising?
2 What happens during that event?
3 Why do cities and towns hold these kinds of event?
4 Does your city or town hold similar events?

3.7 **B LISTEN FOR GIST** Listen to a city council meeting about Car-Free Day and answer the questions.

1 What is Alfred Shaw's view of the Car-Free Day?
2 Do the others at the meeting agree with him?
3 What is Alfred's opinion of cars generally?
4 What two events does Alfred suggest holding instead?
5 What reason does Alfred give for being at the city council meeting?

Glossary

ban (v) to say officially that someone is not allowed to do something
campaign (n) a series of actions intended to produce social change
pedestrian (n) someone who is walking, especially in a town or city, instead of driving or riding

3.7 **C LISTEN FOR DETAIL** Listen again and choose the correct answers.

1 Why don't annual car-free days reduce the amount of traffic?
  a The city has little public transportation.
  b Cars are the most effective type of transportation.
  c You need more than ten car-free days a year.
2 How do car-free days affect pollution levels?
  a They decrease the amount of pollution.
  b They increase the amount of pollution.
  c They do not change the amount of pollution.
3 What might increase the number of people buying electric cars?
  a Providing free electricity-charging stations.
  b Providing opportunities for people to test drive them.
  c Providing online videos showing their advantages.
4 Why do people prefer traveling by car rather than by bus?
  a There are not enough buses.
  b The buses are too slow.
  c The buses are dirty.
5 Why doesn't this city provide bicycles that people can rent?
  a The roads are not very safe.
  b The council has not discussed the idea.
  c It would be too expensive to do.

3.7 **D** Read the information in the box. Now listen again. For 1–7, put the signposting language you hear in the correct position.

Listening for signposting language

When giving a short talk, speakers use signposting language to show the order of points and make their argument easy for people to follow.

- First, I want to talk about the problems.
- [1] First of ________________ …
- To start, …
- Finally, …

They can use it to introduce a new topic:

- Now, let's turn to the solutions.
- Moving on, I'll now discuss my ideas in more detail.
- [2] ________________ look at …
- [3] I'll now ________________ on to …

They can use it to introduce an extra point:

- In addition, …
- [4] Here's another ________________ why …
- [5] And ________________ thing, …
- Also, …

They can also use it to finish a section of a talk or to finish the talk:

- That's all I want to say on that. Any questions?
- In conclusion, …
- [6] In ________________, …
- [7] OK, to sum ________________ …

E SPEAK Work in pairs. Discuss Alfred's arguments and claims. Do you agree or disagree with Alfred?

VOCABULARY

Gradable and ungradable adjectives

A Underline the adjectives in the sentences from the council meeting about the Car-Free Day.

1 Some things about cars are fairly bad.
2 That's very funny.
3 That's a really good idea.
4 This may be extremely difficult.
5 Car-free days have a really tiny effect on driving habits.
6 There was an absolutely enormous traffic jam.
7 People were furious about that.
8 Some of our old buses are really filthy.

B Look at the adjectives in Exercise A. Which are gradable? Which are ungradable? Use the information in the box to help you.

Gradable and ungradable adjectives

Gradable adjectives can be made stronger and weaker. We can use a range of adverbs to change their strength (*fairly, very, extremely, a little, really*). They have a comparative form.

Ungradable adjectives cannot be made weaker. They already mean *very* + adjective. We can use some adverbs to emphasise the adjective (*extremely, absolutely, completely, really*). They do not have a comparative form.

C Write the adjectives from Exercise A in the correct place.

1 very ________ → excellent
2 very small → ________
3 very ________ → terrible
4 very angry → ________
5 very ________ → impossible
6 very dirty → ________
7 very ________ → hilarious
8 very big → ________

D Match the ungradable adjectives (a–g) with some of the adjectives (1–8) in Exercise C.

a wonderful ________
b huge ________
c fabulous ________
d great ________
e awful ________
f superb ________
g massive ________

E Go to the **Vocabulary Hub** on **page 143**.

F **SPEAK** Work in pairs. Describe something you have bought, seen, eaten or done recently using ungradable adjectives.

I saw an awful play last weekend. The lead actor was absolutely terrible. He kept forgetting his words!

SPEAKING HUB

A Go to the **Communication Hub** on **page 151**.

B **DISCUSS** Work in groups. Discuss the proposals and write notes on their advantages and disadvantages. Think of other ideas you can add to each proposal.

C **PLAN** Decide which proposal would be the best for the city and its people as well as being the best value for money.

D **REFLECT** Share your ideas with the class. Was your thinking similar or different?

- Evaluate suggestions and justify a choice
- Talk about why a plan didn't work

Café Hub

3.3 Getting there

F – tell a story P – intonation in responses

COMPREHENSION

A Complete the personal information with *Milly* or *Zac*.

Name:	1 ______	2 ______
Nationality:	American	American
Home town:	Seattle	Seattle
Address:	London	London
Job:	makes video games	owns a clothing store
Hobbies:	playing video games	cycling

B Look at the picture. Where do you think Milly and Zac are going today?

C ▶ Watch the video and check your ideas. Then answer the questions.

1. Which famous people does the cabbie say have been in the back of his cab?
2. Why are Milly and Zac amazed at the cabbie's story about his American girlfriend?
3. How does the cabbie react when Milly asks, 'Are you sure this is the right way?'

D Work in pairs. Discuss the last time you took a taxi.

- Where did you go from and to?
- How much did it cost?
- What did you talk about?

FUNCTIONAL LANGUAGE

Telling a story in five stages

A ▶ Work in pairs. Complete sentences (1–8) in the grey box with the endings (a–h). Then watch the video again and check.

a … went out with an American girl.
b … what happened the other day.
c … I was putting on a shirt and tie.
d … got my cab licence.
e … I miss you, Molly.
f … who I had in the back of my cab the other week.
g … she loved cycling.
h … she stopped answering my calls.

Telling a story in five stages

Introduction

1 You'll never guess … b
2 You won't believe … ___
3 I once … ___

Background

4 It was a few years ago now, when I … ___
The funny thing was she hated driving.
5 It turned out … ___
This is the best part: she used to run this fantastic little vintage clothes shop.

Problem

Well, a couple of months later, everything was going great, then one day, while I was watching the football, she said to me …
6 Before I knew it ___
All of a sudden things started to change.

Resolution

7 In the end … ___

Comment

8 I still love that girl … ___

Glossary

cycling **(v) (British)** = bike riding **(v) (American)**
cabbie **(n) (British)** = taxicab driver **(n) (American)**
football **(n) (British)** = soccer **(n) (American)**

MILLY

SAM

NEENA

ZAC

GABY

B Work in pairs. Look at Milly and Zac's responses in the box. Student A – retell the cabbie's story. Student B – use the responses at an appropriate moment.

> No way! Really? That's awesome! Really? You're kidding! So what happened? That's tough.

C Work in pairs. Student A – use a prompt from the box or your own ideas to begin a conversation. Student B – respond appropriately.

> I found $50 in the street. I earned a perfect score in English. I got tickets to see my favorite band. I won a prize. My dog died. My father lost his job.

USEFUL PHRASES

A Complete the useful phrases with the correct form of the verbs in the box. There are two verbs you do not need.

> be do joke jump let make take(x2)

1 Whatever, ________________ in the back, Jack.
2 Go on, ________________ a guess.
3 Only ________________!
4 I'll ________________ a short cut.
5 ________________ you two an item?
6 ________________ me tell you something.

B How do you say these useful phrases in your language?

PRONUNCIATION

Intonation in responses

3.8 **A** Listen and write the responses in the table below. Then listen and repeat the responses. Copy the stress and intonation.

B Which two types of responses have similar intonation?

Something is very good	Something is difficult	Something is surprising
		I don't believe it!

SPEAKING

A You are going to tell your partner about somebody you used to spend a lot of time with, but now you do not. Answer the questions.

- Who is this person – a childhood friend, a neighbor, a relative?
- When and how did you meet him/her?
- How often did you use to see him/her?
- What sort of things did you use to do / talk about?
- Why did you stop seeing him/her so much?
- When was the last time you saw him/her?
- What is he/she doing now?

B **DISCUSS** Work in pairs. Take turns talking about the person. Use the functional language to structure your story, and if you are listening, respond in an appropriate way.

Tell a story

➤ Turn to page 158 to learn how to write an email of complaint.

Unit 3 Review

GRAMMAR

A Complete the story with the correct form of the verbs in parentheses.

We left home early in the morning because it [1] ______________________ (*snow*) heavily. After we had found a parking space at the airport, we [2] ______________________ (*go*) straight to the check-in desk. That was when Kenny realized he [3] ______________________ (*forgot*) his passport. He thought he [4] ______________________ (*leave*) it on the kitchen table!

I [5] ______________________ (*decide*) to travel without him, but this made me nervous because I [6] ______________________ (*not fly*) on my own before. Luckily, when I [7] ______________________ (*wait*) in the line at the security checkpoint, Kenny [8] ______________________ (*call*) me with some excellent news.

He [9] ______________________ (*find*) his passport in the car and [10] ______________________ (*walk*) back to the check-in desk.

B Correct the mistakes in the following passage by using *a*, *an*, *the* or – (no article).

Japan has the famous network of bullet trains. A network is the world's busiest and connects the major cities of the country. Like many the major train networks, it gets very busy at peak times. It is mainly transportation system for long distances.

C Choose the correct quantifiers to complete the sentences.

1 The town center is full of traffic jams during the day. There are just *too much* / *too many* cars on the road.

2 Our city has a bicycle-sharing system. But at peak times it is difficult to get a bike because there are *not enough* / *too little*.

3 Overall, our town does not invest enough in transportation systems. This is because the council has *few* / *little* money for this.

4 How *many* / *much* of what the council says about the system is actually true?

VOCABULARY

A Choose the best words to complete the traffic reports.

Storm Anna is over, but there are still problems affecting roads and public transportation. You should only travel if it is essential. The central train station is closed, and they have [1]*canceled* / *delayed* all trains. Better news below the roads for the [2]*bus service* / *subway lines*. There [3]*is good service* / *are overcrowded trains* on all lines except for line 3. On that line, there are [4]*severe* / *slight* delays of about ten minutes.

Traffic is building up on Bank Street due to the [5]*roadwork* / *rush hour* at the corner of Bank and Church Street. You can expect [6]*heavy delays* / *heavy traffic* all day there, and probably a [7]*slight delay* / *traffic jam* during [8]*heavy rain* / *rush hour*. That's certainly what happened yesterday.

B Complete the sentences with the nouns in the box.

communication	connection	decision	expectation	inspiration	situation

1 I don't like to make a ______________ too quickly as I may regret it later.

2 It is important to see the ______________ between the job you want and your own experience and knowledge.

3 Many jobs need strong ______________ skills because talking and writing to people is essential.

4 When your ______________ is realistic, you are less likely to be disappointed.

5 When you cannot change a ______________ you are in, you can learn to accept it.

6 You can waste time waiting for ______________ to produce something. Sometimes it's best to take action.

C Find and correct the mistakes in four of the sentences.

1 Tell Stan that joke about the self-driving car. It's very hilarious.

____

2 I'm very angry. The train is late again!

____

3 This road is very bad. They need to repair it.

____

4 Sometimes, the old buses are very filthy.

____

5 These timetables are very impossible to understand.

____

6 The New York City bus tour was very excellent.

____

FUNCTIONAL LANGUAGE

Complete the dialogue with the words in the box.

awesome	best	couple	dear	guess	kidding	sudden	turned	way

A: You'll never [1] ______________ what happened on my last trip with Kate. We got lost on a mountain without a map.

B: Really? You're [2] ______________!

A: No, I'm not! It was a [3] ______________ of months ago in Patagonia. I left the map in our hotel.

B: Oh [4] ______________!

A: And even worse, it was dark when we got to the top. Then all of a [5] ______________ Katie remembers she left the flashlight at the hotel, too.

B: No [6] ______________! I can't believe she did that.

A: Yeah, we were a little stupid. But we were lucky. We met two locals and they helped us get back. And you know the [7] ______________ part?

B: What? Tell me!

A: They invited us for dinner. And it [8] ______________ out they owned the most expensive restaurant in town!

A: That's [9] ______________ .

4 CHANGE

Old and new buildings contrast in modern day Hong Kong.

OBJECTIVES

- talk about resolutions and plans
- talk about a life-changing book or movie
- make and discuss predictions
- discuss problems, reasons and consequences
- clarify and ask for clarification
- make and deal with complaints
- write a short essay

Work with a partner. Discuss the questions.

1 Look at the picture. What change does it show? Is it positive or negative?
2 Read the quote. Do you agree with it?
3 What have been the most important changes in your life?

4.1 Personal change

- Talk about resolutions and plans
- Talk about a life-changing book or movie

G – future forms
V – collocations: goals and resolutions
P – intonation for attitude and mood
S – summarizing

LISTENING

A SPEAK Work in pairs and discuss the questions.

1 Is New Year's Eve an important celebration:
- for you?
- in your country?

2 How do people celebrate the New Year in different parts of the world?

3 Why do people celebrate the New Year?

4.1 **B LISTEN FOR GIST** Listen to a video call between Julia and Shireen. Then answer the questions.

1 What is their relationship and where are they?

____

2 Check (✓) which of these topics they talk about.

a their New Year's Eve activities ☐
b moving ☐
c buying new clothes ☐
d making new friends ☐
e changing jobs ☐
f learning a language ☐

3 What do you think a New Year's resolution is?

____

4.1 **C LISTEN FOR DETAIL** Listen again. Are the sentences true (T) or false (F)? Correct the false sentences.

1 The weather was cold on New Year's Eve at Times Square in New York City. ___
2 Julia's boyfriend has always been very romantic. ___
3 Julia wants to do more physical exercise. ___
4 Julia can't speak Spanish. ___
5 Julia is looking for a new teacher. ___
6 Shireen thinks Julia reads too many advice books. ___
7 Shireen agrees to stop eating chocolate. ___

D SPEAK Work in pairs and discuss the questions.

1 Look at the list of the ten most common New Year's resolutions. Which do you think are the top three? Go to the **Communication Hub** on **page 147** to check your answers.
- get in shape and get healthy
- get organized
- enjoy life to the fullest
- change the foods you eat
- quit unhealthy habits
- help others achieve their dreams
- fall in love
- spend less, save more
- learn something exciting
- spend more time with family

2 What could people do to achieve these resolutions?

3 Which do you think are the hardest to achieve?

GRAMMAR

Future forms

A WORK IT OUT Look at the sentences (1–7) from the conversation between Julia and Shireen. Check (✓) the sentences in which the speaker made a decision or plan before this conversation.

1 Oh! Oops! I'll do it now. Hold on. ☐
2 I've decided to get in better shape this year, so I'm going to join a gym. ☐
3 I did get pretty cold. I'm going to look for a new hat tomorrow. ☐
4 Sophie's coming here to have lunch. ☐
5 I'm meeting a new teacher on Thursday. ☐
6 Make your mind up now! ☐
7 OK, OK. I'll stop eating it every day. ☐

B Complete the rules with the phrases in the box.

already | at a certain time in the future | at the time of speaking

Future forms

1 When we talk about future actions and events, we use *be going to* when we have _______________ decided to do something.

2 We use *will* when we make the decision _______________.

3 We use the present progressive when we have a planned arrangement _______________, usually with another person.

C Go to the **Grammar Hub** on **page 128**.

D SPEAK Work in pairs and discuss the questions.

1 What are you doing tonight?
2 Do you have any plans or arrangements for the weekend?
3 What do you intend to do over the next few months?
4 Imagine you have just realized you left your wallet at home. What will you do?

PRONUNCIATION

Intonation for attitude and mood

Intonation for attitude and mood

We change the tone of our voice to communicate our feelings about or attitude toward something. For example, interested/uninterested, surprised/unsurprised, positive/negative.

Our tone of voice can be in a high, mid or low position.

As we speak, our tone may rise and fall to show mood and attitude.

4.2 **A** Listen and write down the five words and phrases that you hear. They are in a neutral tone.

4.3 **B** Listen to the same five words and phrases. Each phrase is said in two different tones. Match each tone (*a* or *b*) with the moods and feelings below.

1 very positive ___
not very positive ___
2 excited ___
unexcited ___
3 interested and surprised ___
not interested ___
4 serious/determined ___
unsure ___
5 pretty surprised ___
not surprised at all (sarcastic) ___

4.3 **C** Listen again and repeat the sentences.

D SPEAK Work in pairs. Student A – go to the **Communication Hub** on **page 148**. Student B – go to the **Communication Hub** on **page 153**.

VOCABULARY

Collocations: goals and resolutions

A Match the phrases (1–6) with phrases with a similar meaning (a–f).

1 make a resolution
2 keep a resolution
3 break a resolution
4 quit a bad habit
5 reach a target
6 cut down on something

a do less of something
b achieve something
c set (yourself) a goal
d not do what you promised
e stick to a plan
f stop doing something that is not good for you

B Choose the best words to complete the sentences.

1 I've made a resolution *to learn* / *of learning* ten English words a day.
2 He managed to keep his resolution *by* / *in* using a fitness app.
3 He quit *smoking* / *smoke* last year.
4 She wants to cut down on *drink* / *drinking* coffee.
5 His goals are not very *realistic* / *real*. They're too hard to achieve.
6 Stick to your plan *until* / *when* you reach your target.

C Go to the **Vocabulary Hub** on **page 143**.

D SPEAK Work in pairs. Discuss your experiences of making resolutions and achieving goals. Find out:

- about resolutions your partner has made, kept and broken.
- how your partner managed to achieve his/her goals and stick to his/her plans.
- if your partner has ever quit, or cut down on, doing something.

SPEAKING

A Work in pairs. It is New Year's Eve, and you have agreed with your friend to each make eight resolutions. Student A – go to the **Communication Hub** on **page 149**. Student B – go to the **Communication Hub** on **page 150**.

B Talk to your partner about your resolutions, and ask them to make a resolution for each of your topics.

C Compare your resolutions with another pair. Do you think the resolutions will be easy or hard to keep?

READING

A Choose the correct sentence endings.

1 Self-help books …
  a contain instructions for doing something, especially operating a machine.
  b are designed to help you solve your own problems or improve your life.

2 Self-help books are usually written in …
  a a formal style that is for experts only.
  b an informal style for anyone.

B SCAN Read *Life Cycle* quickly. Match the phrases (1–5) with the topics (a–e).

1 Helena Schneiderlin	a a journey
2 *Life Cycle*	b the author's next book
3 Paris to Moscow	c the author's passion
4 cycling	d the author
5 *Inner Pedal Power*	e the author's first book

Life Cycle: How to find what you love and love what you find

About this book

Ten years ago, Helena Schneiderlin was a hard-working mom with no time for herself. Like many people, she didn't know what she really wanted to do with her life. Today, Schneiderlin is a cyclist who is well known for going on long and difficult journeys. She has ridden from Paris to Moscow by herself. She has also ridden across Australia, and last year she rode from the bottom of South America to the top.

Thanks to her cycling experiences, and the effect they have had on her life, Schneiderlin has also become a leading lifestyle expert. Her talks have been watched millions of times online, and she is regularly asked to speak at international lifestyle events and conferences.

In *Life Cycle*, which is her first book, she describes how finding her true passion changed her life, and explains how you can find yours.

'This isn't a book about cycling,' says Schneiderlin. 'It's a book about finding the thing that you enjoy doing most, and helping to make that thing benefit all other areas of your life.'

In *Life Cycle*, Schneiderlin uses her own story as an example for others to follow. She describes how she found her passion for cycling while on vacation with her family, and what it has taught her about commitment, sacrifice and success.

She provides valuable advice and life lessons that apply to all of us, including chapters on getting rid of the things in life that aren't helping, and how to identify the things that make you feel better about yourself.

Schneiderlin says:

> ***I believe that everyone has a passion, but they may not know what it is. I also believe that when you find that passion, you should use it to improve every area of your life. In my case, it was cycling – but it could have been anything. What's important is finding the thing that you love, and then using it in the right way.***

C SUMMARIZE Read the two summaries of the book *Life Cycle*. Which is the best summary? Why? Use the strategies in the box to help you.

Summarizing

A summary gives a brief explanation of the most important parts of the text.

To write a summary, first identify the details in the original text that don't need to be included in a summary. Then find the main points in the original text. Finally, put these together to make a summary, but try not to copy word for word.

1 Helena Schneiderlin has gone on a lot of long bicycle journeys. Once she rode from Paris to Moscow. Another time she rode across Australia. She has also ridden all the way up South America. She is a mom. She is a lifestyle expert and lots of people watch her talks on the internet. This is her first book. This book is about lifestyle changes. This book is about finding the thing you enjoy doing most. It is not about cycling, but she does talk about how she found her passion for cycling while she was on vacation with her family. This book is also about improving your life.

2 Helena Schneiderlin is a top lifestyle expert and a well-known cyclist who has ridden across continents. In this, her first book, she explains how cycling led to a life change and self-discovery, and gives advice on how to find your true passion. Using her own story as a guide, the author explains what she has learned from cycling, and discusses how these 'life lessons' can apply to all of us, in all aspects of life.

D SPEAK Work in pairs. Would you like to read *Life Cycle*? Why/Why not?

LISTENING

A LISTEN FOR GIST (4.4) Listen to four people talking about books or movies that changed their lives. Write *Maya, Lukas, Jody* or *Hassan*.

Who talks about …

1 a non-fiction film? ________
2 a fiction book? ________
3 doing what the book suggested? ________
4 the whole of human history? ________

B LISTEN FOR MAIN IDEA (4.4) Complete the summaries (1–4) with the words in the box. Then listen again and check your answers.

advice characters confident documentary father history impressive journey passion society sport recently

1 Maya read a self-help book about finding your true ________. She followed the ________ in the book and now she feels happier and more ________.

2 Lukas read a book about two ________ on a ________ in a strange place. The book made him think about his own relationship with his ________.

3 Jody learned a lot about the ________ of the human race in a book she read ________. She thinks the book is very ________.

4 Hassan saw a ________ set in the US. He feels that the story is about more than a ________; he thinks it also has an important message about ________.

C SPEAK Work in pairs. Which book or movie from the listening are you most interested in? Why?

SPEAKING HUB

A PLAN You are going to talk about a life-changing book or movie.

1 Choose a book or movie that had a big effect on you.
2 Think about how you can summarize the book/movie:
- What kind of book/movie is it?
- Who wrote/made it?
- What is it about?

3 Think about how it affected you:
- When did you read/see it?
- Why did you read/see it?
- How did it change the way you think/feel?
- Who else do you think should read/see it?

B SPEAK Work in pairs. Tell your partner about the book or movie that changed your life. Listen to his/her description. Ask and answer questions.

Talk about resolutions and plans
Talk about a life-changing book or movie

4.2 Social change

- Make and discuss predictions
- Discuss problems, reasons and consequences

G – making predictions
V – prefixes: *dis-*, *mis-*, *over-*, *re-*, *under-*
P – contraction of *will*; linking final consonant and first vowel sounds
S – paraphrasing

READING

A SPEAK Work in groups. Have you ever predicted something that later came true?

B Look at the headline of the article. Which word means:

a a person who has detailed knowledge about a subject?

b a person who talks about future events and situations?

C READ FOR GIST Read *How super-forecasters could replace professional experts.* Then choose the best summary.

1 Philip Tetlock carried out a study on why experts are good media guests, but make predictions that are generally less accurate than those made by most ordinary people.

2 Philip Tetlock carried out a research project to show that ordinary people who have particular thinking skills usually make better future predictions than experts.

How super-forecasters could replace professional experts

Katy Macnab

'Five minutes left, and Brazil is leading by three goals. They're going to win the World Cup again.' Apart from situations like this, the only certain thing about the future is that our predictions will probably be wrong.

In his early research, Philip Tetlock, of the University of Pennsylvania, showed that professional experts are only slightly better at predicting the future than monkeys. However, his most recent study is more hopeful.

This project involved thousands of ordinary people making predictions about social change. They used the internet, but they did not have detailed knowledge of a topic or access to secret data. Despite this, Tetlock found that 2 percent of them were rather good at it – better than both monkeys and professional experts. These 'super-forecasters' are smart, but not geniuses. However, they do have good thinking skills that anyone can develop.

Super-forecasters are analytical thinkers who update their opinion when they get new information, and they don't let their personal hopes affect their thinking. More importantly, they listen carefully to different views that they then use in their forecast. This perhaps explains why they make their most accurate predictions when working in teams of super-forecasters.

Surprisingly, professional experts usually lack these qualities. They tend to work alone and have strong personal opinions that guide their thinking. They speak with great confidence, stressing they are totally certain: 'I'm sure all cars will be driverless', 'Robots are going to replace office workers', 'We won't have an early election'. This means they are great TV guests and bloggers, but not the best forecasters.

Super-forecasters don't speak in a way that suits TV. They are more cautious: 'There may be an early election', 'People might stop reading newspapers', 'Chinese could become a global language'. They also use percentages to show how likely something is: 'I think this has an 80 percent chance of happening'. In this way, the team can discuss different ideas easily and make a final prediction.

Tetlock also identified three useful techniques, namely looking at current trends, comparing with past events and exploring the possible effects of a prediction: 'If everyone uses electric cars, how will we produce enough electricity?'

In the future, we will definitely develop better computers to make accurate predictions about our society. For now though, teams of super-forecasters are the best crystal balls we have.

Glossary

analytical (adj) using a method of separating things into their parts in order to examine and understand them

genius (n) someone who is much more intelligent or skilful than other people

tend (v) to usually do a particular thing

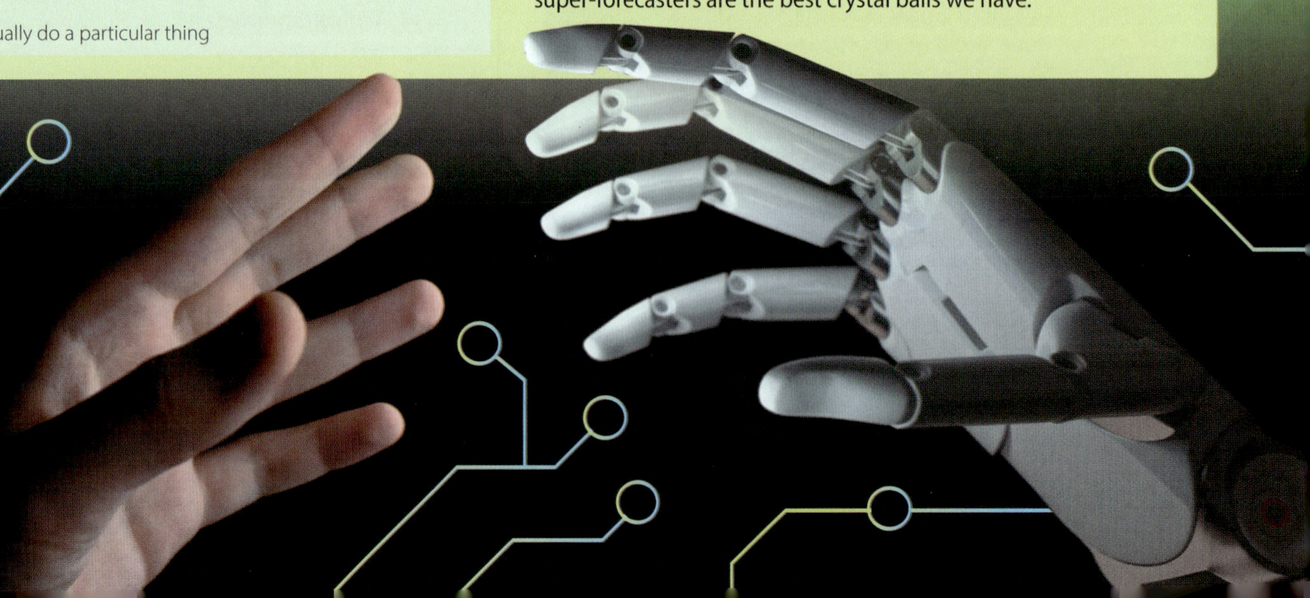

D **READ FOR DETAIL** Read again. Match the sentences (1–6) to the professional experts (PE) or the super-forecasters (SF).

1 They generally work individually. ___
2 They change their ideas when they learn something new. ___
3 They make better predictions when in groups. ___
4 Their personal beliefs influence their thinking. ___
5 They use percentages to show how certain they are. ___
6 The way they speak shows they are really certain. ___

E **SPEAK** Work in pairs. How easy is it to accurately predict these things? Put them in order (1 = easiest, 3 = hardest). Give reasons for your decisions.

a the winner of a soccer competition
b the number of schools we will need in ten years' time
c what life will be like in 100 years' time

GRAMMAR
Making predictions

A **WORK IT OUT** Look at the words in bold in the sentences from *How you could become a super-forecaster.* Which words show that the speaker is less than 100 percent sure of a prediction? Which show that the speaker is 100 percent sure?

1 Brazil is leading by three goals. They**'re going to** win the World Cup again.
2 There **may** be an early election.
3 I'm sure all cars **will** be driverless.
4 Our predictions **will probably** be wrong.
5 Robots **are going to** replace office workers.
6 Chinese **could** become a global language.
7 We **will definitely** develop better computers.
8 People **might** stop reading newspapers.

B Choose the correct words to complete the rules.

Making predictions

1 When we feel certain about a future event or situation, we *use* / *don't use* *be going to*, *will* or *won't*.
2 To show stronger certainty, we can add *definitely* / *probably*.
3 To show we are confident, but not completely certain, we can add *definitely* / *probably*.
4 There is little difference between *will* and *be going to* for predictions. However, if the present provides strong evidence or reasons for our predictions, we usually use *be going to* / *will*.
5 When we feel a future event or situation is possible, but are not completely certain, we *use* / *don't use* *could*, *may* or *might*.

C Go to the **Grammar Hub** on **page 128**.

PRONUNCIATION
contraction of *will*

4.5 **A** Listen to five pairs of sentences. In each pair, which sentence (a or b) uses *'ll*?

1 ___ 2 ___ 3 ___ 4 ___ 5 ___

4.6 **B** Listen and repeat the subject pronouns + *'ll*.

C **SPEAK** Work in pairs. Look at the audio script for Exercise A on **page 148**. Student A – say a sentence. Student B – point to the sentence. Take turns.

SPEAKING

A Follow the instructions.

1 Make two predictions for three of the topics in the box – one prediction for life in ten years' time, the other for life in 50 years.

education	housing and domestic life
free time	national culture
technology	the environment
transportation	work and employment

2 Give each of your predictions a percentage mark to show how likely you think it is.
3 What are the reasons for your predictions and percentages? Write notes.

B Work in pairs. Imagine you are a team of 'super-forecasters'. Explain and discuss your predictions. Practice using super-forecasting language from *How super-forecasters could replace professional experts.*

C Decide on your pair's strongest four predictions. Compare your predictions with another pair.

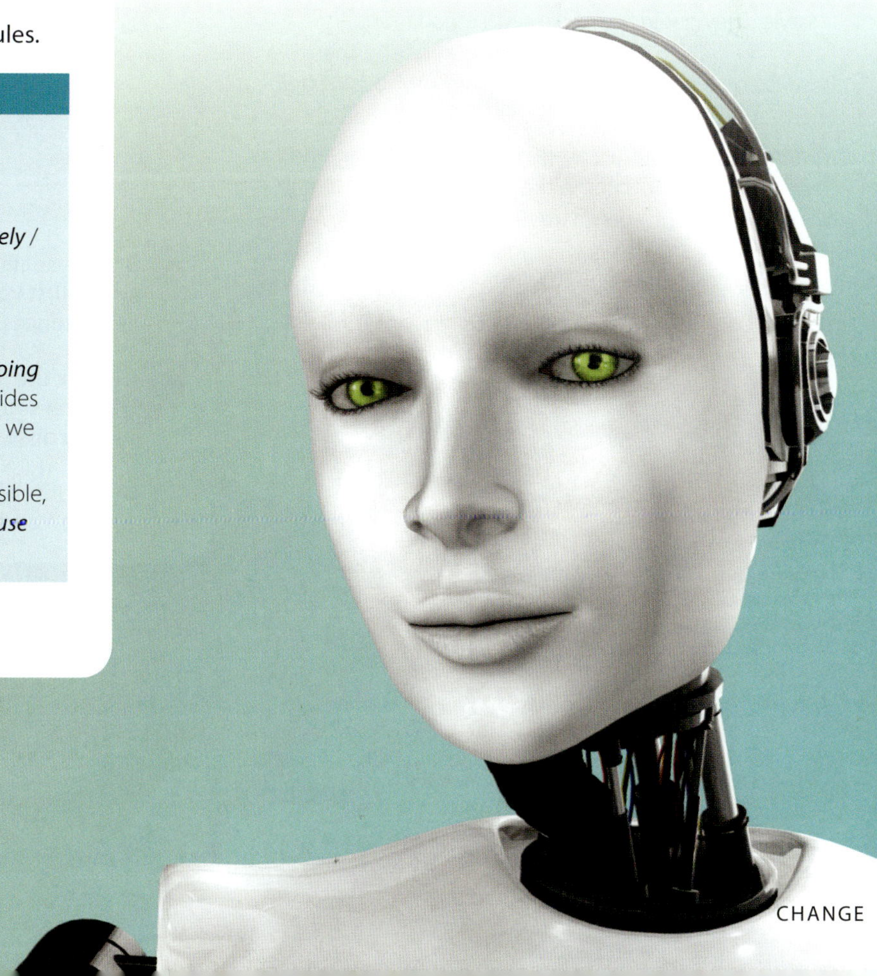

LISTENING

A SPEAK Work in pairs. Student A – describe picture a. Student B – describe picture b. Ask and answer the questions.

1 What are the positive things about living in this place?

2 What are the negative things about living in this place?

4.7 **B LISTEN FOR GIST** Listen to a current affairs radio show. Which is the best description of the show's main topic?

1 They are revealing why a negative prediction, about life in the countryside disappearing, is not very accurate.

2 They are describing the advantages and disadvantages of living in the countryside, in order to understand why the rural population is decreasing.

3 They are reporting on how we can increase the number of people living and working in the countryside in order to stop villages from dying out.

Glossary

expense (n) an amount of money that you spend in order to buy or do something

resident (n) someone who lives in a particular place

4.7 **C LISTEN FOR DETAIL** Listen again. Complete the summaries with the missing word(s) and/or number(s).

Kamiyama, which is [1] ______ from the city, offers a [2] ______ to attract new businesses. Toshi Asaka thinks working in Kamiyama doesn't have any [3] ______ and life is less expensive. Kamiyama is replacing old-style business with [4] ______ companies.

Nakanoshima fishing village provides opportunities for [5] ______ to live and work there for [6] ______ and to discover a more traditional lifestyle. They get inexpensive accommodations and [7] ______ jobs with farmers and fishermen. Because of this program, residents start new businesses, and that helps keep [8] ______ in the area.

Mishima Island gives money to [9] ______ people to pay for romantic dates in the hope that they will stay on the island if they get married and start a family. All [10] ______ receive a young cow. The meat is valuable (it costs [11] ______ per kilo), and these cows are [12] ______ disappearing completely.

D Match the phrases (1–4) with phrases with the same meaning (a–d). Use the strategies in the box to help you.

Paraphrasing

When explaining and describing things, we sometimes paraphrase, which means that we repeat a point, but use different words. We paraphrase for various purposes:

- As the speaker, to make a point clear or to give it extra emphasis.
- As the listener, to check, or show that you understand the speaker's point.
- Both the speaker and the listener may paraphrase to sum up a few points or longer argument.

1 young people are relocating to urban areas

2 offering financial incentives

3 blue-sky thinking

4 these cows are in danger of extinction

a ideas that are different, fresh and unexpected

b they're going to the cities

c offering things like free or cheap housing

d of disappearing completely forever

E SPEAK Work in pairs. Can you think of any other ways to encourage people to move to the countryside?

PRONUNCIATION

Linking final consonant and first vowel sounds

4.8 **A** Complete the sentences from the radio show. Then listen and check your answers.

1 Oh yes, such ______?

2 Tell ______ more.

3 What's the next ______?

4 That sounds like ______ fun thing to do.

5 But, is ______ such a good idea?

6 What ______ did you discover?

7 That isn't ______ lot of money, is it?

8 That's ______ lot of money!

4.8 **B** We usually link the final consonant sound of a word to the first vowel sound of the next word. Listen and repeat sentences 1 and 2 from Exercise A.

4.8 **C** Mark the links between the final consonant and first vowel sounds in Exercise A. Then listen again and check your answers. Repeat the sentences.

D SPEAK Work in pairs. Practice saying the sentences. Listen and check your partner's pronunciation.

VOCABULARY

Prefixes: *dis-*, *mis-*, *over-*, *re-*, *under-*

Using prefixes

We can add a prefix to a verb, noun or adjective to change its meaning. We use prefixes to show the opposite, to indicate a size or to show repetition. For example:

- *do – **un**do* *circle – **semi**circle* *organize – **re**organize*

A Underline the prefixes in the sentences from the radio show.

a Hi, I'm Rita Costa and this is *Rethinking the Future*.
b Many villages and small towns are going to disappear.
c We've talked before about overpopulation in urban areas …
d You've misunderstood the goal of this plan.
e My employees don't feel underpaid now!

B Match the prefixes in the box with their meanings (a–e).

dis- mis- over- re- under-

a bad or wrong
b opposite
c too little or too small
d again, but perhaps in a different way
e too much

C Complete the words in bold with the correct prefixes.

1 There are many things I _________**like** about where I live. I'd like to move.
2 I know someone who usually _________**works**. They should relax more.
3 I regularly _________**place** things and waste time trying to find them.
4 There are some terrible buildings in my town that they should knock down and _________**build**.
5 I usually _________**agree** with my parents, which sometimes leads to arguments.
6 I think that soccer players are _________**paid**. Some get millions of dollars a year. In contrast, I think nurses are _________**paid**.

D Go to the **Vocabulary Hub** on **page 143**.

E **SPEAK** Work in pairs. Rewrite the sentences in Exercise C so they are true for you. Then compare your ideas with your partner.

SPEAKING HUB

A Look at the predicted problems. Think of solutions to these problems. How can we stop this from happening? What could we do? How can we create a better future?

1 The use of robots and artificial intelligence will create massive unemployment because many jobs will disappear.
2 Across the world, air pollution will continue to increase and damage human health.
3 Using social media and digital services will lead to a near total loss of privacy, as companies and governments store and use all the data.

B **DISCUSS** Work in groups. Discuss your ideas. Choose the best two solutions for each problem.

C **REFLECT** Compare your group's solutions with another group. Are they the same or different? Which ideas are good examples of blue-sky thinking?

- Make and discuss predictions
- Discuss problems, reasons and consequences

Café Hub

4.3 Part-time

F – clarify and ask for clarification; make and deal with complaints
P – intonation and stress

COMPREHENSION

A ▶ 00:00–02:30 Work in pairs. Watch the first part of the video without sound and guess the answers to the questions.

1 How is Gaby feeling?
2 What does Sam suggest?
3 How does Gaby respond?
4 What do they decide?
5 What misunderstanding do they have?

B ▶ 00:00–02:30 Watch the first part of the video with sound and check your ideas in Exercise A. What is the main reason Sam gives for taking Gaby on?

C ▶ 02:30–04:49 Watch the second part of the video and answer the questions.

1 What does the customer complain about?
2 What does the customer want Gaby to do?
3 How does Gaby react to the situation?
4 Why does the customer ask to speak to Sam?
5 How does Sam deal with the situation?

FUNCTIONAL LANGUAGE

Clarifying and asking for clarification

A ▶ 01:48–04:49 Complete what Gaby says with the correct form of *get*, *say*, *lose* or *catch*. Then watch the clip and check your answers.

Clarifying and asking for clarification
1 What did you ________?
2 Sorry, I didn't ________ that.
3 I don't ________ what you're saying.
4 So you're ________ you want me to …
5 You've ________ me.
6 Why didn't you just ________ that?

B You are going to role-play a similar situation. Invent a conversation.

Student A: You are Sam. Begin with '… And remember to put the plates under here.'

Student B: You are Gaby. Ask for clarification and use phrases from Exercise A.

MILLY

SAM

NEENA

ZAC

GABY

Making and dealing with complaints

C 02:30-04:49 Put the words or phrases in parentheses in the correct position to complete the sentences. Then watch the second part of the video to check.

Making a complaint	Finding out about a complaint	Apologizing
[1]I'm sorry to bother you, but *I'm afraid* there's a problem with … (*I'm afraid*) I want my money back, please. [2]I'm not happy with the service. (*really*)	[3]What is the problem? (*exactly*) What seems to be the problem?	I'm sorry to hear that. [4]That's no problem. I'm sorry about that. (*so*) [5]I'm sorry for the inconvenience, madam; it won't happen again. (*terribly*)

USEFUL PHRASES

A Match the useful phrases in the box with the phrases before or after them from the video (1–6).

How dare you! How's your first day going? Leave it to me. Something good will come along. The customer is always right. What's up?

1 ______________ / I don't know, Sam.

2 ______________ / It always does.

3 ______________ / Great so far.

4 Excuse me! Hello? Excuse me! / ______________

5 ______________ / Unless the customer is wrong.

6 ______________ / I want to speak to the manager.

B How do you say these useful phrases in your language?

Glossary

madam **(n) (British)** = ma'am **(n) (American)**

PRONUNCIATION

Intonation and stress

4.9 **A** Listen and write down three versions of the question 'What's the problem?'

1 exactly ______________

2 seems ______________

3 appears ______________

B Practice the questions in Exercise A. Copy the stress and intonation.

SPEAKING

A Work in groups of three: the customer, the waiter, the manager. The customer makes one of the following complaints. Write a funny conversation.

- The soup is cold. (The customer has eaten the soup.)
- The steak is tough. (The customer has eaten the steak.)
- The pasta is too salty. (The customer has eaten the pasta.)

B **PRESENT** Perform your conversation in front of the class.

Clarify and ask for clarification

Make and deal with complaints

➤ Turn to **page 159** to learn how to write a short essay.

Unit 4 Review

GRAMMAR

A Choose the best verb form to complete the sentences.

1. I can't tonight, I'm busy. I can't call you tomorrow either. I ***'m visiting*** / ***will visit*** my parents all day. I ***'m calling*** / ***'ll call*** you when I'm free.
2. He ***'s going to*** / ***'ll*** do that this afternoon. It's next on his to-do list.
3. Can I borrow some money? You ***'re getting*** / ***'ll get*** it back tomorrow, if that's OK?
4. Well, let me check. Yes, I ***'m going to*** / ***'ll*** lend you $20. Here you are.
5. We're going now. We ***'re meeting*** / ***'ll meet*** Asif for dinner at seven. Bye!
6. Oh, look – it's raining. Change of plans! I ***'m not bike riding*** / ***won't bike*** today; I think I ***'m going to*** / ***'ll*** take the subway instead.
7. My sister's decided to go to Italy for her vacation this year. She ***'s going to*** / ***'ll*** visit Rome, Florence and Venice.

B Choose the correct words to complete the dialogues.

1 **A:** This game is terrible. Come on – let's leave early.
B: No, let's wait until the end.
A: But there's no point staying. We're losing 5–0. We [1] ***aren't going to*** / ***probably won't*** win.
B: But we [2] ***might*** / ***will*** score one at least. You never know!
A: There's no way that [3] ***may*** / ***will*** happen. Come on. Time to give up.

2 **A:** Flying cars? Of course, I can't say it will [4] ***definitely*** / ***probably*** happen, but it [5] ***definitely*** / ***probably*** will.
B: No, it [6] ***might not*** / ***won't*** happen. I'm sure. Think about it, what would happen if every car were a flying car? It would be too dangerous.
A: But people are definitely [7] ***going to*** / ***might*** want them in the future. The technology can't be far away. I'm sure we [8] ***'re going to*** / ***could*** have flying cars in the future!

VOCABULARY

A Which is the odd-one-out in each set of verb phrases? Why?

1. **a** achieve a target
   b make a resolution
   c set a goal
2. **a** keep a resolution
   b stick to a plan
   c cut down on something
3. **a** do less of something
   b quit a bad habit
   c stop doing something
4. **a** reach a goal
   b break resolutions
   c not do what you promised

B Look at the words in bold. Are the prefixes correct or incorrect? If they are incorrect, write the correct prefix.

1. The fire destroyed a lot of the building. We'll need to **misbuild** it.
2. I'm definitely **overpaid**. Unless I get a pay raise, it'll be time to find a new job!
3. Some money has **reappeared**. It's missing. No one is leaving until we find it.
4. Wait, let me help! It's heavy. Don't **overdo** it. I'll lift it with you.
5. And, don't **disbehave**! We want to impress our school visitors.
6. No, I didn't pass my exam, unfortunately. I have my **overtake** next week.
7. The answer is wrong. You made a **miscalculation**. Do the math again.
8. Urban **underpopulation** isn't a problem now, but it soon will be. The city's population is increasing rapidly.

FUNCTIONAL LANGUAGE

Choose the correct words to complete the dialogue.

A: Hi. I'm sorry to [1] ***excuse*** / ***bother*** you.
B: Not at all, sir. Please sit down. How can I help?
A: I took one of your courses, 'How to change your life in seven days'. I'm [2] ***afraid*** / ***not happy*** there is a problem with the course.
B: Oh, I'm sorry. Could I have your name first?
A: Jim Stevens.
B: Sorry, I didn't [3] ***take*** / ***catch*** the last part.
A: Stevens.
B: Great. What was the problem with the course?
A: I took the course ten days ago. But my life hasn't changed!
B: OK, I'm not sure I [4] ***have*** / ***get*** what you are saying. Do you mean the course was unhelpful?
A: Yes. I expect results for the price. And the teacher was always late.
B: I'm sorry to [5] ***hear*** / ***catch*** that. We will talk to the teacher. That won't [6] ***happen*** / ***bother*** again.
A: And the money?
B: So you're [7] ***saying*** / ***hearing*** you want your money back?
A: Exactly!
B: Ok, just let me check with my manager …

5 WORK AND BUSINESS

A business that makes nothing but money is a poor business.

Henry Ford

Designers making tough decisions at a studio in Berlin.

OBJECTIVES

- discuss and give advice about employment skills and career interests
- discuss and suggest workplace benefits and changes
- describe and evaluate a small business
- talk about environmental business ideas
- structure a presentation
- write a cover letter for a job application

Work with a partner. Discuss the questions.

1 Look at the picture. What do you think they are doing?

2 Read the quote. Do you agree that a business which makes money can still be poor?

3 What kind of business would you like to work for?

5.1 At work

- Discuss and give advice about employment skills and career interests
- Discuss and suggest workplace benefits and changes

V – employment skills and qualities; verbs of influence
G – past habits and states
P – intonation and rhythm: holding your turn
S – following reference links in a text

VOCABULARY

Employment skills and qualities

A SPEAK Work in pairs. Look at the pictures (a–d). What are the people's jobs? What skills do they need to do these jobs?

B SPEAK Work in pairs. Student A – go to the Communication Hub on page 152. Student B – go to the Communication Hub on page 147.

C Read the report about a business survey. Complete the phrases with *be* or *have*.

Many jobs require very specific skills and experience. However, there are also many skills and personal qualities that all employers are looking for. We surveyed **100 Human Resource Managers** to find out which are the most important general employment skills and qualities.

People should:

1 ________ reliable.
2 ________ good communication skills.
3 ________ good digital technology skills.
4 ________ good at time management.
5 ________ good at team work.
6 ________ able to work well under pressure.
7 ________ creative thinking skills.
8 ________ good people skills.

D SPEAK Work in pairs. Match the quiz questions in Exercise B with the employment skills in Exercise C.

E SPEAK For each employment skill in Exercise C, give yourself a percentage score to show your strength. For example, 100 percent = a great strength, no room for improvement. Then work in pairs and explain your answers.

LISTENING

5.1 **A LISTEN FOR KEY WORDS** Listen to the first part of a conversation between Fiona and Michael about work. Choose the correct answer for each question.

1 What is Fiona's job?
 a Human Resources Manager in a company
 b a career advisor
 c a psychologist
2 What is Michael's role in the bank?
 a head of the accounting team
 b a junior member of the property investment team
 c a member of the general management team
3 Why is Michael unhappy in his job?
 a He doesn't work closely with other people.
 b His work doesn't offer enough challenges.
 c He has to meet too many deadlines.
4 In which of these areas hasn't he worked?
 a fashion
 b sports
 c food and drink
5 Which of these things seem most important to Michael?
 a team work
 b digital technology skills
 c time management

5.1 **B LISTEN FOR DETAIL** Listen again. Are the sentences true (T) or false (F)? Correct the false sentences.

1 Michael has worked in five different banks. ____
2 Michael currently uses the skills that the test showed as strengths. ____
3 Michael sometimes bought the clothes that he modeled. ____
4 Michael enjoyed working as a waiter, but not when it was very busy. ____
5 Michael feels positively about training and coaching. ____
6 Michael is interested in setting up his own company. ____

C SPEAK Work in pairs. Look at the pictures (a–d) again. Which job do you think Fiona will recommend for Michael? Why?

5.2 **D LISTEN FOR DETAIL** Listen to the second part of the conversation. Which job does Fiona suggest? Why?

PRONUNCIATION
Intonation and rhythm: holding your turn

5.3 **A** Listen to Michael and Fiona saying *Nice to meet you*. Then answer the questions.

1. Who sounds like they have finished speaking?
2. Who sounds like they are going to continue speaking?
3. What is the difference in how they say *you*?

Holding your turn

We can show that we are going to continue speaking by making a word longer, and sometimes, by using a rising intonation.

We show that we have finished speaking by using a falling intonation on our final word.

5.4 **B** Read the box. Now listen to more examples from Michael and Fiona's conversation. Underline the words the speaker makes longer to show they want to keep speaking.

1. I see you've been there for five years.
2. Well, it's been a good job, but um, I just feel there's something missing.
3. I see, and what is it that's missing exactly?
4. I've recently been made assistant manager, so those skills are important.
5. I mean, you look very neat and well-dressed.

C **SPEAK** Work in pairs. Practice saying the sentences in Exercise B. Listen and check your partner's pronunciation.

GRAMMAR
Past habits and states

A **WORK IT OUT** Look at the sentences from the conversation between Fiona and Michael. Which underlined verbs are state verbs and which are action verbs? Which words are used to show repeated actions and events in the past?

1. I used to be a fashion model.
2. They'd usually give us some of the clothes after the shoot.
3. I used to help new members.
4. At busy times, you would always be under a lot of pressure.
5. I used to be tired but happy at the end of each day.

B **WORK IT OUT** Choose the correct words to complete the rules. Then match the rules (2–5) with the sentences in Exercise A.

Past habits and states

1. We use ***used to*** and ***would*** to describe actions and states in the ***present* / *past***. These are likely to be actions and states that are finished.
2. To talk about repeated actions in the past, we can use *used to* **and / but not** *would*.
3. To talk about temporary repeated states in the past, we can use *used to* **and / but not** *would*.
4. To talk about permanent states in the past, we use *used to* **and / but not** *would*.
5. We usually use adverbs of frequency with ***used to* / *would***.

C Go to the **Grammar Hub** on **page 130**.

D **SPEAK** Work in groups. Discuss some of these topics.

- your childhood vacations
- your grandparents' younger lives
- how you have changed over the years

SPEAKING HUB

A You are going to give and receive some career advice. Think about your employment skills, interests and experience. Then write down three jobs you would like to do.

- What strengths do you have?
- What skills have you used in work, college or your hobbies?
- What is important for you in a job or career?
- What types of work do you like doing?

B **PLAN** Write some interview questions that will help you find out about your partner's employment skills, interests and experience. Use the audio script on **page 171** to help you.

C **SPEAK** Work in pairs. Interview your partner. Listen carefully and make a note of his/her answers. Take turns.

D **DISCUSS** Choose three jobs that you think match your partner's skills and experience. Are they the same jobs that your partner wrote down before?

READING

A SPEAK Work in pairs. Look at the pictures (a–c) and discuss the questions.

1 Which offices would you like to work in? Why?

2 Which wouldn't you like to work in? Why?

B READ FOR MAIN IDEA Read *Are we in the middle of a workplace revolution?* Which is the best subtitle? Why?

1 Why digital technology companies are so successful

2 Why office life is changing and how to manage it

3 Why modern offices and unusual benefits are bad for business

a

b

c

Are we in the middle of a WORKPLACE REVOLUTION?

Pool tables, nap-pods and free food. **They** sound like things at an all-inclusive vacation resort rather than in an office. However, digital tech companies have redesigned the office and provided unusual benefits to make the workplace a more pleasant and productive place to be. Need a massage to help reduce stress? Want to bring your pet to work? No problem. For these companies, the days of individual cubicles where people would work on their own for eight hours a day are no more.

This trend is now spreading outside Silicon Valley. Bob Randell, director of MiCareer, says, 'Everyone's realizing that tech companies don't provide fancy perks or game areas in order to seem cool and trendy. They want their staff to feel good about themselves and their jobs. Happy employees are less likely to leave to work for a competitor and, most importantly, they are more productive.'

This new kind of workplace also encourages people to collaborate and to be creative. Playing table tennis with a colleague you rarely work with can lead to new ways of working and fresh thinking. Thinking over a problem while lying in a hammock might be the best way to find **its** solution.

However, this doesn't mean employers should immediately offer free ice cream, replace desks with couches or let staff bring pets to work. 'Firms have to make sure their perks are of real interest to their employees, and that **they** can afford them for the long term. If a company stops offering a perk, staff happiness goes down and people are less satisfied,' says Anna Tang, head of HR at DigitalForest.

'We advise our managers to monitor the effects of the perks carefully. We now offer free breakfasts instead of free lunches. **This** persuades people to arrive early and to start work with good energy levels, which makes **them** more productive. Large free lunches just made them feel sleepy.'

This revolution in the workplace is unlikely to slow down. As Randell says, 'All businesses can improve by increasing creativity, collaboration and happiness at work. The most successful ones do exactly **that**, and which companies don't want to be successful?'

C Read again. What do the words in bold refer to? Use the strategies in the box to help you.

Following reference links in a text

We use pronouns (for example *it, them, this*) instead of repeating the same word many times. They usually refer to a person or thing, but they can also refer to ideas.

In order to improve your understanding of a text, it is important to understand which idea or thing the pronouns refer to.

1 Line 1: They *pool tables, nap-pods and free food.*
2 Line 21: Its ____________
3 Line 25: they ____________
4 Line 31: This ____________
5 Line 32: them ____________
6 Line 37: that ____________

D READ FOR DETAIL Read again. Answer the questions.

1 According to the article, which of the following are advantages of modern office design and attractive perks?
 a increasing the quality of work that people do
 b attracting high quality people to the company
 c encouraging sharing ideas with different people
 d stopping people from leaving their jobs

2 What should companies who want to update their benefits and office design do?
 a provide benefits that employees really want
 b consider the future costs of extra benefits
 c avoid canceling benefits
 d offer different perks to other companies

E SPEAK Work in groups. Find and underline the innovations and perks in the article. What is your opinion of them?

VOCABULARY
Verbs of influence

A Look at what Sophia, the boss, said to her employees Simon and James. Match the pairs of sentences with the correct meanings (a or b).

1 Yes, of course, you can do that.
2 Do it now!
 a She allowed him to do it.
 b She told him to do it.

3 Of course, no problem. Feel free to do it.
4 I'll explain why it's a good idea, and then you might change your mind.
 a She persuaded him to do it.
 b She let him do it.

5 You must do it. If you don't, I will fire you!
6 I think you should do it this way.
 a She made him do something.
 b She advised him to do something.

7 Don't worry, I'm sure you are good enough. Try to do it.
8 I would like you to do it, not her.
 a She encouraged him to do it.
 b She wanted him to do it.

B Go to the **Vocabulary Hub** on **page 144**.

C SPEAK Work in pairs. Talk to your partner about when you were younger. Use the ideas below to help you.

When I was younger, …		
my parents	didn't let	me …
a friend	used to make	us …
my teacher	encouraged	my parents …
I	advised	a friend …

SPEAKING HUB

A Look at picture b on page 52. Imagine that you work in an office similar to this. You are going to a meeting about improving the workplace and employee motivation. Make a list of ideas to take to the meeting.

B DISCUSS Work in groups. Compare your ideas, giving explanations for each one.

C ORGANIZE Choose the best ideas and make a simple plan to show your office redesign and list your chosen perks.

D PRESENT Show your plan to the class. Then take a class vote to decide which plan is the most popular.

Discuss and give advice about employment skills and career interests

Discuss and suggest workplace benefits and changes

5.2 In business

- Describe and evaluate a small business
- Talk about environmental business ideas

G – the passive voice V – business collocations P – silent consonants S – listening for examples

READING

A SPEAK How much extra do you think you pay when you buy these products? Match the products (1–3) with the percentages in the box. There are two extra percentages. Then work in pairs and compare your answers.

40 percent	300 percent	600 percent	1,200 percent	4,000 percent

1 bottled water rather than tap water
2 pre-cut vegetables and fruits rather than uncut
3 takeout espresso coffee rather than making it at home

B SPEAK Work in pairs and discuss the questions.

1 How often do you buy the items in Exercise A?
2 What's your opinion of these products and the prices charged for them?

C PREDICT You are going to read an article about a new company, Aethaer. Before you read, answer the questions below. Then work in pairs and compare your answers.

1 Look at the picture and the title of the article. What product does Aethaer sell?
2 Which four of the following topics do you think will be in the article?
   a personal information about the owner of Aethaer
   b the production method
   c Aethaer's business model – product, price and target customers
   d full details of how to order, including delivery costs
   e information about other similar businesses
   f why people buy the product

D READ FOR GIST Read *The new bottled water?* Check your answers to Exercise C.

Business Business

News and views on the business of doing business

The new bottled water?

AETHAER (MoreChaos Ltd)

At ***Business Business***, we are always looking for the next bottled water, and we think we have found it – bottled air.

Businessman Leo de Watts is selling jars of fresh air from the British countryside to the residents of polluted cities around the world. He claims Britain has 'designer quality' fresh air, and he sells Aethaer as a luxury product. Each jar costs a breathtaking £95.

The business was launched two months ago. Orders can be made online only, and already 200 jars have been delivered to China. Not many small businesses achieve sales of £16,000 in their first months, and none have a product that is so cheap to produce. With plans to start marketing Aethaer in India, Watts could be made a millionaire by selling almost nothing, nothing but air.

'Air-farming' is incredibly easy. The air is collected from different places in the countryside, from the seaside to the mountains, from the green hills to the forests. The glass jars are held high in the air, and are closed after a few minutes. That's it – the simplest production process ever. Next, a label saying where the air comes from is put on the jars. Then, after they have been packed for delivery, they are sent overseas. Job done.

There are currently 15 different 'airs' in the product range. Watts claims that each one has different qualities, depending on where they were collected. While some customers do buy the air to inhale, many people buy the jars as gifts that will be kept and won't be opened.

Aethaer air is sold as a luxury item for wealthy people, but other new businesses have started selling cans of compressed air for everyday or sports use. Each can contains 200 breaths of air, and they come with a face mask for efficient and easy use.

People laughed when bottled water was first sold in convenience stores, but now everyone buys it. With urban air pollution increasing, it may not be long until you buy a can of clean air as well as a bottle of water every day.

E READ FOR DETAIL Read again. Complete each sentence with a word or phrase from the article.

1 Aethaer's customers usually live in ______.
2 Aethaer air costs £95 per jar because it is a ______.
3 Leo de Watts started the business ______.
4 If you want some Aethaer air, you must buy it ______.
5 There aren't any other businesses with such ______ production costs.
6 He may become ______ in the future.
7 Collecting the air is ______ to do.
8 Before he puts the jars in boxes, Leo adds ______ to each jar.
9 ______ want to breathe the air, but ______ never open the jars.
10 Aethaer's competitors want people to buy air for their ______ lives or when they are playing ______.

F SPEAK Work in pairs and discuss the questions.

1 Why does the article say bottled air is the new bottled water?
2 What do you think of the idea of buying a jar of air for £95?

GRAMMAR

The passive voice

A WORK IT OUT Look at the sentences from *The new bottled water?* and underline the main verb. Which sentences tell us who did the action?

1 Leo de Watts sells Aethaer as a luxury product.
2 The business was launched two months ago.
3 Orders can be made online only.
4 The air is collected from different places in the countryside.
5 Other businesses have started selling cans of compressed air.

B Choose the correct words to complete the rules.

The passive voice

We form the passive voice with *be* + the past participle of the main verb.

We use the passive voice when:

a we *know* / *don't know* or it is *important* / *not important* who or what did the action.
b it is *obvious* / *not obvious* who or what did the action.
c we *want* / *don't want* to focus on the person or thing affected by the action.

C Go to the Grammar Hub on page 130.

SPEAKING HUB

A You are going to choose a business idea as the winner of the *Business Business* Low-cost Business of the Year Award. Read the information about *Fall Memories* below, then compare it to the *Arctic Diamond* on page 152.

B PLAN Write notes to help you present the information in the company profile.

C PRESENT Work in pairs. Present the company to your partner. Then listen to your partner's presentation and write down the key information.

D REFLECT Take a class vote to decide which company (including Aethaer) should win the Low-cost Business of the Year Award.

Basic information

Country: Canada
Business name: Fall Memories
Slogan: 'Bring nature's beauty into your home'
Founded by: Jessica Malone
Products: Fall leaves in a gift box (Three leaves: 1 red, 1 yellow, 1 mixed)
Price: $30

Production process

picked by hand / dried and pressed for ten days / wrapped in tissue paper / packed in a gift box

Sales

Online business: 130 orders in first three days / $12,000 in first year of business
Current customers: People from hot, dry states in the US, e.g. Nevada, Texas
Future markets: India / Saudi Arabia / Dubai

REPAIR, REUSE OR RECYCLE

LISTENING

A SPEAK Work in pairs and discuss the questions.

1 How often do you buy new clothes?
2 Have you ever bought second-hand clothes?
3 Why do you think some people prefer to buy second-hand clothes?

5.5 **B LISTEN FOR GIST** Complete the sentences (1–3) with the words in the box. Then listen to the *Business Business* podcast and check your answers.

marketing outdoor second-hand

1 Patagonia is an ________ clothing company.
2 They launched a ________ campaign called 'Worn Wear'.
3 It encouraged people to return old clothes and buy ________ clothes.

5.5 **C LISTEN FOR MAIN IDEA** Listen again. Are the sentences true (T) or false (F)? Correct the false sentences.

1 Patagonia makes things that people only wear when they are at work or at home. ___
2 Patagonia is one of many companies in this sector. ___
3 'Worn Wear' is a campaign that persuades people to make their own clothes. ___
4 Customers are encouraged to give their old clothes to be sold second-hand. ___
5 'Worn Wear' is the only time Patagonia has launched an environmental campaign. ___
6 As a company, Patagonia is concerned about its effect on the environment. ___

5.5 **D LISTEN FOR EXAMPLES** Listen again. Complete the sentences (1–5) with the missing words and phrases. Use the strategies in the box to help you.

Listening for examples

In longer talks and discussions, speakers give examples to support their claims.

Here are some words and phrases that we usually use to introduce an example:

- *For example, …*
- *… like …*
- *… such as …*
- *As the survey(s) / results / sales figures show …*
- *Another instance …*

Paying close attention to the examples that follow these words will give you a fuller understanding of the speaker's main ideas.

1 There are lots of others, ________ North Face, Berghaus and Columbia.
2 'Worn Wear' encourages customers to buy second-hand Patagonia clothes, ________ old jackets and T-shirts.
3 ________, their sales have increased because of campaigns like 'Worn Wear'.
4 ________, they made record profits on Black Friday.
5 ________ of this is when Patagonia took out a full-page ad in *The New York Times*.

E SPEAK Work in pairs and discuss the questions.

1 Why do you think the 'Worn Wear' and 'Don't Buy This Jacket' campaigns were a success for Patagonia?
2 Would campaigns like these encourage you to buy a company's products? Why/Why not?
3 Can you think of any other environmental business ideas like these campaigns? Give examples.

PRONUNCIATION
Silent consonants

A 5.6 Listen to the sentences from the podcast. Complete the missing words. Which consonant is silent?

1 Patagonia strongly believes in taking care of the e____________.

2 Is 'Worn Wear' the first time Patagonia has used such an unusual marketing c____________?

B 5.7 Underline the silent consonants in each word. Then listen and check your answers.

1 climbing	3 high	5 knowledge
2 design	4 honest	6 write

C Find and correct the mistakes in the sentences.

1 There's no dout the company sold a lot more clothes as a result of the magazine ad.

2 It's rong to say that all businesses are only interested in profits.

3 To understand advertising, you need to understand people's sychology.

4 You can buy second-hand Patagonia clothes at any of their stores with a 'Worn Wear' sain.

VOCABULARY
Business collocations

A Choose the correct verbs to complete the business collocations in the sentences from the podcast.

1 The company *landed* / *launched* a new marketing **campaign** called 'Worn Wear'.

2 That is an unusual way to *run* / *do* a **business**.

3 It's difficult for a clothing company to *have* / *make* a **profit** selling new clothes.

4 They've *run* / *built* a **brand** based on respecting nature.

5 Patagonia is doing a good job of *attracting* / *adapting* **new customers**.

B Match the beginnings of sentences (1–5) with the endings (a–e).

1 Over the last few years, the company has **built**

2 When we **attract**

3 The company tries to **launch**

4 Like any business, we **make**

5 The best way to **run**

a new **investors**, we'll have more money.

b **money** by selling our products for a profit.

c its **reputation** successfully.

d a **company** is to hire good people.

e at least one new **product** every year.

C Go to the Vocabulary Hub on page 144.

D SPEAK Work in pairs and discuss the questions.

1 What can a retailer do to attract new customers?

2 What campaigns have companies that you know launched recently?

SPEAKING HUB

A You are going to talk about an environmental business idea in a podcast. Student A – read the box below about the company *REI stores*. Student B – go to the Communication Hub on page 153.

B PLAN Plan your talk:

- explain the idea.
- include examples and business collocations.
- be prepared to answer questions.

C SPEAK Work in pairs. Role-play presenting a business podcast. Listen to your partner and ask questions about his/her idea. Take turns.

D REFLECT Work in pairs. Which idea do you think is the best? Why?

Student A

Company:	REI stores, US
Retail sector:	Outdoor clothing and equipment
Environmental idea:	Close all stores on Black Friday (the busiest shopping day of the year in the US). Employees are paid to take the day off.
Reason:	To encourage people to spend more time outdoors.
Result:	700 organizations, and 8 million people supported the campaign via social media in its first few years.

- Describe and evaluate a small business
- Talk about environmental business ideas

5.3 Major presentation

F– structure a presentation P– ordering adverbs

COMPREHENSION

A Work in pairs. Which of the following factors are most important for a successful business presentation?

- be nicely dressed
- have neat, organized handouts
- show interesting slides
- have a clear, confident voice
- be relaxed and in good shape
- be punctual

B ▶ 00:00–02:48 Watch the first part of the video. What problems does Matthew Williams have with his presentation?

C Predict what happens next. Do *Jobs, Jobs, Jobs and Jobs* get the contract?

D ▶ 02:48–04:53 Watch the second part of the video and check your ideas. Why does Neena smile at the end?

FUNCTIONAL LANGUAGE

Structuring a presentation

A Put the phrases in the box into a logical order in the table.

Do you have any questions? So first of all, I'd like to talk about So, the next question is That brings us to Today's presentation is all about

Structuring a presentation

Welcome

Good morning and thank you for coming.

Introduction

1 ________ how we can work together in Brazil.

Main points

2 ________ the benefits.
Let's take a look at the first slide.
We have a great deal of experience in the jobs marketplace.

3 ________ how to market ourselves in Brazil.

4 ________ the end of the presentation.

Questions

5 ________

Summary

Great. So to sum up, we see an exciting future …

B ▶ 00:00–02:48 Watch the first part again and check your answers.

C At what stage of a presentation would you expect to hear sentence beginnings 1–5? Use the headings in the box.

1 Let's move on now to look at … ________
2 In conclusion, … ________
3 The purpose of today's presentation is … ________
4 I'd like to finish with … ________
5 The next point I would like to explore is … ________

Glossary

pay rise **(n) (British)** = pay raise **(n) (American)**

MILLY

SAM

NEENA

ZAC

GABY

USEFUL PHRASES

A Rewrite the useful phrases from the presentation less formally. Use the words and phrases in the box.

agree lots write / right away

1 We have a great deal of experience …

____

2 If we can come to an agreement …

____

3 We can put the contract together immediately.

____

B How do you say these useful phrases in your language?

PRONUNCIATION

Ordering adverbs

5.8 **A** Listen and write the ordering adverbs in the correct space.

1 ____________ 4 ____________

2 ____________ 5 ____________

3 ____________ 6 ____________

B Work in pairs. Practice the adverbs in Exercise A. Student A – say a number. Student B – say the adverb.

SPEAKING

A You are going to give a presentation about a personal possession and explain why it is a good one to have. Choose from the personal possessions in the box or your own ideas.

my bag my bicycle my car my coat my laptop/computer my cell phone

B Prepare your presentation. Make presentation slides if possible and think about the following:

- Give a 'history' of your personal possession – when, why, how did you get it?
- Talk about the advantages (and any disadvantages) of owning it.
- Say why it has been a good personal possession to have.
- Use at least six examples of functional language.

C PRESENT Give your presentation to the rest of the class.

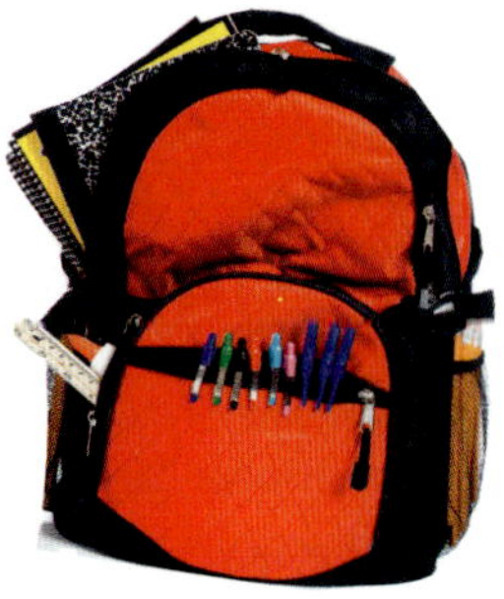

Give a presentation

➤ Turn to page 160 to learn how to write a cover letter for a job application.

Unit 5 Review

VOCABULARY

A Complete the interviewer's comments with the phrases in the box.

communication skills | creative thinking skills | people skills | reliable | teamwork | time management

1 Well, he arrived late, so he isn't very good at ________________.

2 I'd say she has poor ________________ – she didn't offer any fresh ideas.

3 Her presentation showed she doesn't have good ________________ – it wasn't engaging, and her voice was rather flat.

4 I wasn't impressed by his ________________; sometimes he looked annoyed by the questions, and he was a little rude once.

5 But will he be good at ________________? He's only been self-employed before, as a gardener. Not much group work there.

6 I don't think she is ________________. She's left her last few jobs after only two months.

B Choose the best verbs to complete sentences. Use the correct tense.

At first, I didn't [1] ________ (*tell / want*) him to go on the rollercoaster, but he kept asking, and finally he [2] ________ (*persuade / advise*) me to buy his ticket. I certainly didn't [3] ________ (*encourage / make*) him to do it, and I [4] ________ (*tell / let*) him to be careful. In the end, it was fine and he enjoyed it, so I [5] ________ (*let / persuade*) him go again.

My boss [6] ________ (*let / make*) my colleague work over the weekend. I couldn't believe it, but the boss is the boss. I [7] ________ (*advise / let*) him to do it this time, but to say no the next time. My boss has [8] ________ (*allow / let*) him to have two days off later in the week, so it isn't so bad. Personally, I think that if they [9] ________ (*want / make*) us to work overtime, they could [10] ________ (*advise / persuade*) us by offering extra money!

C Complete the sentences with the nouns in the box.

customers | business | profit | campaign

1 The company made a big ________ last year so employees received a bonus.

2 The key to running a successful ________ is to find the right employees.

3 The gyms have attracted ________ because they offer excellent amenities.

4 The health stores launched a ________ about healthy eating.

GRAMMAR

A Find and correct the mistakes in the sentences.

1 A few years ago, I would be an accountant. I loved that job.

____

2 I'd to arrive early most days. I liked it when the office was quiet.

____

3 So I use to have long lunch breaks.

____

4 He didn't used to be such a relaxed boss.

____

5 They would being very quiet when I returned to the office.

____

B Complete the text with the correct form of the verbs in parentheses.

Parmesan cheese, *Parmigiano-Reggiano*, [1] was created (*create*) over 1,500 years ago. It [2] ________ (*have*) a strong and complex savory taste, and its name [3] ________ (*protect*) by EU law since 1955.

Parmesan cheese [4] ________ (*make*) from cow's milk. The cows [5] ________ (*milk*) in the morning, and the milk [6] ________ (*put*) into a large metal container. Key ingredients, such as whey, [7] ________ (*add*), and then the mixture [8] ________ (*heat*) to 35°C. After 15 minutes, the temperature [9] ________ (*raise*) to 55°C for an hour.

FUNCTIONAL LANGUAGE

Complete the conversation with the missing words.

Ian: So, moving on to the next item on the agenda: the new office design. [1] ________ of all, does anyone [2] ________ any questions about the design? No? OK, so …

Kim: Um, just a [3] ________. I just want to say that we should think again. Do we really need a Ping-Pong table?

Ian: I think we've heard enough, Kim. So moving [4] ________ to the next agenda item …

Kim: One minute – I have more to say!

Ian: Sorry, it's time to decide. Before we vote, let's [5] ________ up what we decided. We're saying keep the table, but forget the fish tank, for health reasons and cost reasons. Who agrees?

Kim: No, Ian, you can't make decisions like this. And that [6] ________ me to the next topic we need to discuss: how to make these meetings better.

6 SPORTS AND HOBBIES

A surfer rides the inside of a wave at End of the road Beach, Tahiti.

OBJECTIVES

- describe a sport or game
- give a short, persuasive talk
- talk about hobbies and free time activities
- discuss trying new things
- express your opinion
- write an article for a magazine

Work with a partner. Discuss the questions.

1 Do you agree with the quote?
2 Look at the picture. Why do some people take part in sports like this?
3 How interested are you in these free time activities?

team sports running music collecting

6.1 Take part!

- Describe a sport or game
- Give a short, persuasive talk

G – modals of obligation   V – adjectives ending in *-ive;* sports   P – rhythm: pausing
S – listening for main and supporting points

COMPETITIVE SNOWBALL FIGHTING HITS SCOTLAND!

If you think snowball fights are just for school kids, think again. **Competitive** snowball fighting (*Yukigassen*) is a sport for grown-ups that has just arrived in Scotland.

It began as an official sport in Japan in 1987 and since then it has spread to countries such as Canada, Australia, Norway and Sweden. And this weekend sees the first ever matches in Scotland.

Angus Campbell, the captain of the Glasgow Ice Warriors, says 'I think *Yukigassen* is going to be **massive** here. We have the snow and it's a fun and **inexpensive** sport that's **attractive** to everyone. Each match only lasts nine minutes, so you don't have to be super athletic to take part in a game.'

The snowball fights take place on a small court (40 m x 10 m) between two teams of seven players – each team must include male and female members. To win a game, a team has to capture the other team's flag or take out all their opponents with direct snowball hits. If a player is hit, he or she has to leave the game.

The rules are fairly simple, but Angus insists that having an **effective** strategy is the key to success. 'You must work together as a team, be **decisive** and keep calm when under pressure from your opponents. You shouldn't just run for the flag – you'll soon get hit and be out. You need to be more **creative** than that. Your team only has 90 snowballs, which the referee gives you before the game. You must not make any more during the game.'

Six teams are taking part in the event this weekend, and there will be trial sessions for anyone who wants to try it out. 'It looks a little **aggressive** at first, but you shouldn't feel nervous. It's only snow, and all players have to wear a helmet, which we'll provide. However, you should bring some warm gloves!'

If you're interested in trying something **active** on these cold winter days, you simply must go. The games are **impressive** to watch, and great to play. After all, what's more fun than playing in the snow?

The first game starts at 2 pm, on Saturday, in the city park. Entrance is free. Families are welcome.

READING

A SPEAK Write down the names of the different sports you know in pictures 1–4. Then check with another student. What do you know about these sports? Tell your partner.

B READ FOR GIST Read *Competitive snowball fighting hits Scotland!* Where do you think the article comes from? Why?

- **a** a national newspaper
- **b** a sports science academic journal
- **c** a local news and information website
- **d** a travel blog

C READ FOR DETAIL Put the sentences in the order the information appears in the article.

- **a** New players do not need to bring any safety equipment. ___
- **b** There are two ways to beat the other team. ___
- **c** There are men and women on every team. ___
- **d** Generally, people think children, not adults, have snowball fights. _1_
- **e** A good game plan is important. ___
- **f** Several countries play competitive snowball fighting. ___

D SPEAK Work in pairs. What is your opinion of *Yukigassen*? Would you like to play it?

GRAMMAR

Modals of obligation

A WORK IT OUT Look at the sentences from *Competitive snowball fighting hits Scotland!* Write *nc* (you have no choice, this is 100 percent necessary) or *c* (you have a choice, this is not necessary) next to each sentence.

1 All players **have to** wear a protective helmet. ____
2 You **don't have to** be super athletic. ____
3 You **should** bring some warm gloves. ____
4 You **shouldn't** just run for the flag. ____
5 Each team **must** include male and female members. ____
6 You **must not** make any more during the game. ____
7 You **shouldn't** feel nervous. ____

B Match the beginnings of the rules (1–4) with the endings (a–d).

Modals of obligation

1 We use *must / have to / need to*
2 We use *must not* when
3 We use *don't have to* when
4 We use *should / shouldn't*

a to talk about what is or is not a good idea.
b for rules and situations that are necessary (strong obligation).
c we describe things that are not necessary, but you may still do them.
d we describe something that is not allowed.

C Go to the **Grammar Hub** on **page 132**.

D SPEAK Work in pairs. Compare the pairs of sports below. How are they similar and different? Think about their basic rules and the qualities of good players and successful teams.

baseball and cricket soccer and basketball
marathon running and running a 100 meter race tennis and racquetball

4

3

VOCABULARY

Adjectives ending in *-ive*

A Look at the adjectives in bold in *Competitive snowball fighting hits Scotland!* Then complete the definitions with the correct adjective.

1 A ______________ person makes choices quickly and confidently.
2 A ______________ sport involves two teams trying to beat each other.
3 If something is ______________, it is very big or, in informal English, very popular.
4 An ______________ suggestion or idea is one that people are interested in.
5 An ______________ plan works well and produces the result that is wanted.
6 An ______________ activity doesn't cost a lot of money to do.
7 Having an ______________ lifestyle means you do not sit around all day.
8 ______________ behavior includes being rude or angry in order to get what you want.
9 You admire an ______________ performance because it is very good and shows a lot of skill.
10 A ______________ person thinks of new or unusual ways to do things.

B SPEAK Complete the questions with adjectives from Exercise A. Then work in pairs and interview your partner. Take turns. Give reasons and examples to explain your answers.

1 What is the most ______________ sport that you have played?
2 Are you a very ______________ person? Why do you say that?
3 Which actors do you think are very ______________?

SPEAKING

A You are going to write six sentences to describe a sport or game without naming it. Your classmates will try to guess what it is. Think about:

- reasons why you like it.
- the skills and qualities you need to play it well.
- how it is played and what you need to play it.

B Work in groups. Read your sentences to the group. Can your classmates guess the sport or game?

C Work in groups and discuss the questions.

1 Which of the sports and games described have you played? What do you think of them?
2 Which haven't you played? Would you like to try them?
3 Which is the most popular sport or game?

LISTENING

A SPEAK Work in pairs and discuss the questions. What are the pros and cons of playing video games?

6.1 **B LISTEN FOR GIST** Listen to a talk about eSports and choose the correct answers.

1 What is the best title for the talk?
   - a Video gaming: is it good for you?
   - b Video gaming: the professional sport of the future
   - c Video gaming: nothing more than a free time activity
   - d Video gaming: the next Olympic sport?

2 What is the purpose of the talk?
   - a to give general information about eSports
   - b to encourage people to watch and play eSports
   - c to persuade people to agree with the speaker's opinion of eSports
   - d to give a balanced analysis of eSports

6.1 **C LISTEN FOR DETAIL** Listen again to the introduction. What is the main idea of the talk? What are the supporting points? Use the strategies in the box to help you.

> **Listening for main and supporting points**
>
> When giving a talk, speakers usually give a main idea and then support it with detailed points, in the form of examples, statistics, names or dates.
>
> Listen carefully to identify the main ideas and the supporting points that follow.

6.2 **D** Listen again to another part of the talk. What is the main idea? What are the supporting points?

6.1 **E LISTEN FOR DETAIL** Listen again to the whole talk and choose the correct answers.

1 The speaker thinks that many people in the audience …
   - a play video games at home.
   - b understand how popular eSports are.
   - c don't realize that video gaming is played professionally.

2 She says playing video games is a sport because …
   - a players practice a lot.
   - b the games have clear rules.
   - c there are winners and losers.

3 She says a great eSports player
   - a has a strong mind and body.
   - b plays other traditional sports.
   - c spends all their time training.

4 She says eSports are different from traditional sports because …
   - a they are growing in popularity.
   - b young people like them.
   - c people watch them online.

5 The Olympic Games wants to include sports that …
   - a involve physical activity.
   - b young people like.
   - c have professional players.

F SPEAK Work in pairs and discuss the questions.

1 In your opinion, what is the difference between a sport and a game?

2 Do you agree with the speaker's arguments? Which of her points do you think are strong or weak?

3 Do you think eSports should be an Olympic sport? Why/Why not?

VOCABULARY

Sports

A Check (✓) the nouns that refer to people.

1	champion	☐	6	stadium	☐
2	coach	☐	7	fan	☐
3	final	☐	8	top player	☐
4	league	☐	9	tournament	☐
5	spectator	☐	10	trophy	☐

B Complete the sentences with the correct form of the nouns in Exercise A.

1 In the Olympic Games, the winners receive a gold medal, not a ________________.

2 Usain Bolt and Michael Phelps are two of the most famous Olympic ________________.

3 The FIFA World Cup is a soccer ________________ that is held every four years.

4 If you are a Manchester United ________________, you should wear something red to the game.

5 The Camp Nou, in Barcelona, is the largest soccer ________________ in Europe. It can hold nearly 100,000 ________________.

6 ________________ can earn a lot of money from advertising and sponsorship contracts.

7 If a team loses a lot of games, the ________________ usually loses his or her job.

8 Nothing in sport is certain – you don't always see the two best teams in a ________________.

9 There are 20 teams in the national ________________. Each team plays the others twice, so each team plays 38 games in a year.

C SPEAK Work in groups and discuss the questions.

1 What are the popular spectator sports and sports tournaments in your country?

2 Who are the top sportsmen and women in your country? What do you know about them?

PRONUNCIATION

Rhythm: pausing

Pausing

We use pauses to support the meaning of what we say, and to help the listener follow and understand.

- Use very short pauses to group words that go together in phrases or clauses. This is similar to using a comma in writing, but can be more frequent.
- Use short pauses at the end of sentences and paragraphs. This is similar to using a period in writing.
- Make the pauses a little longer to add emphasis or drama.

6.3 **A** Listen to the beginning of the talk about eSports. Mark where the speaker pauses. The first two pauses have been marked (/) to help you. Which pauses are longer to add emphasis or drama?

Soccer, / basketball, / golf, tennis – four of the world's most popular sports. They are played by millions and watched by millions more, and all four are in the greatest festival of sports, the Olympic Games.

6.4 **B** Where do you think the speaker pauses in the next part of the talk? Mark (/) each pause. Then listen and check your answer.

However, there is one sport that is just as popular as those, but it still hasn't been accepted in the Olympics, and indeed, many people say that it is not even a sport. What sport am I talking about? eSports. Yes, electronic sports, or competitive video gaming.

C SPEAK Work in pairs. Practice saying the extracts in Exercises A and B. Listen and check that your partner pauses in the correct places.

SPEAKING HUB

A You are going to give a short persuasive talk (1–3 minutes). Choose one of the titles and write notes for your talk.

- eSports are not sports and should not be part of the Olympic Games.
- Playing video games is a good activity for children.
- Video games are generally more negative than positive.
- Professional athletes earn too much money. Their pay should be limited.
- ________________ is the best sport to both play and watch.

B PLAN Look at your notes and use these tips on how to improve a persuasive talk.

- Have a good introduction and conclusion.
- Use confident language, e.g. *I strongly believe …; It's undoubtedly true that …*
- Use rhetorical questions, e.g. *Why should we do this?; I'm sure you agree, don't you?*
- Support your main points with good examples and arguments.
- Practice your pausing and rhythm when giving the talk.

C PRESENT Work in groups. Give your talks. Write down the main ideas and supporting points of the other talks.

D REFLECT Work in groups. Did you agree or disagree with the speakers? Which points do you think were strongest?

Describe a sport or game

Give a short, persuasive talk

6.2 Hobbies

- Talk about hobbies and free time activities
- Discuss trying new things

V – hobbies and free time activities
S – identifying tone
G – present perfect progressive; *had to* / *needed to*
P – *been*: unstressed

LISTENING

A SPEAK Work in pairs and discuss the questions.

1 Describe the pictures (a–e). What are the people doing?

2 Which free time activities are you most interested in? Why?

B LISTEN FOR GIST Listen to a radio show about hobbies and free time activities. Match the pictures (a–e) with the guest speakers (1–5). 6.5

1 ___ 2 ___ 3 ___ 4 ___ 5 ___

C LISTEN FOR DETAIL Listen again. Choose the best answers for each person. 6.5

1 Speaker 1
  a buys and sells new cars.
  b spends a lot of money on his hobby.
  c makes enough money from his hobby to pay for his vacations.

2 Speaker 2
  a finds his hobby stressful at times.
  b also works as a photographer.
  c is learning how to do something new.

3 Speaker 3
  a wants her husband to spend more time on his hobby.
  b says her husband spends a lot of time on his hobby.
  c shares her husband's hobby.

4 Speaker 4
  a shares her interest with her friends.
  b has her own social media site about her interest.
  c regularly stays at hotels in Boston.

5 Speaker 5
  a usually has a few hobbies at the same time.
  b finds it hard to get interested in things.
  c has had many different hobbies.

D SPEAK Work in groups and discuss the questions.

1 Are there any hobbies you would like to try? Which ones?

2 What are the benefits of having a hobby?

VOCABULARY

Hobbies and free time activities

A WORK IT OUT Look at the three sets of verb phrases from the radio show. Match the beginnings of the phrases with the endings (a–d).

1	join	a	interest in a hobby
	be	b	a hobby
	lose	c	a society
	take up	d	my thing
2	be	a	into something
	be	b	you in shape
	keep	c	of a singer
	be a fan	d	a member of a fan club
3	get	a	relaxing
	be	b	from daily stress
	collect	c	you out of the house
	escape	d	something, like stamps or art

B Complete the table with the verb phrases from Exercise A.

Show enthusiasm for a hobby	Something you may do as part of a hobby	Benefits of a hobby	Start a new hobby
be into something			

C Go to the **Vocabulary Hub** on **page 144**.

D SPEAK Rewrite these sentences so they are true for you. Then work in pairs and compare your answers. Give reasons and examples.

1 I'm a big fan of the singer Ed Sheeran.

2 I need to find a way to get myself out of the house more frequently.

3 I've collected a lot of different things during my life.

4 I don't do much to stay in shape. I should do more.

5 I've never been a member of a fan club nor joined a society.

6 Cooking isn't really my thing.

7 I've had a few hobbies that I've lost interest in.

8 This year, I've taken up a new hobby.

GRAMMAR
Present perfect progressive

A **WORK IT OUT** Look at the sentences from the radio show and choose the correct answers.

1 Which sentence describes a single action that continues up to now? Which sentences describe an action or activity that is frequently repeated up to now?
   a He's been doing it since his teens.
   b We've been waiting here all day.
   c For the last six months, I've been going to pottery classes.

2 In each sentence, is the main verb a state or an action verb?
   a He's been doing it since his teens.
   b I've had this interest since I was a child.
   c I've been a member of his fan club for a long time.

3 What are the recently completed actions in the sentences? Which sentence focuses on the fact that the action is completed? Which sentence focuses on the duration of the action?
   a I've been working in the studio this afternoon – that's why my hands are so dirty.
   b I've just bought an old Mini, so I'll start working on that tomorrow.

B Complete the rules (1–5) with the words in the box.

progressive long now past present repeated state

Present perfect progressive

1 We usually use the present perfect progressive to talk about an action that started in the ________________ and is continuing ________________. The emphasis is on the unfinished activity.
2 We also use it to talk about a past action that has just finished, but which has a ________________ result.
3 We can use it to talk about ________________ or frequently ________________ actions.
4 We do not use the present perfect progressive with ________________ verbs.
5 We use the present perfect progressive to talk about how ________________ something has been happening.

C Go to the **Grammar Hub** on **page 132**.

D **SPEAK** Work in pairs. Student A – go to the **Communication Hub** on **page 150**. Student B – go to the **Communication Hub** on **page 155**.

PRONUNCIATION
been: unstressed

6.6 **A** Listen to three sentences. What do you notice about the pronunciation of *been* in each sentence? Does it rhyme with *seen* or *thin*?

been

In the present perfect progressive, *been* is an auxiliary verb and it is normally unstressed and pronounced /bɪn/.

The stressed words are usually the main verbs and key information words, not the auxiliary verbs.

6.7 **B** Listen and repeat.

SPEAKING HUB

A Choose one of your hobbies or free time activities and prepare to talk about it. Answer the following questions.

1 When did you take it up and why?
2 How much time and money do you spend on it?
3 What do you like about it?
4 Is there anything you dislike about it?
5 What benefits does it bring to you and your life?
6 Why would someone else enjoy your hobby?

B **SPEAK** Go around the class and interview three or four of your classmates about their hobbies. Write notes.

C **DISCUSS** Work in groups. Tell each other about your interviews. Which hobbies were:

- the most unusual?
- the most interesting?
- the most dangerous?
- the most expensive?

READING

A SPEAK Work in pairs. When was the last time you:

- tried a new food or drink?
- listened to a new singer or group?
- visited a new place?

B READ FOR MAIN IDEA Read the first two paragraphs of *My six months of trying new things*. Then complete the summary with a word in the box.

interesting relaxing

Candie is not very active. She decided to spend the first six months of this year doing different activities because she wants to find a hobby that will make her free time more ______________.

My six months of trying new things

By Candie Carmichael

July 15

I've never been the kind of person who does lots of exciting things in their free time. Paragliding, swimming with dolphins, climbing Mount Everest – not me! My idea of danger is to sit on the couch and watch the latest crime series on TV. The closest I get to nature is when I 'like' my friends' cat pictures on social media. As for climbing Himalayan mountains – forget it! I'd rather climb the stairs to bed.

But at one point toward the end of last year, I started to feel that my life was becoming a little … well … boring. I needed to take up a hobby. But which one? There are so many things out there – how do you know what you will enjoy? So I decided to spend the first six months of this year trying out a new hobby each month. I was a complete beginner at every activity I tried.

Here's what happened:

January: Fly fishing

The first thing I learned was that no flies are harmed in fly fishing. You make a pretty, artificial 'fly' and attach it to a hook on a fishing line. [1]___ When a fish takes a bite you … oh, I don't know. I did NOT do well at this. One month: lots of badly made 'flies', and ZERO fish (apart from the ones I got at the fish and fries place on my way home).

February: Stamp collecting

Why does anyone do this? [2]___ After a whole four weeks of attaching little squares of paper from around the world into a big book with blank pages, I still have no idea.

March: Ping-Pong

This one really surprised me. I'm actually good at it! I joined a club, and I didn't need to spend a lot of time practicing before I started winning games. After only a month, I was already one of the best players in the group. I really can't believe it. [3]___

April: Beekeeping

Surely all I had to do was keep some flying insects in a box? [4]___ About a hundred bee stings later, I realized that a lot can go wrong and beekeeping is a serious (and sometimes painful) business. I think I'll just get my honey from the grocery store in future.

May: Playing the ukulele

The ukulele is like a very small guitar. It has four strings. It makes you look like a giant when you play it. [5]___ I didn't have to be in great shape. It wasn't dangerous and it wasn't painful. And at the end of the month, I could play *Rivers of Babylon* all the way through. If that isn't success, I don't know what is!

C READ FOR KEY WORDS Read the rest of the article. Match the activities (1–6) with Candie's experiences (a–f).

1 fly fishing
2 stamp collecting
3 yoga
4 beekeeping
5 playing the ukulele
6 Ping-Pong

a This hobby caused her pain.
b She wasn't successful at all.
c She was able to complete a whole song.
d She was surprised by how good she was at this activity.
e She learned that she is not able to do this kind of thing well because she isn't athletic.
f She didn't understand why this is a popular hobby.

D READ FOR DETAIL Read again. Fill in the blanks in the article (1–6) with the sentences (a–f).

a Is this really a hobby?
b What could possibly go wrong?
c Maybe there's a chance for me to get in shape after all.
d Then you throw the line on the water.
e I really enjoyed this.
f I am not very flexible.

Identifying tone

An essay or serious news article will usually have a formal or serious tone. Other kinds of text, like emails between friends or some web or magazine articles, may have an informal or humorous tone.

You can identify a text's tone from the way it is written and the author's choice of phrases, adverbs and adjectives, capital letters and punctuation.

E Look at the highlighted words and phrases. What do the capital letters, punctuation and word choice tell us about the article's tone?

F SPEAK Work in pairs. If you had to choose one of these activities to take up for a month, which would you choose? Why? Tell your partner.

June: Yoga

Ouch! I thought yoga was relaxing. I didn't realize I had to be super athletic and flexible. After one month of downward dogs and (falling over!) tree poses, I learned some very important things about me: I am not very athletic. 6___ I do not like yoga.

GRAMMAR

had to / needed to

A WORK IT OUT Look at the sentences from *My six months of trying new things*. Then choose the correct words to complete the rules.

I needed to take up a hobby.
All I had to do was keep some flying insects in a box.
I didn't have to be in great shape.
I didn't need to spend a lot of time practicing before I started winning games.

had to / needed to

1 We use ***had to*** and ***needed to*** when we talk about things that were necessary in the ***present / past***.
2 We use ***didn't have to*** and ***didn't need to*** when we talk about things that were ***not allowed / not necessary but possible*** in the past.

B Go to the Grammar Hub on page 132.

C SPEAK Work in pairs. Tell your partner:

- three things you *had to / needed to* do yesterday. Explain why.
- three things you *didn't have to / didn't need to* do yesterday. Explain why.

SPEAKING HUB

A Think of one or two new activities that you have tried. Use the list to help you or your own ideas.

get a pet
plant flowers or grow a plant
make a birthday present instead of buying one
try a new form of exercise
take language classes
make a photo album
learn a new board game

B PLAN Think about:

- how and why you did it.
- what was easy/difficult about it.
- the things you had to / needed to do.
- the things you didn't have to / didn't need to do.
- why you stopped/continued doing it.

C SPEAK Work in pairs. Tell your partner about the new activity you tried. Then listen to your partner and ask him/her questions about the activity.

- Talk about hobbies and free time activities
- Discuss trying new things

6.3 You got served

F– express your opinion P– intonation for expressing opinions

COMPREHENSION

A Work in pairs. Tell your partner how you prepare for exercising or playing sports. What do you do before you start?

B 00:00–00:32 Watch the first part of the video. Are any of the things you discussed in Exercise A in the video? Who do you think will win the game?

C 00:33–03:15 Watch the second part of the video. Check (✓) *Gaby* or *Sam* or both.

Gaby	Sam	
		thinks it's unusual to put butter on toast.
		thinks British breakfast is more than buttered toast and milky tea.
		thinks Spanish food is better than English food.
		thinks tortilla is boring.
		changes their mind at the end.

FUNCTIONAL LANGUAGE

Expressing your opinion

A Complete the phrases in the table. Then watch the video again and check your answers.

Give an opinion	I [1]_______ that's very strange. [2]_______ you think that's horrible? I [3]_______ British food is better than ever these days. In my [4]_______, British food is still really bad. If you ask [5]_______, it's your opinion that's really bad. Spanish food is so much better. Don't [6]_______ agree? Do you know [7]_______ I think? Tortilla is a bit boring.
Give examples to support an opinion	[8]_______ instance, … To give you an example, …
Agree with an opinion	I agree. You are probably [9]_______. Absolutely!
Disagree with an opinion	I disagree. I [10]_______ don't think that's true. Nonsense. To be brutally [11]_______, no!

B Work in groups. Decide which are the three countries with the best food in the world.

MILLY

SAM

NEENA

ZAC

GABY

USEFUL PHRASES

A Match the useful phrases (1–5) with the phrases that come before or after them (a–e). Then watch the video and check your answers.

1 Game, set and match – Sam!
2 Not hugely.
3 Wake up! Say something!
4 I didn't realize you were so passionate about food.
5 British food is average!

a So you don't like Spanish food?
b Sam, are you OK?
c I'm sorry! I got a bit angry.
d I was right!
e Nonsense!

B How do you say these useful phrases in your language?

PRONUNCIATION

Intonation for expressing opinions

6.8 **A** Listen and repeat the extracts from the video. Copy the stress and intonation.

A: In my opinion, British food is still really bad.
B: Well, if you ask me, it's your opinion that's really bad.
A: Spanish food is so much better – don't you agree?
B: To be brutally honest, no!
A: Do you want to know what I think? I think tortilla is a bit boring.
B: Boring!

B Work in pairs. Make similar conversations. Change the information.

SPEAKING

A Complete the statements with opinion phrases from Functional Language Exercise A.

... eat before exercising.
If you ask me, you shouldn't eat for one hour before exercising.

... do an hour of aerobic exercise every day.

____

... tennis is more exciting to watch than soccer.

____

... the gym is boring.

____

... female athletes should be paid the same as men.

____

... running is the best sport in the world.

____

... boxing is too violent.

____

... eSports are more exciting than real sports.

____

B DISCUSS Work in pairs. Take turns reading out your statements from Exercise A and agree or disagree with your partner's statements.

Express your opinion

➤ Turn to page 161 to learn how to write an article for a magazine.

Unit 6 Review

GRAMMAR

A Complete the conversation between a soccer coach and some new players with the correct modals of obligation.

Coach: The rules say so. You [1] ____________ touch the ball with your hands. It isn't allowed.

Player 1: But what about the goalkeeper? He sometimes [2] ____________ use his hand to stop a shot. I've seen it on TV.

Coach: OK, OK! Everyone except the goalkeeper [3] ____________ follow that rule. And you all [4] ____________ warm up before a game. I insist on that. If you don't warm up, you don't play.

Player 2: I can't get here until 6 pm.

Coach: That's a little late, the game starts at 6:15 pm. You [5] ____________ start warming up at 5:45, by 6 pm at the latest. You bike here, don't you? If so, you [6] ____________ do a big warm-up. But you [7] ____________ be here by six, OK?

B Complete the TV interview with the present perfect or present progressive form of the verbs in parentheses.

Reporter: Hi, everyone. I'm with champion surfer Sally Gowen. Sally, [1] ____________ you ____________ (*surf*) here all day?

Surfer: Hi, Maisie. Yes, I sure have. The water [2] ____________ (*be*) excellent all day. I love it here. I [3] ____________ (*come*) here a lot recently.

Reporter: What [4] ____________ you ____________ (*practice*) today? Some new moves?

Surfer: No, no. Nothing too special. OK, I'm going back on the surf now.

Reporter: Oh, I [5] ____________ (*finish*) yet. Just one more … Sally? Sally! Oh, she [6] ____________ (*go*).

C Complete the text with *had to*, *didn't have to*, *needed to* or *didn't need to*. Sometimes more than one answer is possible.

I remember my first year at college well. It was so different from being at high school. Finally, we [1] ____________ wear a uniform every day, and I [2] ____________ tell my parents where I was all the time. I enjoyed that new freedom, and I [3] ____________ grow up quickly, too. I [4] ____________ take more responsibility for everyday things. I was lucky though because I lived in a student residence. I [5] ____________ live there, but I chose to because I wanted to meet other people easily. It was a good decision. We [6] ____________ follow a few rules, but having a housekeeper was great. I mean, we still [7] ____________ wash the dishes and keep things clean, but a housekeeper every week was good.

VOCABULARY

A Choose the best adjectives to complete the sentences.

1 Don't delay any more. Make your mind up. It's time to be ***decisive / aggressive***.
2 Stop yelling! You're being very ***effective / aggressive***.
3 He's very ***creative / competitive***. He hates losing.
4 eSports are already ***massive / expensive***. They'll definitely be in the Olympics soon.
5 You won 7–2? That's ***impressive / aggressive***!
6 Running with the ball is not very ***effective / competitive***. It's better to pass it quickly.

B Complete the text about sports with the missing words.

I loved my time as a soccer player. I only played for one club in the national [1]**l** _e_ _a_ _g_ _u_ _e_, but what a club! I had great [2]**c** _ _ _ _ _ _ who really improved my game, and our [3]**f** _ _ _ were amazing, always singing and cheering us on. It was a great feeling walking into the [4]**s** _ _ _ _ _ _, to hear that noise at the beginning of the game. And, of course, I played for the national team at three World Cup [5]**t** _ _ _ _ _ _ _ _ _ _ _, and the 2018 one was the highlight of my career. How can anything be better than winning the [6]**f** _ _ _ _ and lifting the [7]**t** _ _ _ _ _ _, knowing you are the [8]**c** _ _ _ _ _ _ _ _ _ of the world? I bet all the [9]**s** _ _ _ _ _ _ _ _ _ _ watching in the stadium and on TV were jealous! I think I can safely say I was a [10]**t** _ _ _ _ _ _ _ _ _ _. After all, I won the 'Player of the Year' award twice! I certainly miss those days. I don't get the same feeling from running a restaurant.

C Complete the radio vox-pop with the words in the box.

am	been	collect	get	joined	lost	took

Yes, I [1] ____________ stamps. I've [2] ____________ into stamp collecting for a long time. I [3] ____________ it up when I was just a kid. Some people think it is boring, but I have never [4] ____________ interest in it, and I'm 45 now. Of course, I [5] ____________ a member of my local stamp collecting society. I [6] ____________ that ten years ago. The weekly meetings [7] ____________ me out of the house.

FUNCTIONAL LANGUAGE

Complete the TV discussion with the correct phrases to express opinions.

Mario: Let's ask our panel of experts. You first, Tim, what do you think?

Tim: Well, in my [1] ____________, they should be banned.

Asif: If you [2] ____________ me, we shouldn't ban them.

Ana: As far as I'm [3] ____________, a ban is the answer.

Sue: I think we should do more research. Don't you [4] ____________?

Tim: To be [5] ____________, I disagree completely. We already know enough. To [6] ____________ you an example, there were five different stories about them in the newspapers last week.

7 FOOD

So long as you have food in your mouth, you have solved all questions for the time being.

Franz Kafka

Lunch in Marrakesh: Rainbow salad bowl, falafel and mint tea.

OBJECTIVES

- talk about eating out
- make speculations and deductions about food
- compare different types of food
- compare a range of solutions and choose the best one
- make suggestions
- write a reply in an online discussion forum

Work with a partner. Discuss the questions.

1 Look at the photo. How many types of food can you name?

2 Read the quote. What do you think it means?

3 Do you think it is important to eat with your family or friends? Why/Why not?

7.1 Eating out

- Talk about eating out
- Make speculations and deductions about food

P – diphthongs; word stress with modals
G – modals of speculation and deduction
V – phrasal verbs; adjectives to describe food
S – hidden contrasts

READING

A SPEAK Work in groups and discuss the questions.

1 Do you usually eat out in a restaurant? Why/Why not?
2 Do you usually leave a tip to thank the waiter for good service?

B READ FOR MAIN IDEA Read *Super supper clubs*. What are supper clubs? Why do many customers prefer supper clubs to traditional restaurants?

C Complete the notes on the differences between supper clubs and traditional restaurants. Use the strategies in the box to help you.

Paragraph	Supper clubs	Traditional restaurants
Choosing a dish (2)	*the chef chooses*	*you choose from a menu*
Where customers sit (2)		
Choosing when to go (2)		
What to cook (4)		
The food (4)		
The experience (5)		

Hidden contrasts

In articles about new or unusual things, writers frequently use words like *instead*, *just* and *even* to show contrasts with more normal things. These contrasts are usually hidden, so it's difficult to notice them. But they help you to understand the points that the writer wants to make.

SUPER SUPPER CLUBS

1 Anti-restaurants. Underground restaurants. Pop-up restaurants. Guestaurants. Whatever you call them, there's no doubt that supper clubs are one of the hottest trends in eating out today.

2 The idea is simple: instead of going to a traditional restaurant, you eat in the chef's home. Instead of choosing a dish from a menu, you eat what the chef gives you. And instead of sitting quietly at separate tables, all the customers eat together, talking and making friends. But if that sounds like your perfect evening, there's some bad news . You can't just show up when you're feeling hungry; you'll need to join a waiting list and then wait for an invitation from the chef.

3 The modern idea of supper clubs took off in Cuba in the 1990s. Cuba now has a huge amount of supper clubs, or *paladares*. Most of them started off as simply a room in the chef's home. They're popular with tourists, as well as people who want a simple home-cooked meal at a fair price. One of Cuba's best *paladares* is Castas y Tal, on the 11th floor of a large apartment building in central Havana. The main restaurant area has only eight seats, but there are wonderful views of the city below.

4 For chefs, supper clubs clearly seem like a great idea. They're fairly cheap and easy to set up because the chef can do everything at home. Instead of having to cook the same food again and again, supper clubs give chefs control over what to cook. Customers don't mind giving up some choice because they know they'll eat amazing food that they've never eaten before. They might not like it, but at least it won't be boring.

5 At the St. Jude Project in Mumbai, India, Chef Gresham Fernandes tries out ideas while he's cooking ... and even while he's serving up the meal! He cooks in front of the guests, explaining what he's doing as he works.

6 So next time you're feeling adventurous, why not visit a supper club? It's sure to be an experience you won't forget!

PRONUNCIATION
Diphthongs

7.1 **A** Look at the underlined words in *Super supper clubs*. Match the words with their correct pronunciation (1–8). Then listen and check your answers.

1 weɪt ______ 5 hoʊm ______
2 ju ______ 6 daʊt ______
3 dʒɔɪn ______ 7 nuwz ______
4 maɪt ______

B WORK IT OUT The words in Exercise A all contain diphthongs. Choose the best word or phrase to complete the rules.

Diphthongs

1 Diphthongs are long *vowel* / *consonant* sounds made from *two* / *three* short sounds.
2 We pronounce diphthongs by **moving quickly from one sound to the next** / **saying the two sounds separately**.
3 American English has *seven* / *ten* diphthongs: /eɪ/, /aɪ/, /oʊ/, /ɔɪ/, /aʊ/, /ju/, and /uw/.

C SPEAK Work in pairs. Make sentences using at least three of the words from Exercises A and B. Then practice saying your sentences.

VOCABULARY
Phrasal verbs

A Look at *Super supper clubs* again. Find sentences that have the same meaning as the ones below. Which words are used instead of the underlined words?

1 You can't just arrive without making a reservation when you're feeling hungry.
2 The modern idea of supper clubs really became popular in Cuba in the 1990s.
3 Most of them began their existence as simply a room in the chef's home.
4 They're fairly cheap and easy to get ready to start.
5 Customers don't mind losing some choice.
6 Chef Gresham Fernandes experiments with ideas while he's cooking … and even while he's putting the food on plates.

B WORK IT OUT Read the rules about phrasal verbs. Then complete the examples with phrasal verbs from Exercise A.

Phrasal verbs

1 Phrasal verbs are usually made of two parts: a verb (e.g. *work, try*) and a particle (e.g. *out, up*).
2 Sometimes it's possible to guess the meaning from the two words, but usually you just need to learn the meaning of the whole phrasal verb:
- *You can't just* [a] ______ ______ *at their house! Always call first to check it's OK.*

3 Some phrasal verbs can have an object. When the object is short (e.g. a pronoun or one or two words), it usually comes in the middle:
- *I have lots of ideas and I like to* [b] ______ *them* ______ *while I'm cooking.*

But when the object is a longer phrase, it usually comes at the end:
- *I like to* [c] ______ ______ *lots of new ideas while I'm cooking.*

C Go to the **Vocabulary Hub** on **page 145**.

D SPEAK Complete the questions with the correct phrasal verbs. Then work in pairs and ask and answer the questions.

1 Do you think supper clubs will take ______ in your country?
2 Do you ever try ______ new meals while you're cooking or do you always plan carefully before you start?
3 Have your cooking skills ever let you ______? What went wrong?

SPEAKING

A Work in pairs. You are going to plan your own supper club. Write notes about:

- name
- location
- type of food
- cost
- number of guests
- what makes your supper club unique

B PRESENT Work in groups. Take turns presenting your supper club to the group.

C REFLECT Decide which supper club you would like to attend and why.

VOCABULARY
Adjectives to describe food

a

b

c

A Work in groups. Look at the pictures and discuss the questions.

1 Where do you think each dish is from?
2 What do you think it contains?

B Go to the **Vocabulary Hub** on **page 145**.

C Many food adjectives end in *-y* (e.g. *spicy*). Complete the sentences with the missing adjectives. Use the words in bold to help you.

1 I didn't think this soup would **taste** very nice, but in fact it's really ___*tasty*___!
2 Honey is very ________. It **sticks** to the bread like glue!
3 I really love ________ pizza, so I always ask for extra **cheese** on the top.
4 This ________ sauce is too rich for me. How much **cream** did you put into it?

D SPEAK Work in pairs. Think of some types of food and drinks that these adjectives might describe. Use the glossary to help you.

buttery chocolatey fatty fruity oily meaty milky nutty peppery runny salty watery

E SPEAK Work in pairs. Use adjectives to describe:

1 your favorite soft drink.
2 your favorite flavor of ice cream.
3 your perfect breakfast.
4 your least favorite types of food.

LISTENING

A SPEAK Work in pairs. If you are invited to eat dinner at somebody's house, do you bring:

- flowers
- a gift
- something to drink
- dessert
- nothing

B Complete the description with the words in the box.

course dessert ~~dinner party~~ dishes host appetizer surprise

A [1] ___*dinner party*___ is an event where one person (the [2] ________) invites a group of friends to eat a meal at his or her house. At a traditional dinner party, the host cooks the food: an [3] ________ and a main [4] ________. But the guests usually bring something to drink, and perhaps also a [5] ________. In a pot luck dinner party, everybody (the host and guests) prepares one or two [6] ________. It's called pot luck because it's always a [7] ________: nobody knows what the others will bring.

7.2 **C LISTEN FOR SPECIFIC INFORMATION** Listen to a conversation at a pot luck dinner party. Match the people (1–5) with the dishes (a–e).

1	Vicky (the host)	a	cheesy chicken pasta surprise
2	Charlie	b	cream of chicken soup
3	Tina	c	spicy buffalo wings
4	Felipe	d	cheese and chilli salad
5	Markus	e	chicken curry in a creamy sauce

Glossary

allergic (adj) affected by an allergy (a medical condition in which you become sick or your skin becomes covered with red marks as a reaction to something you eat, breathe or touch)
buffalo (n) a large African animal similar to a cow, with curved horns
dairy products (n) foods that are made from milk (e.g. cheese, butter, ice cream)
spicy (adj) food that has a strong hot flavor

D Listen again. Check (✓) the correct name(s).

7.2

	Vicky	Charlie	Felipe	Tina	Markus
1 Who arrived late?					
2 Whose dish needs to be heated up?					
3 Who is allergic to dairy products?					
4 Who doesn't like spicy food?					
5 Who doesn't like chicken?					

E SPEAK Work in groups and discuss the questions.

1 What went wrong with the pot luck dinner party?
2 Does it matter if some things go wrong at a party like this?

GRAMMAR
Modals of speculation and deduction

A WORK IT OUT Choose the correct meaning for the sentences from the conversation at the pot luck dinner party.

1 They **can't be** buffalo wings. Buffaloes don't have wings!
  a Maybe they aren't buffalo wings.
  b I'm sure they aren't buffalo wings.
2 They **could be** chicken or something like that.
  a It's possible that they're chicken.
  b It was possible that they were chicken.
3 You **must think** I'm so disorganized!
  a I'm sure you think this.
  b It's necessary for you to think this.
4 Well, they **might not be** chilies.
  a It isn't possible that they're chilies.
  b Maybe they aren't chilies.
5 Uh … you **may have** a problem there.
  a Maybe you have a problem.
  b I'm sure you have a problem.

B Look again at the sentences in Exercise A. Complete the rules (1–4) with the words in the box.

Modals of speculation and deduction

can't could may may not might might not must

1 We use ______ when we are sure something is true.
2 We use ______, ______ or ______ when we think something is possibly true, but we are not sure.
3 We use ______ or ______ when we think something possibly isn't true, but we are not sure.
4 We use ______ when we are sure something is not true.

C Go to the **Grammar Hub** on **page 134**.

PRONUNCIATION
Word stress with modals

A Listen to the sentences (1–4) from the conversation at the pot luck dinner party. Then match the sentences with the rules (a–d).

7.3

1 Oh, that must be Felipe, right?
2 Hang on … that can't be right.
3 The name must come from the city, not the animal.
4 They might not be chilies.

a We usually place extra stress on the word *not* or a negative modal verb. ___, ___
b Modal verb + *be*: We usually stress the modal verb, not *be*. ___, ___
c Modal verb + main verb: We usually stress both verbs about the same. ___
d When we're speaking quickly, we usually don't pronounce the *t* in *must*. ___, ___

B Look at the highlighted words in the sentences below and underline the stressed words. Then listen and check your answers.

7.4

1 You're such a great host. You must have a lot of dinner parties!
2 'What's wrong with the oven?' 'I don't know. It might not be turned on.'
3 I made a lot of soup because some people may want two or three bowls.
4 Oh, no! Felipe can't be here already! The party doesn't start for another 20 minutes!

C Listen again and repeat the sentences. Then work in pairs and practice saying the sentences. Listen and check your partner's pronunciation.

7.4

D SPEAK Work in pairs. Make deductions and speculations about the people at the dinner party. Think about these questions.

1 How do they know each other?
2 What is the surprise in Tina's cheesy chicken pasta surprise?

SPEAKING HUB

A You have been invited to a pot luck dinner party. Write a short description of the dish you would like to bring.

B SPEAK Work in groups. Choose one person to be the host and give him/her your description. In your groups, decide:

- who brought which dish.
- which dishes you want to try.

C REFLECT Tell the class about your pot luck dinner party. Which dishes were the most popular?

Talk about eating out
Make speculations and deductions about food

7.2 Food fads

- Compare different types of food
- Compare a range of solutions and choose the best one

G – comparatives and superlatives; *the …, the …* P – vowel + *w* V – waste S – identifying people's opinions

READING

A SPEAK Read the definition of *fad*. Then work in pairs and discuss the questions.

fad – definition and synonyms
NOUN Pronunciation /fæd/
1 something that is popular or fashionable for only a short time

1 Can you think of any current food fads? Which foods are fashionable now?
2 Are there any food fads connected with different ways of cooking? Or different ways of eating?
3 Which older food fads have gone out of fashion?

B READ FOR GIST Read *Food fads* quickly. What is the writer's opinion about superfoods?

a They're just a fad – they aren't really very good for you.
b Expensive superfoods are much healthier than cheaper food.
c You don't need to spend a lot of money to buy some superfoods.
d Most superfoods are actually bad for your health.

FOOD FADS

Hi again! This week, I've decided to look at one of the biggest food fads of the 21st century: superfoods. Let's try to sort the facts from the fiction!

Quinoa has a long history as a superfood: it was known to the ancient Incas as 'the mother of all grains' because it was so healthy. Even today it's recommended by NASA as the perfect food for long space flights. Like all whole grains, it can help your body fight a variety of diseases, and it contains lots of vitamins, minerals and fiber. It's also one of the best sources of protein, so it's perfect for vegetarians and vegans, too. Amazing!

Goji berries are another great source of plant-based protein. These sweet berries have been used in China for centuries as a way to protect against illness. They contain less sugar than other fruits, so they're one of the healthiest snacks around. Unfortunately, they can be dangerous for some people, so always check with your doctor before eating them.

Açaí berries are perhaps the most successful superfoods of all: not long ago, they were unknown outside of Brazil. Now, açaí products are big business. Why are they so popular? Well, some people believe these berries will help them to grow old more slowly … or even to live longer. Like goji berries, they're full of chemicals which seem to protect our hearts and our brains. Sounds good, right?

Chia seeds are known as the healthiest food on the planet. The name 'chia' comes from the ancient Mayan word for 'strength'. Out of all the foods in the world, chia seeds contain some of the most nutrients for the fewest calories. They're also one of the best sources of fiber, which is great for your digestive system. Even better, they make you feel full … so you'll eat fewer snacks!

C READ FOR SPECIFIC INFORMATION Read again. Write *A* (açaí berries), *B* (broccoli), *C* (chia seeds), *G* (goji berries) or *Q* (quinoa).

According to the blog post, which superfood …

1. isn't only eaten on our planet? ____
2. is much cheaper than other superfoods? ____
3. might help you stay younger for longer? ____
4. can help you digest your food more effectively? ____
5. might not be safe for everybody? ____
6. has become popular very quickly? ____
7. helps you to eat less food between meals? ____

D SPEAK Work in groups and discuss the questions.

1. Do you think it's worth paying more money for superfoods? Why/Why not?
2. Do you think it is more important for you to eat healthy food or tasty food? Why?
3. What are some simple ways that we can eat more healthily?

But before you all rush out to buy superfoods from your local health food store, remember that superfoods are usually super expensive, too! And do you know what? Strawberries are probably just as good for you as goji berries and açaí berries. Similarly, quinoa and chia seeds are great because they're whole grains. But you can get all that fiber far more cheaply by eating plenty of brown bread, brown rice and whole grain pasta. And what's the best superfood of all? Broccoli! It's cheap, tasty and incredibly good for you. It isn't as exciting as quinoa, but it's a lot less expensive!

Glossary

fiber (n) the parts of fruit, vegetables and grains that your body cannot digest (= turn into substances it can use); it helps food to pass through your body

nutrient (n) a substance in food that plants, animals and people need to live and grow

protein (n) a substance in food, such as meat, eggs and milk, that people need in order to grow and be healthy

GRAMMAR

Comparatives and superlatives

A Cover the *Food fads* article. Complete the sentences with one word in each space. Then check your answers in the blog post.

1. This week, I've decided to look at one of ___*the*___ biggest food fads of the 21st century: superfoods.
2. They contain ________ sugar ________ other fruits, so they're one of ________ healthiest snacks around.
3. Chia seeds contain some of the ________ nutrients for the ________ calories.
4. Even better, they make you feel full … so you'll eat ________ snacks!
5. Some people believe these berries will help them to grow old ________ slowly … or even to live ________.
6. It isn't ________ exciting ________ quinoa, but it's a lot ________ expensive!

B Go to the **Grammar Hub** on **page 134**.

C SPEAK Work in pairs. Compare each set of ideas.

1. quinoa vs white rice
2. broccoli vs ice cream
3. grocery stores vs health food stores
4. fast food vs superfoods
5. cooking vs eating out
6. eating alone vs eating in a large group

A: Quinoa is much tastier than white rice.
B: Yes, but it's a lot more expensive.

SPEAKING

Work in pairs. Use the superlative form of the words and phrases in the box to ask and answer questions.

bad	expensive	far (to travel for a meal)	few ingredients	little money (to spend on food)	much time (to spend preparing a meal)	spicy

A: What's the farthest you've ever traveled for a meal?
B: Not very far. I usually buy all my food in the local store. But once I spent an hour bike riding to the 'best ice cream store in town'. But it wasn't as good as I expected.

LISTENING

A Work in pairs. Take the **Reduce Your Waste** quiz. Then go to the Communication Hub on page 153 to check your answers.

7.5 **B** You are going to listen to part of a radio show about a family who is trying to waste less food. Look at the pictures (1–6) and guess the answers to the questions. Then listen and check your answers.

REDUCE YOUR WASTE

1 How long can you store these things before they go bad?

- a fresh milk in a fridge
- b frozen vegetables in a freezer
- c fresh bananas
- d dry food (e.g. pasta)
- e an opened bottle of apple juice in a fridge
- f a plate of leftovers in a fridge

2 True or false?

- a You can safely reheat food as many times as you like.
- b Most food is still safe to eat after it has passed its best if used by date.
- c You must eat rice within 24 hours of cooking it.

1 How much money does the average person lose from food waste every year?

2 Do ugly carrots taste as good as beautiful carrots?

3 What's the problem with growing lettuce in a greenhouse?

4 How many buckets of water does it take to make a loaf of bread?

5 What can you do with your leftovers if you don't want to waste them?

6 How can a cell phone app help us waste less food?

C Who expressed each of these opinions: *Mrs. Taylor*, *Mr. Taylor*, *Alison* or *Philip*? Use the strategies in the box to help you.

Identifying people's opinions

When you're listening, pay attention to whether people are just describing a situation or expressing an opinion about it. Adjectives like *great* and *awful* usually show that the person is expressing an opinion.

1 Food doesn't need to be beautiful. Mrs. Taylor
2 I like collecting and studying detailed information about our experiment. ______
3 Food waste is bad for our planet. ______
4 I didn't like eating the same food the next day. ______
5 I enjoy cooking meals to use up the food in the fridge. ______
6 Money isn't the most important reason for reducing waste. ______

D **SPEAK** Work in pairs. How much food do you think you waste in your family?

GRAMMAR

the …, the …

A **WORK IT OUT** Look at the sentences from the radio show. Match the beginnings of the sentences (1–5) with the endings (a–e).

1 The more I researched the topic,
2 The less food we throw away,
3 The less we cook,
4 The longer we do it,
5 The more carefully you count things,

a the more normal it feels.
b the better.
c the more I realized that we aren't just throwing away food.
d the more accurate your results will be.
e the less we waste.

B Read the rule and complete the example. Use the words in parentheses to help you.

the …, the …

To show that two changes are closely connected, we use *the* + comparative, *the* + comparative. As one thing changes, it makes the other thing change.

As far as I'm concerned, the ______ *(ugly), the* ______ *(good)!*

C Go to the Grammar Hub on page 134.

PRONUNCIATION
Vowel + *w*

7.6 **A** How do you pronounce these words? Use the strategies in the box to help you. Then listen and repeat the words.

chew cow own raw stew

Vowel + *w*

Three vowels, ***a***, ***e*** and ***o***, when combined with ***w***, make a new sound. There are two possible sounds for ***e*** + ***w*** and ***o*** + ***w***.

a + *w* /ɔː/ for, draw, awful, ________, ________

e + *w* /juː/ you, few, view, ________

e + *w* /uː/ too, jewelry, threw, ________, ________

o + *w* /oʊ/ go, low, owe, ________, ________, ________, ________, ________

o + *w* /aʊ/ out, how, wow, ________, ________, ________

7.7 **B** Look at the bold words in these sentences. Write them in the correct place in the box in Exercise A. Then listen and check your answers.

1 'Have you ever **flown** in a helicopter?' 'Yes, I **flew** in one a **few** weeks ago. It was **awesome**.'

2 You aren't **allowed** to **throw** away your trash here! Don't you **know** it's against the **law**!

3 The **flowers grew** fairly **slowly** at first, but **now** they're fully **grown**.

C SPEAK Work in pairs. Practice saying the sentences in Exercise B. Listen and check your partner's pronunciation.

VOCABULARY
Waste

A Match the definitions (1–8) with the words and phrases in the box.

garbage can cut down get rid of recycle reduce reuse garbage throw away use up ~~waste~~

1 to not use something that you could use ________ *waste*

2 a container for putting garbage in ________

3 things that you throw away because they are no longer useful ________

4 to use all of something, so there's no waste ________

5 to change waste materials such as newspapers and bottles so that they can be used again ________

6 to use something again ________

7 to use less of something ________, ________

8 to get rid of something that you no longer want ________, ________

B SPEAK Complete the questions with one word in each space. Then work in pairs and discuss the questions.

1 Do you ________ plastic and glass containers so they can be turned into new products, or do you just get ________ of them?

2 Do you ________ plastic bags again and again, or throw them in the ________?

3 How could restaurants cut ________ the amount of ________ they throw ________ each week?

SPEAKING HUB

A Work in pairs. How could you reduce food waste in your home by fifty percent? Write notes about:

- shopping habits (how often? how much?)
- meal planning (weekly menus)
- leftovers
- food storage (fridge? cupboard? special containers?)
- apps and gadgets

B PRESENT Use your notes to prepare a short presentation on how you can help people reduce their food waste. Present your ideas to the class.

C DISCUSS Work in groups. Use these questions to compare your ideas from Exercise B. Then choose the best two or three ideas.

- Which ideas will be easiest for people to understand and follow?
- Which ideas will make the biggest difference?
- Which ideas might cost people more money? Which ideas might save them money?

D REFLECT Work in groups and discuss the questions.

1 Are you going to try to reduce your own food waste? How?

2 Will you try to persuade others to cut their food waste? How?

- Compare different types of food
- Compare a range of solutions and choose the best one

Café Hub

7.3 Comfort eating

F– make suggestions P– suggestions

COMPREHENSION

A Work in pairs and discuss the questions.

What do you do when you're feeling upset or worried?

Do you cook, go for a run, call a friend, watch a good movie or something else?

B 00:00–01:30 Watch the first part of the video and answer the questions.

1 What is Gaby's big news?

2 What does Milly think about her news?

3 What is Gaby upset about?

C 00:56–01:21 Find and correct five mistakes in the story that Gaby told Milly. What advice do you think Milly will give? Watch to check your answers.

It was about a week ago. Last Wednesday, Sam had to leave work early and so he asked me to look after the café. I had decided to tell him how I felt, and so before I locked up, I wrote a poem expressing my true feelings for him. ... And I left it on the doormat for him to find. He can't have seen it.

FUNCTIONAL LANGUAGE

Making suggestions

A Match the two halves of the extracts from the video.

Making a suggestion

1 Have you tried
2 What about
3 The best thing might be
4 If I were you, I'd
5 Why don't we
6 We could

a cook something delicious.
b take some time to think about it.
c talking to him about it?
d put on some whipped cream and sprinkles?
e sending a text or an email or something?
f to just ask him if he got the letter.

B Complete the phrases in the table.

Saying no to a suggestion	Saying yes to a suggestion
No, I ________________. I don't know what to say.	That's a good ________________.
No, that wouldn't ________________. To say what?	It's worth a ________________.
That's a ________________ idea. I'm already really embarrassed.	Good ________________.

C 01:21–04:13 Watch the second part of the video and check your answers to Exercises A and B.

MILLY

SAM

NEENA

ZAC

GABY

USEFUL PHRASES

A Match the useful phrases (1–4) with the screenshots (a–d).

1 What's up? ____
2 Great timing! ____
3 It'll help take your mind off Sam. ____
4 He's been acting like nothing happened! ____

B How do you say these useful phrases in your language?

PRONUNCIATION
Suggestions

7.8 **A** Listen to the extracts from the video and underline the stressed/key words. Does the intonation rise or fall at the end of each phrase?

Milly: Have you tried talking to him about it?
Gaby: No, I can't. I don't know what to say.
Milly: Or, what about sending him a text or an email or something?
Gaby: No, that wouldn't work. To say what?
Milly: I don't know exactly. The best thing might be to just ask him if he got the letter?
Gaby: No, no, no, no, no, no, no, no! That's a terrible idea. I'm already really embarrassed.
Milly: If I were you, I'd take some time to think about it.

B In pairs, practice the conversation. Copy the stress and intonation.

SPEAKING

A Work in pairs. Think about possible solutions to the problems below.

1 I'm having a dinner party, but I hate cooking.
2 I want to eat more healthily, but superfoods are too expensive.
3 I want to save some money, but I love going out to restaurants!
4 I frequently have leftover food, but I don't want to waste it.
5 I want to grow vegetables, but I live in an apartment.

B DISCUSS Take turns reading out a problem and make suggestions using the phrases in Functional Language Exercise A.

A: I'm having a dinner party, but I hate cooking.
B: What about getting takeout?

Make suggestions

➤ Turn to page 162 to learn how to write a reply in an online discussion forum.

Unit 7 Review

GRAMMAR

A Choose the best words to complete the conversation.

A: Do you want some of this pot luck stew? I made it from all of last week's leftovers: fish curry, cheesy chicken pasta, spicy vegetables …

B: Yuck! That [1]*can't / might not / must* taste disgusting!

A: Well, no, it actually tastes very good. Try it – you [2]*can / might / must* like it.

B: Really? OK. I guess it [3]*couldn't / might not / must not* be so bad. But don't forget I'm allergic to peanuts.

A: Don't worry, it [4]*can't / may not / might* contain any peanuts. I never cook with them. But it [5] *couldn't / may / must* contain some other types of nuts – I'm not sure. Is that OK?

B: Yes, that's fine. Hmm … this [6]*can't / could / must* be a big mistake, but … OK, I'll try it.

B Complete the sentences with the correct form of the words in parentheses.

1 I want to cook the most food for the ______________________ (*little*) money. Any ideas?
2 Açaí berries are really good for you – they're much ______________________ (*healthy*) than I thought.
3 If you want to lose weight, you need to eat ______________________ (*few*) candy.
4 You should come to the restaurant on a Tuesday at lunchtime – that's the ______________________ (*crowded*) time.
5 You baked this cake too quickly! Next time, try baking it ______________________ (*slowly*).
6 Cooking for ten people is far ______________________ (*stressful*) than cooking for one!
7 There's too much cream in this sauce. Can you make it a little ______________________ (*creamy*) next time?

C Match the beginnings of the sentences (1–6) with the endings (a–f).

1 Bring all your friends to our dinner party – the more people who come,
2 The earlier you arrive at the restaurant,
3 The older I get,
4 The more sugar you add,
5 Natural food is much better for you; the fewer chemicals it contains,
6 Don't boil vegetables for too long; the longer you cook them,

a the more I prefer to stay in and cook at home.
b the less flavor they'll have.
c the more fun we'll have.
d the more likely you are to get a table.
e the sweeter it will be.
f the healthier it is.

VOCABULARY

A Complete the sentences with the correct form of the phrasal verbs in the box.

keep on | clean up | end up | put off | figure out

1 I can't ______________ how to turn on the microwave. Can you help me?
2 Sorry to interrupt your meal, but I need to go out for a minute. Please ______________ eating while I'm away.
3 I'm happy to cook dinner, but could you ______________ the dirty plates afterward?
4 If you want to learn to cook, don't ______________ it ______________! Join our cooking classes today!
5 I was planning to cook a big meal, but then the oven broke so I ______________ buying takeout pizzas for everybody.

B Choose the best adjectives to complete the sentences.

1 I think we need to cook this meat a little longer – it's still *delicious / mild / raw* in the middle.
2 I don't really like sweet snacks. Do you have anything *bitter / rich / savory*, like a sandwich?
3 Don't worry. This soup is very *buttery / mild / spicy* – there are no chilies or strong flavors in it.
4 The food was great, but it wasn't very *chewy / filling / spicy*. We were still hungry at the end of the meal!
5 I don't like dark chocolate – it's too *fatty / bitter / creamy* for me. I prefer something sweeter.
6 If you want a cheap and *disgusting / sour / tasty* lunch, Kate's café is the best place to go.

C Complete the advice about food waste with words in the box. There is one extra word.

garbage cans | get | recycle | reduce | reuse | throw | use

Try these tips:

- Don't [1]__________ rid of yesterday's bread just because it isn't fresh. Make toast to [2]__________ up the last few pieces.
- Don't [3]__________ old plastic away. You can [4]__________ the same shopping bags again and again.
- Use two (or more) [5]__________: one for food waste and one for containers that you can [6]__________.

FUNCTIONAL LANGUAGE

Find and correct the mistakes in the sentences.

1 I don't feel like cooking tonight. Why ~~we~~ don't ^we eat out tonight?
2 Yes, why not? What about go to The Food Zone?

____

3 Again? We went there last week. Could we going to that new supper club, The Spicy Kitchen, instead?

____

4 Good idea! The best thing might be call them. They might have a free table tonight.

____

5 Yes, that's worth to try. Can you call them and ask?

____

8 INNOVATION

To invent, you need a good imagination and a pile of junk.

Thomas Edison

A helicopter mechanic double checks some wiring, Germany.

OBJECTIVES

- explain how an invention works
- suggest and evaluate creative ideas
- use positive language to promote a new product
- give a friend advice about choosing a gadget
- give and follow instructions
- write a biography

Work with a partner. Discuss the questions.

1 Look at the picture. What characteristics would be helpful to have as a mechanic?

2 Look at the quote. Do you think you have to be imaginative to be an inventor?

3 Talk about a situation where you have been imaginative or innovative in your life.

8.1 Making a difference

- Explain how an invention works
- Suggest and evaluate creative ideas

V – word families; creative thinking G – adjective clauses P – adjective clauses
S – listening for problems and solutions

Eden Full Goh:

the inventor who is making a big difference

Eden Full Goh is perhaps not a name that you immediately recognize, but she is one of the most exciting and creative inventors of the 21st century.

Eden, who was born in Calgary, Canada, started to show talent at the age of nine, when she built a solar-powered toy car. That is where her interest in solar power began but certainly not where it stopped. She had not yet graduated from college when she came up with a very simple, but highly efficient, solar panel system that produces energy at low cost.

Eden's invention, which has won many prizes, is now used in 19 countries, where it makes a real difference to thousands of people's lives. Here is how to use it.

1. The SunSaluter is like a table. The top of the table is a solar panel, which can face in different directions.
2. Get up early in the morning when it's still dark. Fill one plastic bottle with sand and two more bottles with dirty water.
3. Attach the water bottles to the filter. At the bottom of the filter is a tube that takes clean water to a large container. At the top there's a hook that attaches the filter to the SunSaluter.
4. Hang the filter on one end of the SunSaluter, which will then go down. Hang the bottle that you filled with sand on the other end of the solar panel. Make sure the solar panel is facing the east, where the sun will rise.
5. At sunrise, when the sun comes up, the solar panel will start catching sunlight from the east.
6. During the day, the water will flow very slowly through the filter to the container, where it is stored. As the water bottles become lighter, the heavy sand bottle slowly pulls the other end of the SunSaluter down. At noon, when the sun is high in the sky, the solar panel will face upwards.
7. In the evening, when the water bottles are empty, the solar panel will face west. You can now drink the clean water that you collected during the day.

Glossary

solar panel (n) a piece of equipment that uses energy from the sun to create power

READING

A SPEAK Work in pairs and discuss the questions.

1. What famous inventors do you know? What did they invent?
2. What skills do inventors need?

B READ FOR GIST Read *Eden Full Goh: the inventor who is making a big difference*. What is special about Eden and her invention?

C READ FOR DETAIL Read again. Match the explanations (1–7) in the text with the pictures (a–g).

D SPEAK Make a list of your own life goals. Use the ideas in the box to help you. Then work in pairs and compare your lists.

awards and prizes career experiences family helping other people certifications

VOCABULARY

Word families

A Read the box. Then complete the word families. Use *Eden Full Goh: the inventor who is making a big difference* to help you.

Word families

Word families can help you learn many words together, not just one at a time. Here's an example:

innovation (n) = a new idea or product
innovator (n) = someone who thinks of new ideas or products
innovate (v) = to invent or begin using new ideas or products
innovative (adj) = an adjective to describe an innovator or an innovation

Noun (thing/idea)	Noun (person)	Verb	Adjective
a success	a success	to succeed (in something)	1 successful
an 2 ______	an 3 ______	to invent something	inventive
a design	a designer	to 4 ______ something	–
a product	a producer	to 5 ______ something	productive
6 ______	a scientist	–	scientific
engineering	an 7 ______	to engineer something	–

B Complete the sentences with words from the same family as the words in bold.

1 You don't need to be **successful** every time. You just need to *succeed* in the most important things.

2 I could never **invent** something – I'm not a very ________ person.

3 You can only call yourself an ________ after studying **engineering** in college.

4 A ________ should concentrate on **designing** things that work well. That's more important than making them look beautiful.

5 I always think like a **scientist**. Being ________ means checking the facts before making a decision, and not focusing on opinions and feelings.

C **SPEAK** Work in pairs. Which sentences in Exercise B do you agree or disagree with? Tell your partner. Then make the sentences true for you.

GRAMMAR

Adjective clauses

A **WORK IT OUT** Look at *Eden Full Goh: the inventor who is making a big difference.* What do the highlighted words in the article refer to?

1 who = *Eden*
2 when = ________
3 where = ________
4 which = ________
5 that = ________

B Read the rules and complete the examples with adjective clauses from the article.

> **Adjective clauses**
>
> Essential adjective clauses tell us which person, thing, place or time we are talking about. Without the adjective clause, the sentence isn't complete.
>
> Eden Full Goh: the inventor [1] ________.
>
> Non-essential adjective clauses give extra information about a person, thing, place or time. We can cut the adjective clause and the sentence is still complete. We use commas to separate the adjective clause from the rest of the sentence.
>
> Eden's invention, [2] ________, is now used in 19 countries.

C Go to the Grammar Hub on page 136.

PRONUNCIATION

Adjective clauses

A 8.1 Listen to the two sentences. What do you notice about the pronunciation of essential adjective clauses and non-essential adjective clauses?

1 The person who invented the SunSaluter has made a big difference to people's lives.

2 Eden Full Goh, who invented the SunSaluter, has made a big difference to people's lives.

B 8.2 Listen and repeat the sentences.

1 Solar panels, which turn sunlight into electricity, are becoming cheaper all the time.

2 I've hidden my plans in a place where they'll be safe.

3 My favorite inventor is Mária Telkes, who created the first 100 percent solar-powered house in 1947.

C **SPEAK** Work in pairs. Practice saying the sentences in Exercise B. Listen and check your partner's pronunciation.

SPEAKING

A Work in pairs. Write down three sentences using adjective clauses. They should describe:

- a famous person
- a place
- an object

B Join another pair and take turns reading out your sentences, saying 'Beep' in place of the subject. The other pair must guess who, where or what you are talking about.

A: Beep, who is American, invented the light bulb.
B: Is it Thomas Edison?

Thinking outside THE BOX

Thinking outside the box means looking at a problem in a new way. It means forgetting about 'the way we normally do things', taking away unimportant rules and experimenting with new ideas. So for example, in the 'nine dots' problem, we see 'rules' that don't actually exist. Who said your lines have to stay inside the red box? In fact, do the lines even need to go through the middle of each dot?

It's the same with the light bulb problem. We can't stop ourselves from thinking of a light bulb as something that we see with our eyes, as something that can only be in two states, off or on. But what if we think of it as something we can touch with our hands? Are there still only two states?

Thinking outside the box also helps with brainstorming tasks, like the 'uses for old tickets' exercise. The key to successful brainstorming is to break it into two stages: generating ideas in the first place, and then evaluating those ideas to see if they're useful or not. We need to keep those stages separate; if we try to do both at the same time, we only generate boring, sensible ideas. But sometimes it's the silly ideas that help us to find excellent ideas. For example, a single bus ticket wouldn't make a great poster for your wall, but what about a poster made from 100 bus tickets from around the world?

READING

A SPEAK Work in pairs. How creative are you? Follow the instructions to find out.

1 Take an object from your pocket/bag (e.g. a used bus ticket). Try to think of as many different uses as possible for this object. Your ideas can be sensible or silly. What's your best idea?

A: We could cut it up to make a tiny jigsaw puzzle.
B: Why don't we write a short shopping list on the back?

2 Draw four straight lines to connect all the dots without taking your pen off the page. Now try again with only three straight lines.

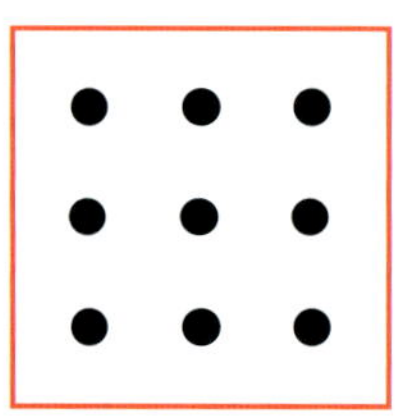

3 You're inside a room with three light switches on the wall. One of these switches turns on a light in a room on the other side of the house, but you don't know which switch. How can you find out? You can go to the other room to check only once.

B READ FOR GIST Read *Thinking outside the box*. How does it help with the questions in Exercise A?

C READ FOR DETAIL Choose *Do* or *Don't* for each piece of advice.

1 *Do / Don't* look at a problem in a new way.
2 *Do / Don't* do things the way you normally do them.
3 *Do / Don't* experiment with new ideas.
4 *Do / Don't* guess the rules and follow those rules.
5 *Do / Don't* evaluate ideas while you're generating them.

D SPEAK Work in groups. When do you need to brainstorm ideas? How could brainstorming silly ideas help you to think of useful ideas?

LISTENING

A SPEAK Work in pairs. The pictures show some techniques for becoming more creative. What do you think the techniques are?

8.3 **B LISTEN FOR GIST** Listen to a conversation between two friends, Caroline and Toby, to check your answers to Exercise A. Number the pictures in the order they are mentioned.

Glossary

wander (v) if your mind or thoughts wander, you stop concentrating and start thinking about other things

8.3 **C** Listen again. What was the solution to each problem? Use the strategies in the box to help you.

Listening for problems and solutions

When you're listening, it's useful to organize information into a set of problems and solutions. This usually makes it easier to understand a lot of information and to remember it better later.

Listen carefully when you hear people talking about problems because they'll probably present a solution next.

1 You don't learn how to be creative at school.
   - a Write stories and design clothes.
   - b Go to creativity classes.
   - c Read books about creativity.

2 You're too busy to stop working.
   - a Take a break to make yourself more productive.
   - b Work in the evenings so you can have a break during the day.
   - c Relax – your work isn't as important as you think.

3 Your brain is filled with too much information.
   - a Get some physical exercise.
   - b Watch TV and play games on your phone.
   - c Turn off your computer.

4 You need to think outside the box.
   - a Go to the library to get some ideas.
   - b Look at blue things.
   - c Listen to some music.

5 You have no ideas at all.
   - a Discuss your ideas with a group of friends.
   - b Close your eyes for a few minutes.
   - c Use letters of the alphabet to generate ideas.

D SPEAK Work in pairs. Which of Caroline's techniques have you used? Which might you use in the future? Tell your partner.

VOCABULARY
Creative thinking

A Match the beginnings of the sentences (1–10) with the endings (a–j).

1 I'm terrible at **coming up**
2 You can actually learn to **use your**
3 A break actually **boosted my**
4 You need to **unplug**
5 You need to **let your mind**
6 They're all good for **generating**
7 Whenever I need to **think outside**
8 You're letting your emotions **block**
9 You should **look at a problem**
10 **My mind's**

a **the box**, I go to the beach.
b **wander freely**.
c **imagination** better.
d **your creativity**.
e **gone blank**.
f **creativity**.
g **with new ideas**.
h **from the outside**.
i **completely**.
j **new ideas**.

B Look at the sentences in Exercise A. What do the phrases in bold mean?

C SPEAK Choose the best words to complete the questions. Then work in groups and ask and answer the questions.

1 Does your mind ever *boost* / *generate* / *wander* during boring activities? Think of some examples.
2 Is it possible to *come up* / *unplug* / *block* completely from the things that make you stressed? How can you do it?
3 What can you do when your *mind* / *creativity* / *imagination* goes blank in a stressful situation (e.g. when you're in an exam, giving a presentation or speaking English)?

SPEAKING HUB

A Work in groups. You have decided to create a website that will make a big difference to people's lives. Use the alphabet technique to generate some ideas – silly or serious!

Write down three letters of the alphabet.
- 1st letter: Who is your website for?
- 2nd letter: What problem do those people have?
- 3rd letter: How will you solve that problem?

B PLAN Think of five ideas for each of the questions below. Remember to think outside the box!

1 What will you call your website?
2 How can you make money from your website?
3 How will you tell the world about your website?

C ORGANIZE Look at your ideas from Exercise B. Turn your silly ideas into excellent ideas. Choose your best idea.

D PRESENT Present your idea to the class. Which teams' websites would you visit?

- Explain how an invention works
- Suggest and evaluate creative ideas

8.2 Must-have gadgets

- Use positive language to promote a new product
- Give a friend advice about choosing a gadget

V – positive adjectives
G – zero and first conditionals; conditionals with modals and imperatives
P – *'ll* and *won't*
S – topic sentences

LISTENING

A SPEAK Work in pairs. Look at the pictures of inventions (a–d) and discuss the questions.

1 What do you think the gadgets in the pictures do?
2 How useful are they?
3 Do you like gadgets? What gadgets do you own?

8.4 **B LISTEN FOR MAIN IDEA** Listen to a podcast about new gadgets and answer the questions.

1 Which gadgets from the pictures do the people discuss?
2 What is special about them?

8.4 **C** Listen again. Which gadgets do these sentences describe? Write *O* (Oombrella), *C* (CleverPet) or *B* (both).

1 It looks beautiful. ______
2 It's connected to the internet. ______
3 It sends messages to your phone. ______
4 It's useful for many years. ______
5 It gets more difficult to use over time. ______
6 It can lead to a longer life. ______

D SPEAK Work in groups and discuss the questions.

1 What is good about the two gadgets? Which one is more useful?
2 Who do you think will buy the gadgets? Why?

VOCABULARY
Positive adjectives

Using positive adjectives

As your English improves, try to avoid using words like *good* or *nice* too frequently. There are many other positive words that you can use like *amazing*, *excellent* and *wonderful*.

A Match the positive adjectives (1–10) with the meanings (a–j).

1 gorgeous
2 sensible
3 practical
4 unforgettable
5 impressive
6 unique
7 sophisticated
8 incredible
9 suitable
10 fascinating

a you admire it because it is very good, large or shows great skill
b making you very interested or attracted
c right for a particular purpose, person or situation
d not the same as anything or anyone else
e reasonable and practical
f will be remembered for a very long time
g surprising, or difficult to believe
h very beautiful
i complicated and advanced in design
j intended to be useful

B Go to the **Vocabulary Hub** on **page 145**.

C SPEAK Work in pairs. Write down the names of your favorite three possessions. Use positive adjectives to tell your partner why you like each one. Ask questions about your partner's possessions.

a

b

GRAMMAR

Zero and first conditionals

8.5 **A** Look at the extracts from the podcast about new gadgets. Match the beginnings of the sentences (1–4) with the endings (a–d). Then listen and check your answers.

1 I never go for a walk
2 Will it keep me dry
3 If this Oombrella lasts for years,
4 Pets stay healthier and they live longer

a if there's a storm tomorrow morning?
b if they keep busy.
c I'll be very happy.
d unless the sun's shining.

B WORK IT OUT Choose the correct words to complete the rules.

Zero and first conditional

1 Conditional sentences usually have ***two*** / ***four*** clauses: the *if*-clause and the result clause.
2 When the *if*-clause comes first, we ***always*** / ***never*** need a comma between the clauses.
3 We can use ***unless*** instead of *if*. It means ***if not*** / ***because***.
4 We use the zero conditional to talk about things that are always true. We use ***past*** / ***present*** tenses in both clauses.
5 We use the first conditional to talk about possible situations in the ***future*** / ***past***. We usually use ***will*** in the result clause.

C Go to the Grammar Hub on page 136.

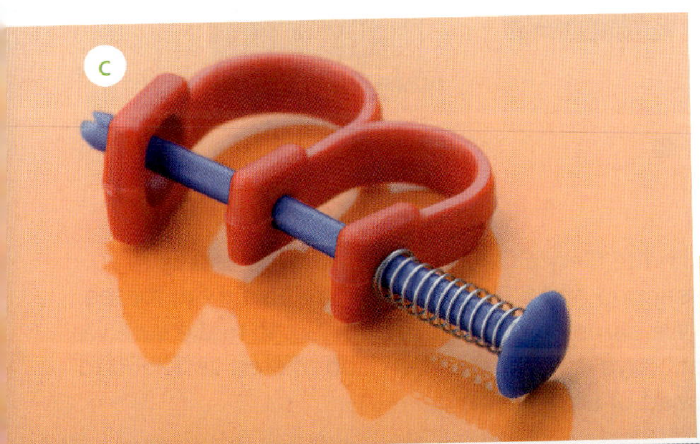

PRONUNCIATION

'll and *won't*

'll* and *won't

It's sometimes hard to hear the difference between words such as *you* and *you'll*, or *I* and *I'll*. It's also sometimes hard to hear the difference between *won't* and *want*. The rules for conditionals will help you figure out what you hear.

8.6 **A** Listen and circle the words you hear.

1 If you ***want to go*** / ***won't go*** to the grocery store, ***you*** / ***you'll*** need to bring a bag.
2 ***I lend*** / ***I'll lend*** you my raincoat if you ***want to borrow*** / ***won't borrow*** it.
3 If ***you*** / ***you'll*** like gadgets, ***you*** / ***you'll*** love this.
4 ***You learn*** / ***You'll earn*** a lot more if ***you*** / ***you'll*** listen carefully.

8.6 **B** Listen again and repeat the sentences.

C SPEAK Work in pairs. Imagine you are going to lend your partner a gadget tonight. Follow the instructions.

1 If you have a gadget with you (e.g. a phone, a smartwatch), show your partner what to do. Ask questions about your partner's gadget.
2 If you don't have a gadget, use an everyday object (e.g. a pen, your car keys) and pretend it's a gadget. Invent some cool functions for it.

SPEAKING

A You are going to invent a new gadget and then promote it to the class. Use the ideas below and your own ideas to invent a gadget.

What is it?	What's innovative about it?
a book, a chair, a food bowl, a hat, swimming goggles, a mirror, a light bulb, a plastic bottle, a puzzle, shoes, a toy, a TV, an umbrella	It can fly/talk/move by itself. It's connected to the internet. It contains a GPS device / a camera. It's for pets/birds/fish. It's very big/small.

B PLAN Work in groups. Choose the best idea for your group's gadget and answer the questions:

- What is special about your gadget?
- What problem does it solve?
- What else can you use to help you promote your gadget (e.g. pictures, stories)?
- What questions might people ask about your gadget?

C PRESENT Promote your gadget to the class. At the end of each presentation, ask questions about other groups' gadgets.

D REFLECT Take a class vote to find out the most popular gadget. Would you like to buy the other groups' gadgets? Why/Why not? Do you think your gadgets could become real products?

READING

A SPEAK Work in pairs. Look at the picture and answer the questions.

1 What do you think the people are doing? Why?

2 Have you ever done something similar? Why/Why not?

B PREDICT Work in pairs. Before you read *If you really can't wait …*, look at the five topic sentences (a–e) and discuss the questions. Use the strategies in the box to help you.

Topic sentences

The topic sentence is usually the first or second sentence in a paragraph. It tells you what the whole paragraph will be about.

You can usually understand a lot about a text just by reading and thinking about the topic sentences.

You can also use them to make predictions before reading the whole text to check.

a Marketers have a name for people who buy new gadgets before everyone else: innovators.

Why do you think marketers have a special name for these people? Why are marketers interested in them?

b A little further back in the line, I meet some fans who aren't just there to buy a phone.

Why do you think these fans are in the line?

c Near the back of the line, some people are feeling less positive.

Why do you think they're feeling less positive?

d It's five o'clock in the morning, and there are already over 200 people in the line outside the phone store.

Why do you think they're there so early in the morning?

e I decided to speak to some people in the line outside the phone store to find out … and I got a few surprises.

What surprises do you think the writer got?

If you really *can't wait …*

1 ___ It's cold and dark, but the people seem happy. In a few hours, the doors will open and they'll finally get their hands on the gadget of their dreams: a gorgeous new cell phone. Of course, if you don't want to stand in line all night, you can come to the store this afternoon when the lines will be gone. Even better, if you can wait six months or so, the same phone will cost half the price. But if you really need that phone right now, come and join the back of the line.

2 ___ I've always thought that was a terrible name – innovation normally means doing something extremely smart, like inventing a new machine. But what's innovative about buying expensive gadgets just because they're new? Of course, marketers love 'innovators' for two reasons: innovators are happy to spend a lot of money and they persuade the rest of us to buy those gadgets a few months later.

So why do they do it? 3 ___ The biggest surprise was that the people at the front of the line were actually being paid to be there. 'I work for a gadget store, Gary's Gadgets. My boss, Gary, is paying me,' said Bob, who is right at the front of the line. 'It's good for business because when the doors open, I'll be on TV around the world – wearing a T-shirt with the Gary's Gadgets logo.' Janice and Damian, who are second and third in the line, are also there for the money. 'We came here ten days ago, just to make sure we were first,' says Janice. 'But then Bob offered us $2500 to move ahead of us.'

4 ___ 'For me, it's a social event,' says a man named Mo. 'It's a great way to meet people who share my love of gadgets. I've had some amazing conversations in this line. Many of us come every year, so it feels like meeting old friends.' A woman named Ruby agrees, 'It's like going to a pop concert or a live sports game. I love the feeling of being at an important place at an important time.'

5 ___ 'I'm only here because of the special offer: 25 percent off for the first 200 customers,' explains a stressed-looking young woman named Lucy, 'so I'll be really annoyed if I'm number 201!' Her best friend, Fiona, looks annoyed already. 'I'm only here to keep Lucy company,' she says. 'I actually think it's a waste of time and money. I've been here all night and I'm really cold. I mean, this new phone looks exactly the same as last year's!' But Lucy looks shocked. 'There's only one difference that counts: the difference between the best … and second best.'

C READ FOR GIST Read the article. Match the topic sentences (a–e) with the paragraphs (1–5).

D READ FOR DETAIL Read again. Write *B* (Bob), *J* (Janice), *M* (Mo), *R* (Ruby), *L* (Lucy) or *F* (Fiona).

Which person …

1 has met people from the line at events like this before? *M*
2 paid to be at the front of the line? ____
3 doesn't want to buy a phone at all? ____
4 compares the experience to other exciting events? ____
5 arrived before anyone else? ____
6 enjoys talking to other people about gadgets? ____
7 is hoping to save some money? ____

E SPEAK Work in groups. Do you think it is right to call people who buy the latest gadgets *innovators*? Why/Why not?

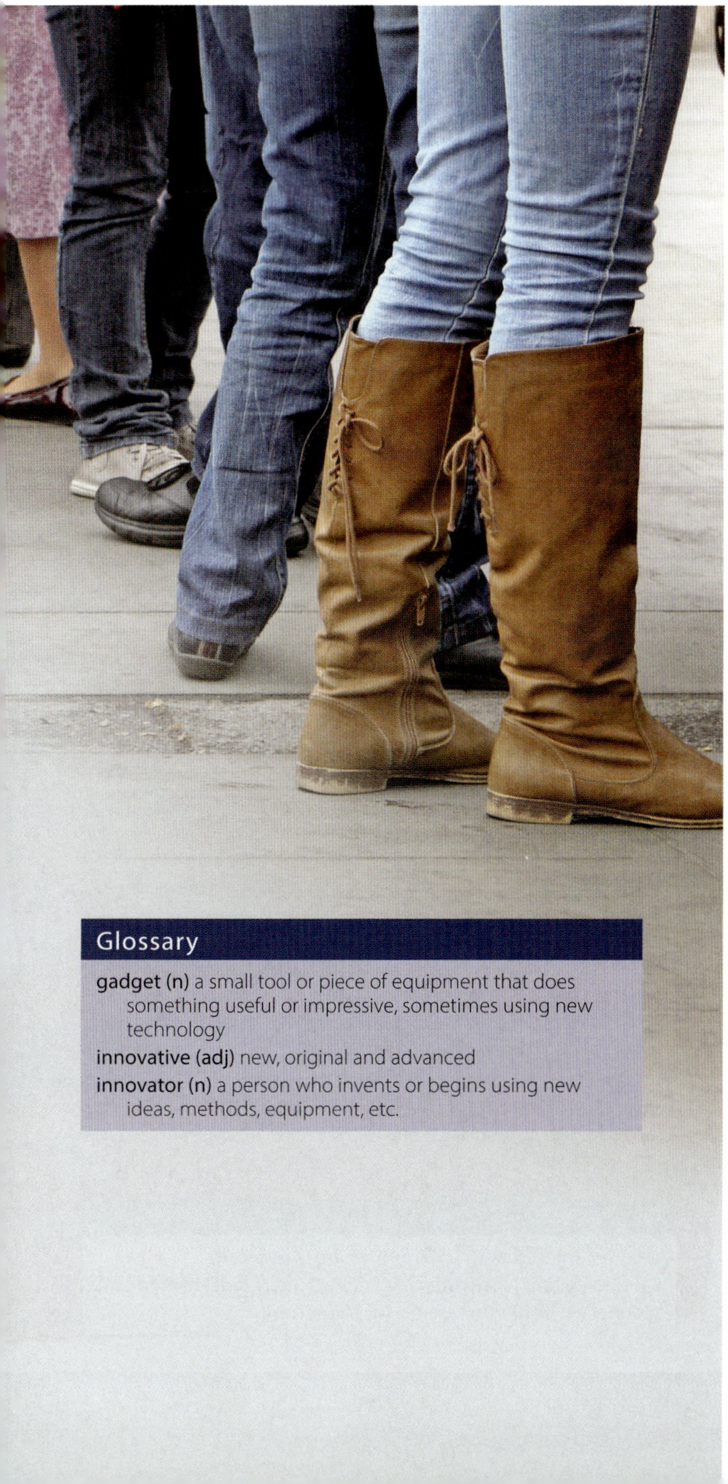

Glossary

gadget (n) a small tool or piece of equipment that does something useful or impressive, sometimes using new technology
innovative (adj) new, original and advanced
innovator (n) a person who invents or begins using new ideas, methods, equipment, etc.

GRAMMAR

Conditionals with modals and imperatives

A WORK IT OUT Read the rules. Then look at paragraph 1 of *If you really can't wait …* again and complete the examples.

Conditionals with modals and imperatives

Zero conditionals and first conditionals are very common. They can be very varied. Many patterns are possible.

For example, we can use imperatives in the result clause:

If you really need that phone right now, [1] ____________ *the back of the line.*

We can use modal verbs (e.g. *should, might, can, must*) in the *if*-clause or the result clause:

If you don't want to stand in line all night, you [2] ____________ *to the store this afternoon.*

If you [3] ____________ *six months or so, the same phone will cost half the price.*

B Go to the **Grammar Hub** on **page 136**.

C SPEAK Work in pairs. Write five pieces of advice for people who are thinking of standing in line for the latest cell phone. Use these ideas and your own ideas:

- If you want to be at the front of the line, you should …
- If you can't afford a new phone right now, …
- If somebody offers you $2500 for your place in the line, …

SPEAKING HUB

A Work in pairs. Choose a gadget you both know well (e.g. phone, camera, laptop, webcam). You are going to give some advice to a friend who wants to buy one of these gadgets. Write notes on:

- price (simple version / best version?)
- features (what must/should it have?)
- risks (what might go wrong with it?)

B SPEAK Work in new pairs. Take turns role-playing the conversation. Student A is the friend who needs advice. Student B gives advice.

A: I don't know anything about photography. Do you have any recommendations for a new camera?
B: Well, it does really depend on how much you want to spend …

C DISCUSS What was the best advice you received? Would you buy the gadget your partner recommended?

Use positive language to promote a new product

Give a friend advice about choosing a gadget

Café Hub

8.3 Flat-packed

F – give and follow instructions   P – sentence stress

COMPREHENSION

A Work in pairs and discuss the questions.

- Have you ever tried to build a piece of furniture or put up a shelf?
- How would you describe the experience – successful, frustrating, etc?
- Are you good at giving and following instructions?

B Match the words in the box with the tools in the pictures (a–d). Which tools do you think Sam and Zac will need to build a shelf?

allen key   drill   hammer   helmet
pliers   screwdriver   spanner   tape measure

C ▶ 00:00–02:53 Watch the first part of the video. How many tools do they use?

D ▶ 00:00–02:53 Put the instructions in the correct order (1–5). Watch the first part again and check your answers.

___ Lay out all the pieces in a row.
___ Insert the screws on both sides.
___ Put the screws into the correct holes.
___ Take the packet of screws.
___ Organize all of the pieces into the correct order.

E ▶ 02:54–04:13 How is Sam feeling and why? Watch the second part of the video to check your ideas.

FUNCTIONAL LANGUAGE

Giving and following instructions

A ▶ 02:54–04:13 Complete the phrases with the words in the box. Then watch the second part of the video again to check your answers.

after   again   correct   do   how   let   sure   that   thing

Sequencing

1 The first ________ to do is …
2 When you've done ________ …
3 ________ that, you …

Explaining

4 Make ________ you …
5 ________ me show you …
6 This is how you ________ it.

Checking

7 Sorry, can you say that ________.
8 Is this ________ you do it?
9 Are you sure this is ________?

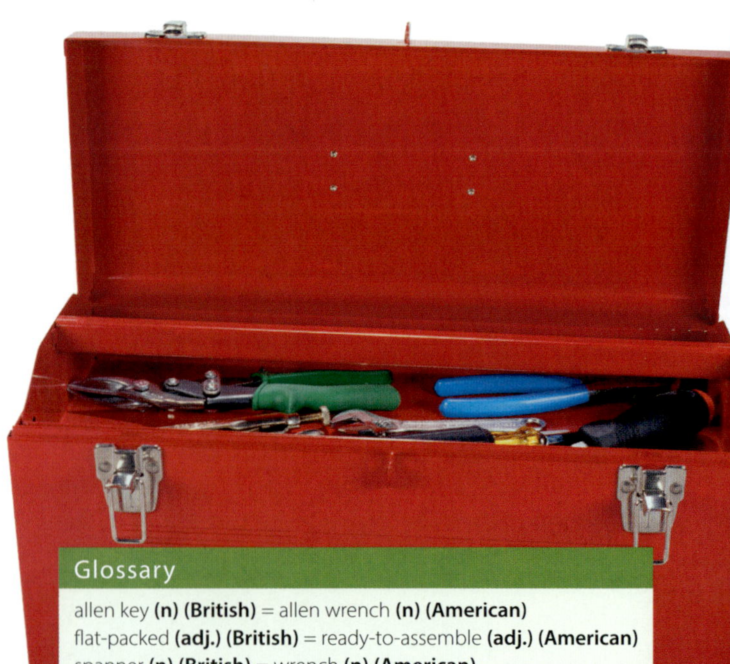

Glossary

allen key **(n) (British)** = allen wrench **(n) (American)**
flat-packed **(adj.) (British)** = ready-to-assemble **(adj.) (American)**
spanner **(n) (British)** = wrench **(n) (American)**

MILLY

SAM

NEENA

ZAC

GABY

B Work in pairs. Cover the functional language in Exercise A, and add sequencing phrases to the instructions in Comprehension Exercise D.

1 *The first thing to do is to organize all of the pieces into the correct order.*
2 ______________________________
3 ______________________________
4 ______________________________
5 ______________________________

USEFUL PHRASES

A Who says it? *Sam*, *Zac* or *Gaby*?

1 I know when something's wrong with you. ____________
2 It's complicated. ____________
3 She's been acting strangely around me. ____________
4 A bit cold and unfriendly. ____________
5 Whatever! ____________

B How would you describe how each person feels in Exercise A? Choose the most appropriate adjective for each phrase.

concerned confused puzzled uninterested upset

C How do you say these useful phrases in your language?

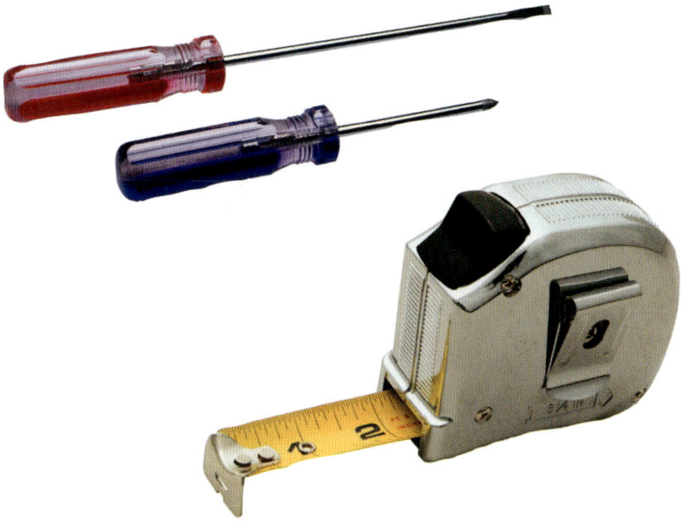

PRONUNCIATION
Sentence stress

8.7 **A** Underline the stressed words in the sentences (1–7). Then listen and check.

1 The first thing to do is to organize all of the pieces into the correct order.
2 Sorry, can you say that again?
3 What did you say?
4 When you've done that, take the packet of screws.
5 After that, you put the screws into the correct holes.
6 Is this how you do it?
7 Are you sure this is correct?

B Work in pairs. Practice saying the instructions in Exercise A, paying attention to the sentence stress.

SPEAKING

Work in pairs. Student A – go to the Communication Hub on page 155. Student B – go to the Communication Hub on page 151. Follow the instructions.

Give and follow instructions

➤ Turn to page 163 to learn how to write a biography.

Unit 8 Review

GRAMMAR

A Complete the dialogue with the adjective clauses in the box.

when which who

A: Hey, I like your watch. Is it new?

B: Yeah, I bought it last week [1] ________ I was in Boston. It has a built-in phone and a button [2] ________ you press to connect to the internet.

A: Cool. So what's the time?

B: Uh … I don't know. It worked for the man [3] ________ sold it to me, but when I took it home, it didn't work at all.

B Choose the correct words to complete the article.

The liter of light

If [1]***you want / you'll want*** to make a difference in people's lives, a good, simple idea is best. Brazilian engineer Alfredo Moser noticed that many people in his country live in houses with no electricity. Of course, if [2]***there'll be / there's*** no electricity, the houses are usually very dark. It's hard for people to read or study at home [3]***if / unless*** they have enough light. Alfredo's solution? Cut a hole in your roof and put a plastic water bottle through the hole. If [4]***you do / you'll do*** it properly, the light will fill your house.

C Match the beginnings of the sentences (1–5) with the endings (a–e).

1 If you can't think of any good ideas,
2 If you must have the new phone today,
3 If you wear your smartwatch in the bathtub,
4 You shouldn't watch TV all the time
5 Don't worry

a if you're late – I'll wait for you.
b it might stop working properly.
c if you want to be more creative.
d join the line outside the store.
e go for a long walk.

VOCABULARY

A Complete the sentences with the correct form of the words in parentheses.

1 My old website looked horrible, so I asked my sister to ________ (*designer*) a new one for me.
2 A great ________ (*produce*) is one that makes a difference.
3 This machine's broken again! Can you call an ________ (*engineering*) to come and fix it?
4 We've tried really hard, but we haven't had much ________ (*succeed*) yet.
5 You just copied all my ideas! That isn't very ________ (*innovate*), is it?

B Complete the advice with one word in each space.

Do you find it hard to come up [1] ________ new ideas? Try these techniques to boost your creativity!

- If your mind goes [2] ________, you probably need to take a break.
- Too much TV can block your creativity. Try to [3] ________ completely.
- Try to relax and [4] ________ your mind wander freely.
- Don't follow rules that don't exist! Learn to think outside the [5] ________!
- Talk to a friend. This will help you to look at your problems [6] ________ the outside.

C Complete the sentences with the best adjectives from the box.

gorgeous impressive sensible sophisticated suitable unique

1 Each user has a ________ username and password – it can't be the same as anybody else's.
2 **A:** 'I built a laptop computer in my garage when I was ten years old.'
B: 'Wow! That's ________!'
3 This camera isn't really ________ for taking underwater pictures. If water gets into the electronics, it might break.
4 The best thing about my watch is that it looks ________. Isn't it beautiful!
5 You can buy a simple microphone in the grocery store, but if you need something more ________, with lots more options, you need to go to a specialist store.
6 It's fine to use another person's computer, but you need to be ________. For example, don't use it to check your bank account.

FUNCTIONAL LANGUAGE

Correct the mistake in each part of the dialogue.

1 **A:** OK, here are the instructions for the table. Let's build this! The first thing do is take everything out of the box.
2 **B:** After that, put the legs on. Careful don't to lose the screws.
3 **A:** This is how you do it?
4 **B:** No, no, no! Those are the wrong screws. Let show you how to do it.
5 **A:** Are you sure this correct is? It looks wrong! Give me the instructions.

9 THE ARTS

Art is unquestionably one of the purest and highest elements in human happiness.
John Lubbock

A young man comes face to face with nature in a London gallery.

OBJECTIVES

- suggest improvements to a proposal
- plan an arts event
- report a conversation
- create a collaborative story
- talk about movies and books
- write a review

Work with a partner. Discuss the questions.

1 Look at the picture. Do you think this is art?

2 Look at the quote. Do you agree? Why/ Why not?

3 Which of the arts do you like? What do you not like? Why? Are the arts important? Why/Why not?

9.1 Art for everybody

- Suggest improvements to a proposal
- Plan an arts event

V – the arts; verbal idioms G – second conditional P – /tʃ/, /ʃ/ and /k/
S – using linking words to understand the writer's opinion

A NEW ARTS VENUE FOR THE CITY CENTER

After the recent closure of a furniture factory in the city center, the city council has become the owner of a large warehouse. Council members voted last week to turn the warehouse into a major public arts venue. There will be a competition to choose the best use of the space. Please visit the council website for information on how to submit a proposal.
The warehouse consists of a large empty hall (120 m x 150 m), with offices upstairs.

LISTENING

A Look at the picture and read the article above. What would you like to use the warehouse for?

9.1 **B LISTEN FOR GIST** Listen to the three finalists from the competition speaking at a council meeting. Match the finalists (1–3) with the pictures (a–c).

1 Leon MacGregor ___
2 Violet Spring ___
3 Florian Quirk ___

9.1 **C LISTEN FOR DETAIL** Listen again. Choose the correct answers.

1 Who does Leon mostly want to help?
   a people who don't work now
   b professional musicians
   c people who go out frequently
2 What exactly is Leon's dream?
   a to teach people to play musical instruments
   b to bring people together to learn new skills
   c to make money by selling tickets to concerts
3 Why do people travel to other cities to visit the theater?
   a because they are open every day
   b because there's no theater in their own city
   c because they don't want to spend their money at the Grand Theater
4 What is special about immersive theater?
   a The audience is on the stage with the actors.
   b Tickets are a lot more expensive than for other plays.
   c The audience doesn't just watch the play.
5 Why does Florian think art is important?
   a It makes money that can be spent on roads and schools.
   b It helps you to understand new ideas.
   c It helps you to relax when you're stressed.
6 How will Florian's idea help the people of the city?
   a It will give them a place to perform.
   b It will help the city's artists to sell their paintings.
   c It will make them think in a different way.

D SPEAK Work in pairs. Which proposal sounds the most interesting? Explain why.

a

b

c

VOCABULARY
The arts

A Complete the table with the words in the box. Some words can go in more than one place.

~~an audience~~ a choir a display an exhibit a gallery an instrument a live concert a musician an orchestra to perform live a performance a recording studio a rehearsal room to rehearse a scene a spectator a stage

Theater	Art (e.g. paintings)	Music
an audience		an audience

B What other words can you add to each group? Think about people and places connected with each topic.

C **SPEAK** Work in pairs and ask and answer the questions.

1. Do you ever rehearse what you are going to say before you say it? Think of examples.
2. Do you prefer to be a performer on a stage or a member of the audience? Why?
3. Can you play any musical instruments? Would you like to?

GRAMMAR
Second conditional

A **WORK IT OUT** Work in pairs. Look at the sentences (a–d) from the council meeting and discuss the questions (1–3).

a. If we open a community music center, it will change thousands of people's lives.
b. If we turned the warehouse into a theater, it would make a lot of money.
c. If we had a good, modern theater in this city, it would be extremely popular.
d. If the city council had three warehouses, maybe we could do all of those wonderful things.

1. Sentences **a** and **b** are both about the future. Which speaker is more certain that their plans will really happen?
2. In sentence **c**, does the city have a theater right now?
3. In sentence **d**, does the city council have three warehouses? Can they do all three things?

B Complete the rules with the words in the box.

could base past unreal were

Second conditional

1. Conditional sentences usually have two clauses: the *if*-clause and the result clause. To make second conditional sentences, we use ***If*** + simple ________ and ***would*** + ________ form of the verb.
2. With the verb ***be***, we use ________ instead of *was*.
   If I were you, I'd vote for the first proposal.
3. We use the second conditional to talk about ________ or impossible situations in the present or future.
4. If we are not sure of the result, we can use ***might*** or ________ instead of ***would*** in the result clause.

C Go to the **Grammar Hub** on **page 138**.

D **SPEAK** Work in pairs and discuss the questions.

1. How would you feel if somebody asked you to sing in public?
2. If you were a successful musician, what sort of music would you play?

SPEAKING

A Work in pairs. Student A – read the box below. Student B – go to the **Communication Hub** on **page 152**. Student C – go to the **Communication Hub** on **page 154**. Read about one of the proposals for the Warehouse Project. Write about the advantages and disadvantages.

Proposal 1: Community music center

Costs (= money going out)		Income (= money coming in)
Building work: $450,000	Employees: $50,000/year	None – everything will be free for community groups
Equipment: $350,000	Other costs (e.g. electricity): $100,000/year	

- The community music center will save money by only opening for a few hours each day.
- Rehearsals/Workshops: Mondays, Wednesdays and Fridays, 10 am to 3 pm
- Concerts: Tuesdays and Thursdays, 12 pm to 2 pm
- Evenings and weekends: closed

B Tell your partner about your proposal. Then discuss what you like about each one. Suggest some improvements.

C Decide which proposal should win the competition. Why? Then share your ideas with the class.

READING

A SPEAK Work in pairs. Imagine you are watching a traditional play. What would you do if a character on the stage spoke to you? Would you be happy or would you feel uncomfortable?

B READ FOR MAIN IDEA Read the first paragraph of *The best (and the worst) of immersive theater*. Why has the writer written the article?

C READ FOR GIST Read the rest of the article. Match the recommendations (a–g) with the sections (1–6). There is one extra recommendation.

a Keep it simple.

b Tell a story.

c Make the audience feel special.

d Make it an experience for all the senses.

e Keep ticket prices as low as possible.

f Keep the rest of the audience out of sight.

g Make good use of the space.

The best (and the worst) of **immersive theater**

For most people, going to the theater is a chance to relax and let the actors do all the work. But in recent years, a new type of theater has appeared where the audience takes part in the play! When it works well, immersive theater can be breathtaking. But when it goes wrong, it can be awful. Here are my six recommendations based on my favorite (and least favorite!) immersive plays.

1 ____

Sometimes the building itself is part of the experience. A good example is *Hotel Impossible*, which took place in a real hotel building. Similarly, *The Dark Tunnels* took place inside real tunnels, which created a very scary atmosphere. However, a great location isn't everything. *Dangerous Heart* was in a beautiful palace, but the play didn't really take advantage of the space.

2 ____

In *Step by Step*, the audience was limited to 15, so we could interact one-on-one with the characters. During the play, the audience had to solve a crime, so we really had to pay attention to what we saw and heard. By the end, I was terrified and exhausted, but it was an unforgettable experience.

3 ____

Some immersive plays feel far too complicated, with too many characters and storylines. For example, *Yellow and Blue* had amazing special effects, but I couldn't keep track of who was who. In *The Quiet Visitors*, however, there were only six characters in a large empty room. We had to use our imaginations, and the effect was incredibly powerful.

4 ____

The worst thing about immersive theater? Other members of the audience! The play *Life with the Lions* got rid of this problem by making the audience wear animal costumes. I felt silly in my zebra costume, but at least we couldn't tell the difference between actors and spectators. In *The Dark Tunnels*, we all wore black clothes and masks so the members of the audience were almost invisible to each other.

5 ____

Without a strong story, immersive theater can easily fall flat – it feels like something's missing. In *Hotel Impossible*, for example, lots of interesting things happened, but the whole play didn't really go anywhere. In *The Quiet Visitors*, however, there was a clear beginning, a middle … and a shocking surprise at the end.

6 ____

It isn't just about what the audience sees and hears. The best immersive plays make use of the senses of taste, smell and touch, too. In *Dangerous Heart*, we enjoyed a delicious meal as part of the experience. Similarly, in *The Dark Tunnels*, the unpleasant underground smell added to the sense of danger. And in *The Quiet Visitors*, when the room suddenly went as cold as ice, the effect was terrifying.

D Look at the highlighted words in the article. What is the writer's opinion? Use the strategies in the box to help you. Choose + (positive) or – (negative).

Using linking words to understand the writer's opinion

When you're trying to figure out the writer's opinion, don't just look for positive words (e.g. *amazing*, *interesting*) and negative words (e.g. *unpleasant*, *terrifying*).

Writers regularly use words like *for example*, *similarly* and *however* to link their opinions to earlier sentences.

1 the location for *The Dark Tunnels* + / –
2 the characters and story in *Yellow and Blue* + / –
3 the characters and story in *The Quiet Visitors* + / –
4 the story in *Hotel Impossible* + / –
5 the experience for the senses in *The Dark Tunnels* + / –
6 the experience for the senses in *The Quiet Visitors* + / –

E **SPEAK** Work in pairs. Which of the plays from the article would you most like to see? Which would you least like to see? Why? Tell your partner.

VOCABULARY
Verbal idioms

Verbal idioms

Verbal idioms are fixed phrases that work as verbs with a single meaning.

A Go to the **Vocabulary Hub** on **page 146**.

B **SPEAK** Complete the sentences so they are true for you. Then work in pairs and tell your partner what happened.

1 I had an opportunity to … but I didn't take advantage of it, because …
2 Everything went wrong when I …
3 I'm planning to get rid of …
4 I once tried to (tell a joke/story, etc.), but it fell flat, because …

PRONUNCIATION
/tʃ/, /ʃ/ and /k/

9.2 **A** How do you pronounce *ch* in these words? Listen and repeat.

character charge chef choice choir orchestra

ch

ch is usually pronounced /tʃ/ (as in *cheese*). But there are also a few words where *ch* is pronounced /ʃ/ (as in *mustache*) or /k/ (as in *chemist*).

B Find and underline *ch* in these sentences. Then write /tʃ/, /ʃ/ or /k/ above each example.

/tʃ/
1 My <u>ch</u>ildren didn't go to school today – they both had bad stomachaches.
2 If I were a mechanic, I might be able to fix this machine, but I don't know anything about technology.
3 My sister is a chemist; she's doing some research into new techniques for recycling harmful chemicals.

9.3 **C** Listen and check.

D **SPEAK** Work in pairs. Practice saying the sentences. Listen and check your partner's pronunciation.

SPEAKING HUB

A Work in groups. Discuss ideas for an immersive theater performance. Think about:

- story: Will you use an existing story or create your own?
- location: Where will it take place? How could you make use of the location?
- interactivity: How will the actors interact with the audience?

B **PLAN** Choose your best idea and add more details. Follow the advice in *The best (and the worst) of immersive theater* on page 100.

C **PRESENT** Present your idea to the class.

D **REFLECT** Which immersive play would you most like to watch? Why?

Suggest improvements to a proposal
Plan an arts event

9.2 Tell me a story

- Report a conversation
- Create a collaborative story

G – reported speech **V** – reporting verbs **P** – using your voice to make a story more interesting
S – listening for definitions of new words

Francis Scott Key Fitzgerald (1896–1940) was one of the most important American writers of the 20th century. His best-known novel, *The Great Gatsby* (1925), is an American classic. It paints a powerful portrait of life in 1920s America, a period known as the Jazz Age. For many young people in America, this was a time for partying and having fun, with new types of music, new ways of dancing and new fashions.

READING

A Work in pairs. Read about F. Scott Fitzgerald and look at the pictures. Have you read *The Great Gatsby*? Why do you think it is 'an American classic'?

I haven't read the book but I have seen the movie starring Leonardo DiCaprio.

9.4 **B** Listen to a conversation between two friends, Joe and Nadia. Answer the questions.

1 Who is Jay Gatsby?
2 Why doesn't Joe want to borrow the book? Why does he change his mind?
3 Why does Nadia like the book?

CHAPTER 3: I MEET GATSBY

PART 1

One day, I was invited to one of Gatsby's parties. As soon as I arrived, I began to look for Gatsby to thank him for his invitation. But no one knew where he was.
As I went to get a drink, I saw Jordan Baker. I walked toward her, glad to see someone I knew.
'I thought you might be here,' Jordan said.
We took our drinks and sat down at a small table under a tree. Jordan began to talk to a girl in a yellow dress.
'Do you come to these parties often?' Jordan asked her.
'I come when I can,' the girl said. 'No one cares what I do, so I always have a good time. Last time I was here, I tore my dress. Do you know, Gatsby sent me a new one! It cost him 265 dollars!'

PART 2

Supper was now being served. Jordan and I left our table and went to look for Gatsby.
People were dancing now. The voices and the laughter were very loud. The moon was high in the sky.
Jordan and I sat down at a table with a well-dressed man of my own age. I was enjoying myself, now. The music stopped for a moment. The man at our table looked at me and smiled.
'I think I know your face,' the man said. 'Weren't you in France during the War?'
'Yes, I was.'
'Me, too,' he said. We talked about the War for a few minutes. Then the man told me that **he had a new motorboat.**
'Want to go out with me in the morning, old sport?' he asked.
'Sure, what time?'
'Let's say nine o'clock.'
I looked at the yard and smiled.
'This is an unusual party,' I told the man. 'I haven't seen my host yet. Gatsby sent me an invitation this morning. I ought to thank him.'
The man stared at me in surprise.
'I'm Gatsby,' he said. 'I thought you knew, old sport. I'm not a very good host, am I?'
Gatsby smiled. He had a pleasant smile. His smile made me feel important. I looked at Gatsby with interest. He was a tough-looking young man, but he had beautiful clothes and beautiful manners.

PART 3

A few guests were standing near Gatsby. I went up to him to say goodbye.
'Don't forget we're going out in the boat, old sport,' he said. 'At nine o'clock.'
Gatsby smiled at me.
'Goodnight, old sport, goodnight.'
I walked across the lawn in the moonlight. The cars drove away. The yard was quiet and empty.
All alone, Gatsby stood on the white steps, waving goodbye.

Glossary

old sport (phrase) a popular way of saying 'my friend' in the 1920s

C READ FOR DETAIL Read *The Great Gatsby*, Chapter 3, Part 1. Are the sentences true (T) or false (F)? Correct the false sentences.

1 Gatsby invited Nick Carraway (the storyteller) to his party. ____
2 Nick already knew most of the people at the party. ____
3 Jordan was surprised to see Nick. ____
4 Gatsby is very careful with his money. ____

D Read Part 2. What do we learn about Gatsby? Write notes on:

1 his appearance (= his clothes and the way he looks).
2 his manners (= the way he treats other people).
3 his background (= what he has done in the past).

E Read Part 3. Why do you think Gatsby has so many parties?

GRAMMAR

Reported speech

A WORK IT OUT Look at the phrase in bold from *The Great Gatsby*, Chapter 3, Part 2. What do you think Gatsby actually said?

Direct speech: 'I ________________ a new motorboat.'

B Complete the examples in the correct tense.

Direct speech	Reported speech
Simple present 'My name's Jay Gatsby.'	Simple past He told me his name 1 ________________ Jay Gatsby.
Present progressive 'I'm really enjoying the party.'	Past progressive I told him I 2 ________________ really enjoying the party.
Present perfect 'I've never met Gatsby.'	Past perfect He said he 3 ________________ never met Gatsby.
Simple past 'Gatsby sent me a new dress.'	Past perfect She said Gatsby 4 ________________ sent her a new dress.
can 'I can't see the host.'	*could* I told him I 5 ________________ see the host.
will 'We'll have a great time on my boat.'	*would* He said we 6 ________________ have a great time on his boat.

C Go to the Grammar Hub on page 138.

D Report the sentences (1–5) from *The Great Gatsby*.

1 'Do you come to these parties often?' Jordan asked her.
Jordan asked the girl if she came to these parties often.
2 'I come when I can,' the girl said.
____
3 'I think I know your face,' the man said.
____
4 'This is an unusual party,' I told the man. 'I haven't seen my host yet.'
____
5 'Gatsby sent me an invitation this morning.'
____

E SPEAK Work in pairs. Use your imagination to tell the next part of the story. Report the conversation between Jay and Nick the next morning.

SPEAKING

A Think about the questions below. Write notes.

1 Do you read a lot of novels? What sort of books do you enjoy? Which books would you recommend? Why?
2 Do you ever read books in English? What have you read? Did you find it easy or difficult? Do you need to understand every word or can you simply relax and enjoy the story?

B Work in pairs. Ask and answer the questions from Exercise A. Ask follow-up questions and give examples.

C Work with a new partner. Tell your new partner about your conversation.

LISTENING

A SPEAK Work in groups and discuss the questions.

1 What are some situations where people tell each other stories?

2 Are stories just for fun, or do they have a serious purpose?

3 Do you like telling stories? What kind of stories?

4 What skills do you need to tell great stories? When was the last time you told a story?

- Where were you?
- Who did you tell it to?
- Why did you tell it?
- What was the story about?

9.5 **B LISTEN FOR GIST** Listen to the conversation between two friends, Zoe and Jacob. They are talking about storytelling. Put the pictures (a–c) in the order that they discuss them (1–3).

1 ____ 2 ____ 3 ____

Glossary

dice (n) a small block of wood or plastic with six sides marked with spots that you roll or throw to play a game

end up (with) (phrasal verb) to be in a particular place or state after doing something or because of doing it

a

b

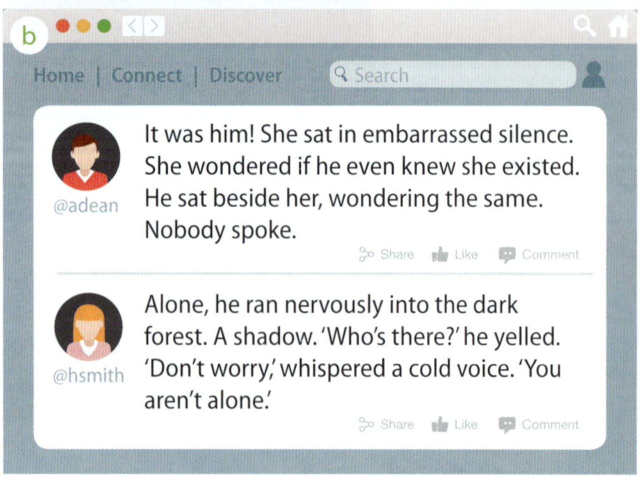

9.5 **C LISTEN FOR KEY WORDS** Listen again and complete the definitions of the new words. Use the strategies in the box to help you.

Listening for definitions of new words

Speakers usually pause before and after an important new word. They usually place extra stress on the word itself.

When you hear an important new word, listen carefully for a definition or explanation.

1 Flash fiction: A story with a word limit, usually ________________ words.

2 Micro-stories: These are stories on social ________________ sites (e.g. Twitter). A whole story told in a ________________-character message.

3 A twist: When something happens in the story that you didn't ________________.

4 Collaborative stories: Stories that are created by a large group of people working ________________.

5 Pass the paper: You write one line of a ________________ on a sheet of paper, fold it down and pass it to the next player, who writes the next ________________, and so on.

6 Add a word: You sit in a ________________. The first person says the first ________________ from a sentence, and then the next person says the next word.

7 Story dice: A set of ________________ dice, and each one has six ________________, one on each side.

D SPEAK Work in groups. Play *Add a word*.

E DISCUSS Work in groups and discuss the questions.

1 Have you ever played any of the games or tried any of the story techniques mentioned in the conversation? Would you like to?

2 Do you think word limits make it easier or harder to write a good story?

3 Do you prefer working collaboratively or by yourself?

c

VOCABULARY

Reporting verbs

A Look at the examples of micro-stories in Listening Exercise B, picture b. Which verbs are used instead of *say* and *think*? Why?

B Look at the information in the box. Use a dictionary to check any new verbs.

> **Reporting verbs**
>
> Instead of using *say* and *tell*, we can use more interesting and descriptive reporting verbs.
>
> verb (+ *that*) + reported speech: *add, admit, agree, argue, explain, insist, mention, predict, promise, repeat, reply, say, yell, warn, whisper*
>
> verb + somebody (+ *that*) + reported speech: *advise, persuade, promise, remind, tell, warn*
>
> verb + reported question: *ask, explain, wonder*
>
> verb + infinitive: *agree, ask, promise, refuse*
>
> verb + somebody + infinitive: *advise, ask, persuade, promise, remind, tell, warn*

C Choose the best reporting verbs to complete the sentences from the conversation between Zoe and Jacob.

1. Zoe asked how Jacob's creative writing class was going, and he *added* / *reminded* / *replied* that it was going really well.
2. Zoe *agreed* / *mentioned* / *wondered* whether Jacob was joking about micro-stories.
3. Jacob *persuaded* / *warned* / *whispered* Zoe that it's usually better if the writer provides less information.
4. Zoe *agreed* / *insisted* / *predicted* that the second story was really powerful.
5. Zoe *added* / *explained* / *persuaded* how 'Pass the paper' works.
6. Zoe *agreed* / *promised* / *yelled* that Jacob would enjoy playing 'Pass the paper', but Jacob *admitted* / *insisted* / *refused* to play.
7. Jacob *admitted* / *predicted* / *yelled* that most of the stories are trash.
8. Zoe *argued* / *explained* / *mentioned* that she had been a student in California.
9. Jacob *argued* / *predicted* / *reminded* Zoe that the story could have up to 1,000 words.
10. Jacob *insisted* / *warned* / *whispered* Zoe that it wouldn't be easy to write the story.

PRONUNCIATION

Using your voice to make a story more interesting

9.6 **A** Listen again to Jacob reading the two micro-stories. How does he use his voice to make the stories sound more interesting? Think about:

- speaking quickly, slowly, loudly or quietly.
- showing emotions.
- pausing.

B **SPEAK** Work in pairs. Look at the audio script on page 176. Take turns reading the two stories aloud. Try to use your voice to make the stories sound more interesting.

C **SPEAK** Look at the story you wrote in Listening Exercise D. How can you use your voice to make it sound more interesting? Read your story to the class.

D **REFLECT** Work in groups. Which is the best story? Which storyteller used his/her voice most effectively?

SPEAKING HUB

A You are going to tell a story based on four pictures. Student A – go to the Communication Hub on page 147. Student B – go to the Communication Hub on page 154. Look at the pictures and spend one minute thinking about your story. Do not worry if your story is not very good yet!

B **SPEAK** Work in pairs. Take turns telling your story. While your partner is talking, listen carefully to his/her story. You can help if your partner runs out of ideas.

C **PLAN** Work together to improve your stories and make them longer. Can you join your two stories together into a single story? Use these ideas to help you:

- Who exactly were the people?
- What were the characters trying to do?
- How did they feel?
- What did they say?
- What happened next?

D **PRESENT** Share your stories with the class. Use your voice to make them as interesting as possible.

E **REFLECT** Work in groups. Which story did you like best? Why? Who was the best storyteller?

- Report a conversation
- Create a collaborative story

Café Hub

9.3 Leaving London

F– talk about movies and books   P– words connected to movies

COMPREHENSION

A Work in pairs and discuss the questions.

- What kind of movies do you like and dislike?
- Do you ever cry at movies? When was the last time?
- Do you prefer reading a book or watching the movie based on the book?

B Think of a movie you have seen recently and answer the questions.

1 What kind of movie was it? Romantic comedy, horror, etc?

2 Who was in it?

3 What kind of ending did it have?

C 00:00–03:36 Watch the first part of the video and answer the questions in Exercise B. Why is Gaby so emotional?

D 03:36–05:03 Watch the second part of the video with the volume turned off. What do you think is happening? Discuss with a partner and then watch with the volume turned up and check your ideas.

FUNCTIONAL LANGUAGE

Talking about movies

Match the two halves of phrases you can use to talk about movies. Watch the video again and check your ideas.

Talking about movies	
1 If you like sad and romantic films,	a sad ending.
2 It's got Jessica Brune in it.	b tearjerker.
3 It's a real	c where he writes the letter to her.
4 That was a really	d reading.
5 It's really worth	e amazing performance.
6 I thought the plot was good	f Oh really, she's a brilliant actor.
7 What an	g then this is the one for you.
8 I loved the scene	h and it felt like real life.

USEFUL PHRASES

A Match the useful phrases (1–6) with the phrases that have a similar meaning (a–f).

1 Yeah, right!

2 Things don't always work out perfectly.

3 There's something I've been meaning to tell you.

4 We're going to miss you.

5 Do you want a hand?

6 Just finishing up here.

a There isn't always a happy ending.

b I've almost done all my work.

c We don't believe you.

d I've been waiting for the right time to say this.

e We don't want you to leave.

f Can I help you?

B How do you say these useful phrases in your language?

Glossary

brilliant **(adj.) (British)** = great/fabulous/excellent **(adj.) (American)**
film/s **(n) (British)** = movie/s **(n) (American)**

MILLY

SAM

NEENA

ZAC

GABY

PRONUNCIATION

Words connected to movies

9.7 **A** These are some of the words connected to movies that appear in the video. Put them in the correct column according to the word stress. Listen and check your answers.

actor amazing brilliant comedy ending horror movie performance ~~review~~ romantic tearjerker terrible

•●	●•	•●•	●••
review			

B Work in pairs. Complete the sentences so that they are true for you. Compare with your partner.

1 The most terrible movie I've ever seen was …
2 My favorite comedy is …
3 The most fabulous actor in my country is …
4 I'd give the Oscar for the most amazing performance to …
5 The best place to read movie reviews is …

SPEAKING

A Think of your favorite movie of all time and write notes.

1 What's the title of the movie?
2 What kind of movie is it?
3 Who stars in the movie?
4 What happens and how does it end?
5 What do you particularly like about the plot and characters?
6 How did the movie make you feel?

B **DISCUSS** Work in pairs. Take turns describing your favorite movie.

Talk about movies and books

➤ Turn to page 164 to learn how to write a review.

Unit 9 Review

A Correct the four mistakes in the sentences.

1 I'd feel really strange if one of the actors start talking to me.

____

2 If I had a little more time, I'll come and watch the movie with you, but I'm much too busy.

____

3 If I'd know the answer, I'd tell you, but I don't so I can't.

____

4 You'd be a better actor if you can remember your lines!

____

B Change the direct speech into reported speech.

1 'My daughter is a talented artist.'
He said that _______________ a talented artist.

2 'Immersive theater is becoming a lot more popular all the time.'
She said that immersive theater _______________ a lot more popular all the time.

3 'Do you prefer reading books or watching movies?'
He asked me _______________ reading books or watching movies.

4 'I can't paint, but I can draw fairly well.'
She told me she _______________ fairly well.

5 'How much will the tickets cost?'
She asked me _______________.

6 'Be quiet! We're trying to rehearse!'
They told me _______________ because they _______________ to rehearse.

7 'Have you ever seen a famous band live in concert?'
He asked me _______________ a famous band live in concert.

VOCABULARY

A Complete the sentences with the words in the box.

choir display gallery orchestra scene spectators

Reviews

1 We went to an amazing classical music concert last week. The _______________ had over 50 musicians!

2 The play was very smart. There was an unexpected twist in the final _______________.

3 The Japanese Culture Week ended with a wonderful _______________ by a group of traditional dancers.

4 I'm a member of a _______________. There are 30 of us, and we practice singing three times a week.

5 I'm really excited. There's going to be an exhibit of my paintings at the local _______________!

6 It was such an amazing tennis game. The _______________ clapped for ten minutes!

B Read the conversation and choose the correct verb to complete the idioms.

A: So? What did you think of my short story?

B: Well, I thought it was a little too complicated. I couldn't [1]***stay / keep*** track of who was who.

A: Really? So do you think I should [2]***get / go*** rid of some of the main characters?

B: Yes, that would be much better. And some of your characters were too similar to each other. It needs to be much easier for the reader to [3]***tell / talk*** the difference between them.

A: OK, that's a good point. I'll try to [4]***hold / pay*** attention to things like that in future. Anything else?

B: The beginning was excellent, and I loved the fact that the whole story [5]***takes / starts*** place on a train, but then you didn't really [6]***do / make*** use of that idea later in the book. I think you should definitely try to [7]***take / make*** advantage of the train trip more.

A: OK. What did you think of the ending?

B: I thought the ending was fairly weak, so the story kind of [8]***falls / keeps*** flat at the end. But … apart from that, it was great.

C Match the beginnings of the sentences (1–7) with the endings (a–g).

1 'Shhh! Don't talk during the play,'
2 'You must keep your promise and come to watch the show,'
3 'The gallery might be fairly crowded tomorrow,'
4 'Don't forget to buy a ticket,'
5 'Yes, you're absolutely right,'
6 'I didn't write my story – I copied it from the internet,'
7 'Where is everybody?'

a she reminded him.
b he admitted.
c she predicted.
d he insisted.
e she wondered.
f he agreed.
g she whispered.

FUNCTIONAL LANGUAGE

Choose the correct words to complete the conversation.

A: I want to go to the movie theater tonight, but all the new movies look a little boring.

B: Really? What about *Silly Story 2*? I thought the lead actor, Max Connor, was great [1]***at / in / on / with*** it. If you like funny movies, it's definitely the movie [2]***by / for / of / to*** you.

A: Oh, yes, I saw the ad for it. But I didn't like *Silly Story 1*. The plot was really difficult to [3]***follow / mention / predict / record***, and it was very sad at the end.

B: Yeah, I know what you mean. But this one's much better, and it really [4]***had / did / made / took*** me laugh. And it has a really happy [5]***ending / finishing / starting / stopping***.

A: Don't tell me how it ends! You'll spoil it for me!

B: OK, sorry, but I think it's really [6]***worth / love / miss / recommend*** seeing. Definitely watch this movie.

10 PSYCHOLOGY

The purpose of psychology is to give us a completely different idea of the things we know best.

Paul Valéry

A hiker watches a storm approach in New South Wales, Australia.

OBJECTIVES

- talk about different versions of past events
- talk about past mistakes
- talk about your wishes and regrets
- plan a to-do list
- make and accept apologies
- write a report

Work with a partner. Discuss the questions.

1 Look at the picture. Where do you go when you want to think?

2 Look at the quote. Do you agree?

3 Work in pairs. Tell your partner what you do when you need to reflect on a problem.

10.1 Making up your mind

- Talk about different versions of past events
- Talk about past mistakes

V – psychology verbs; expressions with *mind*
P – third conditional
G – third conditional; *should have* + past participle
S – listening for phrases that support an argument

READING

A SPEAK Work in pairs. Go the Communication Hub on page 150.

B READ FOR MAIN IDEA Read *Do you think you think rationally? Think again!* What is the connection between the three sub-headings and pictures 1–3 above?

C READ FOR DETAIL Read again. Are the sentences true (T) or false (F)? Correct the false sentences.

1 New research has shown that we're good at making rational decisions. ____
2 After we've thought about a hook number, it's easy to think of a number that's a long way from that hook. ____
3 We would probably make better decisions if we ignored hook numbers. ____
4 If we were more rational, we would worry more about buried costs. ____
5 In the example about the weekend break, the money you've spent on the hotel and travel is a buried cost. ____
6 Filtering involves presenting a situation in a way that makes it sound better (or worse) than it really is. ____

D SPEAK Work in pairs. Can you think of any examples of hook numbers, buried costs or filtering from your own life? Tell your partner.

DO YOU THINK YOU THINK RATIONALLY? THINK AGAIN!

For centuries, psychologists assumed that people think rationally and make decisions based on facts. But we're actually much less rational than we think.

HOOK NUMBERS

Look again at the quiz. Question 1a is clearly nonsense: of course we have more than 70 thoughts per day! So it shouldn't affect our answers to question 1b. But for most people, the number 70 acts as a hook. It encourages us to think of a number that isn't too far from 70. But if the hook number had been much higher, say 70 million, it would have made us think of a number in the millions. And if we hadn't seen a hook at all, we might have chosen a more likely answer: around 70,000 thoughts per day.
Sales people use hook numbers to persuade us to spend much more than we should, for example, by tricking us into believing a watch must be worth thousands of dollars.

BURIED COSTS

A buried cost is time, money or effort that we've already spent and can't get back. It would be rational to ignore buried costs when making decisions; they're gone, so we should forget about them. But for most of us, waste feels like physical pain, and we usually spend even more time, money and effort trying to avoid that pain. Look back at question 2 in the quiz. The money you've spent is gone. Instead of regretting the past, we should forget it and focus on the future. When you're sick, you should stay home and get better.

VOCABULARY
Psychology verbs

A Match the beginnings of the definitions (1–8) with the endings (a–h). Use *Do you think you think rationally? Think again!* to help you.

1 If something **affects** or **influences** you,
2 If you **assume** that something is true,
3 If something **attracts** you,
4 If you **avoid** doing something,
5 If you **encourage** or **persuade** somebody to do something,
6 If you **regret** something,
7 If something **tempts** you,
8 If somebody **tricks** you into doing something,

a you say something that makes him/her want to do it.
b you feel bad about something you did (or didn't do) in the past.
c they make you do it by lying or hiding the truth.
d you believe it although you haven't checked for sure.
e you are careful not to do it.
f you want it, even though it might be bad for you.
g it changes the way you think or behave.
h you like it and want to have it.

B Choose the correct verbs to complete the questions.

1 How do marketers and advertisers *avoid* / *tempt* us to buy things we don't really want or need?
2 When you go shopping, which things *attract* / *influence* your decision to buy something? Is it possible that the stores use psychological tricks to affect your choices?

C **SPEAK** Work in pairs. Ask and answer the questions in Exercise B.

FILTERING

In question 3 from the quiz, were you tempted by School A? That 75 percent pass rate sounds great, doesn't it? What about School B, with all those failures? No, thanks! Of course, your rational side knows that School B is better – a 20 percent failure rate means there's an 80 percent pass rate. But we can't help being influenced by words like *pass* and *fail*.
We're strongly attracted to positive words like *success*, *save* and *free*. But negative words are even more powerful. We hate *losing*, *wasting* or *missing* things. So if you see an ad that warns, 'Don't miss your last chance to save,' remember that someone is trying to trick our irrational minds.

Glossary

bury (v) to put something in the ground and cover it with earth
filter (v) if you filter a photo, you change or improve the appearance of the image before posting it on social media
hook (n) a curved piece of metal or plastic fixed to a pole or with a handle at the other end, used for catching hold of something

GRAMMAR
Third conditional

A **WORK IT OUT** Work in pairs. Look at the sentence from *Do you think you think rationally? Think again!* Then choose the correct words to complete the rules.

If the hook number had been much higher, say 70 million, it would have made us think of a number in the millions.

Third conditional

1 We use the third conditional to talk about imaginary situations in *the past / the present*.
2 Conditional sentences usually have *two / three* clauses: the *if*-clause and the result clause. To make a third conditional sentence, we use:
if + past perfect, *would* + *have* + past participle
3 We *can / can't* use *might* or *could* instead of *would* in the result clause.

B Find and underline another third conditional sentence in the article.

C Go to the **Grammar Hub** on **page 140**.

D **SPEAK** Work in pairs. Write three third conditional sentences that are true for you. Tell your partner about the situations in your sentences.

PRONUNCIATION
Third conditional

10.1 **A** Listen and repeat the third conditional sentence. What do you notice about the pronunciation of *had*, *would* and *have*?

If I'd thought about it more carefully, I'd have made a better decision.

B **SPEAK** Work in pairs. Practice saying the sentences you wrote in Grammar Exercise D. Listen and check your partner's pronunciation.

SPEAKING

Work in pairs and discuss the questions.

1 Think of a time in the past when you paid too much for something or bought something you didn't really want or need. What happened? Why? What would have happened if you'd thought more carefully?
When I bought my first car, I thought it was perfect. But I didn't check whether it actually worked properly! In the end, I spent a lot of money fixing it and sold it again. If I'd …

2 Think of a time in the past when you made a bad decision because you didn't have enough information or experience. What would you have done differently if you'd known then what you know now?
I received an email from my bank last week telling me to click on a link to change my password. Luckily, I noticed that the link was to a completely different site. But if I hadn't noticed …

LISTENING

A SPEAK Work in groups and discuss the questions.

1 Do you find shopping relaxing or stressful? Why?

2 When you're shopping for clothes and shoes, do you find it easy to decide what to buy?

10.2 **B LISTEN FOR MAIN IDEA** Listen to a conversation between two friends, Robert and Vicky. What do they say about the items in the pictures (a–d)?

Glossary

common sense (n) the ability to use good judgment and make sensible decisions

paradox (n) a statement consisting of two parts that seem to mean the opposite of each other

perfectionist (n) someone who always wants things to be done perfectly

10.2 **C** Listen again. How does Robert support his arguments? Use the strategies in the box to help you.

Listening for phrases that support an argument

Sometimes when you listen, you need to decide how strong a person's arguments are. Pay attention to the techniques they use to support their argument.

Common sense:

- *Surely, Of course, Obviously, Clearly, As you can imagine, …*

Facts and statistics:

- *In fact, …; The researchers found that …*

Examples and details:

- *For example, …; For instance, …*

Expert opinions:

- *According to Professor Schwartz …; He's shown that …*

10.2 **D LISTEN FOR DETAIL** Listen again. Complete the notes about the conversation.

1 **The Paradox of Choice:** According to Professor Barry Schwartz (an ___American___ psychologist), too many ________ makes us ________.

2 **Shampoo company:** Cut choices from ________ to ________. Sales went up by ________ percent.

3 **Robert's experience of buying a laptop:** He went to a small store with ________ laptops to choose from. Took ________ minutes to choose and buy a laptop.

4 **Perfectionists regret their choices:** Vicky bought ________ different pairs of shoes, but took each pair back to the store.

5 **Quick deciders don't worry about perfection:** When Robert finds jeans that are ________ enough, he buys them and stops worrying. Only takes them back to store if they're ________.

E SPEAK Work in groups and discuss the questions.

1 Have you ever experienced the Paradox of Choice? Think about the following situations:
   - shopping
   - choosing what to watch on TV or online
   - making important life decisions
   - cooking or eating

2 Are you a perfectionist or a quick decider? What about other people in your family?

3 How can stores, websites and other businesses help us deal with the Paradox of Choice?

GRAMMAR
should have + past participle

A WORK IT OUT **Look at the sentences from the conversation between Vicky and Robert. Then choose the correct words to complete the rules.**

So with your laptop, you **should have gone** to a smaller store.

I realized that they weren't perfect and I **shouldn't have bought** them.

should have + past participle

1 We write *should* (*not*) + *have* + past participle / base form.

2 We use *should have done* to talk about mistakes that we *make* / *made* in the past and imagine how we could have avoided those mistakes.

B **Go to the Grammar Hub on page 140.**

C SPEAK **Work in pairs. Use *should/shouldn't have done* to talk about these situations.**

1 Angela went shopping for a new coat. She found a great coat in the first store, but she went to ten more stores to make sure it was the best one. When she went back to buy it, somebody else had bought it.

2 Kasia bought a used computer five years ago, but it didn't work properly. Although she had enough money to buy a new one, she kept using the old one for years.

VOCABULARY
Expressions with *mind*

10.2 **A** **Complete the sentences (1–8) from the conversation with the expressions in the box. Then listen again and check your answers.**

all in the mind	bear in mind	change my mind	of two minds	made up my mind	never mind	put your mind to	would you mind if

1 ______________________ I borrowed your laptop for a few minutes?

2 Just ______________________ that it's really slow.

3 I found two that I liked, but I was ______________________ and I couldn't decide which one to buy.

4 But ______________________. I still have my old computer, so it isn't so bad.

5 Once I've ______________________, I stick with my decision.

6 You think it's impossible, but maybe it's ______________________.

7 I think you can become a quick decider – you just need to ______________________ it!

8 But what if I ______________________ later?

B SPEAK **Work in pairs. What do you think the expressions in Exercise A mean?**

C SPEAK **Work in pairs and discuss the questions.**

1 Quick deciders are generally less stressed, but there are some dangers connected with making quick decisions. What should they **bear in mind** before making a decision?

2 How long does it usually take you to **make up your mind** about whether you can trust somebody? What might make you **change your mind** about them?

SPEAKING HUB

A **Read the sentences about regrets. Do you agree or disagree with them? Why?**

1 You should never regret anything. Your mistakes are part of who you are.

2 You should regret the things you haven't done more than the things you have done.

B **Think about two or three mistakes you have made in the past. What did you do? What did you not do? What should or should you not have done?**

C **Work in pairs. Tell your partner about some of the mistakes you have made. While your partner is talking, listen carefully, and then ask questions to find out more information.**

Finding out more information

Really? So what did you do? Why did you do that?

What do you think you should have done?

But if you hadn't done that, what do you think would have happened?

D **Work in pairs and discuss the questions.**

1 What can you learn from the mistakes you have made in the past?

2 What would you do differently if you were in the same situation in the future?

3 Is it good to talk about past mistakes?

— **Talk about different versions of past events**

— **Talk about past mistakes**

10.2 Wish lists

- Talk about your wishes and regrets
- Plan a to-do list

V – reflexive verbs; staying organized
S – bridge sentences
P – emphasis and reflexive pronouns
G – hopes and wishes

LISTENING

A SPEAK Work in pairs and discuss the questions.

1 Do you have any habits that you'd like to stop?
2 Are there any good habits that you'd like to start?
3 How easy is it to change your habits?
4 Look at the diagram. What do you think it shows?

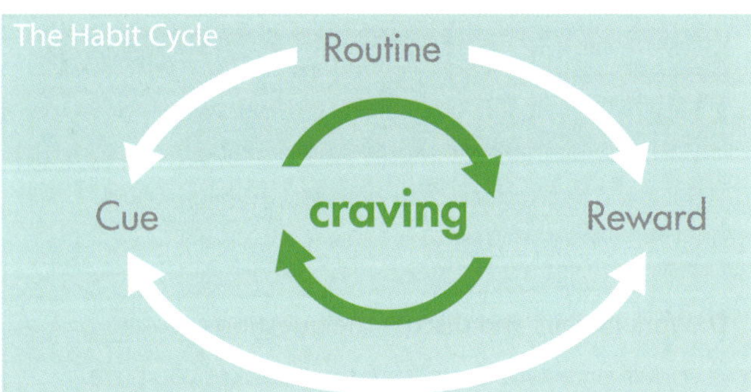

10.3 **B LISTEN FOR GIST** Listen to a radio show about habits. Which habits in the pictures do the speakers talk about?

10.3 **C LISTEN FOR DETAIL** Listen again and choose the correct answers.

1 What is David's main cue for eating fast food?
 a He sees a sign while he's driving.
 b He smells food in a shopping mall.
2 What happens when a routine is part of a true habit?
 a You can follow the steps without thinking.
 b You do it although you don't want to.
3 Why are cravings dangerous?
 a Because you don't want the reward any more.
 b Because you feel that you need the reward.
4 What's the only way to change a habit?
 a Change the routine.
 b Change the reward.
5 Why does Leo make coffee when he arrives at work?
 a Because he loves the taste of coffee.
 b Because he's tired and he needs a break.

D SPEAK Work in pairs and discuss the questions.

1 What are some cues for bad habits? What routines and rewards can we use to change those bad habits?
2 What cues and rewards can we use to start good habits?

VOCABULARY

Reflexive verbs

10.4 **A** Complete the sentences from the conversation (1–8) with the words in the box. Then listen and check your answers.

blame	control	get	help	make	reward	set	treat

1 When I drive past a sign for a fast-food restaurant, I ________________ myself to a snack from the package.
2 'Can I try one of those?'
'Sure! ________________ yourself.'
3 I wish I could stop, but I can't ________________ myself.
4 I always ________________ myself a cup of coffee before I check my emails.
5 I suppose I could ________________ myself a glass of water.
6 I always ________________ myself goals, but nothing seems to work.
7 First of all, Alice, don't ________________ yourself.
8 How will you ________________ yourself for being good?

Reflexive verbs

A reflexive verb is a verb + a reflexive pronoun (*myself, yourself, himself, herself, itself, ourselves, yourselves, themselves*).

Some reflexive verbs have a special meaning:

Help yourself! = Please take as much as you want; there's no need to ask.

B Go to the **Vocabulary Hub** on **page 146**.

C **SPEAK** Work in pairs and discuss the questions.

1 Where do you see yourself in ten years?
2 How do you amuse yourself when you're on a long trip?
3 Can you think of any situations where you can't trust yourself?

PRONUNCIATION
Emphasis and reflexive pronouns

10.5 **A** Listen to the sentences from the radio show. For each sentence, decide if the reflexive pronouns are stressed or unstressed.

1 I treat myself to a snack from the package.
2 I always make myself a cup of coffee before I check my emails.
3 Don't blame yourself.
4 How will you reward yourself for being good?

B Now choose the best word or phrase to complete the rules.

Emphasis and reflexive pronouns

1 When a reflexive pronoun follows a verb, the pronoun **is / is not** usually stressed.
2 But when we want to emphasise the subject at the end of a clause, we **can / can't** stress the pronoun.

C **SPEAK** Work in pairs. Practice saying the sentences in Exercise A. Listen and check your partner's pronunciation.

GRAMMAR
Hopes and wishes

A **WORK IT OUT** Match the sentences from the conversation (1–5) with the explanations (a–d).

1 **I wish I'd known** about all this a few years ago! But I guess it's too late for me now.
2 I **hope your new routine works** for you, Leo.
3 **I wish we had time** to talk about your other seven cups of coffee, but we need to go to our next caller.
4 **I wish I could** run a marathon next year.
5 I really **wish I were** better organized.

a The speaker is talking about something that's likely to happen in the future.
b The speaker is talking about something that's unlikely to happen in the future.
c The speaker is imagining a different present situation.
d The speaker is imagining a different past situation.

Hopes and wishes

When we talk about hopes and wishes, we use very similar structures to the first, second and third conditionals.

	Conditional sentences	Hopes and wishes
Likely future	It'll be good if your idea works.	I hope your idea works.
Unlikely future	I'd be happy if I could find a new job. (or: … if I found a new job.)	I wish I could find a new job. (NOT: I wish I found a new job.)
Unreal present	It would be nice if I were taller.	I wish I were taller.
Unreal past	It would have been better if you'd told me.	I wish you'd told me.

B Go to the **Grammar Hub** on **page 140**.

C Complete the sentences with *hope* or *wish*. Then choose the correct words to complete the hopes and wishes.

1 I ______ you *have* / *had* / *could have* a great time on vacation next week.
2 I started playing tennis last year and I love it, but I'm too old to become a top player. I ______ I *start* / *started* / *'d started* playing when I was younger.
3 It's great that you're coming to my city next week. I ______ I *met* / *could meet* / *'d met* you while you're here, but unfortunately I'll be away all week.
4 I'm a little worried about Frank and Donna. They should have arrived an hour ago. I ______ they *arrive* / *'d arrived* / *arrived* soon.
5 I never have time to do all the things I need to do each week. Sometimes I ______ there *were* / *are* / *had been* eight days in a week!
6 My main regret is that I didn't spend enough time with my children when they were younger. I ______ I *don't spend* / *didn't spend* / *hadn't spent* so much time working in those days!
7 My dream is to be the first person to travel to Mars! I really ______ I *went* / *could go* / *'d gone* there one day, but I know it's never going to happen.

SPEAKING

Work in pairs and discuss the questions.

1 Do you have any regrets about your habits? What do you wish you'd started earlier? What do you wish you'd never started?
2 What do you wish you could change about yourself?
3 What are your hopes for the future? Think about next week, next month and next year.
4 What are your dreams for the future? What do you wish you could do one day?

READING

A SPEAK Work in pairs and discuss the questions.

1 What is a to-do list? What information does it contain?

2 Why do you think psychologists are interested in to-do lists?

3 Do you keep a to-do list? Why/Why not?

B READ FOR GIST Read *The psychology of to-do lists*. Match the headings (a–g) with the paragraphs (1–7).

a Organization, motivation and satisfaction

b The benefits of forgetting

c Not as difficult as it sounds

d An experiment over dinner

e Keeping tasks small and simple

f Using to-do lists to cut stress

g The stress of not finishing things

The psychology of to-do lists

1 ____

One day in the 1920s, a large group of psychologists were having a meal at their favorite restaurant. They were discussing the waiter's amazing memory: he always remembered everybody's orders perfectly, but he never wrote anything down. One of the psychologists, Bluma Zeigarnik, decided to try an experiment. She told everyone to cover their plates. Then she asked the waiter to come back to the table, and to try to remember what was on each plate. Amazingly, he couldn't remember anything, even though he himself had put the plates on the table only a few minutes earlier. How was it possible that a man with such an amazing memory had forgotten everything a few minutes later?

2 ____

Zeigarnik realized that there was in fact nothing special about the waiter. In fact, we're all good at remembering current <u>tasks</u> – things that we still need to do. But as soon as they're finished, we forget all about them. The 'Zeigarnik effect', as it's now called, is our brains' way of <u>cleaning up</u> and <u>sorting</u> information. If we had to remember everything forever, our brains would soon run out of space.

3 ____

But there's a dark side to the Zeigarnik effect. Studies have shown that people perform badly in tests when they're worrying about other unfinished tasks. It seems that we can't stop thinking about what we still need to do. This makes us stressed and prevents us from focusing on new tasks.

4 ____

Is there anything we can do about this problem? Recent research suggests that we can reduce our stress levels by <u>keeping a record</u> of all our current tasks in a to-do list. This simple action tells our brains to stop worrying about the task, which means we can give our full attention to other tasks.

5 ____

To-do lists have three additional benefits. First, they help us to stay organized. Second, they are a useful record of what we've achieved and when. It can be highly motivating to look back at our past achievements – especially because the Zeigarnik effect usually makes us forget them. However, the best thing about to-do lists is the satisfying feeling you get when you cross each item off the list.

6 ____

The key to successful to-do lists is to break large <u>objectives</u> into smaller <u>action points</u>. Instead of writing 'Learn to drive' on your list, focus on small and practical jobs that you can achieve very quickly, such as 'Find a list of driving schools in my city' and 'Read a website with reviews of different schools'. The smaller the tasks, the better. Dave Allen, a time-management expert, also recommends an archive to <u>store</u> all the things you might need and a system of 43 folders to <u>schedule</u> when to do each task.

7 ____

If that sounds like too much hard work, think again. With a good system, life is much easier. You can relax and enjoy the rest of the day, happy in the knowledge that everything is under control.

Glossary

archive (n) a place where you store documents and records

C Read the box about bridge sentences. What is the connection between bridge sentences and topic sentences (see Unit 8)? What's the difference between them?

Bridge sentences

The first sentence in a paragraph is usually a bridge sentence, which shows how the paragraph is connected to the previous paragraph. For example, it might use words like *however* to introduce a contrast, or words like *another* to add extra information.

Not all paragraphs have a bridge sentence.

D READ FOR KEY INFORMATION Read the first sentence in each paragraph again. Which five are bridge sentences? Underline the words and phrases in the sentences that refer back to the previous paragraph. What exactly do they refer to?

E SPEAK Work in pairs and discuss the questions.

1 Have you ever experienced the Zeigarnik effect? Think about:
- preparing for a test.
- learning a speech, a song or a poem.
- remembering people's names and faces.

2 Do you ever look back at your past achievements? Would you find it motivating?

VOCABULARY

Staying organized

A Look at the underlined words in *The psychology of to-do lists*. Find words or phrases that mean the following.

1 a job that you need to do
a t a s k
2 to keep something in a safe place
to _ _ _ _ _ something
3 to put things back in the right places
to _ _ _ _ _ up
4 to plan exactly when you will do something
to _ _ _ _ _ _ _ _ something
5 a small thing that you're going to do
an _ _ _ _ _ _ point
6 to put things in the right order
to _ _ _ _ things
7 a large thing that you want to achieve
an _ _ _ _ _ _ _ _ _
8 to write something down
to keep a _ _ _ _ _ _ of something

B SPEAK Work in pairs and discuss the questions.

1 How many **tasks** are on your to-do list?
2 Do you **keep a record** of the tasks you need to do? Would you like to start?

SPEAKING HUB

A PREPARE Write a short wish list. Use the ideas below or your own ideas.
- a problem that you would like to solve
- a good habit that you hope you will start / wish you could start
- a way to become less stressed or better organized
- how you'll continue learning/using English after this course

B PLAN Work in groups. Discuss your wish lists. As a group, choose the most interesting items from your wish lists and create a to-do list. Try to:
- plan cues, routines and rewards for any habits you want to change.
- turn your objectives into tasks and action points.

C PRESENT Stand up and tell the class what you plan to do and when. When others are speaking, listen carefully and be positive about their plans.

D REFLECT Work in groups and discuss the questions.

1 How will you make sure you'll do the things on your list?
2 How will you motivate each other to do those things?

Talk about your wishes and regrets
Plan a to-do list

Café Hub

10.3 Come home

F– make and accept apologies P– vowel sounds

COMPREHENSION

A When was the last time you had to say goodbye to someone? How did you feel? How long was it before you saw that person again?

B Number the pictures in the order you think they happened. What do you think happened?

a ☐

b ☐

c ☐

d ☐

e ☐

f ☐

C ▶ 00:00–02:25 Watch the first part of the video and check your ideas. How do you think the video will end?

D ▶ 02:25–04:29 Complete the letter that Sam wrote to Gaby by choosing the correct words below. Watch the second part of the video and check your answers. Does the video end how you predicted?

1 leaving / in / over
2 words / time / pen
3 should / usually / never
4 city / life / home
5 business / Madrid / yourself

Dear Gaby,

I've just heard that you're [1] __________ London and … I wish I had said this to you in person, but I just couldn't find the [2] __________. I'm so sorry, but I [3] __________ know the right thing to say. I know you've already made your mind up about leaving, and I'm going to miss you so much. The thought of not having you in my [4] __________ hurts because … I love you. I always have. I just didn't know how to say it before. Take good care of [5] __________.

MILLY

SAM

NEENA

ZAC

GABY

FUNCTIONAL LANGUAGE

Making and accepting apologies

A Put the words in the correct order. Then put each phrase under the correct heading in the table.

1 quickly / leave / sorry / to / so / I'm / really

2 you'll / worry / be / don't / fine

3 apologize / need / no / there's / to

4 worry / don't / it / about

5 just / things / of / those / one / it's

6 OK / all / to / be / it's / going

7 my / it's / fault

8 not / fault / fault / it's / it's / my / your

9 nothing / about / worry / there's / to

10 great / is / this / to / be / going

Making an apology	Accepting an apology	Giving reassurance
I'm really sorry to leave so quickly.		

B Watch the video again and check (✓) each phrase as you hear it.

Glossary

housemate **(n) (British)** = roommate **(n) (American)**

USEFUL PHRASES

A Match the useful phrases (1–5) with the phrases that come before or after them (a–e).

1 It's time to go.
2 I wish I had said this to you in person.
3 I'm such an idiot!
4 I've changed my mind about leaving.
5 I'm scared.

a What about your plane? You're going to miss it.
b I can't believe that I missed her.
c You'll be fine; don't worry.
d But I just couldn't find the words.
e There's nothing to worry about.

B How do you say these useful phrases in your language?

PRONUNCIATION

Vowel sounds

A Match words with the same vowel sounds from boxes A, B and C.

A airport roommate <u>mind</u> person sorry worry

B apologize <u>guys</u> hurt love strangely thought

C gone <u>my</u> of course paying under words

10.6 **B** Listen, check and repeat the words. Copy the sounds.

SPEAKING

A Work in pairs. Write conversations about the following situations or your own ideas. Student A – apologize. Student B – accept the apology and reassure Student A.

arrive late / for meeting break / chair forget / to call miss / party spill / coffee

A: I'm really sorry about breaking your chair.
B: Oh, don't worry about it – it's not your fault. It's just one of those things.

B **PRESENT** Act out your conversations. Take turns being Student A and Student B.

Make and accept apologies

➤ Turn to page 165 to learn how to write a report.

Unit 10 Review

GRAMMAR

A Complete the third conditional sentences. Use the correct form of the underlined verbs.

1 The waiter forgot our order because he didn't write it down.
If the waiter *had written* down our order, he *wouldn't have forgotten* it.

2 You didn't finish anything on your to-do list. Maybe it's because all the items were too big.
You might ________ some things on your to-do list if they ________ a little smaller.

3 I saw a sign for a fast-food restaurant, so I felt a need to eat.
If I ________ a sign for the fast-food restaurant, I ________ a need to eat!

4 I didn't have time to try on these jeans, but I bought them anyway.
I ________ these jeans if I ________ them on first! They're much too small!

B Write sentences with *should/shouldn't have done*.

1 I wish you'd been more careful.
You *should have been more careful*.

2 I regret buying these shoes.
I ________.

3 Why didn't they listen to us?
They ________.

4 It was a mistake to go out yesterday.
We ________.

C Complete the conversation with the correct form of the verbs in parentheses.

A: Hey! I'm having a dinner party tomorrow night. I hope you [1] ________ (*can come*). It's going to be excellent.

B: Oh, I wish I [2] ________ (*can come*), but I can't. I have tickets for a soccer game tomorrow, and it's the final.

A: Oh, I didn't know it's the final tomorrow! I wish I [3] ________ (*know*)! I'd have arranged the party for a different night. Anyway, I hope your team [4] ________ (*win*)!

B: Well, my team isn't in the final. I wish we [5] ________ (*be*)! But we lost in the semi-final last week. I wish I [6] ________ (*not buy*) a ticket – then I could come to your party!

VOCABULARY

A Choose the correct verbs to complete the sentences.

1 I got an email from somebody who tried to ***persuade / trick*** me into giving my bank account number.

2 I didn't want to buy a camera at all, but the saleswoman ***affected / persuaded*** me to buy one.

3 Whenever I walk past a fast-food restaurant, I'm ***regretted / tempted*** to go inside.

4 For a long time, businesses ***assumed / influenced*** that more choice meant more sales.

B Find and correct one mistake in each underlined phrase.

[1]Would you mind that I asked you for some advice? You see, I want to go somewhere new this weekend, but I'm [2]of three minds about where to go. This morning, I [3]made my mind and decided to go bike riding in the forest, but then I heard the weather is going to be horrible, so I [4]changed the mind and decided to go to the new museum instead. But … I don't really like museums. What should I do? [5]Bear to mind, I don't have a car, so it needs to be somewhere with good bus connections.

C Match the beginnings of the tips for staying organized (1–5) with the endings (a–e).

1 Don't do everything at once. Focus
2 Remember to schedule
3 Use a to-do list to keep
4 Break big objectives into smaller action
5 Use an archive to store

a a record of your tasks.
b important old documents.
c some time to relax!
d on one task at a time.
e points.

D Choose the correct reflexive verb to complete the sentences.

1 You shouldn't ***blame / control*** yourself. It's not your fault.

2 ***Help / get*** yourself to anything you want.

3 I always go into fast food restaurants when I see them. I can't ***make / control*** myself.

4 He's trained so hard for the race. Why doesn't he ***treat / set*** himself to a night off and just relax?

FUNCTIONAL LANGUAGE

Complete the conversation with the words in the box. There are two extra words.

about apologize blame fault not so those worry

Dimitri: Hey, Igor! Have you eaten my pizza?

Igor: Don't [1] ________ me! I've been out all day. I don't know anything about it.

Dimitri: Oh … I'm [2] ________ sorry. I shouldn't have blamed you.

Igor: It's OK. Don't [3] ________ about it. So I wonder who ate your pizza …

Rob: Uh, sorry, but it's my [4] ________. I was really hungry when I got home last night and I hadn't gone to the store!

Dimitri: Oh, there's no need to [5] ________. It's just one of [6] ________ things.

Irregular Verbs

Base form	Simple past	Past participle
be	was/were	been
become	became	become
begin	began	begun
break	broke	broken
bring	brought	brought
build	built	built
buy	bought	bought
can	could	been able to
catch	caught	caught
choose	chose	chosen
come	came	come
cost	cost	cost
cut	cut	cut
do	did	done
drink	drank	drunk
eat	ate	eaten
fall	fell	fallen
feel	felt	felt
find	found	found
forget	forgot	forgotten
get	got	got
give	gave	given
go	went	gone/been
grow	grew	grown
have	had	had
hear	heard	heard
hit	hit	hit
hold	held	held
hurt	hurt	hurt
keep	kept	kept
know	knew	known
leave	left	left
lend	lent	lent
let	let	let

Base form	Simple past	Past participle
lose	lost	lost
make	made	made
mean	meant	meant
meet	met	met
must	had to	had to
pay	paid	paid
put	put	put
read	read	read
ride	rode	ridden
run	ran	run
say	said	said
see	saw	seen
sell	sold	sold
send	sent	sent
set	set	set
shut	shut	shut
sing	sang	sung
sit	sat	sat
sleep	slept	slept
speak	spoke	spoken
spell	spelled	spelled
spend	spent	spent
stand	stood	stood
steal	stole	stolen
take	took	taken
teach	taught	taught
tell	told	told
think	thought	thought
throw	threw	thrown
understand	understood	understood
wear	wore	worn
win	won	won
write	wrote	written

PHONETIC SYMBOLS											
Single vowels			Diphthongs			Consonants					
/ɪ/	fish	/fɪʃ/	/uw/	news	/nuw/	/p/	pen	/pen/	/s/	snake	/sneɪk/
/iː/	bean	/biːn/	/eɪ/	face	/feɪs/	/b/	bag	/bæg/	/z/	zoo	/zuː/
/ʊ/	foot	/fʊt/	/ɔɪ/	boy	/bɔɪ/	/t/	tea	/tiː/	/ʃ/	shop	/ʃɒp/
/uː/	shoe	/ʃuː/	/oʊ/	nose	/noʊz/	/d/	dog	/dɒg/	/ʒ/	television	/ˈtelɪvɪʒən/
/e/	egg	/eg/	/ju/	use	/juz/	/ʧ/	chip	/ʧɪp/	/m/	map	/mæp/
/ə/	mother	/ˈmʌðər/	/aɪ/	eye	/aɪ/	/ʤ/	jazz	/ʤæz/	/n/	name	/neɪm/
/ɜː/	word	/wɜːrd/	/aʊ/	mouth	/maʊθ/	/k/	cake	/keɪk/	/ŋ/	ring	/rɪŋ/
/ɔː/	talk	/tɔːk/				/g/	girl	/gɜːrl/	/h/	house	/haʊs/
/æ/	back	/bæk/				/f/	film	/fɪlm/	/l/	leg	/leg/
/ʌ/	bus	/bʌs/				/v/	verb	/vɜːrb/	/r/	road	/roʊd/
/ɑː/	arm	/ɑːrm/				/θ/	thing	/θɪŋ/	/w/	wine	/waɪn/
/ɒ/	top	/tɒp/				/ð/	these	/ðiːz/	/j/	yes	/jes/

Grammar Hub

1.1 Simple present and present progressive

	Positive	Negative	Question
Simple present	**He gets up** early.	**It doesn't look** good.	**Do you take** the bus?
Present progressive	**I'm taking** a selfie.	**She isn't watching** TV. **She's not watching** TV.	**Are they smiling**?

- We use the simple present to talk about actions that always/ usually/never happen.
  I don't always get up early.
- We use the present progressive to talk about actions that are in progress at the moment of speaking or writing.
  They aren't working this week.
- We also use the present progressive to describe actions in a photo or video.
  What is he doing in this photo?
- We also use the present progressive to describe trends.
  More and more people are getting worried about money.
- We use the simple present, not the present progressive, to talk about our everyday routines.
  Do you write many emails at work?
  NOT ~~Are you writing many emails at work?~~
- We usually use these adverbs of frequency with the simple present: *always, never, rarely, sometimes, usually*.
  *Do you **usually** post photos of yourself on social media?*
- We use stative verbs to describe feelings and ideas. We use the simple present (not the present progressive) with stative verbs.
  *I **love** taking selfies!*
- Some verbs (e.g. *have, look, speak, think*) can be used as both dynamic and stative verbs, depending on the situation.
  *have: She **has** a perfect life. / **Are** you **having** fun?*
  *look: Your new kitchen **looks** really good! / **I'm looking** for a new job.*

1.2 Subject and object questions

Subject questions		
Question word/ Subject	Main verb	Rest of question
What	is	your first language?

Object questions				
Question word	Auxiliary verb	Subject	Main verb	Rest of question
What	do	you	want	to study?

- We use these question words to ask for information: *who* and *whose* (for people), *where* (for places), *when* (for times), *why* (for reasons), *what* (for things), *which* (for two or more different choices), *how* (for the way something is done) and *how long/many/much*/etc (for time, quantity, etc).
  ***Whose** blog is this?*
- We frequently use an auxiliary verb (*be, can, do* or *have*) to form questions. We put the auxiliary verb before the main verb.
  ***Are** they practicing their English?*
  ***Can** I ask you a question?*
  *Why **do** you want to learn English?*
  *How long **have** you known Liam?*
- In subject questions, the question word is the subject of the sentence. We use subject questions when we don't know what/who/which/whose something/someone is. We don't use an auxiliary verb in subject questions and we don't change the word order in the answer.
  Who interviewed him? Mona interviewed him.
- In object questions, the question word is the object of the sentence. We use object questions when we want to know more information about something/someone. We always use an auxiliary verb in object questions. In the answer, we use the normal word order for a sentence.
  Where did he learn to speak English?
  NOT ~~Where he learned to speak English?~~
  What do you want to study? I want to study modern languages.
- With subject questions, the answer is the subject.
  Who told you? Someone told you.
- With object questions, the answer is the object.
  Who did you tell? You told someone.
- With questions using *do, does* or *did*, we don't change the form of the main verb.
  Does she speak English? NOT ~~Does she speaks English?~~
- When a question word is the object of a preposition, the preposition usually comes at the end of the sentence.
  What did you have problems with?

1.1 Simple present and present progressive

A Choose the correct option.

1. Sarah *is showing* / *shows* me her vacation photos. They're amazing!
2. *Are they working* / *Do they work* today?
3. *Are you always getting up* / *Do you always get up* early on weekdays?
4. They *are relaxing* / *relax* on the beach in this picture.
5. We *are not usually* / *don't usually* watch TV but this show is really good!
6. I *am becoming* / *become* more worried about my social media posts.

B Complete the email with the correct form of the verb in parentheses. Use contractions where possible.

Hi Sarah!

We [1] ______ (*have*) a great time here in Spain! The sun [2] ______ (*shine*) and the country is beautiful. We [3] ______ (*have*) a nice room in a little hotel with a view of the beach. I [4] ______ (*sit*) on the balcony to write this email and I can see Paul down on the beach. He [5] ______ (*play*) soccer with the boys on the sand. The children [6] ______ (*like*) it here – they say they [7] ______ (*not want*) to go home! Hope you [8] ______ (*not work*) too hard!

See you next week!

Love, Mary

➤ Go back to page 3.

1.2 Subject and object questions

A Read the answers and write questions. Use the question words in the box.

how what where which who why

1. *Why are you taking an umbrella?* — Because it's raining!
2. ______ — My house is close to the school.
3. ______ — I'm watching the news.
4. ______ — I get to work by bus.
5. ______ — I want to visit Poland.
6. ______ — David is helping me.

B Put the words in order to make questions.

1. you / want / about / to talk / do / what / ?
   What do you want to talk about?
2. I / am / pronouncing / right / this word / ?
3. please / say / you / that again, / can / ?
4. usually / do / at work / use English / you / ?
5. this / phone / whose / is / ?
6. the graph / what / does / show / ?
7. you / me / help / this / article / with / can / ?
8. hours / how / you / English / study / week / do / many / each / ?

C Correct the mistakes in each question.

1. How long you have your phone?
   How long have you had your phone?
2. Where you are working right now?
3. You understand these words?
4. Who laptop is this?
5. Where you keep your English books?
6. How many people do they speak English in the world?
7. How long it takes you to get to work?
8. Who you met yesterday?
9. Where they are learning English?
10. Does he uses the app to practice his pronunciation?

➤ Go back to page 7.

Grammar Hub

2.1 Present perfect and simple past

	Positive	Negative	Question
Present perfect	**Wilhelm has climbed** Mt. Everest before. **We've visited** the Pyramids already.	**I haven't been** sailing before. **Paula hasn't made** a bucket list yet.	**Have you** ever **met** a movie star? **Have they bought** the tickets already?
Simple past	**Wilhelm climbed** Mt. Everest last month. **We visited** Yosemite National Park a year ago.	**I didn't go** sailing last weekend. **Paula didn't move** out of her parents' house a week ago.	**Did you meet** a movie star yesterday? **Did they buy** the tickets?

- We use the present perfect for actions completed during a period of time that continues to now.

  *Juan **has been** in Asia for three months so far.*
  = He's still there.

- We also use the present perfect for actions completed before now when we don't say exactly when.

  *She **has** already **written** out a bucket list.*
  NOT ~~She already wrote out her bucket list.~~

- We frequently use time expressions such as *before*, *already*, *just* and *yet* with the present perfect.

  Have you finished your exams yet?

- We use the simple past for actions completed during a finished period of time or at a specific time in the past.

  ***Did** you **stop** using your social media account last week?*

- We frequently use time expressions such as *yesterday*, *two days / a week / a month ago*, or *last week/month/year* with the simple past.
- If we use a specific time reference, we usually use the simple past.

  *She's **just won** a free vacation. / She **won** a free vacation **a moment ago**.*
  *Henri **has already booked** a flight to India. / Henri **booked** a flight to India **yesterday**.*

2.2 Present and past ability

can

	Positive	Negative
I/you/he/she/it/we/they	**Rosa can ride** a horse.	**They cannot drive.** **They can't drive.**

Question	Positive short answer	Negative short answer
Can you fish in the lake?	Yes, **I can**.	No, **I can't**.

***be able to* (simple present)**

	Positive	Negative
I/you/he/she/it/we/they	**I am able to book** a taxi online.	**Sven isn't able to fly** a plane.

Question	Positive short answer	Negative short answer
Are Tomas and Jaime able to work as volunteers?	Yes, **they are**.	No, **they aren't**.

***manage to* (simple present)**

	Positive	Negative
I/you/he/she/it/we/they	**He manages to remember** new words every day.	**We don't manage to meet** our friends very regularly.

Question	Positive short answer	Negative short answer
Does Laura manage to stay calm when she presents?	Yes, **she does**.	No, **she doesn't**.

- We use *can*, *can't*, *(not) be able to* and *(not) manage* to talk about our ability or skills in general in the present.

could

Subject	Positive	Negative
I/you/he/she/it/we/they	**I could cook** when I was young.	**Paolo couldn't take on** more work.

Question	Positive short answer	Negative short answer
Could your cousin swim as a baby?	Yes, **he could**.	No, **he couldn't**.

- We use *could*, *couldn't* or *(not) be able to* when we talk about our ability or skills in general in the past.
- We use *couldn't*, *(not) be able to* and *(not) manage to* when we talk about our ability to do a specific task on a particular occasion in the past. We usually do NOT use *could*.

  We couldn't solve the problem at that time.
  BUT NOT ~~We could solve the problem at that time.~~
  We were/weren't able to solve the problem at that time.
  We managed / didn't manage to solve the problem at that time.

- When a verb is followed by *-ing* or the infinitive, we can't use *can*. We use *be able to* instead.

  Sebastian enjoys being able to cook.
  NOT ~~Sebastian enjoys can cook.~~

2.1 Present perfect and simple past

A Choose the correct option.

1 I *have swum* / *swam* with dolphins before.
2 Martin *dreamed* / *has dreamed* about the pyramids last night.
3 We *haven't climbed* / *didn't climb* Mt. Everest yet.
4 *Did you hear* / *Have you heard* Leon's good news already?
5 *Did Zac learn* / *Has Zac learned* how to make a fire at camp last summer?
6 *Have you ever taken* / *Did you ever take* a trip to another country?

B Correct the mistakes in each sentence. Use contractions where possible.

1 She ~~has seen~~ saw a beautiful sunset last week.
2 They made a sci-fi movie already.
3 Molly didn't prepare a list yet.
4 Mohammed traveled never around Asia before.
5 Did you deal with a serious problem before?
6 He has come up with a smart plan yesterday.

C Complete each sentence with the correct form of the verb in parentheses.

1 Giralt has never been (*never / be*) to America.
2 Dan ________ (*just / finish*) a charity walk.
3 Katerina worked hard but she ________ (*not / achieve*) her goal.
4 When the time was right, the chess champion ________ (*put*) his plan into action.
5 ________ (*you / read*) other people's bucket lists before?
6 I ________ (*already / do*) two parachute jumps this year.

➤ Go back to page 15.

2.2 Present and past ability

A Complete the sentences with the words in the box.

can could couldn't manage managed wasn't

1 She didn't manage to make it to the interview on time.
2 Amazingly, Diego ________ read when he was two and a half years old.
3 They ________ to find a solution to the complicated problem.
4 We were discussing something important, so I ________ able to answer my phone.
5 Francisco ________ stop his hands from shaking because he was so nervous.
6 Michela is amazing because she ________ work three jobs and not be tired.

B Put the words in order to make sentences.

1 can't / Helena / egg / an / boil
Helena can't boil an egg.
2 a / manage / I / cook / meal / didn't / tasty / to
____
3 our / we / goals / long-term / were / to / able / achieve
____
4 system / very / can / quickly / analyze / the / data
____
5 manage / speech / to / give / Aisha / her / did / ?
____
6 couldn't / easier / suggest / an / plan / they
____

C Choose the correct option.

1 Marina ________ raise enough money for her trip.
a wasn't able b didn't manage c couldn't
2 Olaf ________ paint great pictures of animals.
a can b manages c is able
3 I ________ watch TV all day as a kid.
a was able b can c could
4 They ________ to deal with any more problems.
a couldn't b weren't able c can't
5 Hana ________ to find a good cooking video.
a can't b didn't manage c couldn't
6 She forgot her lines, but she ________ stay calm.
a could b managed to c was able
7 She ________ to find the theater with the help of her app.
a was able b manages c can't
8 Fred ________ sing to other people – he gets too nervous.
a couldn't b manages c can't
9 Poppy ________ work and study, but she's usually tired.
a manages to b able to c can't
10 I ________ take my English exam because I was on vacation.
a couldn't b didn't manage c wasn't able

➤ Go back to page 20.

Grammar Hub

3.1 Narrative tenses

	Positive	Negative	Question
Simple past	They **went** to Spain last year.	The train trip **didn't take** long.	Where **did** you **go** on vacation?
Past progressive	It **was raining** when we left the house.	Anna **wasn't enjoying** the trip.	Where **were you going** when I saw you yesterday?
Past perfect	I **had just arrived** at the hotel. We **had missed** the train.	Ben **hadn't arrived** at the office.	What time **had** they **left** the house? **Had** you ever **been** there before?

- We use the simple past to talk about finished actions or situations, and things that happened one after another.

  I waited at the bus stop until my bus came.
- We use the past progressive to describe the background to a story.

  It was snowing and the traffic was moving very slowly.
- When we are talking about two events in the past, we use the past perfect to show that one event happened before the other.

past ← *I had left the train station when I saw a bus.* → present

I left the train station. — I saw a bus.

- We use the past progressive for actions or situations that were unfinished at a past time and which were interrupted by shorter events (described using the simple past).

  *While we **were going** through town, the bus **started** making a strange noise.*

3.2 Articles and quantifiers

Articles

a/an, *the*, no article

a/an	We use *a/an* the first time we talk about a singular noun.	I have **a ticket** for the train. There was **an accident** on the main road.
the	We use *the* when we have already mentioned the person or thing.	There was an accident. **The accident** wasn't serious.
	We use *the* with singular nouns when it is clear what we are talking about or when there is only one.	I usually take **the bus** that leaves at 6:15.
	We use *the* with plural nouns when it is clear what we are talking about.	**The trains** that leave in the mornings are overcrowded.
no article	We use no article with the names of people, companies, cities and countries (except *the UK*, *the US*, *the Netherlands*).	My cousin's name is **Sam**. He recently flew to **Colorado**, which is in **the US**.
	We use no article when we talk about things in general.	Do you like **traveling**? **Buses** are sometimes faster than **trains**.

- We use *an* before a vowel sound. We use *a* before a consonant sound, even if the word begins with *a*, *e*, *i*, *o* or *u*.

  an hour, an expensive trip, a university town
- We sometimes use *the* before a type of transportation.

  *We always take **the** bus / **the** train / **the** plane.*
- We use *the* before the names of oceans and rivers and countries whose names are plural.

  ***the** Atlantic Ocean / **the** Nile River / **the** United States / **the** Philippines*

Quantifiers

	Countable nouns	Uncountable nouns
Question	**How many people** use the subway?	**How much traffic** was there on the road?
Positive number	There are **a few people** on the train.	There is **a little ice** on the roads so drive carefully.
	There are **a lot of / lots of people** waiting for the bus.	There is **a lot of / lots of information** in this booklet.
	There are **enough seats**.	There is **enough space**.
	There are **plenty of buses**.	There is **plenty of time**.
Negative number	There are **few people** on the train.	There is **little chance** of us getting there on time.
	There aren't **many people** here.	There isn't **much traffic** today.
	There aren't **enough seats**.	There isn't **enough space**.
	There are **too many people** on this train. It's **too small**.	There's **too much noise** on the train. It's **too noisy**.

3.1 Narrative tenses

A Complete each sentence with the correct form of the verb in parentheses.

1 We got to the station but we *had already missed* (already / miss) the train.

2 When I arrived at the station, my cousin ________________ (wait) for me.

3 The car left the road and ________________ (hit) a tree.

4 ________________ (you / go) to Berlin before or was it your first time?

5 What ________________ (your friend / say) when you finally arrived?

6 We ________________ (just / arrive) at the station when we saw our train coming in.

B Choose the correct option.

1 We were excited because we ***didn't visit*** / ***had never visited*** South America before.

2 ***Did anyone wait*** / ***Was anyone waiting*** for you when you got there?

3 Tom arrived at the hotel and ***had gone*** / ***went*** straight to his room for a nap.

4 The reason we were lost was that we ***were taking*** / ***had taken*** the wrong subway line.

5 What ***did you do*** / ***had you done*** when you realized you'd lost your ticket?

6 Didn't you know the train ***was being*** / ***had been*** canceled?

C Correct the mistakes in each sentence.

1 The accident happened because the driver had ~~fell~~ *fallen* asleep at the wheel.

2 I was late, but luckily for me the meeting wasn't starting.

3 We missed the beginning because we were getting stuck in a traffic jam.

4 They had already went to Paris so they decided to go somewhere else.

5 I was worried because I wasn't hearing from my brother for several hours.

6 The traffic didn't move at all so we got out of the taxi and walked.

➤ Go back to page 27.

3.2 Articles and quantifiers

A Find eight more mistakes with articles and correct them.

The trip from my house to my office only takes me about half hour. There is the quicker way – I could take bus – but I prefer to walk. There are many reasons for this. First, the walking is healthy and I find it puts me in good mood. I usually arrive at office awake and ready for work. Going by the bus, on the other hand, leaves me feeling tired and stressed before a day begins!

B Write one word in each blank. Sometimes more than one answer is possible.

1 How *much* time do we have before the train comes?

2 Sometimes we take ____________ taxi and share the cost between us.

3 There weren't very ____________ passengers on my bus this morning. I wonder why.

4 I find that bike riding is ____________ easy way to get through traffic jams.

5 Very ____________ people in the town have cars, so the bus service is really important to them.

6 There aren't ____________ places to park, and that's why there are traffic problems.

C Check (✓) the sentences that are correct. Write *of* in the right place in the sentences that are incorrect.

1 There are very few buses that go near my house. ✓

2 It will take a little time for the public to get used to the new system.

3 Not enough people used the bus service so they stopped running it.

4 A lot passengers complain of overcrowding on the buses.

5 I don't usually take taxis because they cost too much money.

6 There are plenty people who take their cars to work every day.

7 There are lots taxis where I live.

8 There's plenty money to improve the bus system.

9 There were few free seats on the train today.

10 Is there too much traffic on our streets?

➤ Go back to page 31.

Grammar Hub

4.1 Future forms

- We use *will* when we make a decision at the time of speaking.

  I'll get my coat and we can leave now.
  I won't buy this dress because it's too small.

- We use *be going to* for our intentions (the things we want to do or have already decided to do).

  Salma is going to cut down on the amount of chocolate she eats.
  We aren't going to have a New Year's party this year.
  Are you going to keep your New Year's resolutions?

- We use the present progressive when we have made an arrangement for a certain time in the future, usually with another person.

  Aisa is going shopping with her sister tomorrow.
  He isn't coming out with us tonight.
  What are you doing on New Year's Eve?

Be careful!

- We don't use the present progressive for intentions that haven't been arranged yet. We use *be going to.*

  I'm going to write a book one day.
  NOT ~~*I'm writing a book one day.*~~

4.2 Making predictions

- When we are certain about a future event or situation, we can use either *be going to* or *will.*

  Panit is going to keep his New Year's resolutions.
  The company won't reach its sales target this month.
  Will the forecaster's predictions be accurate?

- Although there is little difference between the use of *be going to* and *will* for predictions, if there is strong evidence or a good reason for our prediction, we usually use *be going to* rather than *will.*

  Caitlyn is going to have a baby.
  NOT ~~*Caitlyn will have a baby.*~~

- To add even greater certainty to our prediction, we can use the adverb *definitely.*

  The other team has a lot of points – they're definitely going to win.

- We can use the adverb *probably* to show that we are not completely certain.

  I'll probably stay at home on New Year's Eve.

- We usually use these phrases with *will* when we're making a prediction: *I (don't) think …, I expect …, I'm sure …*

  I don't think the media experts will predict the election results accurately.

- When we feel that a future event is possible, but we are not completely certain, we use *could, may* or *might.*

  You could make some new friends by joining the gym.

Be careful!

- We put the adverbs *definitely* and *probably* after the auxiliary verb in sentences with *be going to* or *will.*

  They're definitely going to win the World Cup.
  NOT ~~*They're going to definitely win the World Cup.*~~
  I'll probably take part in the project.
  NOT ~~*I'll take part probably in the project.*~~

4.1 Future forms

A Match the sentences (1–6) to the answers (a–f) to make short dialogues.

1 The phone's ringing! ___
2 Are you staying at home tonight? ___
3 Would you like anything else? ___
4 Josh is having a fireworks party tomorrow. ___
5 I've lost my wallet! ___
6 What time are you meeting the others? ___

a Oh no! What are you going to do?
b Sometime tomorrow morning.
c Sounds amazing. Can I come?
d OK. I'll get it!
e Yes, I'll have a coffee, please.
f No, I'm having dinner with Kate.

B Choose the correct option.

1 **A:** 'I've just heard it's Dan's birthday today.'
B: 'Oh! ***I'll get*** / ***I'm getting*** him a present at lunchtime, then.'
2 Next year, I'm ***going to try*** / ***trying*** to keep my New Year's resolutions.
3 It's all arranged. ***We'll move*** / ***We're moving*** next Tuesday.
4 I made a big decision last week. ***I'll*** / ***I'm going to*** look for a new job.
5 **A:** 'I don't think I'll ever fall in love.'
B: 'Don't be silly. It's ***happening*** / ***going to happen*** soon, I'm sure.'

C Complete the dialogue with the correct form of the words in parentheses. Sometimes more than one answer is possible.

Ashanti: What are you doing on the weekend, Camilla?
Camilla: I [1] ___ (*not / do*) anything special. Why?
Ashanti: Well, I'm going to a two-day self-help course. Come with me!
Camilla: Self-help?
Ashanti: Yes. I've decided I [2] ___ (*change*) my life.
Camilla: It doesn't sound like my kind of thing. What time [3] ___ (*leave*) tomorrow?
Ashanti: Early – at about eight o'clock.
Camilla: In that case, I definitely don't want to come! Tomorrow's Saturday and I [4] ___ (*not / work*). I [5] ___ (*sleep*) until eleven o'clock and then have breakfast in bed!
Ashanti: All right. If you're sure. In that case, I [6] ___ (*call*) you on Sunday evening and tell you all about it.
Camilla: OK. Have a good time!

➤ Go back to page 39.

4.2 Making predictions

A Reorder the words to make sentences.

1 the future / for our children / is / going to / what / be like / ?
What is the future going to be like for our children?
2 probably / in college / study / Modern Languages / Gareth / will
___
3 going / she / buy / definitely / to / a new cell phone / is
___
4 soon / will / he / sure / be here / I'm
___
5 will / don't / to the party / Dimitris / I / come / think
___
6 Jamie / going / is / a new suit / to buy / for the interview / ?
___

B Write a word from the box in each blank to complete the sentences. Sometimes more than one answer is possible.

could definitely is might think won't

1 The score is 4-0 – they're ___ going to lose.
2 She ___ make a lot of money one day – anything's possible!
3 Don't worry – you ___ have any problems.
4 She ___ going to compete in a national sports competition.
5 I ___ she will need some help moving.
6 The weather's bad today; some people ___ arrive late.

C Choose the correct option.

1 I'm sure people ___ fewer hours in the future.
a are working b will work
2 Hundreds of people ___ their jobs when the factory closes.
a are losing b are going to lose
3 Look out! That driverless car ___ crash!
a will b is going to
4 People ___ reading newspapers in the future, maybe, but I don't think they'll stop reading books.
a are stopping b will stop
5 I think Magda ___ a good mother when she's older.
a is going to be b is being
6 I don't expect that he ___ get good grades because he never studies.
a will b won't

➤ Go back to page 43.

Grammar Hub

5.1 Past habits and states

	Positive	Negative
I/you/he/she/it/we/they	**I used to be** a waiter in a restaurant.	**They did not use to work** here. **They didn't use to work** here.

Question	Positive short answer	Negative short answer
Did you use to work from home?	Yes, **I did**.	No, **I didn't**.

- We use *used to* to talk about past situations that do not exist now. These include past habits and past states.

  *Past habit: We **used to meet** at the station on the way to work.*

  *Past state: He **used to be** a manager but he left his job.*
- We use *use to* with the auxiliary verb *did*.

  *I didn't **use** to work here.*
  NOT ~~I didn't used to work here.~~

  *Did you **use** to do voluntary work?*
  NOT ~~Did you used to do voluntary work?~~
- In the negative, we can also say *never used to*.

  *I **didn't use** to work here. OR I **never used** to work here.*

- We can use *would* when we talk about past actions. We do not use it for permanent states in the past.

  When I was younger, I would visit London regularly on business. NOT ~~When I was younger, I would live in London.~~
- We usually use *would* when we are telling a story or talking fondly about the past.

  Every year, the boss would take us all out to eat.
- When talking about the past, we rarely use *would* in the negative or question form.

  I didn't use to like it here. NOT ~~I wouldn't like it here.~~
  Did you use to work part time? NOT ~~Would you work part time?~~

5.2 The passive voice

	Positive	Negative	Question
Simple present	**I am expected** to work on weekends.	**You are not allowed** to take time off. **You aren't allowed** to take time off.	**Is he paid** a lot of money?
Present progressive	**The goods are being delivered** now.	**The workers are not being trained** right now. **The workers aren't being trained** right now.	**Is the product being sold** at full price?
Simple past	**I was told** to wait at the front desk.	**They were not asked** to work on weekends. **They weren't asked** to work on weekends.	**Were you given** instructions?
Past progressive	**The product was being used** all over the world.	**She was not being paid** very much. **She wasn't being paid** very much.	**Was bottled water being sold** here 30 years ago?
Present perfect	**The product has** just **been launched**.	**Your order has not been received**. **Your order hasn't been received**.	**Have the workers been told**?

- We use the passive voice when we don't say who or what causes the action (usually because the person or thing is not known, not important or obvious).

  *The business **was launched** last year.*
- We can sometimes say the same thing in the active or passive voice. The choice frequently depends on the topic we are talking about.

  *Active: The company **sells** the product as a luxury item. (The topic is the company.)*

  *Passive: The product **is sold** as a luxury item. (The topic is the product.)*

- We use *by* when we know who does/did an action and we want to mention it.

  *This product was bought **by** both young and old customers.*
- We can use the passive voice with modal verbs.

  *Orders **can be made** online or at one of our stores.*
  *The product **might be launched** in the New Year.*
- We don't use *by* + the agent unless it is important, useful information.

  The product is sold all over the world. NOT ~~The product is sold by store owners all over the world.~~

5.1 Past habits and states

A Complete the sentences with *used to* or *would* and the verb in parentheses. If both options are possible, write both.

1 When I was younger, I *used to dream / would dream* of running my own business. (*dream*)
2 In my old job, I ______ events. (*plan*)
3 The office has moved. It ______ closer to my home. (*be*)
4 I ______ that management skills were important. (*not think*)
5 Joel ______ his job but he hates it now. (*love*)
6 Work ______ at eight and nobody dared to be late! (*start*)

B Make questions with *used to*.

1 you / live / New York City / ?
Did you use to live in New York City?
2 Sally / work / restaurant / ?
______
3 things / be better / in the past / ?
______
4 where / you / spend / your childhood vacations / ?
______
5 what / you / do / in your old job / ?
______
6 when you walked to work / how long / it / take you / ?
______

C Make sentences with *used to*. Put a check (✓) or an (✗) to show whether the same idea can be expressed with *would*.

1 when / I / be / younger / I / have / my own business
When I was younger, I used to have my own business. ✗
2 in the past / our manager / not have / good communication skills
______
3 every afternoon / I / try / finish / all the letters
______
4 years ago / people / laugh / at the idea / computers in the home
______
5 you / enjoy / your job / more / ?
______
6 we / not take / a summer vacation
______

➤ Go back to page 51.

5.2 The passive voice

A Correct the mistakes in each sentence.

1 The office *is* located in the center of Manchester.
2 The business was start by two brothers in Cape Town in 2018.
3 The company is knowing for its luxury goods and excellent website.
4 Is the plan been considered right now or is there a delay?
5 The items you have ordered can delivered within two working days.
6 The managers agreed. A decision was taken by them yesterday.

B Choose the correct option.

1 When will we ______?
a paid (b) be paid c paying
2 My order ______ yesterday.
a was made b is make c made
3 We ______ what to do.
a haven't told b didn't tell c weren't told
4 When you called me, I ______ for a job.
a was being interviewed b was interviewed c am interviewing
5 The food for tonight ______.
a has been delivering b has just been delivered c was been delivered
6 Is everything ______ in the box?
a provide b provided c providing

C Rewrite the sentences in the passive voice. Use *by* only when necessary.

1 They usually give us our tasks in the morning.
We are usually given our tasks in the morning.
2 The manager is studying Rob's business plan.
______
3 They started the business last year.
______
4 They have only delivered three jars.
______
5 Matt presented details of the plan.
______
6 When I started, they were making some big changes.
______

➤ Go back to page 55.

Grammar Hub

6.1 Modals of obligation

should

	Positive	Negative
I/you/he/she/it/we/they	**I should choose** the best team.	**We shouldn't yell** at the players.

must

	Positive	Negative
I/you/he/she/it/we/they	**They must find** a better place to train.	**You must not be** so aggressive on the field.

have to

	Positive	Negative
I/you/we/they	**You have to wear** a helmet.	**They don't have to play** the game on the computer.
he/she/it	**She has to perform** well today.	**He doesn't have to win** every match.

- We use *should/shouldn't* when we describe what is or is not a good idea now, in the future or generally.
- We use *must* and *have to* when we describe rules and situations that are necessary.
- There is sometimes no difference between them. However, we usually use *must* and *must not* in written rules, and *have to* in speech.
- We use *must not* when we describe something that is not allowed.
- We use *don't/doesn't have to* when we describe things that aren't necessary, but you may still do them.
- There is a difference in meaning between *must not* and *don't have to*.

  must not *= not allowed*

  don't have to *= not necessary*
- In questions, we use *have to* instead of *must*.
- We can use *don't/doesn't need to* instead of *don't/doesn't have to* when we describe things that aren't necessary.

6.2 Present perfect and present perfect progressive; *had to / needed to*

Present perfect

Positive	Negative	Question
I've joined a sailing club.	**They haven't made up** their minds about joining the league.	**Have you met** your opponent yet?

- We use the present perfect for actions completed during a period of time that continues to now.
- We also use the present perfect for actions completed before now when we don't say exactly when.
- See Grammar Hub 2.1 for more information about the present perfect.

Present perfect progressive

	Positive	Negative
I/you/we/they	**I have been collecting** stamps for years.	**We haven't been doing** our best in every game.
he/she/it	**She's been training** hard every single day.	**Zain hasn't been training** hard enough.

Question	Positive short answer	Negative short answer
Have they been playing tennis for long?	Yes, **they have**.	No, **they haven't**.
Has Anika been watching the game on TV?	Yes, **she has**.	No, **she hasn't**.

- We use the present perfect progressive to talk about an action that started in the past and continues in the present. It can be a single or a frequently repeated action.

  He has been cooking all afternoon.
- We can use both the present perfect and the present perfect progressive to describe a recently completed activity.

  She has posted the videos on social media. She has been posting the videos on social media all morning.
- We use the present perfect progressive to find out the duration of an activity.

  How long have you been waiting for your teammates?
- We do NOT use the present perfect progressive with state verbs.

  I have known my coach for years.

had to / needed to

	Positive	Negative
I/you/he/she/it/we/they	**They had to** practice for four hours each day. **He needed to wear** safety equipment.	**You didn't have to train** for the snowball fight. **She didn't need to buy** a new helmet.

Question	Positive short answer	Negative short answer
Did you have to take a lesson first?	Yes, **I/we did**.	No, **I/we didn't**.

- We use *had to* and *needed to* to talk about things that were necessary in the past. They mean the same thing.
- We don't use *must* to talk about the past.

  They had to pay for the skiing lessons last winter.
- We use *didn't have to* and *didn't need to* to talk about things that were not necessary but possible in the past.

6.1 Modals of obligation

A Choose the correct option.

1 We *don't have to* / *must not* be competitive to have fun playing sports.
2 He *must* / *doesn't have to* wear a helmet. It's required.
3 I *must* / *must not* eat a massive meal before playing a sport.
4 They *shouldn't* / *don't have to* practice today because the coach isn't going to be here.
5 *Do you have to* / *Must you* train every day?

B Complete the sentences with the correct words and phrases from the box.

don't have   doesn't have   has
must not   don't need   should

1 You ________________ to buy a ticket. Dad's bought them already.
2 She ________________ ask her coach for advice on how to play better.
3 I ________________ to go to practice today. It's been canceled.
4 For a helmet to work, it ________________ to fit on your head properly.
5 You ________________ run while holding the ball. It's against the rules.
6 He ________________ to wear protective gear because his sport isn't dangerous.

C Choose the correct option to complete the dialogue.

Anna: I'm excited about Saturday's game. It starts at 1 pm. I think we [1] ________________ meet in front of the entrance, shouldn't we?

Vincenzo: I [2] ________________ take my little sister to her lesson first, so I might be a little late. You [3] ________________ wait for me outside. Just go on inside and I'll find you.

Anna: Well, I don't mind waiting for you outside. I [4] ________________ be in my seat when the game starts. Besides, it's a big place. We [5] ________________ go in together so we don't get lost.

Vincenzo: OK, fine.

	a	b	c
1	don't need to	must	(c) should
2	have to	should	don't have to
3	must	don't have to	have to
4	should	must	don't have to
5	must	should	don't need to

➤ Go back to page 63.

6.2 Present perfect and present perfect progressive; *had to / needed to*

A Choose the correct option.

1 I've never *played* / *been playing* racquetball before. Is it fun?
2 Have you *been watching* / *watched* sports on TV all day?
3 I've just *finished* / *been finishing* a really difficult exercise class.
4 Sorry about my appearance. I've *run* / *been running*.
5 Do you think he's *understood* / *been understanding* the rules yet?
6 Lee hasn't *worked out* / *been working out* for a long time but he's already *increased* / *been increasing* his muscle strength.

B Complete the sentences in the present perfect or progressive with the correct form of these verbs. Sometimes more than one tense is possible.

follow   join   stay   lose   play   spend

1 Tom has ____lost____ interest in playing soccer.
2 The coach has ________________ a lot of time with the players lately.
3 Have you ________________ the tennis competition? It's getting good!
4 Georgia has ________________ in shape these days using a new exercise program.
5 Eli and Greta haven't ________________ the club yet.
6 I've ________________ this video game all day and there's still a lot left.

C Correct the mistakes.

1 He had to ~~left~~ leave the game because he broke his leg.
2 I must yell so the other players could hear me.
3 You hadn't to yell. I couldn't hear you on the field.
4 I didn't needed to tell my friend about the game.
5 **A:** Why they didn't have to buy a paddle?
B: Because they already had one.

➤ Go back to page 69.

Grammar Hub

7.1 Modals of speculation and deduction

- We use *could*, *might* or *may* when we think something is possible, but we are not sure.

  This dish is very hot – it could contain a lot of chilies.
  Carla might be allergic to nuts – don't add any walnuts.
  Paul may want sugar in his coffee.
- In the negative, we use *might not* and *may not* but NOT *could not*.

  This restaurant may/might not be very good.
  NOT ~~*This restaurant could not be very good.*~~
- We use *must* when we are sure something is true because we have strong evidence for our belief.

  This cake is burned – it must taste horrible!
- We use *can't* when we are sure something is not true because we have strong evidence for our belief.

  These cookies are white – they can't be chocolate chip cookies.
- We don't use *must* and *can't* for facts we are 100% sure about.

7.2 Comparatives and superlatives; *the ..., the ...*

Comparatives and superlatives

	Comparative	Superlative
Short adjectives (one syllable)	adj + *-er* (+ *than*) cheap → cheap**er**	*the* + adj + *-est* cheap → **the** cheap**est**
Longer adjectives	*more* + adj (+ *than*) popular → **more** popular	*the most* + adj popular → **the most** popular
Irregular adjectives	good → **better** (+ *than*) bad → **worse** (+ *than*)	good → **the best** bad → **the worst**
Adverbs	*more* + adv (+ *than*) quickly → **more** quickly	*the most* + adv quickly → **the most** quickly
Irregular adverbs	badly → **worse** far → **farther/further** fast → fast**er** hard → hard**er** well → **better**	badly → **the worst** far → **the farthest** / **the furthest** fast → **the** fast**est** hard → **the** hard**est** well → **the best**
Countable nouns	many nutrients → **more** nutrients few nutrients → few**er** nutrients	many nutrients → **the most** nutrients few nutrients → **the** few**est** nutrients
Uncountable nouns	much protein → **more** protein little fiber → **less** fiber	much protein → **the most** protein little fiber → **the least** fiber

- We use comparative adjectives and adverbs to say how two or more things or actions are different.
- We use superlative adjectives and adverbs to say that something is the top or bottom of a group.
- For adjectives ending in *-e* or *-y* the rules differ a little.

  Your meal is larger than mine, but Harry's is the largest.
  Carrot soup is tastier than pea soup, but chicken soup is the tastiest of all.
- For adjectives which end with one vowel and one consonant, we double the final consonant before adding *-er* or *-est*.

  These melons are ***bigger*** *than those ones.*
- To make negative comparatives and superlatives, we use *less* instead of *more* and *the least* instead of *the most*.
- We never use *more* or *the most* together with *-er* or *-est*.

  I think juice is healthier than coffee. NOT ~~*I think juice is more healthier than coffee.*~~
- We only use *than* when it is followed by the thing we are comparing.

  This dish is good but this one is better. NOT ~~*This dish is good but this one is better than.*~~
  This dish is better than that dish.

the ..., the ...

the + comparative adjective + noun, *the* + comparative adjective + noun	**The fresher** the ingredients, **the better** the dish.
the + comparative adjective + clause, *the* + comparative adjective + clause	**The more tasty** it is, **the more satisfied** they will be.
the + comparative adverb + clause, *the* + comparative adverb + clause	**The faster** it boils, **the more quickly** it will be ready.
the + *more/less* + noun + clause, *the* + *more/less* + noun + clause	**The more recipes** you learn, **the more food** you can cook.
the + *more/less* + clause, *the* + *more/less* + clause	**The more I practiced**, **the less I needed** a cookbook.

- We use *the ..., the* to show that two changes are closely connected. As one thing changes, the other thing changes too.
- Sometimes we use the very simplest form of this structure, using comparative adjectives only, and no verb.

  The more, the merrier.
- We don't have to use only the forms shown in the table above. We can also combine different parts of the structures.

  The more complicated the recipe, the longer it takes.
  The less we spend on food, the more money we have.

7.1 Modals of speculation and deduction

A Decide if the statements are true or false.

1 'Kitty may serve fruit salad for dessert tonight.'
Dessert will definitely be fruit salad. **True / False**

2 'I've been invited to three pot-luck dinners. They must be popular.'
Pot-luck dinners are popular. **True / False**

3 'This can't be tomato soup – it isn't red!'
It almost certainly isn't tomato soup. **True / False**

4 'Bitter chocolate could be good in a cake.'
The speaker really doesn't like bitter chocolate. **True / False**

5 'If you left the milk out all night, it could be sour.'
It's possible that the milk is sour. **True / False**

B Choose the correct option.

1 **A:** 'Are you going to order soup?'
B: 'No, I'm very hungry and it ***must not / might not*** be very filling.'

2 **A:** 'Lara said she wants chicken.'
B: 'But she doesn't eat meat. She ***can't / must not*** want chicken.'

3 **A:** 'What's 'scampi'?'
B: 'I don't know really. It ***could / can*** be some kind of fish.'

4 **A:** 'Dinner is at seven tonight.'
B: 'I ***could / may*** not get there in time because I have to work late.'

5 **A:** 'Look at that man! He's ordered three pizzas!'
B: 'He ***can / must*** really like pizza!'

6 **A:** 'I've ordered sushi for lunch.'
B: 'Hector ***might / could*** not eat that but we'll see.'

➤ Go back to page 77.

7.2 Comparatives and superlatives; *the ..., the ...*

A Complete the sentences with the correct form of the adjectives and adverbs in parentheses.

1 The ________________ (*fast*) the pizza delivery man can get here is 15 minutes.

2 You can buy cheese ________________ (*cheaply*) in the street market than in the stores.

3 The food in the airport was bad, but the meal on the plane was ________________ (*bad*).

4 I made the soup with ________________ (*few*) ingredients than it says in the recipe.

5 The ________________ (*good*) way to serve this dessert is with a little cream.

6 I would prefer to try a ________________ (*mild*) sauce than the one you're eating.

B Complete the sentences with the words and phrases in the box.

less meat	more times	more quickly	the better	the more money	the sweeter	you disagree

1 The ________________ you eat, the healthier it is for your heart.

2 The more sugar you add, ________________ the sauce will be.

3 The ________________ you eat your salad, the sooner you'll have dessert!

4 The more ________________ with me, the less likely I am to change my mind!

5 The ________________ you reheat food, the more unsafe it becomes.

6 The less food we throw away, ________________ we'll save.

➤ Go back to page 80.

C Correct the mistakes in each sentence.

1 The peas will cook more fast than the potatoes.

2 I think the most sourest taste of any food is vinegar.

3 Salad is the least filling than pasta.

4 First prize in the competition will go to the person who cooks the more creatively.

5 I put very little sugar in Jim's coffee, but he wanted even little!

6 Chia seeds have much protein than some foods, but quinoa has the most.

D Write one word in each blank to complete the sentences.

1 Is fast food ________________ popular than home cooking in your country?

2 My old mixer worked fairly well, but this one works much ________________.

3 Water is the ________________ fattening drink you can have because it has zero calories!

4 Raw food is generally healthier ________________ cooked food.

5 All these curries are spicy, but this one is the hottest ________________ all!

6 The older the wine is, ________________ better it gets.

7 The salad plates are pretty large, but the dinner plates are ________________.

8 Mmm! This is ________________ most delicious meal I've ever had!

➤ Go back to page 81.

Grammar Hub

8.1 Adjective clauses

Essential adjective clauses

	Relative pronoun	
Person	who/that	The person **who/that** first had the idea was named Smith.
Thing	which/that	The thing **which/that** stops it being a success is the price.
Possession	whose	The man **whose** design won first prize was from China.
Place	where	The company **where** I work makes a difference to people's lives.
Time	when	Early in the morning is the time **when** I have my best ideas.

- We use an essential adjective clause to give information about and identify a noun (person or thing).
- We use *who* or *that* for people, and *which* or *that* for things.
- With *who*, *which* and *that*, we can leave out the relative pronoun if it's followed by a subject + verb rather than just a verb.

  The design (that) he suggested was very good.

- When the relative pronoun is the subject of the adjective clause, we don't add another pronoun.

  *Do you know the name of the man **who invented** this?* NOT ~~*Do you know the name of the man who he invented this?*~~

Non-essential adjective clauses

	Relative pronoun	
Person	who	Carol Taylor, **who** presents science programs, is a university professor.
Thing	which	The idea, **which** I first read about in the newspaper, is really very simple.
Possession	whose	Miriam, **whose** dad is a designer, would like to become an inventor.
Place	where	London, **where** her grandparents live, is where Sophie would like to find work.
Time	when	On Sundays, **when** Andrew isn't working, he likes to catch up with his reading.

- We use a non-essential adjective clause when we want to include two pieces of information in the same sentence. The adjective clause is usually an additional piece of information and is always separated by commas.
- We do not use *that* with non-essential adjective clauses.
- When we remove a non-essential adjective clause, the sentence still makes sense.

8.2 Zero and first conditionals; Conditionals with modals and imperatives

Zero conditional

Condition	Result
If **you listen**,	**you learn**.
If **you like** science,	**it helps**.

Question	Positive short answer	Negative short answer
If **I win**, **do I get** a prize?	Yes, **you do**.	No, **you don't**.
Does it help if you like science?	Yes, **it does**.	No, **it doesn't**.

- We use the zero conditional to talk about things that are always true.
- We can put the *if*-clause or the result clause first. The only difference is we do not use a comma if we begin with the result clause.
- We can use negatives and *unless* (which means *if not* or *except if*) in the zero conditional.

  If you don't pay attention, you make mistakes.
  = *Unless you pay attention, you make mistakes.*

First conditional

Condition	Result
If **you try** hard,	**you'll succeed**.
If **it doesn't work**,	**we'll start** again.

Question	Positive short answer	Negative short answer
If **we win** the award, **will we be** famous?	Yes, **we/you will**.	No, **we/you won't**.
Will we be famous if **we win** the award?		

- We use the first conditional to talk about possible situations in the future.
- We can put the *if*-clause or the result clause first. The only difference is we do not use a comma if we begin with the result clause.
- We can use negatives and *unless* (meaning *if not* or *except if*) in the first conditional.

  If you don't listen, you won't understand.
  = *Unless you listen, you won't understand.*
- We never put *will* in an *if*-clause.

Conditionals with modals and imperatives

- We can use other modal verbs (e.g. *can*, *could*, *might*, *should*) instead of *will*.

  *If you work hard enough, you **can** do it!*
  *I **might** visit the science museum if it's open tomorrow.*

- We can use an imperative instead of a result clause.

  *If you see smoke, **call** for help.*
  ***Call** me if you have any questions.*

8.1 Adjective clauses

A Choose the correct option.

1 There are a lot of students *which* / (*who*) have great ideas.
2 The last century was the time *when* / *where* technology really progressed.
3 The magazine *who* / *that* I like best is called *New Scientist*.
4 Princeton is the place *where* / *which* I studied for my degree.
5 I want to find a job *that* / *who* helps others.
6 John is the boy *who* / *whose* father is a doctor.
7 I don't know anyone *who* / *which* works in technology.
8 He was born at a time *when* / *where* computers didn't exist.

B Match to make sentences.

1 California is where ___b___
2 The computer is an invention ______
3 Steve Jobs was the person who ______
4 The experiences ______
5 Myra is the woman ______
6 My phone is the one thing ______
7 I really enjoyed the time ______

a started Apple Computers.
b most software industries started.
c which I would hate to lose.
d which has changed many people's lives.
e that I had were more important than the money I made.
f when I was studying at college.
g who helped me choose my career.

C Join the two sentences to make one. Use non-essential adjective clauses.

1 My aunt is a scientist. She lives in Boston.
My aunt, who lives in Boston, is a scientist. / My aunt, who is a scientist, lives in Boston.
2 The invention is very simple. It has made a big difference to people's lives.
______
3 Justin is 23. He has just won a prize.
______
4 Carl spoke to us from Lisbon. He lives there.
______
5 The invention won first prize. It is sold in many countries.
______
6 Marie loves inventing things. Her husband is also an engineer.
______
7 Next week the results come out. We'll see if you win anything.
______

➤ Go back to page 87.

8.2 Zero and first conditionals; Conditionals with modals and imperatives

A Find and correct the mistakes with the zero conditional.

1 If you ~~will~~ read a lot, you understand things better.
2 It's better if you called me in the evenings.
3 Unless you don't try, you don't learn.
4 The roads will more dangerous if it rains.
5 It doesn't work if you won't turn it on.
6 I'll never go out if it's cold.

B Complete the first conditional sentences using the information in parentheses.

1 The machine will not work if you don't press this button.
(*you / not / press this button*)
2 If you find it at the right price, ______
(*you / buy it?*)
3 What will we do ______
(*it / not work?*)
4 How will you get home ______
(*you / miss the bus?*)
5 If it rains tomorrow, ______
(*you / still / play soccer?*)
6 If you take an umbrella with you, ______
(*it / keep you dry*)
7 I won't help him ______
(*he / not ask*)

➤ Go back to page 91.

C Choose the correct option.

1 If you see Jimmy, ______
a will give him this note.
(b) give him this note.
2 You will save money if ______
a you can wait a few months.
b you will wait a few months.
3 If you don't like it, ______
a you can go home.
b will you go home.
4 If you have any problems, ______
a will call me.
b call me.
5 If I feel like it, ______
a I might go to the pop concert.
b I can go to the pop concert.
6 Ask me if there's anything ______
a you don't understand.
b you won't understand.
7 If you want to have a good time, ______
a you will come and join us on Saturday night!
b come and join us on Saturday night!

➤ Go back to page 93.

Grammar Hub

9.1 Second conditional

Condition	Result
If **you submitted** a proposal,	**they would accept** it.
If **she didn't teach** music,	**she'd be** a full-time musician.
If **the show were** expensive,	**I wouldn't go** to it.
If **we didn't have** an art venue,	**we wouldn't see** much art.

Question	Positive short answer	Negative short answer
If **you had** more free time, **would you spend** it creatively?	Yes, **I would**.	No, **I wouldn't**.
Would you spend your free time creatively if **you had** more of it?		

- We use the second conditional to talk about present situations that aren't real and future events that are unlikely but possible.
- Although it uses the simple past, the second conditional is NOT about the past.
- We use *if* + simple past in the *if*-clause and *would* + base form in the result clause.
- We can use *might* or *could* in the result clause if we are not sure of the result.

  If she rehearsed every day, she might improve her skills.

  We could display community art if we had a local arts venue.
- With the verb *be*, we generally use *were* instead of *was* with all subjects, including *I*.

9.2 Reported speech

Direct speech	Reported speech
simple present	simple past
'**We enjoy** live concerts the best.'	They said (that) **they enjoyed** live concerts the best.
present progressive	past progressive
'**We are learning** how to write a short story.'	They said (that) **they were learning** how to write a short story.
will	*would*
'**I will** read my book later.'	She said (that) **she would** read her book later.
may	*might*
'**Elle may** sing in the play.'	He said (that) **Elle might** sing in the play.
can	*could*
'**We can** film our daily lives.'	They said (that) **they could** film their daily lives.
should	*should* (no change)
'**He should try out** for that role.'	She said (that) he **should try out** for that role.
For commands and instructions	*tell* + object (+ *not*) + infinitive
'**Rehearse** the scene again.'	He told them **to rehearse** the scene again.
'**Don't look** at the camera.'	She told me **not to look** at the camera.

- We use reported speech to report what people say. We use a reporting verb in the simple past (e.g. *said*, *asked*, *told*).
- When we report what someone says, the reported verb usually goes back one tense.
- When we report questions, the subject comes before the verb (the same as in sentences).

  *Alain: 'Where **is he** acting?' → Alain asked where **he was** acting.*
- With yes/no questions, we start the reported question with *if* or *whether*.

  *Chloe: 'Will Tom attend the show?' → Chloe asked **if/whether** Tom would attend the show.*
- We change some pronouns from direct speech to reported speech depending on the speaker (*I* to *he/she*, *you* to *me*, *my* to *his/her*, etc).

  *Kieran: 'I've given **you my** ticket already.' → He said **he** had given **me his** ticket already.*
- We sometimes also need to change words which refer to time and place.

Direct speech	Reported speech
tomorrow	*the next day / the following day*
today	*that day*
here	*there*
this	*that/the*

- We usually don't change the verb tenses if we are reporting facts that are still true in the present.

  *Our coach said that acting **requires** a great deal of time and effort.*

9.1 Second conditional

A Choose the correct option.

1 If I *knew* / *know* the words to the song, I would sing it.
2 If she had a better idea for the story, she *uses* / *would use* it.
3 If we *would hold* / *held* an art competition, many people would take part.
4 The public *liked* / *might like* his proposal if he presented it to them.
5 If you *invite* / *invited* Monique to the play, would she come?
6 If they allowed the public behind the stage, the actors *weren't* / *wouldn't be* pleased.
7 I'd study art at Kingston University if I *were* / *am* you.

B Correct the mistakes in these second conditional sentences.

1 If you ~~get~~ got rid of your guitar, you would miss it later.
2 If we bought cheaper tickets, we would saved a lot of money.
3 If they interact with the audience, the play would be more exciting.
4 I won't be terribly upset if my bandmates and I didn't make up.
5 Will Chanda enjoy it more if she spent more time in her studio?
6 If the show took place outdoors, more people can come.
7 Everyone would be very unhappy if it rains the day of the concert.

C Write the correct form of the verbs in parentheses. Use *would* if necessary.

1 If the city ___built___ (*build*) a new theater, many people would attend it.
2 If we rehearsed every day, we ________ (*become*) the best!
3 If my favorite musician ________ (*perform*) for free, thousands would go to see it.
4 Jean-Philippe ________ (*sell*) millions of copies if he recorded his songs.
5 The public would be disappointed if the gallery ________ (*close*) its doors.
6 If I ________ (*be*) a famous artist, could I sell my paintings for $1 million?
7 If you ________ (*tell*) your story, I think people would show an interest in it.
8 Most people ________ (*not like*) it if I sang in public!

➤ Go back to page 99.

9.2 Reported speech

A Choose the correct option.

1 Maya: 'I'm going to an outdoor concert tonight.'
She said she *is* / *was* going to an outdoor concert that night.
2 Dan and Tracy: 'We're rehearsing all day tomorrow.'
They said they *were rehearsing* / *will rehearse* all day the following day.
3 Joe to Lyn: 'I can give you my proposal.'
He said he *can* / *could* give her his proposal.
4 Nadia to me: 'I will ask the doorman to let you in for free.'
She said she *asked* / *would ask* the doorman to let me in for free.
5 The teachers: 'We've chosen a local warehouse.'
They said they *will choose* / *had chosen* a local warehouse.
6 Me: 'I'm not writing a review of the play this evening.'
You said you weren't writing the review *this* / *that* evening.
7 John to Isabel: 'Come to the concert hall at 7 pm.'
John *said* / *told* Isabel to come to the concert hall at 7 pm.

B Report the statements.

1 Hanna: 'I'm performing at the theater tomorrow.'
She said (that) she was performing at the theater the next/following day.
2 Alexis: 'I've never written a novel before.'
He said ________
3 Marcia: 'I'll buy my tickets online.'
She said ________
4 Davide and Maria: 'We're meeting a famous actor today.'
They said ________
5 Anastasiya: 'I can't hear from the back row.'
She said ________
6 Hussein: 'I gave Sonia my seat.'
He said ________

C Choose the correct option.

1 Sara: 'When is the concert?'
She asked ________.
a if the concert was today
b when the concert was
c when is the concert
2 Elena to Jim: 'You'll love Paulina's performance.'
She promised that Jim ________ Paulina's performance.
a loves
b will love
c would love
3 Soraya to me: 'Have you read *The Great Gatsby*?'
She asked me ________ *The Great Gatsby*.
a whether I read
b if I had read
c why I had read
4 Georgia and Hans: 'Are our seats at the front?'
They asked ________.
a if our seats are at the front
b if our seats were at the front
c if their seats were at the front

➤ Go back to page 103.

Grammar Hub

10.1 Third conditional; *would have* + past participle

Third conditional

Condition	Result
I would have made a better decision	if **Daniel had done** the research.
If **I had known** all the facts,	**he wouldn't have made** his discovery.

Question	Positive short answer	Negative short answer
If **you had thought** about it more, **would you have made** the same decision?	Yes, **I would (have)**.	No, **I wouldn't (have)**.
Would they have passed the exam if **they had answered** correctly?	Yes, **they would (have)**.	No, **they wouldn't (have)**.

- We use the third conditional to imagine a situation in the past that didn't actually happen.

  *If I had set my alarm clock, I wouldn't have been late for work. (= I **didn't** set my alarm clock and I **was** late for work.)*
- As with other conditionals, we only use a comma when the *if*-clause comes first.
- We can use *could have* or *might have* instead of *would have* to express possibility.

  I could have answered correctly if I'd had more time.
- In answer to a third conditional question, we can use either *I would* or *I would have.*

  Would you have made the same decision if you'd known all the facts?
  Yes, I would. / Yes, I would have. / No, I wouldn't. / No, I wouldn't have.

would have + past participle

should have + past participle

Positive	Negative	Question
I would have told her about my exam results.	**He wouldn't have bought** me such an expensive gift.	**Why would they have left** the house already?
She should have bought the first pair.	**You shouldn't have spent** so much money.	**Should I have changed** my mind?
They should have offered more choice.	**I shouldn't have bought** these shoes.	How much **should they have paid**?

- We use *should/shouldn't have* + the past participle of the main verb to talk about mistakes that we made in the past. We regret those actions and try to imagine how we could have acted differently.

  *She shouldn't have changed her mind. (= She **did** change her mind and this was a mistake.)*
- We always put the past participle of the main verb after *should/ shouldn't have.*

  They should have thought about their decision more carefully. NOT ~~*They should have think about their decision more carefully.*~~

10.2 Hopes and wishes

wish + simple past	imagining a different present situation (unreal present)	**I wish she were** more organized. **I wish I weren't** so hungry! **He wishes he knew** the answer.
wish + past perfect	imagining a different past situation (unreal past)	**We wish our son had won** the race. **They wish they hadn't eaten** so much.
wish + *could*	imagining an unlikely future possibility (unlikely future)	**I wish I could stop** drinking coffee.
hope (that) + simple present/ present progressive	imagining a likely future possibility (likely future)	**I hope that you enjoy** yourself tomorrow. **I hope that you are enjoying** yourself on vacation! **We hope that she doesn't make** the wrong decision.

- We can use *wish* to talk about ourselves or other people.

  I wish I had more friends. / I wish Sarah had more friends. / Sarah wishes her brother had more friends.
- We usually use *were* instead of *was* after *I wish* or *He/She wishes.*

  I wish I were better organized.
- We use *wish* + *could* to talk about something that we want to be different in the future. However, by using *could*, we express a belief that our wish probably won't come true.

  I wish I could treat myself to a vacation. (= I know that I won't be able to do this because I don't have the money, time, etc.)
- Although *hope* refers to the future, it is followed by a verb in the present tense. You can include the word *that*, but it is usually omitted.

  I hope (that) the snacks aren't too salty.
  We hope (that) the fast food restaurant is open tomorrow.
- We use the negative for the verb which **follows** *wish* or *hope.*

  I hope it doesn't rain tomorrow.
  NOT ~~*I don't hope it rains.*~~
  I wish I hadn't spent so much money.
  NOT ~~*I don't wish I had spent so much money.*~~

10.1 Third conditional; Would have + past participle

A Read the sentences and choose the option which is true.

1 He should have made a decision based on the facts.
 a He considered the facts. b He didn't consider the facts.
2 She could have avoided the other car if she'd stopped in time.
 a She avoided the other car. b She didn't avoid the other car.
3 If you had listened to me, you wouldn't have made a foolish decision.
 a You made a foolish decision. b You didn't make a foolish decision.
4 If David had gone to a smaller store, he would have felt less stressed.
 a David went to a small store. b David went to a big store.
5 You shouldn't have encouraged her to spend all that money!
 a She spent a lot of money. b She didn't spend a lot of money.
6 We wouldn't have bought this house if we'd known it was so noisy here.
 a We bought the house. b We didn't buy the house.

B Correct the mistakes in each sentence.

1 I shouldn't paid so much for this cell phone.
2 If our teacher gave us time to review, we would all have earned better grades.
3 Will the show have attracted more people if we had advertised it better?
4 I'm sorry – I would have listened to your advice.
5 If you have bought your shoes in the first store, you would have saved time!
6 Should we have count the sunk costs?
7 Would you had agreed to take part if you had known it was a trick?
8 I should realize that the watch was made of plastic!

➤ Go back to page 111.

C Choose the correct option.

The sneakers were fashionable, attractive and cheap, so I bought them. However, I [1]*shouldn't* / *wouldn't* have been so easily influenced by the saleswoman. A few days later, I searched for that brand online and discovered that they were made by child workers! If I [2]*had known* / *would know* that they were made by children, I would never [3]*buy* / *have bought* them. In fact, I [4]*had avoided* / *would have avoided* that store completely! If I [5]*would discover* / *had discovered* the truth sooner, I would have complained to the store. And of course I [6]*hadn't encouraged* / *wouldn't have encouraged* my friends to buy them either! It's really important that, as shoppers, we act responsibly. I've found an online group which persuades customers not to buy products like these. I joined it right away. If I [7]*had heard* / *heard* about it sooner, I [8]*would* / *will* have joined months ago!

➤ Go back to page 113.

10.2 Hopes and wishes

A Match the situations to the people's comments.

1 Brett's too short for the basketball team.
2 Dad is always losing his keys.
3 I don't know any of the answers.
4 Josh's drive to work takes 90 minutes.
5 I want to stop eating sugar completely.
6 Phoebe feels lonely.
7 Anna is really tired.

a 'I wish I didn't have to drive so far.'
b 'I wish I had studied more.'
c 'I wish I had more friends.'
d 'I wish I were taller.'
e 'I wish I hadn't stayed up all night.'
f 'I hope you achieve your goal.'
g 'I wish I wasn't so disorganized.'

B Choose the correct option.

1 I *wish* / *hope* to achieve everything on my to-do list.
2 Do you wish you *don't give* / *hadn't given* in to your cravings?
3 The children wish they *could stay* / *stayed* up late to watch the movie.
4 I wish I *have* / *had* more money to spend on clothes.
5 Kate wishes her husband *is* / *were* more focused on his career.
6 They wish they *didn't live* / *couldn't live* near a noisy shopping mall.
7 Jared *wishes* / *hopes* he could take a vacation.
8 I wish you *didn't persuade* / *hadn't persuaded* me to eat this burger – it's horrible!

C Complete the sentences with the correct form of the verb in parentheses.

1 I never have enough time. I wish there ________________ (*be*) more hours in the day!
2 I hope this snack ________________ (*not* / *be*) high in salt.
3 The children are full of energy. I wish they ________________ (*not* / *eat*) so many sugary snacks!
4 My children wish I ________________ (*not* / *work*) such long hours.
5 I hope Pam ________________ (*not* / *change*) her mind!
6 Alisha wants to buy a laptop but wishes she ________________ (*know*) more about them.
7 I wish my best friend ________________ (*be*) here to help me make the right choice!
8 She ________________ (*wish*) she could give up drinking sugary drinks but says it's very difficult.

➤ Go back to page 115.

Vocabulary Hub

1.1 Seeing and hearing

Match the beginnings of the sentences (1–5) with the endings (a–e).

1 If you **spot** somebody,
2 If you **recognize** somebody,
3 If you **notice** something,
4 If you **observe** something,
5 If you **stare at** something,
a you look at it for a long time, maybe too long.
b you see him/her by chance.
c you see it for the first time.
d you watch it carefully over a long time.
e you see him/her and know who he/she is.

➤ Go back to page 5.

1.2 Languages

A Put the letters in bold in the correct order to make words about language learning.

1 Which is more important when you're speaking English? Speaking **uelcartyac** or **tnulylfe**? Why?
2 Do you know any **midosi** in English? What's your favorite?
3 Are most people in your country **nanoliomlgu** or **ialinglub**? What about in your family?
4 Can you tell where somebody is from just by listening to their **cectna**? In your language? In English?

B SPEAK Work in pairs. Ask and answer the questions in Exercise A.

➤ Go back to page 9.

2.2 Problems and solutions

Complete the advice with the correct form of the verbs in the box. Sometimes more than one answer is possible.

agree on	analyze	come up with	deal with	solve	suggest

1 If you really want to ________ a problem, you'll find a way. If you don't, you'll find an excuse.
2 If you are stuck and can't ________ a solution, go and do something different until you have some fresh ideas.
3 It is best to ________ a problem in as much detail as you can. This will make it easier to solve.
4 It is not always difficult to say what the problem is at work. The real challenge is to ________ a solution to your colleagues.
5 People frequently have different ideas about how to solve problems. In those situations, you should find a solution everyone ________.

➤ Go back to page 21.

3.1 Collocations: travel information

Complete the sentences with the correct travel collocations.

1 We are sorry to announce there are ________ on line 1, of approximately 45 minutes.
2 Let's leave really early, before rush hour, to avoid the ________.
3 Don't go that way. It's closed due to ________ – they're replacing the pavement.
4 It's always very crowded on the trains during ________, with lots of people standing for a long time.
5 Following the earlier delays, we now have ________ on all lines. All lines are running normally.
6 We're stuck in a ________ on the highway; we'll be at least half an hour late.
7 Look, they've just ________. We'll have to wait another hour now, for the next one.
8 The first ________ opened in 1863 and went from Paddington station to Farringdon Street station, in London.

➤ Go back to page 27.

3.1 Nouns ending in *-ion*

Complete the sentences with the nouns in the box.

communication connection decisions expectation expression inspiration reaction situations

1 I think ________________ between the engineer and the passengers is important when a train is delayed.
2 In my country, there has been a negative ________________ to driverless cars.
3 Environmental issues don't change the ________________ that I make about transportation.
4 I think it is important to have a ________________ with the people you see every day.
5 There are some travel ________________ that make me annoyed or angry.
6 I generally have a blank ________________ when out in public. I never smile at others.
7 I find people that can talk to strangers an ________________. I wish I were so confident.
8 When I was on vacation, the transportation system was better than my ________________.

➤ Go back to page 29.

3.2 Gradable and ungradable adjectives

Complete the sentences with the adjectives in the box.

enormous excellent filthy furious good hilarious terrible tiny

1 Your hands are absolutely ________________. Wash them before dinner.
2 ________________ work. You made no mistakes at all.
3 We had a really ________________ time on vacation. We really didn't want to come back home!
4 Don't talk to him now. He's absolutely ________________ because you lost his bike. Let him calm down first.
5 Don't go to that restaurant. The food's really ________________.
6 Charlie thought the show was absolutely ________________. He laughed from the beginning to the end.
7 The Gobi Desert is extremely large, but the Sahara Desert is ________________; it's seven times bigger!
8 Compared to Russia, the UK is absolutely ________________. Russia is 70 times bigger!

➤ Go back to page 33.

4.1 Collocations: goals and resolutions

Complete the sentences with the correct collocations.

1 He didn't stop drinking soda completely but he ________________ to two cans a week.
2 When I make a plan I stick to it. I've ________________ I made last year.
3 She finally ________________ of running for thirty minutes every day.
4 He ________________ eating sugary food three months ago and he already feels healthier.
5 He ________________ to quit eating chocolate last New Year.

➤ Go back to page 39.

4.2 Prefixes: *dis-*, *mis-*, *over-*, *re-*, *under-*

Choose the correct prefix to complete the word.

1 I ***dis*** / ***mis*** like working late and try to make sure I finish on time each day.
2 I moved out of that city because it is ***re*** / ***over*** populated. There are just too many people.
3 I didn't mean that. You ***mis*** / ***dis*** understood what I was trying to say!
4 Many people at the company feel they don't earn enough. Personally I agree that they are ***under*** / ***mis*** paid.
5 I don't think this is the best strategy. We should ***under*** / ***re*** think this.

➤ Go back to page 45.

Vocabulary Hub

5.1 Verbs of influence

A **Match the beginnings of the sentences (1–4) with the endings (a–d).**

1 My boss persuaded me ___
2 My boss made me ___
3 I told him ___
4 My friend advised me not ___

a to work on the weekend, but he refused.
b to work at home because I might feel lonely.
c to work overtime by offering me some extra money.
d apologize to the customer for being rude.

B **Match the beginnings of the sentences (1–4) with the endings (a–d).**

1 Our company lets us ___
2 I want my boss ___
3 My colleague encouraged me ___
4 My company allows us ___

a to use our personal social media at work.
b to apply for the job, and now I'm her boss!
c to go on vacation forever. I can't stand him.
d leave early on Fridays.

➤ Go back to page 53.

5.2 Business collocations

Which noun cannot be used to complete each sentence?

1 Over the last few years, the company has built its … very successfully.
a brand b reputation c customers

2 Recently, we have done a lot of … overseas.
a money b deals c business

3 The … was launched at the end of last year.
a reputation b product c campaign

4 The sales team are very good at making …
a business. b money. c a profit.

5 The media attention has helped us to attract new …
a customers. b investors. c expenses.

➤ Go back to page 57.

6.2 Hobbies and free time activities

Complete the texts with the verb phrases in the box.

collect escape from daily stress get you out of the house is a fan is into is relaxing isn't my thing joined a society keeps you in shape lost interest in took up

My brother [1] ______________ soccer. He [2] ______________ of Liverpool Football Club and he goes to almost all their games. To be honest, soccer [3] ______________, so I've only been to one game with him. I like to [4] ______________ stamps. I've recently [5] ______________ for that, and I'm going to my first meeting with the other members now. Who says stamp collecting doesn't [6] ______________?!

Last year, I [7] ______________ sailing as a hobby. I live in the city, and sailing is a great way to [8] ______________. Being out on the lake with the wind in your hair [9] ______________, and it [10] ______________ too because you have to do a lot of physical work. I used to go to the gym, but I soon [11] ______________ that. The running machines were too boring!

➤ Go back to page 66.

7.1 Phrasal verbs

Work in pairs. Match the underlined phrasal verbs (1–9) with the definitions (a–i) .

1 I can't figure out what ingredients you've used here. What are they?

2 A: 'Maybe I'll start studying for my exams next week …'
B: 'Don't put it off! Start today!'

3 We've eaten out every night this week. Let's stay in this evening and cook some food at home.

4 Sorry to let you down, but I can't come to your party.

5 I asked everybody to be quiet for a few minutes, but most people just kept on talking.

6 Can you turn the oven down to 150°C in ten minutes? If you leave it at 220°C for too long, the food will burn.

7 I don't mind cooking, but can you clean up afterward?

8 Can you put your phone away, please! It's really rude to check your messages while we're eating dinner!

9 Great job! Keep up the good work!

a continue without stopping

b take something that's in the wrong place and put it in the right place

c continue at the same high level

d make everything clean and neat again after making a mess

e not go out

f find the answer by thinking carefully

g decide to do something later, not now

h make something lower/colder/quieter

i make somebody feel sad because you don't do something that you promised to do

➤ Go back to page 75.

7.1 Adjectives to describe food

A Complete the sentences with the adjectives in the box.

delicious disgusting filling mild savory sour

1 Our bakery sells a mix of sweet products, like cakes and fruit pies, and ______________ products, like bread and meat pies.

2 Do you prefer strong flavors or ______________ flavors?

3 Mmm … I love this meal. It's absolutely ______________!

4 I love ______________ food like lemons, grapefruit and pickled cabbage.

5 Ugh! How long has this milk been in the fridge? Two weeks? It tastes ______________!

6 This meal is great but it's very ______________ – I feel completely full already.

B Label the pictures with the adjectives in the box.

bitter raw rich spicy

1

2

______________ ______________

3

4

______________ ______________

➤ Go back to page 76.

8.2 Positive adjectives

Choose the best adjectives to complete the sentences.

1 A: My dog pressed six buttons in the right order!
B: That's so ***unique*** / ***impressive***!

2 I just want an umbrella that's ***incredible*** / ***practical*** – if it keeps me dry, I'm happy.

3 I read a ***fascinating*** / ***gorgeous*** article about the dangers of technology.

4 The party was ***sensible*** / ***unforgettable*** – I'll remember it for the rest of my life.

5 It's ***unique*** / ***incredible*** that people waste so much money on stupid gadgets!

6 It looks like a normal umbrella, but it contains very ***sophisticated*** / ***gorgeous*** electronics.

7 The CleverPet is ***sophisticated*** / ***suitable*** for small pets, like cats and dogs, but not large animals, like horses.

8 A: I lost my Oombrella. I forgot to take my phone with me.
B: Well, that wasn't very ***sensible*** / ***unique***, was it?

➤ Go back to page 90.

Vocabulary Hub

9.1 Verbal idioms

A Complete the sentences with the underlined verbal idioms in *The best (and the worst) of immersive theater.*

1. I can't really **tell** ________ ________ ________ immersive theater and interactive theater. Aren't they the same?
2. I tried to tell a joke, but it **fell** ________. Nobody understood it.
3. If you agree to help people all the time, they might **take** ________ ________ your kindness. You need to say 'no' more often.
4. Do you still have your old guitar, or did you **get** ________ ________ it?
5. Immersive plays usually **take** ________ in unusual locations.
6. They have a nice big yard, but they don't really **make** ________ ________ it.
7. Six actors **took** ________ ________ the play: four adults and two children.
8. I always write down the money I spend to help me **keep** ________ ________ my finances.
9. Everything is **going** ________ today! My computer stopped working and my car broke down!
10. If you don't **pay** ________ ________ your teacher, you won't learn very much.

B Complete the verbal idioms with the words in the box.

attention friends fun note sure true

1. I've always dreamed of being a chef, but I'm not sure my dream will ever **come** ________.
2. You shouldn't **make** ________ **of** other people's mistakes. They aren't funny at all.
3. When someone gives you good advice, always **take** ________ **of** what they say.
4. I **made** ________ **with** Alissa when we were at school, and we've liked each other ever since.
5. I didn't notice the sculpture in the corner. They should put it in the middle of the room to **draw** ________ **to** it!
6. I think I know the answer, but I need to check the internet to **make** ________.

➤ Go back to page 101.

10.2 Reflexive verbs

Complete the sentences with the correct reflexive pronouns. What do you think the reflexive verbs mean?

1. Can you all please behave ________! You're making too much noise!
2. Daisy bought ________ a box of chocolates this morning and ate every single one!
3. Where do you see ________ ten years from now, Hannah? Will you still be doing the same job?
4. Many people find it difficult to express ________ when they're speaking a foreign language. They know what they want to say, but they can't say it.
5. Look at that dog! It's having a good time playing in the water! It's really enjoying ________!
6. I want to do some exercise every day, but I don't trust ________. I'll probably give up after a week!
7. I need to go out for half an hour. Can you all amuse ________ while I'm gone?

➤ Go back to page 115.

Communication Hub

4.1 Students A and B

The top ten most common New Year's resolutions (in descending order):

1 change the food you eat
2 get organized
3 spend less, save more
4 enjoy life to the fullest
5 get in shape and get healthy
6 learn something exciting
7 quit unhealthy habits
8 help others achieve their dreams
9 fall in love
10 spend more time with family

➤ Go back to page 38.

5.1 Student B

A Take the quiz. Choose the answer that is most true for you.

1 When you get a new piece of picture editing software or an app, do you
- **a** just use the basic functions?
- **b** teach yourself how to use all of its functions?
- **c** ask a friend to show you how to use it?

2 When your teacher suddenly tells you that you are going to do an important speaking test in the next lesson, do you
- **a** get nervous and make extra mistakes?
- **b** enjoy the challenge and do your best?
- **c** say it is not fair and ask to do the test the next day?

3 When you disagree with someone's suggestion, do you usually
- **a** say nothing?
- **b** explain your opinion clearly, and listen carefully to their views?
- **c** tell them directly that it is a bad idea?

4 If you are brainstorming ideas in a group, do you suggest
- **a** similar ideas to other people?
- **b** many, and usually different, ideas?
- **c** very little?

B Ask your partner the questions and take note of his/her answers. Then answer his/her questions.

C Go to page 149 to find out your score and what it means!

➤ Go back to page 50.

9.2 Student A

➤ Go back to page 105.

4.1 Student A

You can only see your side of the conversation. Read through your lines, and practice your intonation. Role-play the conversation with your partner. You will start the conversation. Listen carefully in order to speak at the right time.

A: Hi, [name].

B: ______________________________

A: Oh! Oops! I'll do it now. Hold on. There we go.

B: ______________________________

A: And happy New Year to you!

B: ______________________________

A: Great. We had a good time on New Year's Eve.

B: ______________________________

A: That sounds amazing!

B: ______________________________

A: Oh! I bet it was freezing, too. I'm glad I was at a party.

B: ______________________________

A: Is that one of your New Year's resolutions?

B: ______________________________

A: You haven't? I've made several.

B: ______________________________

A: Well, I've decided to get in better shape this year, so I'm going to join a gym. Also, I'm going to study English more seriously.

B: ______________________________

A: Well, not good enough. In fact, I'm meeting a new teacher on Thursday, for private lessons.

B: ______________________________

A: Well, there's no point in putting things off. What about your chocolate habit?

B: ______________________________

A: You eat some every day, don't you?

B: ______________________________

➤ Go back to page 39.

2.1 Student A

Has your partner done these things? If he/she has, find out more details.

- go surfing
- climb a tree
- hold a snake
- relax in a natural hot spring
- take a bike riding vacation
- bake some bread
- give blood
- see a lion in the wild
- stay in an ice hotel
- learn to fly a plane

➤ Go back to page 15.

2.2 Personality test scores

In general, the higher your score in this test, the better your attitude toward challenging situations and the better your problem-solving skills. The highest possible score is 30.

A low score for a question shows an area to consider improving in order to become a truly effective problem solver.

Questions 1–3 reveal your attitude toward problems.

Questions 4–6 reveal your problem-solving skills.

➤ Go back to page 21.

4.2 Students A and B

1 **a** I'll make a lot of money.
  b I make a lot of money.

2 **a** You have many friends at college.
  b You'll have many friends at college.

3 **a** She'll shut the window because she hates the cold.
  b She shut the window because she hates the cold.

4 **a** He put solar panels on his roof.
  b He'll put solar panels on his roof.

5 **a** They use cell phones in English classes.
  b They'll use cell phones in English classes.

➤ Go back to page 43.

3.1 Students A and B

SPEAK Work in pairs. Put the pictures in the correct order and use them to retell the two stories.

Junko's story

Alan's story

➤ Go back to page 27.

1.2 Student A

A **SPEAK** Work in pairs. Ask and answer questions to complete the information about the percentage of people with English as a first language in different countries around the world.

Percentage of people with English as a first language	
....	93 percent
UK	92 percent
New Zealand	.... percent
US	79 percent
....	57 percent
Singapore	37 percent
Jamaica	.... percent
South Africa	9.3 percent
Sierra Leone	.... percent
Pakistan	8 percent

*Where **do** 93 percent of people **speak** English as a first language?*
*How many people in New Zealand **speak** English as a first language?*

B **SPEAK** Work in pairs. Are you surprised by any of the information?

➤ Go back to page 7.

5.1 Student A and B

Score 2 points for every time you chose answer b. Score nothing for all other answers.

6–8: You have a very good set of general skills and qualities for employment. Reflect on which are stronger than others, and look for jobs that use your clear strengths. What other employability skills do you have? Can you improve them?

2–5: You have some key skills that are important to employers, but there is room for improvement. Identify those skills, and find out what employers are looking for in those areas. What improvements could you make?

0–1: Employers want people to use their skills in certain ways in the workplace. Learn more about employability skills, and find opportunities to practice, for example group projects or leadership roles. Which skills could you focus on first?

➤ Go back to page 50.

4.1 Student A

A Make a resolution for each of these topics:

- studying English
- money
- food and diet
- house and home

B Tell your partner about your resolutions and why you have made them.

C Ask your partner to make resolutions for these topics.

D Make resolutions for your partner's topics.

➤ Go back to page 39.

1.2 Student B

A SPEAK Work in pairs. Ask and answer questions to complete the information about the percentage of people with English as a first language in different countries around the world.

Percentage of people with English as a first language	
Ireland	93 percent
UK	________ percent
New Zealand	86 percent
________	79 percent
Canada	57 percent
________	37 percent
Jamaica	17 percent
South Africa	________ percent
Sierra Leone	8.5 percent
Pakistan	________ percent

*How many people in the UK **speak** English as a first language?*
*Where **do** 79 percent of people **speak** English as a first language?*

B SPEAK Work in pairs. Are you surprised by any of the information?

➤ Go back to page 7.

10.1 Students A and B

Take the quiz.

Psychology quiz

1 **a** Do we have more than 70 thoughts per day or fewer than 70?
b How many thoughts do we have each day?

2 You have paid for a weekend break in an expensive hotel. On the morning of your long journey, you feel sick and you just want to stay in bed. But it's too late to cancel your trip and get your money back. What do you do?

3 You're choosing a language school to help you pass an important exam. You know that 75 percent of School A's students passed the exam last year. You also know that 20 percent of School B's students failed the exam. Which school sounds better?

➤ Go back to page 110.

4.1 Student B

A Make a resolution for each of these topics.

- work or study
- family and friends
- physical fitness
- the internet and digital media

B Tell your partner about your resolutions and why you have made them.

C Ask your partner to make resolutions for these topics.

D Make resolutions for your partner's topics.

➤ Go back to page 39.

6.2 Student A

Look at the table. Do you currently do these things? Complete the table so it is true for you. Then ask your partner questions and write down his/her answers.

	You		Your partner		
Activities	Yes/No?	How long?	Yes/No?	How long?	Other details
Use an app to study English					
Follow a celebrity on social media					
Regularly go to a favorite café					
Play a sport					
Collect something					
States					
Be a member of an online-only group					
Know someone from another country					
Have a desktop computer					
Have a car					

➤ Go back to page 67.

8.3 Student B

Use the pictures and notes to write instructions for making a paper heart. Use sequencing phrases. Then read out your instructions so that Student A can make a paper heart.

How to make a heart

You will need a square piece of paper.

Fold the piece of paper in half both ways, and unfold it so that you see the fold marks.

Turn the piece of paper around so that the point is at the top, and fold the top corner down to the middle.

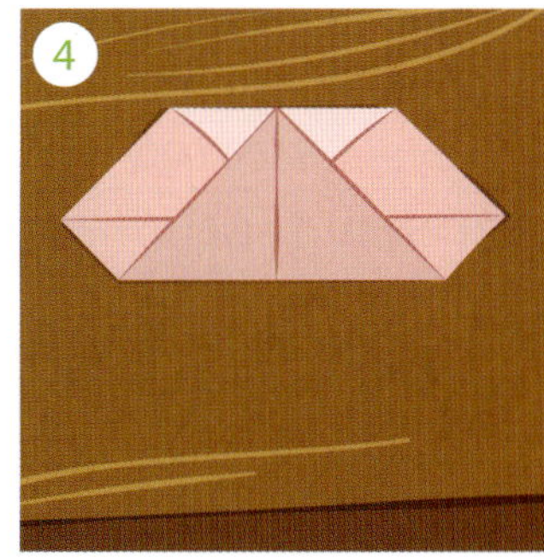

Fold the bottom corner to the top.

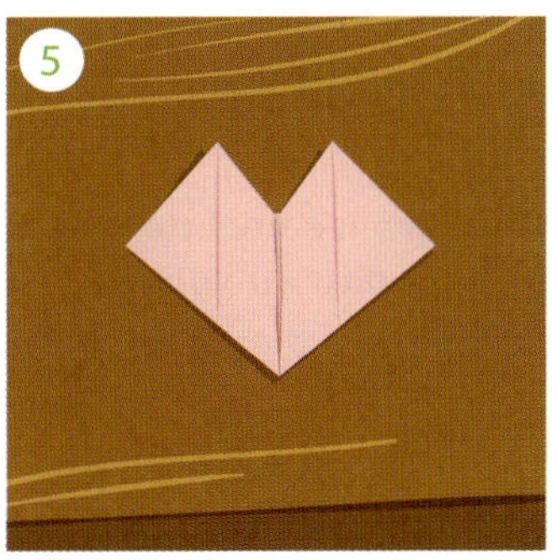

Fold the bottom edges to the middle.

Turn the paper over and fold the two top corners down.

Fold the corners down on both sides.

The heart is ready.

➤ Go back to page 95.

3.2 Students

The local mayor has decided to cancel the city's Car-Free Day. She wants a new project and campaign to reduce the traffic problems and pollution. Read the proposals.

TRANSPORTATION PROPOSALS

1 Reduce your car use!

Encourage people to leave their car at home. Run a media publicity campaign to promote:

- shopping locally, not using out-of-town grocery stores.
- walking or biking for short trips.
- working from home.
- setting up a city council app for car-sharing on common trip.
- increasing city center car parking fees.

2 Go electric!

Encourage the purchase and use of electric cars:

- Install car-charging points around the city.
- Provide cheap loans for the purchase of electric cars.
- Allow free parking for electric cars.

3 A wheely good future!

Encourage biking:

- Run a media publicity campaign to promote riding your bike to work.
- Introduce a city bike rental system.
- Hold 'Bike Fun Days' in local park.

➤ Go back to page 33.

Communication Hub

9.1 Student B

Proposal 2: Immersive theater

Costs (= money going out)		Income (= money coming in)
Building work: $100,000	Marketing: $150,000/year	Ticket sales: $1,500,000/year
Equipment: $150,000	Other costs (e.g. electricity): $150,000/year	Sponsorship: $500,000/year
Employees: $500,000/year		

- Sponsorship: Companies pay for their names/logos to be in the theater, on posters, etc.
- Ticket prices: $50–$100
- 80–100 tickets/performance; 400 performances/year (evenings and weekends only)
- No plans to help the community (e.g. free tickets for schools)

➤ Go back to page 99.

5.1 Student A

A Take the quiz. Choose the answer that is most true for you.

1 When two friends are arguing about what to do on the weekend, do you
- **a** ignore them until they finish?
- **b** calm them down and help them decide?
- **c** tell them to stop and make the decision for them?

2 When you have many things to do next week, do you
- **a** start doing them this week and see how many you can finish?
- **b** make a plan before starting?
- **c** do nothing at first and then rush to do them late next week?

3 When you work on a group project, do you
- **a** focus on your personal tasks?
- **b** do your tasks and support others with theirs?
- **c** do little, and let others do a lot?

4 When you borrow a little money from someone and say you will return it the next day, do you
- **a** pay it back a few days later?
- **b** pay it back the next day?
- **c** need reminding to pay it back.

B Ask your partner the questions and take note of his/her answers. Then answer his/her questions.

C Go to **page 149** to find out your score and what it means!

➤ Go back to page 50.

5.2 Students

Basic information

Country: Finland
Business name: Arctic Diamond
Slogan: 'Luxury chilling'
Founded by: Mika Hakala
Products: Ice cubes from the Arctic
Price: $50 for 100 grams

Production process

collected by hand / packed in freezer boxes / delivered by air and courier

Sales

Online business: 15 orders in first two weeks / $20,000 in first year of business
Current customers: European restaurants and bars, hotels in Abu Dhabi and Dubai
Future markets: China, United States

Arctic Diamond

➤ Go back to page 55.

4.1 Student B

You can only see your side of the conversation. Read through your lines, and practice your intonation. Role-play the conversation with your partner. Listen carefully in order to speak at the right time. Your partner will start the conversation.

A: ______________________________

B: Hi, [name]. I can't see you – I don't think you've clicked the video button.

A: ______________________________

B: That's better. Good to see you. Happy New Year!

A: ______________________________

B: How's everything going in Spain?

A: ______________________________

B: Well, lucky you! We went to see the fireworks.

A: ______________________________

B: Yeah, it was great! Mind you, it was a long wait. We got there at nine.

A: ______________________________

B: Yeah! Lucky you. I didn't have a hat or anything. In fact, I'm going to look for one tomorrow.

A: ______________________________

B: Actually, I haven't made any resolutions yet.

A: ______________________________

B: Really? What have you decided?

A: ______________________________

B: That's a surprise! I always thought your English was really good.

A: ______________________________

B: Really? That's quick!

A: ______________________________

B: My chocolate habit? What do you mean?

A: ______________________________

B: Well, just a little.

➤ Go back to page 39.

5.2 Student B

Company:	H&M stores, Sweden and worldwide
Retail sector:	Fashion clothing
Environmental idea:	Customers hand in their old clothes (even ones they didn't buy at H&M). The company either sells them as second-hand clothes from, or turns them into other clothing items.
Reason:	To stop old clothes from going to waste.
Result:	In a four-year period, the company received more than 40,000 metric tons of clothing items (enough material to make 150 million T-shirts).

➤ Go back to page 57.

2.1 Student B

Has your partner done these things? If he/she has, find out more details.

- go sailing
- climb a mountain
- hold a monkey
- relax on a beach all day
- take a camping vacation
- bake a cake
- give someone flowers
- see a tiger in the wild
- stay in an underwater hotel
- learn to drive

➤ Go back to page 15.

7.2 Students A and B

1 **a** about a week
b 8–10 months
c 4–5 days
d 18–24 months
e about 3 days
f about 2 days

2 **a** False. You should only reheat food once.
b True. After the best if used by date, the food may lose some taste or color, but it's probably still safe to eat for a little longer.
c True. Rice sometimes contains very strong bacteria which aren't killed by cooking. So after cooking, put any leftover rice in the fridge and eat within 24 hours.

➤ Go back to page 80.

9.1 Student C

Proposal 3: Modern art gallery

Costs (= money going out)	Income (= money coming in)
Building work and equipment: $150,000	Gift shop and snack bar: $150,000/year Sales of paintings, etc: $200,000–$500,000/year
Employees: $150,000/year	
Marketing: $50,000/year	
Other costs (e.g. electricity): $100,000/year	

- Two major exhibits each year (international artists, etc.)
- Smaller exhibits each month (local artists, etc.)
- Free entry for all people to all exhibits
- The gallery will take 40 percent of the sale price of any paintings (e.g. by local artists) that it sells.

➤ Go back to page 99.

3.1 Students

A Look at the list of annoying behavior on public transportation. Number them in order of how annoying they are (1 = most annoying, 9 = least annoying). Think about the reasons for your choices.

___ people talking loudly on the phone
___ people playing loud music and not using headphones
___ people walking too slowly
___ people eating takeout food
___ people not lining up or not waiting their turn to board
___ people leaving trash behind
___ people not giving up their seats to people who need them
___ people coughing and sneezing because of a cold
___ people trying to talk to me

➤ Go back to page 29.

9.2 Student B

➤ Go back to page 105.

6.2 Student B

Look at the table. Do you currently do these things? Complete the table so it is true for you. Then ask your partner questions and write a note of his/her answers.

	You		Your partner		
Activities	Yes/No?	How long?	Yes/No?	How long?	Other details
Use an app to order food					
Write a blog					
Regularly go to a favorite movie theater					
Play a musical instrument					
Work for a company					
States					
Be a member of a club or society					
Know someone famous					
Have a laptop computer					
Have a pet					

➤ Go back to page 67.

8.3 Student A

Use the pictures and notes to write instructions for making a paper airplane. Use sequencing phrases. Then read out your instructions so that Student B can make a paper airplane.

How to make a paper airplane

Put a piece of paper on the table.

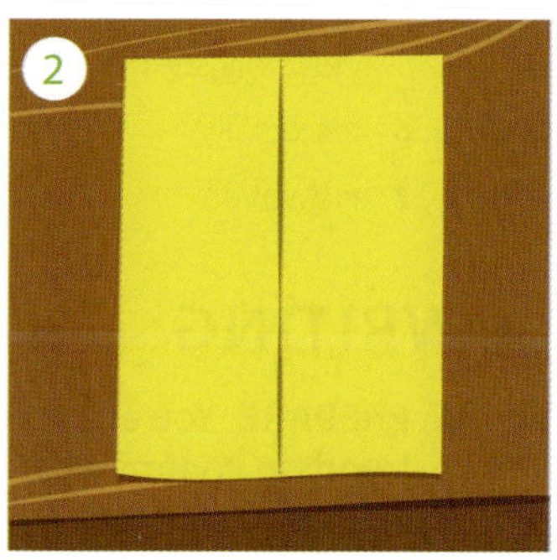

Fold the piece of paper in half lengthways, then unfold it.

Smooth it down.

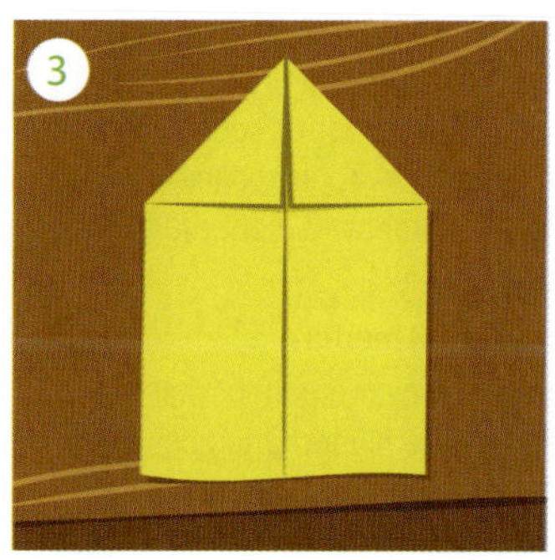

Form a point at the top of the paper.

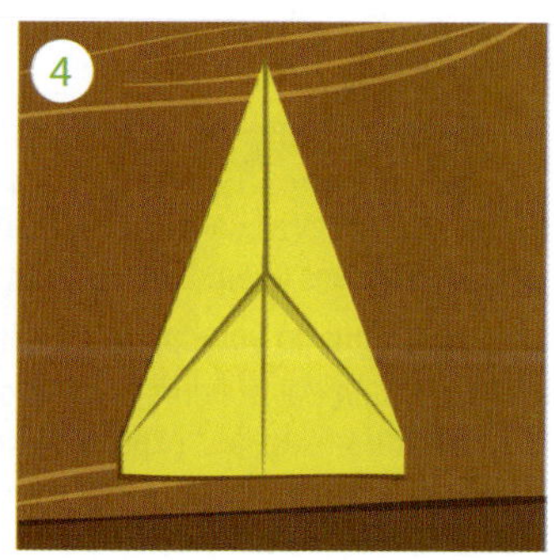

Fold the edges again.

Smooth down the edges with a ruler.

Fold the right side of the paper over the left side.

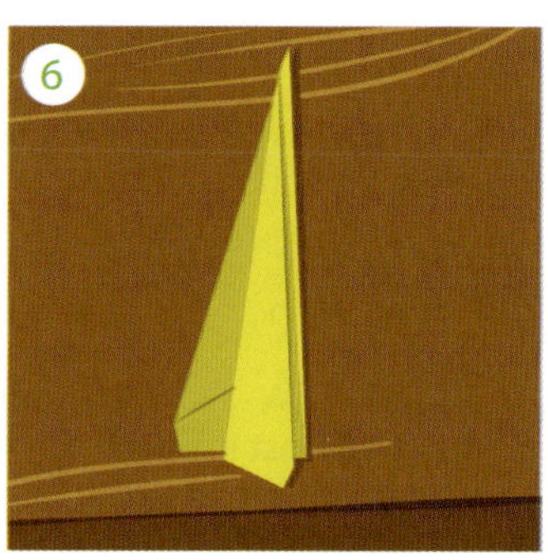

Create the wings.

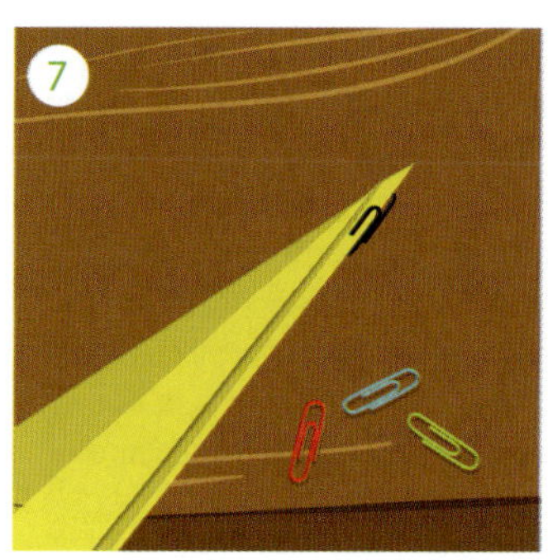

Attach a paperclip to the nose of the airplane – it will make it fly better.

Unfold the wings and you're ready for takeoff.

➤ Go back to page 95.

1 Writing — Write a report about trends

W — using formal language in reports

A Work in groups of three. Discuss the questions and complete the *Me, Partner 1* and *Partner 2* columns in the table.

1 How much time do you spend doing each activity in the table each week?

2 Are you spending more (↑), less (↓) or the same (↔) time on each activity at the moment, compared to last year?

	Me hours	Partner 1 hours	Partner 2 hours	Average hours
checking social media				
sending instant messages				
studying online				

B Now figure out the average number of hours spent doing each activity. Are people spending more or less time on each activity compared to last year? Complete the *Average* column of the table in Exercise A.

C Read the *Report about online trends* and answer the questions.

1 What trends did the writer find? Did you find the same trends?

2 What was different?

3 What is the writer's main prediction for the future?

Report about online trends

[1]These days, online communication is more and more important in our daily lives. [2]But are we actually spending more time online? [3]This report examines the number of hours that people spend on various online activities and explores some recent trends. [4]I interviewed eight members of my English class about their online habits.

How much time do you spend checking social media?

The average number of hours in my group is just over one hour per day. This is surprising, as I expected the total to be higher. One possible reason is that several popular social media sites are showing more advertisements these days.

How much time do you spend sending instant messages?

The average number of hours here is approximately 1.5 hours per day. Almost everybody said that this number is increasing for them. It seems that many people are using instant messaging services for conversations that they had on social media before.

How much time do you spend studying online?

The average number of hours here was 4.3 per week. Two people in my group never study online, and this trend is not changing. Two people study online a lot: 12 and 15 hours a week. This trend is also not changing, as these people both study on long-term courses. However, the other three people's answers were especially interesting: they all spend two to three hours a week studying, but this is increasing very fast, from zero last year. They all use language learning apps to study for pleasure.

Conclusion

There certainly seems to be a trend away from social media and towards messaging apps. However, the main trend I noticed is the increase in online studying, especially the use of language apps. I expect this trend to continue into the future.

D Look at the introduction to the *Report about online trends*. Match the sentences (1–4) with the descriptions (a–d).

a Explain where you got your information, e.g. *Who did you ask?*

b Ask a rhetorical question to make the reader think about the topic.

c Present your reason for writing the report: what does the report do?

d Start by introducing the general topic of your report.

E Look at the box and complete the tips about using formal language in reports. Then find examples of each tip in the report.

Using formal language in reports

We ***use / don't use*** contractions (e.g. *there's, isn't*).

In general, most sentences are fairly ***long / short***.

Most sentences have ***a human subject, e.g. I, Two people / a non-human subject, e.g. It, This trend***.

F Match the formal phrases (1–7), which are underlined in the *Report about online trends,* with the less formal phrases (a–g).

1 This report examines ...
2 various
3 One possible reason is that ...
4 approximately
5 It seems that ... / There certainly seems to be ...
6 especially
7 However, ...

a but
b more or less
c Maybe this is because ...
d In this report, I look at ...
e I think ...
f a few different
g very

WRITING

A PREPARE You are going to write a report about current trends in communication. What trends do you notice? You can use the ideas in Exercise A or your own ideas.

B PLAN Choose two or three points to include in your report. These will be your main paragraphs.

C WRITE Write your report (150–200 words). Remember:

- to start with an introduction.
- when you present numbers, show what they mean and how they're connected together.
- to use formal language.
- to end with a conclusion.

D REVIEW Work in groups. Share your reports. Who found the most interesting information? Were you surprised by any of the trends he/she found?

2 Writing

Write an informal email

W informal writing

A SPEAK Work in pairs. Read the email from Sophie to Marta. What is their relationship?

a family members **c** elementary school friends
b new friends **d** business colleagues

To: Marta
Subject: Hello and good news

Hi Marta,

How are you? I hope everything has been OK since you left New York. Did you have a good vacation with your family? I guess you're back at college now. Studying or partying hard? [1]___ 🙂.

Sorry I haven't written sooner – I can't believe it's been two months since our course finished! I really miss New York. My English really improved, and I loved getting to know you, Sato and the others. [2]___

Anyway, I have some good news! I have a new job and I've moved to Paris. I'm working for a web design agency. I'm so happy. It's only a small company, but everyone's really nice and [3]___

So, how about coming to Paris to visit me? Would you like to? I remember that you haven't been to Paris before, so now's your chance. Come for a weekend and stay at my place – it's easy to get here from Rome! What do you think? [4]___

Let me know what you think, and let me know when you finally get on Facebook – [5]___

Hugs and all the best.

Sophie

B Read again. Answer the questions.

1 Where did Sophie and Marta meet each other?
2 When did they last see each other?
3 Where do they live?
4 How has Sophie's life changed recently?
5 What does Sophie want Marta to do?

C Complete Sophie's email with the sentences (a–e).

a I'm enjoying the work.
b Or both?
c Have you heard from anyone else from our class?
d I can't believe you haven't done that yet!
e I'd love to see you.

D Put the sections in the order they appear in Sophie's email.

telling Marta about what she has done recently ___
making a suggestion/plan for the future ___
asking about Marta's life ___
talking about a shared experience ___

E Look at the box. Find and underline features of informal writing in the sentences (1–4).

Informal writing

In emails and letters to friends and family, we usually use an informal writing style. We use:

- contractions, such as *You'll …*
- incomplete grammar, such as *How you doing?*
- informal words and phrases, such as *buddy* (= *friend*).
- informal punctuation, such as *!*, *–*.
- emojis/emoticons, such as 🙂.
- informal opening and closing expressions, such as *Hi*, *Hugs*.

1 I'm going on vacation soon – can't wait!
2 I've just passed my driving test 🙂.
3 All fine here. It's great to be back at college!
4 Big hug and say hi to your mom.

WRITING

A PREPARE You are going to write an informal email to a friend. Think of a friend you want to write to or imagine you are writing to a new friend.

B PLAN Write notes. Think about:

- What can you ask your friend about?
- What shared experience can you write about?
- What news do you have? What have you done recently?
- What suggestion or request can you make?

C WRITE Write your email (150–200 words). Use Sophie's email and the skills box to help you.

D REVIEW Work in pairs. Read your partner's email. Ask for more information about his/her news.

3 Writing

Write an email of complaint

W using adverbs to give emphasis

A Work in pairs. Add to the list of common causes of complaint for travelers.

- trash on buses and trains
- poor quality in-flight entertainment
- a lack of space
- delays due to technical problems

B Work in pairs. Have you experienced any of the problems you wrote down in Exercise A? Did you make a complaint? Why/Why not?

C Read Asaf King's email of complaint. Are the sentences true (T) or false (F)? Correct the false sentences.

1 When he made the reservation, Asaf paid more money to guarantee his seat. ___
2 Asaf went quickly to check-in because he didn't have much time left. ___
3 There were no seats available on the flight to London. ___
4 Asaf was not able to travel to Bangkok. ___
5 Asaf did not tell the airline staff about his seat reservation. ___
6 He wants the airline to give his money back and to pay extra for his problems. ___

To: LuxAir Customer Services
Subject: A serious complaint:
Reservation Reference No. 589RT

Dear Sir or Madam,

a I am writing to complain about the mistakes your airline made with my reservation that meant I missed two flights and lost important business.

b On April 17, I made a reservation with your airline for flight Y33 from Dublin to London on May 23. I also paid extra to reserve my seat.

c I arrived at Dublin airport two hours before the flight and immediately went to the check-in desks. Since I had arrived early, I certainly wasn't expecting any problems, but sadly this was not the case. At check-in, I was told that the flight had been overbooked and was completely full, which meant I couldn't board the plane.

d This was extremely disappointing and incredibly inconvenient because it meant that I also missed my connecting flight, an international departure from London to Bangkok. The new flight to Bangkok cost me $500, and I missed an important meeting.

e The simple fact is that I had paid in advance to confirm my reservation, but you failed to hold my seat. I found your customer service at the airport completely unsatisfactory as your staff totally ignored my seat reservation.

f Because of the extra flight costs, my lost time and the effect on my business, I would like to ask for a full refund for my flight and for additional compensation.

I hope to hear from you soon regarding this matter.

Kind regards,

Asaf King

D Match the descriptions (1–6) with the paragraphs (a–f) in Asaf's email.

1 a detailed description of the main events ___
2 the reason why you are writing the email ___
3 the result you want from your email ___
4 the key dates and places ___
5 a summary of the main complaint ___
6 the effects of the event and problems it caused ___

E Look at the box. Then match the adverbs (1–3) with those that have a similar meaning (a–c). Use the email to help you.

Using adverbs to give emphasis

In the email, the writer uses adverbs to make a word stronger. An adverb usually goes before the adjective or verb that it describes.

- *The flight ... was* ***completely*** *full.*
- *This was* ***extremely*** *disappointing.*

1 certainly	a incredibly
2 extremely	b totally
3 completely	c definitely

WRITING

A PREPARE Choose one of the situations to write an email about.

- Your recent flight was terrible.
- A member of staff gave you the wrong information.
- You experienced a long travel delay.

B PLAN Write detailed notes about what happened. Think about:

- where and when did it happen?
- what result do you want?

C WRITE Write a semi-formal email of complaint (150–250 words).

- Use Asaf's email and Exercise D to help you.
- Use adverbs to explain your problem.

W using linking words to introduce reasons and consequences

A Read the advertisement for a competition. What can you win? How can you win it?

Happy New Year with Digital Express and Tinto Phones

Enter our New Year competition and win a TINTO X cell phone.

Digital technology has already changed our lives in many ways, and this is going to continue in the future. We want to know how you think digital technology is going to change our lives over the next 20 years.

Write a short essay describing a change that digital technology will bring to our lives, explaining why this will happen and any consequences it will have.

The five winning entries will be published online.

B Read a competition essay entry. Put the paragraphs (a–d) in the correct order (1–4).

1 introduction (what the writer thinks the change will be) ___
2 reason 1 ___
3 reason 2 ___
4 conclusion ___

a Digital technology supports a sharing economy, and that means people will not need to buy so many things. Owning a car will not be necessary **as** you will simply use an app to book a driverless car when you need one. People will share things like bicycles and gardening equipment within their local community by using an app to find what they need. **As a result**, people will own fewer things, but they will have more contact with other people.

b People are always buying things **because** they want to get the latest products. However, in the future, people will probably buy fewer things **because of** the development of digital technology.

c To sum up, digital technology will definitely continue to change our lives, and one of those changes will be that we won't need to own so much stuff.

d In the past, new inventions brought many products into our houses, but digital technology usually replaces these things with a single device. For example, your cell phone can now be your television, radio, music player and alarm clock. In the future, children may play all their games on a phone or tablet, **and so** traditional board games will disappear. **Consequently**, people will have less stuff in their house, although they will spend a lot on digital services.

C SPEAK Work in pairs. Read again and discuss the questions.

1 What two reasons are given for why people will own fewer things?
2 How many examples illustrate each reason?
3 What other things will happen?
4 What do you think of the predictions?

D Look at the linking words in bold in the essay. Write them in the correct column.

Introduce a reason	Introduce a consequence
because	

E Look again at the linking words in bold in the essay. Write them in the correct place in the box. Use each of them twice.

Using linking words to introduce reasons and consequences

We use linking words and phrases to show the relationship between information and ideas.

1 Some linking words connect ideas inside one sentence. For example, ___*because*___, ________, ________, ________.

2 Some connect ideas across two sentences. For example, ________, ________.

3 Some linking words are followed by a clause (subject + verb). For example, ________, ________, ________, ________, ________.

4 Others are followed by noun phrases (such as the increase in pollution). For example, ________.

F SPEAK Work in pairs. Complete the sentences with your own ideas. Then compare your answers with a partner.

1 All cars should be electric because …
2 Children are using social media. As a result, …
3 Every year, more people are only paying for things electronically. Consequently, …
4 Cities are unhealthy places to live because of …
5 People are watching less TV as …
6 Online shopping continues to increase, and so …

WRITING

A PLAN Make a prediction about how digital technology will change the future. Think of the reasons why this change will happen and any consequences it will have.

B WRITE Write your competition entry (150–200 words).

C REVIEW Work in groups. Read and discuss your essays. Have a vote to decide on the two winning entries.

5 Writing — Write a cover letter for a job application

W— paragraph structure

A Read the job advertisement. Is it the type of work you are interested in? Why/Why not?

> **Events Team Assistant (Ref: 783G)**
> **ICE: International Charity Events**
> This is an exciting opportunity to join our lively and dynamic Events Team. We organize and promote fundraising events and programs for charities across Europe. Typical events include sports, cultural events and adventure challenges and tours.
> **Essential requirements:**
> - excellent organizational, communication and marketing skills
> - a great team player
> - good digital technology skills
> - able to meet deadlines
>
> **Desired experience:**
> - experience of working internationally
>
> To apply, email a cover letter and résumé to Marta Safin: M.Safin@ice.nett

B Read Peter O'Malley's application. In which paragraph (1–4) does he cover each topic (a–d)?

a why he is a good candidate for this job ____
b when he is able to attend an interview ____
c why he wants to work for this company ____
d what job he is applying for and why ____

To: Ms. Safin
Subject: Events Team Assistant (Ref: 783G)

Dear Ms. Safin

1 I am writing to apply for the position of Events Team Assistant, currently advertised on Euro_Recruit.com (Ref: 783G). I have attached my résumé. I recently graduated with a degree in Marketing, and I wish to start a career in events organization.

2 The experience and skills that I gained from college make me the perfect candidate for this role. I was a member of the Student Social Committee and I was responsible for our International Food Festival. This demanded excellent organizational skills and demonstrated my ability to meet deadlines. I also improved the marketing for the event, which led to the largest ever attendance at the festival. In addition, I attended frequent meetings, which required good communication skills and the ability to work on a team.

3 Working for your company would be a great opportunity for me to begin my career. I am interested in the wide range of events that you organize and I would love the opportunity to work for an international company.

4 Thank you for considering my application. I am available for an interview at any time, and I look forward to hearing from you.

Sincerely yours,
Peter O'Malley

C Look at the advice about writing a cover letter. Find and underline examples in Peter O'Malley's cover letter.

> **Writing a cover letter**
> Write in a professional, formal style that suits a business letter. Do not use informal language such as contractions. Follow a clear structure:
> - If possible, address the letter to a named person. Use Dear Mr./Mrs. Do not use the person's first name.
> - State where you saw the job advertisement and give its reference number.
> - Show your interest in the position on offer and the company.
> - Describe the key skills and experience that you have for the role and give examples to support your claims.
> - Use standard closing sentences.

D Look at the box. Then read paragraphs 2 and 3 of the cover letter again. Identify the topic sentence and examples for each paragraph.

> **Paragraph structure**
> The paragraphs in the main body of a cover letter should focus on a single topic and be carefully organized and well structured. Always:
> - start with a topic sentence that makes a clear, relevant point.
> - support that point with examples to show how your skills and experience meet those listed in the job ad, or to show your genuine interest in the role.
> - only add extra points if they relate to the topic sentence.

WRITING

A PLAN You are going to write a cover letter for the job advertisement below. Think about:

- what language style you need to use.
- the best way to organize the letter.
- what your topic sentences will be and how you will structure each paragraph.

> **Catering Management Assistant (Ref: 812C)**
> **SCC: Superior Conference Catering**
> High quality catering for events and conferences in the southeastern United States.
> **Essential requirements:**
> - excellent organization and time management skills
> - excellent communication and team-working skills
> - strong digital technology skills
>
> **Desired experience and interests:**
> - event organization
> - food and drink
> - languages

B WRITE Write the letter (150–200 words).

C REVIEW Work in pairs. Read your partner's letter. Has he/she covered the key points in the ad and organized the letter well?

Write an article for a magazine

W– introductory clauses

A Work in pairs. Read the magazine ad. Then look at the free time activities in the box. Which three do you think would be good subjects for an article? Why?

> Share your stories with Life & *Style*.
>
> In our Free time section, we're going to publish a new series of reader's articles, called *'Why everyone should …!'*
>
> Send us your short articles about ideas for free time activities and hobbies – things that you think everyone should try doing at least once in their lifetime.

arts and crafts   playing soccer   skydiving   stamp collecting   stargazing (astronomy)   team video gaming

B Read *Why everyone should … go stargazing!*. Put the sentences (a–f) in the order they are mentioned in the article (1–6).

a It is a good way to meet people. ___
b It is a simple hobby to start. ___
c Stargazing events at night are enjoyable. ___
d Cellular digital technology is useful. ___
e There is a place to go to use good equipment. ___
f You can join a club. ___

Why everyone should … go stargazing!

Wow! That's all I can say as I look at the rings of Saturn, or see a shadow pass across the sun. I'll never regret taking up stargazing.

Besides the wonder of discovering the universe, the great thing about stargazing is that it is an easy hobby to take up. You only have to look up into the sky at night and you've already become a stargazer. The cool thing is that there are many cell phone apps to help you when you start, telling you exactly what you are looking at.

It is also easy to visit your local observatory. The wonderful thing about going there is that you can use powerful telescopes to see deep into the universe. You'll see the mountains of Mars, the moons of Jupiter and the stardust of the Milky Way.

A nice thing about stargazing is that it is actually very sociable. There are local societies all over the country, and enthusiasts frequently meet up for 'star parties'. They are like having a picnic at night and are a lot of fun. One thing to remember is that you should bring hot chocolate rather than juice – it's important to keep warm!

Everyone wants to put a little 'wow!' into their lives, and stargazing is a surprisingly simple, inexpensive and enjoyable way to do that. There's so much to discover in the universe, so isn't it time to start exploring?

C Read the tips on writing articles. Then look at the article again. Which tips did the writer follow? Give examples.

Top tips for writing a magazine article

1 In the introduction, clearly give the topic, and grab the reader's attention and interest.
2 Use a more relaxed and personal style than in a newspaper report.
3 Show your passion for the subject.
4 Give each paragraph a clear topic.
5 Use direct quotes from interviews.
6 Use humor.
7 In the conclusion, summarize the key points in the article.
8 Finish with a memorable sentence, giving the reader something to think about.

D Look at the box. Find and underline the introductory clauses in the highlighted sentences in the article.

Introductory clauses

We can begin a sentence with an introductory clause that provides, and draws attention to, the topic for the rest of the sentence.

E Work in pairs. Complete the sentences with information about a hobby, sport or activity that you do. Then compare your answers with a partner.

1 One good thing about ______________ is that ______________.
2 Something that I like about ______________ is that ______________.
3 A good reason to ______________ is that ______________.
4 One problem with ______________ is that ______________.
5 One thing to remember is that ______________.

WRITING

A PREPARE You are going to write a short magazine article. Choose a hobby, sport or free time activity as the subject of your article. Why do you think everyone should try it?

B PLAN Write notes for your article. Read the tips in Exercise C again to help.

C WRITE Write an article (150–200 words).

D REVIEW Work in groups. Read the other students' articles. Which activities would you choose to do? Why?

Write a reply in an online discussion forum

W– comparing and recommending

A Work in pairs and discuss the questions.

1 Have you ever …
   a read an online discussion forum?
   b asked a question on an online discussion forum?
   c written a reply to somebody on an online discussion forum?

2 What kind of online discussion groups are you interested in? Use the ideas in the box and your own ideas.

current affairs   financial matters   food
health and fitness   music and movies   personal matters
product reviews and recommendations   travel

3 What's good about using these websites? What's bad about them?

B Read the forum post and the three replies. Which reply offers the best advice? What is the worst advice?

Message from Jo493

Hi. We have some relatives from another country coming to stay next week. I want to take them out to eat when they arrive after their long flight. I'm not sure whether to take them to an expensive restaurant or a fast-food joint.

I've asked them which they prefer, and they say they don't mind … but maybe they're just being polite. What do you recommend?

3 Comments

Reply from Miss Orange

It depends. Expensive restaurants serve better food, but of course they're much more expensive than fast-food joints. On the other hand, I like fast food because it's a lot faster than food from a restaurant. Why don't you ask them what they want to eat? Or how about cooking a meal for them instead?

Reply from hungry_al

I strongly recommend taking them for a good meal at an expensive restaurant. It'll make them feel special and welcome, and it should make an excellent first impression on them. They might be stressed after their flight, so they might want to go somewhere quiet and relaxing. You could always take them to a fast-food joint later during their stay with you – it's a nice thing to do with somebody you already know well. But for that first meeting, an expensive restaurant is far better.

Reply from Stewpot

I think you should take them for some fast food. After a long flight, they'll be tired and hungry, so they'll want to eat as quickly as possible. Another thing to remember is that your visitors might not feel very fresh and clean after their flight, and they may not have suitable clothes for a fancy restaurant. So you'll have to take them home first so they can change their clothes … and that could take hours. It's much quicker and easier if you take them for some simple food at a fast-food joint. After all, you can always take them to your favorite restaurant the next day. Good luck!

C Read again. Which reply or replies …

1 started with a clear recommendation?
2 ended with a clear recommendation?
3 introduced a third option?
4 thought about how the visitors will feel after their trip?
5 missed some important information in the original message?
6 gave reasons to explain why their recommendation is better?
7 suggested a way of using both options?

D Look at the box. Choose *Do* or *Don't* for each rule.

Comparing and recommending

1 **Do / Don't** start with a clear recommendation. (I think you should …; I strongly recommend …)
2 **Do / Don't** say it depends. The writer is asking you for a recommendation, so don't make their decision more complicated.
3 **Do / Don't** use comparatives to show why your option is better. (It's much quicker and easier …)
4 **Do / Don't** just talk about what you prefer.
5 **Do / Don't** show that you have thought about the people in the situation. (They might be stressed after their flight, so …)
6 **Do / Don't** give reasons for your recommendation.
7 **Do / Don't** add extra suggestions.
8 **Do / Don't** end with a clear recommendation. (… is far better.)

WRITING

A PLAN Read the forum post. What are the two options? Write notes on some arguments for and against each option.

I want to organize a dinner party for about 20 people from work and their families. I like the idea of a pot luck dinner party, but I've heard they don't always work well. Maybe I should just cook all the food myself. What do you recommend?

B WRITE Which option will you recommend? Write your reply (100–150 words).

C REVIEW Work in groups. Read each other's replies. Did everyone follow all the rules in the skills box? Who wrote the best recommendation?

8 Writing — Write a biography

W — using linking words to show contrast

A SPEAK Work in pairs. Read the short biography *Sal Khan, founder of the Khan Academy*.

1 Who is Sal Khan?
2 What are the main events in his life?
3 How innovative is he? Why?

Sal Khan, founder of the Khan Academy

1 Sal Khan is one of the most innovative people in education today. The Khan Academy, which he started in 2006, makes free online videos to teach people around the world about math, science and many other things.

2 Sal was born near New Orleans, US, in 1976. After college, he found a well-paid job in finance. However, he soon realized there was more to life than money.

3 Sal's life changed in 2004, when he started giving math lessons to members of his family. To save time, he decided to record his lessons and post them on YouTube. Despite the simple quality of the videos, they soon became popular around the world. Suddenly, he was teaching millions of people and making a real difference to their lives.

4 Although Sal didn't invent video-based learning, he helped make it popular and successful. His main innovation was to give everything away for free. As a result, he can really help those people who need it.

5 Sal's story teaches us that we don't need to be an inventor to be innovative, and we don't need to be powerful to change the world. In fact, we just need to do something we love. Hopefully, we can help other people along the way.

B Read again. Are the sentences true (T) or false (F)? Correct the false sentences.

1 You can only watch the videos in the US. ____
2 Sal's first job was as a teacher. ____
3 He made videos because he wanted to be famous. ____
4 Sal was the first person to teach using YouTube videos. ____
5 The writer thinks that Sal loves his work. ____

C A good biography usually has five sections. Match the sections (1–5) with the explanations (a-e). Use the biography of Sal Khan to help you.

1 introduction
2 backstory
3 turning point
4 impact
5 conclusion

a the story of the person's early life: family, education, first jobs, etc.
b why the person is special; how they changed the world
c lessons for our own lives
d who you are writing about and that person's biggest achievements
e something happened that changed the person's life

D Look at the box. Add an example of each linking word from Sal Khan's biography.

Using linking words to show contrast

We use linking words (*although, despite, however*) to link two different or contrasting ideas, one of which is unexpected, surprising or seems to be contradictory.

although + subject + verb

- ***Although*** *Sal Khan isn't an inventor, he's very innovative.*
- *Sal Khan is very innovative,* ***although*** *he isn't an inventor.*

1 ________________________________

despite + noun

2 ________________________________

despite + (*not*) + verb + *-ing*

- ***Despite*** *not being an inventor, Sal Khan is very innovative.*

despite the fact that + subject + verb

- ***Despite the fact that*** *he isn't an inventor, Sal Khan is very innovative.*

however

- *Sal Khan isn't an inventor.* ***However,*** *he's very innovative.*
- *Sal Khan is very innovative;* ***however,*** *he isn't an inventor.*

3 ________________________________

E Complete the sentences with the correct linking words.

1 ________________ the fact that he had no experience as an engineer, he solved an extremely difficult engineering problem.
2 Nobody was interested in her ideas at first, ________________ they became a lot more popular later.
3 Her invention was gorgeous and extremely innovative. ________________, it was far too expensive at first.
4 She ended up changing the world ________________ some very serious challenges at the beginning.
5 ________________ he was only 14 at the time, he managed to win the design competition.

WRITING

A PREPARE You are going to write a short biography of a famous innovator or an innovative friend or family member.

B PLAN Use the five-section plan in Exercise C to help you.

C WRITE Write your biography (about 200 words). Try to use linking words to show contrasting ideas. Use the skills box to help you. Check your grammar and spelling.

D REVIEW Work in groups. Read the other students' biographies. Which biography is about the most innovative person?

9 Writing

Write a review

W– using colons to introduce explanations

A Look at the pictures and read the reviews. Which event was better, the exhibit or the concert?

Robert Gonsalves exhibit at the TACA

One of my favorite artists is Robert Gonsalves (1959–2017). I fell in love with his incredible paintings years ago, so I was delighted to visit an exhibit of his work last month at the Toronto Academy of Contemporary Art.

His paintings show beautiful scenes with a twist: they all show two different worlds coming together. This means you can enjoy the paintings on two levels: first as objects of beauty, and then as amazing ideas to help you see the world differently.

However, I visited the exhibit on a Saturday afternoon, when it was extremely crowded. At times, it was difficult to get close to the paintings. Also, the space felt too small for so many paintings. If there were only one painting on each wall, it would create a much more powerful impression.

Overall, I would strongly recommend the exhibit, but you should go when it is less crowded.

Mel Montuno in concert at the City Arena

Last night I attended a concert by Mel Montuno, one of today's most exciting young musicians.

I became a fan of Mel's music two years ago, when I saw her performing live for an audience of 30. Now she is an international star – she usually has audiences of 10,000!

Although Mel is still an incredible songwriter with a beautiful voice, I definitely preferred her before she was famous. Last night's concert felt 'too big': she looked uncomfortable with such a large audience and hardly interacted with her fans at all.

More seriously, the music was too loud and the lights were painfully bright. After half an hour, I had to leave, to give my ears and eyes a break!

Mel Montuno is currently on an eight-city tour of the country. If you like huge concerts, you might want to buy a ticket. But if, like me, you prefer calm, beautiful music, I recommend buying Mel's new CD, *My Jazz Age*, instead.

B Read again and answer the questions.

1. Why did the writer decide to go to the exhibit/concert?
2. What did the writer like?
3. What wasn't so good?
4. What does the writer recommend? Why?

C What is the purpose of the paragraphs in each review? How are the two reviews similar? How are they different?

D Read the advice about writing reviews. Find examples of each piece of advice in the reviews.

1. Add a personal touch to describe how you felt.
2. Include practical information.
3. Don't be too negative – write about how you would do things differently or why people might not mind the problems.
4. Avoid repeating words like *beautiful* or *amazing*. Try to include a range of words instead.
5. Always end with a clear recommendation for your readers.

E Look at the box. Find three colons in the reviews. Underline the explanations after each colon. Circle the key phrase before each colon.

Using colons to introduce explanations

We can use colons (:) to join two sentences together and show how they are connected. The information after the colon provides an explanation for the key phrase before the colon.

F Match the beginnings of the review writers' sentences (1–3) with the endings (a–c).

1. There were three problems with the restaurant:
2. My recommendation couldn't be clearer:
3. When I arrived at the festival, I got an unpleasant surprise:

a. go and buy tickets for this concert immediately.
b. the food was bad, the service was slow and the prices were too high.
c. half of the musicians had canceled their live shows because of the bad weather.

WRITING

A PREPARE You are going to write a review of an art event. Write about a real event that you attended or invent one.

B PLAN Write notes. Think about:

1. What was good about the event?
2. What would you improve? How?
3. Would you recommend the event to other people?

C WRITE Write your review (150–200 words).

D REVIEW Work in groups. Read some of your classmates' reviews. Which events would you like to attend?

W writing a report

A Work in pairs and discuss the questions.

1 Why do people write reports? What are some situations where non-business people write reports?

2 Why do people read reports? What information do they need?

B Read the *Report on charity auction* and answer the questions.

1 Why has the writer written the report?

2 What went well with the auction? What went wrong?

3 What did the writer learn from the experience?

REPORT ON CHARITY AUCTION

Summary:
On December 15, we held a charity auction to raise money for the local hospital. The auction raised less money than expected. This report explores what we did wrong.

Background:
We asked 24 local celebrities (e.g. sportspeople, TV presenters) to donate gifts for our auction. We received 55 gifts, including many valuable items (e.g. a signed soccer ball, a beautiful painting). We expected to raise around $5,000. 720 people attended our auction event. The auction only raised $322. Many of the items were not sold.

Analysis:
1 **Paradox of choice:** There were too many items, so people could not decide. If we had limited the auction to around ten items, we would probably have made more money.
2 **Hook numbers:** We wanted to attract large numbers of people to the auction, so in our marketing materials, we showed pictures of the best items with low starting prices, e.g. $2 for the signed soccer ball. We shouldn't have done this because it encouraged people to make offers of a few dollars, not hundreds of dollars.

Recommendations:
- For future auctions, limit the number of items to around ten.
- In marketing materials, show the value of the items (e.g. *Worth over $500*) rather than the starting price.

Glossary

auction (n) a public occasion when things are sold to the people who offer the most money for them

donate (v) to give something such as money or goods to an organization, especially to a school, hospital, political party or charity

C Look at the box. Match the features of a report (1–8) with the explanations (a–h). Find examples in the report.

Writing a report

A report describes a past event or a present situation and ends with recommendations for the future.

1 title	5 numbered lists
2 summary	6 full forms
3 headings	7 facts and figures
4 bullet points	8 examples

a Use these small black circles to make it easier to read lists of items.

b Your report should include dates, names, numbers, etc.

c In the first paragraph, say briefly what happened and why you've written the report.

d The reader can see immediately what the report is about.

e You can use these to show that the order of items in a list is important.

f Use words like *Analysis* and *Recommendations* to show you're starting a new section.

g Include these to explain important points. You can put them in parentheses: (e.g. …).

h Reports are usually fairly formal, so it's best to write separate words (e.g. *do not*) instead of contractions (e.g. *don't*).

D Find examples of the third conditional and *would have* or *should have done* in the report. Which section are they in? Why?

WRITING

A PREPARE You are going to write a short report about an event where some things could have been better. Think about:

- will you write about a real event or will you invent one?
- what event will you describe? Something from your work or studies? An accident that you had?
- who will read your report? Why?

B PLAN Write notes under these headings:

- Background: What happened?
- Analysis: What went wrong? Why?
- Recommendations: What should happen differently in the future?

C WRITE Write your report. Remember to use headings, bullet points or numbered lists. When you finish writing the three main sections, write a short summary at the beginning.

D REVIEW Work in groups. Read some of your groups' reports. Do you agree with their recommendations?

Audio scripts

UNIT 1

Lesson 1.1, Listening, Exercise C

1.1 **J = Jackson O = Olivia**

J: Hello. Welcome to the Tec-cast. I'm Jackson, and this is my big sister, Olivia.

O: Hello. In this week's podcast, we're looking at phones. Or rather, we're not looking at our phones for a whole week!

J: Yes, that's right. Our experiment runs for seven days. We started on Monday and today's Thursday, so we're halfway through it.

O: Exactly. And instead of our phones, we're both carrying around one of these voice recorders all week, so we can record our experiences. And it's been an interesting week! I arranged to meet Jackson outside the university on Monday afternoon, but it didn't really work, did it, Jackson?

J: Uh, no. Sorry. Let's listen to our recordings from earlier in the week.

Lesson 1.1, Listening, Exercise D

1.2 **J = Jackson O = Olivia S = Sebastian**

O: Hi. Olivia here. It's 4:20 on Monday afternoon and I'm waiting for Jackson. We arranged to meet here, outside the university, at four o'clock, but I can't see him and it's starting to rain. So it looks like he isn't coming and I'm not sure what to do. Hmm, I can't call him because I don't have my phone. OK, I know. I'll go and wait in that bakery over there – at least I'll stay dry, and I'll be able to see Jackson through the window when he arrives.

J: Hi. This is Jackson. It's Monday afternoon and I'm late meeting Olivia. I think. I don't actually know the time because I never wear a watch; I always use the clock on my phone. Anyway, I missed my bus and I couldn't check the time of the next one – the timetables are all online now. So I decided to walk. But then I got lost because I didn't have a map – I usually use the map on my phone! And I couldn't call Olivia to tell her I'd be late. And now it's raining! OK, so I'm just arriving at the university now and I'm looking for Olivia, but I can't see her. Hmm, now I don't know what to do.

S: Excuse me. Are you looking for Olivia?

J: Uh, yes. Why?

S: Hi. I'm Sebastian. I'm a student here at the university. I listen to your podcast every week, and I watch all your videos. I love them!

J: Really? Wow! Thanks. Uh … but how do you know I'm looking for Olivia?

S: I spotted her here a few minutes ago. I recognized her from your videos. She went into that bakery over there.

J: Oh, excellent. Thank you so much. Look, do you want to come and join us? I'll buy you a cupcake to say thank you, and you can tell us what you think of our podcasts.

S: Yeah, that sounds like a great idea. Thanks a lot.

Lesson 1.1, Listening, Exercise E

1.3 **J = Jackson O = Olivia**

O: Hi. Me again. It's eleven fifteen on Tuesday morning, and yes, I'm waiting for Jackson, again. He's 15 minutes late, again, but it's OK because we arranged a plan B: what to do if something goes wrong. So I'm enjoying a nice outdoor concert in the park right now, by a really cool band. Maybe you can hear the music in the background. Our new friend Sebastian told us about the concert yesterday – he plays the guitar in the band, and he sounds really good. It's strange because all the other people in the audience are filming the concert on their cell phones, but I think they're missing half the fun! I'm just listening and enjoying it – and it's much better. In fact, I think I'll stop recording now so I can listen!

J: Hi. It's Tuesday morning, and I'm late for a meeting with Olivia, again, but it's OK because we discussed where she'll be at 11, 11:30, 12:00 and 12:30. And yes, I'm wearing a watch today – an old one from when I was a teenager. It doesn't look great, but it's good for telling the time! Anyway, today I decided to walk the same way I came yesterday – so I checked a map before I left home! I wanted to come back to this part of town because I noticed that the buildings are really beautiful and interesting. I don't normally look at the buildings around me – I usually just stare at my phone. But it's really nice to look around and think about where I am and … how to get to the park from here. So I'm not exactly lost again; I'm just exploring the city a little more than usual.

Lesson 1.1, Listening, Exercise F

1.4 **J = Jackson O = Olivia**

O: Hello again. So, as I said, it's now Thursday, and we're halfway through our experiment. How's it going for you, Jackson?

J: Surprisingly well! I mean, I think I'm seeing a lot more than usual – now I'm looking at the real world, not my phone all the time.

O: Yeah, me too. I really enjoyed observing all the people outside the university on Monday! So what about those amazing buildings? Did you take any pictures?

J: Uh, no. Because I didn't have my phone! But I can tell you about them, if you want.

O: Wow! You usually just show me your pictures. You see! We're talking more than before, too! Our experiment is working! So tell me about those buildings!

Lesson 1.2, Listening, Exercise B

1.8 **M = Mona J = Juan**

M: Hey, Juan. I'm writing a blog post for our website. I thought it might be good to interview you. Can I ask you a few questions?

J: Yes, of course. Go ahead. But why do you want to talk to me? What do you want to talk about?

M: Well, I hear you've just returned from a trip across Europe. It'd be nice to hear about your experiences of using English during your trip.

J: Oh, right. Yes, no problem.

M: Great. I'll just turn on my microphone … OK, so thanks, Juan, for agreeing to talk to me today about your recent trip to Europe. Which countries did you visit?

J: Well, I started in Russia, and then I traveled through Belarus, Poland, Germany, the Netherlands and England. It was a long journey, but I met a lot of great people and I had some amazing conversations. It was a good way to practice my English.

M: Yes, I'm sure it was! It sounds like a great way of practicing. Was it hard to communicate in English?

J: No, actually I found it really easy to communicate all the way from Russia to the Netherlands. But when I got to England … well, it was terrible!

M: Really? What happened in England?

J: Everybody spoke so fast! And they used really strange words and phrases – lots of idioms that I'd never heard before. Plus, the people had very strong accents, so I couldn't understand very much at all!

M: Oh, no! So what did you do?

J: I just asked people to slow down. 'Can you say that again, please?'; 'Could you speak slowly, please?', and so on!

M: And did that help?

J: Yes. I mean, the people were very nice, and they were happy to talk to me. But they speak very strange English! I guess it's because English is changing all the time.

M: Really? How is English changing? Can you give me an example?

J: Yes, of course. When I was in London, I heard many people speaking a new variety of English called MLE – Multicultural London English. It's becoming extremely popular.

M: Really? I've never heard of it. Who uses MLE?

J: Mostly young people in London.

M: So how is MLE different from normal English?

J: Well, it's mostly a question of pronunciation. But there are also grammar differences. For example, in MLE, they don't say 'you were'; they say 'you was.' 'I was', 'you was', 'he was', 'she was', 'we was', 'they was'. And then in negative sentences, it's 'I weren't', 'you weren't', 'he weren't', 'she weren't', and so on.

M: What? That's terrible! But isn't that a mistake?

J: Well, it isn't Standard English, of course. But millions of people speak like that, so how can it be wrong?

M: Hmm ... what do you mean by 'Standard English'?

J: Well, Standard English is the form they use in books and newspapers. It's a kind of cleaned-up version of English. But it isn't the only form of English, and most native speakers don't speak Standard English – at least, not all the time. There are hundreds of other forms of English all over the world – like Jamaican English, Nigerian English, Indian English and so on. They're all different, but I think that's really cool!

M: OK, but isn't it just a question of good English and bad English? Surely Standard English is better, isn't it?

J: No. I don't think so. 'Standard' doesn't always mean 'the best'. When I traveled by train across Europe, I went by 'standard class', not 'first class'. And I think Standard English is like 'standard class' in a train: simple and basic, but a little boring. I think non-standard English is much more interesting.

M: So are you saying we need to learn non-standard English?

J: No, not at all. Standard English is perfect for international communication. As I say, Standard English worked well for me all the way from Russia to the Netherlands. I only had a problem when I got to England. So it depends what you need English for. I think for most learners of English around the world, it's better to learn Standard English. We don't need to speak like native speakers. In fact, as I learned on my trip, it's usually better when we don't speak like native speakers.

M: Wow! Yes, I see what you mean, and I certainly agree with you on that last point. OK, so thanks a lot for that interview, Juan. You've given me a lot to think about ... and to write about on the blog.

UNIT 2

Lesson 2.1, Listening, Exercise C

2.2 **I = Interviewer E = Emma**

I: Welcome to *Dreams Come True*, the podcast that finds out about people's life-long dreams and how they've turned them into reality. My guest in the studio today is Emma Sykes from New York.

E: Hello, thanks for having me!

I: Glad you could be here. Now, Emma, you are 35 and you are the owner of a successful advertising agency, is that right?

E: Yes, that's right.

I: So you've already had a lot of success in your life.

E: Yes, you could say that. I've worked very hard and the agency is doing well, but I still have dreams – well, one dream anyway.

I: And I believe that dream involves big plans on water! Tell us a little more about it.

E: That's right, John. Ever since I was young, I've been fascinated by the water. I love swimming and diving, and for the last few years I've been learning how to sail. My ultimate dream, the thing I've wanted to achieve my whole life, is to live on a yacht and sail around the world.

I: Wow, that's a big dream! And it doesn't sound easy. Tell us, just how have you made this dream a reality?

E: Well, that's the thing ... I haven't. Not yet. Not completely.

I: So, you haven't sailed around the world?

E: No, I haven't. It's just not practical at this time in my life. Yachts are very expensive. I've saved a fair amount of money, but not enough yet. Plus, I don't have enough skills or knowledge yet to go sailing on my own across the oceans.

I: Well, that does sound very complicated! So how do you keep going with your plan when it seems so far away?

E: For me, the most important thing is to make a decision to put a plan into action. Once you've made the decision, you can set short-term and long-term goals that will help you achieve your dream.

I: I see. Yes, that's a good point. So what are some of your short-term goals? How are you going to work toward that ultimate goal?

E: Well, there's the sailing lessons, obviously. But actually, I've turned one part of the dream into reality already.

I: Really? What's that?

E: A year ago, I sold my house and used some of the money to buy a houseboat. It isn't a yacht, and it won't take me around the world, but it's a home and it's on the water. OK, I'm on freshwater, not saltwater, but I now live on a boat.

I: Wow, that's already a pretty big change! But does living on a houseboat really prepare you for sailing around the world?

E: Yes, I think so. The important thing here is to stay motivated and not lose heart, and this step helps me to do that.

I: And of course, you're getting some experience of what it's like to live on the water.

E: Exactly! I'm learning to live in a small space, and I'm also finding out what it's like to live in a home that can move from place to place. OK, I'm cruising along canals, not crossing oceans, but doing something similar to my dream – it's a start.

I: And now that you've made that start, do you think your plan to sail around the world is more achievable?

E: Absolutely. On the whole, I think the hardest part of any journey is the first step. Now that I've made the break from the land to the water, I'll be able to take the next step of my journey with more confidence.

I: Well, thank you for coming to talk to us, Emma. I hope you can join us again once you've achieved your ultimate dream. Will you do that?

E: Yes, of course. I look forward to it.

I: Thank you, Emma. Now, next up, I'll be speaking to ...

Lesson 2.2, Listening, Exercise B

2.4 **M = Matt S = Suzanna N = Nancy R = Roberto**

M: You know, when you move away from home, arrive in a new place, there are lots of different challenges, and for me the biggest one was eating. Well, not eating, but cooking. I mean, I could make a salad or a sandwich, but not cook anything, like, I couldn't boil an egg. I know that sounds silly, but I simply had no idea. Anyway, I looked at some books and also found some excellent 'how to cook' videos online. To be honest, the books didn't help, but I started to teach myself with the videos. I wasn't very good at first – the first time, I didn't manage to make anything at all; I just watched the video and then ordered a takeout! But, I never gave up. I kept practicing. And when my parents came to see me six months later, I managed to cook them a really tasty meal. They were so surprised.

S: I really hate standing up in front of people to give a talk or a presentation. So, when my brother asked me to make a speech at his wedding, I didn't know what to do. I couldn't say no to him. Luckily a friend of mine, an actor, helped me. Basically, we created a character for me to play when giving the speech, so that I didn't think it was actually me standing up to speak. Also, I learned my speech by heart so that I didn't need to use any notes. Just like an actor. On the big day, I wasn't able to stop my hands from shaking, but I remembered everything and I played that character. And, incredibly, I was able to complete the speech. That was a big day for me, as well as for my brother.

N: I worked as a volunteer in a village school in China for about six months, and the language was my biggest problem. I was able to speak very basic Chinese, but I couldn't remember many new words. I studied each day, but didn't achieve much – the words went in one ear and then straight out the other! Then, I had a great idea. I had my guitar with me, so I started to write simple songs with all the new words. They were kind of like children's songs. I asked a

Chinese friend to check my grammar was correct, and then tried to learn the songs. And, you know what, it worked. Each day, I was able to remember those new words, and I even started singing the songs to the kids. I was actually pretty nervous the first time I sang to them, but I managed to do it without mistakes, although I think my pronunciation was pretty poor, from the way the kids were laughing at me.

R: When I was a child, I never learned to swim, and, when I started going on beach vacations, I really regretted that. My friends spent all day swimming in the ocean, but I wasn't able to swim. All I could do was sunbathe! So, I asked my sister to teach me. She was very patient, but, after a few months, I gave up because I still couldn't swim. Then, after another vacation just sitting on the beach, I decided to try again. This time, I paid for lessons at the local pool. And yes, after a few more months, I finally managed to swim 50 meters. That felt so good. And then, that next vacation, I was finally able to swim in the ocean with my friends – that felt incredible. A real achievement!

UNIT 3

Lesson 3.1, Listening, Exercise B
3.1 **B = Presenter (Bobby) J = Junko A = Alan**

B: OK, our first caller is Junko. Hello, Junko.

J: Hello, Bobby. Well, my story happened some time ago, when I first came to the US to study English. I was only 18 then.

B: OK. Can I ask, where are you from, Junko?

J: Japan.

B: Japan? OK, but you aren't calling from there, are you?

J: No, no. I've lived here for ten years now.

B: OK. Well, Junko, thank you for calling. Tell us your story. What problem did you have?

J: Well, the problem was a public holiday. New Year's Day to be exact!

B: New Year's Day was a problem? That is pretty unusual. What happened?

J: Well, I'd arranged to go to a classmate's house for dinner. Of course, I knew it was a holiday. But what I didn't know was there was no public transportation. So in the afternoon, I went to the subway station. It was snowing, not very heavily, but it was really cold. Anyway, the station was closed when I got there, so I couldn't get a train. I thought it was because of the snow, but the roads were OK, so I decided to try to get a bus.

B: But there were no buses either?

J: Mmm, exactly. But I didn't know. Anyway, I found a bus stop and sat down to wait.

B: Oh, no! Did you wait for long?

J: Actually, not so long. I was very lucky.

B: You got a taxi?

J: Not exactly. A police car was driving by when it suddenly stopped and one of the officers got out. She asked me if I was OK and explained there were no buses today. I felt so embarrassed and stupid. But then, guess what?

B: What?

J: She told me to get in the car. I was worried. Had I done something wrong? But they were both smiling, so I just asked why.

B: So then what?

J: They took me to my friend's place.

B: What? Like a taxi?

J: Exactly. I couldn't believe it. So kind. You know, we went right across the city. When I arrived, my friends hadn't started dinner. So, I wasn't late at all. Perfect!

B: How nice, Junko. I guess it was a quiet day for everyone, even the police. A great example of the New Year's spirit in action. Thank you. OK, now let's hear from Alan. Hello, Alan. Tell us your story.

A: Sure. Hi, Bobby. Yeah, so, I'd been out of work for a few months when I got this interview for a job in another city. I really needed the job, so I decided to leave really early – you know, I didn't want to be late and all that.

B: Not for an interview, no!

A: Right! Well, it was raining when I left, so I took a taxi to the station. That didn't take long, but when I got there, I found out that they'd canceled my train. I wasn't too worried though – the next one was in half an hour, and I had plenty of time. So I took the next train, but after about 30 minutes, that train broke down and we were just stuck there. Not moving or anything. And, stupidly, I'd left my phone at home. Yes, I'd changed my jacket just before I left, and my phone was in that first jacket, so I couldn't even call the company.

B: How unlucky, Alan. So how long were you stuck there?

A: About an hour! And all that time I was getting more and more stressed. The train started moving again, but really slowly, and we arrived about two hours late, and that meant I had already missed the interview by over an hour. So, I jumped in a taxi, but that only made things worse.

B: In what way?

A: The traffic was awful – you know, it was still raining. We ended up stuck in a traffic jam. After about 20 minutes we were still not moving, so I got out and walked. So, when I finally got to the office, I was really late, stressed and wet from the rain. I looked like a mess.

B: I can imagine. Nightmare! Did they still interview you?

A: Well, that's the funny thing. I was standing at the reception desk, waiting to make my excuses to the receptionist when this guy stepped in front of me. I was about to complain when the receptionist said 'Mr. Hammond, you've arrived. At last'. And, can you guess who he was?

B: Another candidate?

A: Oh, no, not another candidate. He was the manager, the interviewer! It turned out he'd been on the same train as me! I introduced myself immediately, and we had a laugh about the whole trip.

B: Amazing! What a coincidence. And so I have to ask: did you get the job?

A: Well, after all that bad luck, things had to change, and yes, I got the job.

Lesson 3.2, Listening, Exercise B
3.7 **C = Chairperson A = Alfred C1 = Councilor 1 C2 = Councilor 2**

C: OK, everyone, before we make our final decisions on this year's Car-Free Day, I'd like to invite some members of the public to give their views. First, let me introduce Alfred Shaw, a lecturer in business studies.

A: Thank you. OK, well, it's clear what most of you think about a car-free day. An absolutely wonderful idea, right? However, I'm here to disagree. Actually, it's a really terrible idea.

C1: What? You can't be serious!

C2: Nonsense, it's an excellent idea.

A: OK, you say that, but it really isn't. Let's look at the facts. First of all, they don't solve the traffic problem. And, anyway, cars are, very simply, great.

C2: Great? Come off it! We know they cause some awful problems.

A: OK, some things about cars are fairly bad, but they're clearly the best way to get around, and so they're never going to disappear. We've held this Car-Free Day 15 times before, but the rush-hour traffic jams have not gone away. Car-free days have a really tiny effect on driving habits, if any at all.

C1: But it's still better than doing nothing.

A: Is it? Here's another reason why we should think again. Car-free days don't even help the environment. Think about it. Although there may be no cars in the city center for that one day, those cars are still out there on the roads, just on different roads. So, all you're doing is moving the pollution.

And another thing, the car-free day causes massive traffic problems in the city, as drivers have to find other ways to go. Remember what happened last year, when that truck got stuck under the railroad bridge because we'd closed the main road? Because of that, there was an absolutely enormous traffic jam, trains were canceled and thousands of dollars of damage was caused. People were furious about that, and rightly so.

In short, car-free days are absolutely useless because they change nothing, and they create huge problems, not solutions. I'll now move onto what we should do instead.

C1: About time!

C2: Like what? A pedestrian-free day?!

C1: Ha ha. That's very funny.

A: Hmm, hilarious. You're clearly missing my point. We shouldn't ban anything, we should just improve everything.

First, we should start a campaign to encourage people to buy greener cars. Let's get more people using electric and hybrid cars. This may be extremely difficult, but it isn't impossible. We could hold an e-car festival and give people a chance to try the cars out in order to see their benefits. That would be a superb way to change things.

Also, we need to improve public transportation and get people using it. We need more buses, and cleaner buses – some of our old buses are really filthy, so it's no wonder people choose cars first. Let's invest some money, and then, why don't we run a 'Use Public Transportation Week', instead of banning cars for a day?

C1: Actually, that's a really good idea.

A: Thanks – an extremely good idea, I'd say. Finally, we should encourage a healthier and greener lifestyle all year round, rather than just for one day a year. Let's get people back on bikes. Let's teach people of all ages how to bike safely. Other cities have city bike rental systems – why don't we? We haven't even had a meeting to discuss it because you're too busy planning for car-free day.

OK, to sum up, there are alternatives to car-free days that are actually better for the environment and that actually reduce car use. Let's try them out, instead of holding another useless car-free day. OK, any questions?

C2: Um, isn't it true that your brother runs an electric car dealership? Maybe that's …

A: Hey, what's that got to do with anything? Really! I just want our city to be a great place to live, that's all.

UNIT 4

Lesson 4.1, Listening, Exercises B and C

4.1 **J = Julia S = Shireen**

J: Hi, Shireen.

S: Hi, Julia. I can't see you; I don't think you've clicked the video button.

J: Oh! Oops! I'll do it now. Hold on. There we go.

S: That's better. Good to see you. Happy New Year!

J: And happy New Year to you!

S: How's everything going in Spain?

J: Great. We had a good time on New Year's Eve; there's a real party atmosphere in Madrid. We were at a house party, and then out on the streets at midnight, eating grapes, dancing and drinking hot chocolate – just wonderful!

S: Well, lucky you! Sounds better than mine. We went to see the ball drop at Times Square in New York City.

J: But that sounds amazing!

S: Oh, I'm sure it was – it's just we never actually saw it.

J: Oh no! What happened? You didn't get lost again, did you?

S: Not exactly – we just weren't early enough. There was a massive crowd and we got stuck on a side road. We could hear the countdown, but couldn't see a thing.

J: Oh! I bet it was freezing, too. I'm glad I was at that party and had that hot chocolate at midnight.

S: Yeah, I can imagine. We were outside for hours, and I lost my hat. To be honest, I did get pretty cold. I'm going to look for a new hat tomorrow; Sophie's coming here to have lunch, and then we're going shopping.

J: That's nice. Is that one of your New Year's resolutions? Are you going to finally buy some new clothes? No more going out in your sister's old ones?

S: Haha, very funny. Actually, I haven't made any resolutions yet.

J: You haven't? I've made several.

S: Really? What've you decided?

J: Try and guess.

S: OK, OK! Let me see. So, are you going to get married this year? Time to copy me?

J: Ooh, that's a big question to ask! No, no plans yet, but Alberto's said he's going to buy me flowers every month. He's going to try to be more romantic, for a change.

S: That's great. He sounds sweet. Let's hope he keeps that one. So, what are yours?

J: Well, I've decided to get in better shape this year, so I'm going to join a gym. Also, I'm going to study Spanish more seriously. I find it pretty hard to follow Alberto's friends.

S: That's a surprise! I always thought your Spanish was really good.

J: Well, not good enough. In fact, I'm meeting a new teacher on Thursday, for private lessons.

S: Really? That's quick!

J: Well, there's no point in putting things off. Just get started and then stick to the plan. I was reading a self-help book about this the other day: *How to Reach Your Goals and Change Your Life*.

S: Another self-help book? I think you should make a resolution to stop reading them.

J: Well, I think you should read some. It'd be good for you.

S: Really? I'll leave that to you, I think.

J: Oh, come on – now's the time to make some resolutions. What do you want to achieve this year? Or change? What about your chocolate habit? Resolutions are a great way to quit bad habits.

S: My chocolate habit? What do you mean?

J: You eat some every day, don't you?

S: Well, just a little. At work, you know.

J: Shireen, I really think you should cut it out of your diet. I was reading about how we've all become sugar addicts and …

S: That's a surprise! Another book! But, yeah, I know what you mean. It's just that I get really bored at work. I don't think I can totally quit, but I'll cut down on the amount I eat. Happy now?

J: Cut down by how much? There's no escape – make your mind up now!

S: OK, OK, I'll stop eating it every day. I'll have chocolate on Fridays only, as a treat.

J: Great, and I'll make sure you don't break that resolution.

S: Great, and how are you going to do that? Going to come to work with me each day?

J: Hmm, I'll put a webcam on your office desk.

S: Well, at least you can see how boring my job is then.

Lesson 4.1, Listening, Exercise A

4.4 **A = Announcer M = Maya L = Lukas J = Jody H = Hassan**

A: Maya

M: I never usually bother with self-help books. I usually prefer fiction, especially things like sci-fi and fantasy. But last year, I read a book that totally changed the way I feel about myself. It's called *Life Cycle* and it's by a famous cyclist and lifestyle expert named Helena Schneiderlin. The book explains how you can find the real you and be a happier person when you find your true passion. It gives you advice on how to find the thing that you love and how to use it to improve the quality of your life. I followed the advice in the book, and since then I've become much happier. It's definitely changed how I feel about myself. It's changed my life really. I'm much more confident now.

A: Lukas

L: I think the one thing that changed my life most of all was a book called *The Road*. It's by Cormac McCarthy and it's about a father and son on a journey through a strange and unwelcoming place. It might be the future after a terrible event – the book doesn't say exactly. Really, I think it's about the relationship between the two characters. Even though their situation is very bad, the love they have keeps them strong. I'll never forget the first time I read this book. It made me think about my own relationship with my father. We don't always get along, but I think *The Road* has helped me to understand him better.

A: Jody

J: There's a book called *Sapiens*. I only read it last year, but honestly, I can't think of another book that has had such a strong effect on me. It's a history book, and it tells the story of the human race – everything, from how we started as hunters, and then became farmers, on to how we developed cities and industry. It's written by Yuval Noah Harari. He talks about religion, money, countries, law – everything. It's a very impressive piece of work, and it really helped me to see things in context. I feel I have a better understanding about who we are now that I've read that book.

A: Hassan

H: Seeing *Hoop Dreams* was a life-changing moment for me. It's a documentary about two teenagers in Chicago who want to be professional basketball players. It follows six years of their lives, as they try and make it to the top. Both boys come from poor backgrounds, and the film is about a lot more than just basketball. It's about society, and it's about how a life can change in an instant. I was really into basketball when I was young, and I went into the movie theater that day wanting to be a basketball player, but by the time I walked out of the movie theater I wanted to be a film-maker instead. And that's what I am now. *Hoop Dreams* inspired me to make documentaries.

Lesson 4.2, Listening, Exercise B
4.7 R = Rita Costa J = John Malone T = Toshi Asaka

R: Hi, I'm Rita Costa, and this is *Rethinking the Future*, when we look at how we can stop pessimistic predictions from coming true.

OK, so, today's prediction is that rural life has no future. Many villages and small towns are going to disappear, or only have older residents because young people are relocating to urban areas – that is, they're going to the cities to find work and a new, modern life. We've talked before about overpopulation in urban areas, but what about the problem of under-population in rural areas? Like many countries, Japan faces that problem, but it is trying to deal with it. Our reporter John has been there to find out more. Hi, John.

J: Hi, Rita. Yes, I visited several places and saw some great ideas for repopulating small villages, for getting people to exchange their life in the city for one in the country.

R: I guess that means offering financial incentives, you know, offering things like free or cheap housing, low business taxes and relocation expenses.

J: Yes, and some local governments are certainly doing that, but I'm talking about examples of blue-sky thinking, and by that I mean ideas that are different, fresh and unexpected.

R: Oh yes, such as?

J: Well, the fresh thinking involves foreigners, the internet, cows and love.

R: That sounds fascinating. Tell us more.

J: Sure. My tour started in the small mountain town of Kamiyama, where the city feels far away. At first, it all seems very traditional and underdeveloped – you know, there are very few signs of modern life. However, to encourage companies to relocate from urban areas the town council provides a super-fast internet service, faster than Tokyo's. And now, if you look inside some of those traditional buildings, you'll see signs of a growing digital start-up economy, teams of young designers and programmers working away on their computers.

R: Do you mean like small digital design and app companies? Like in those urban creative business centers?

J: Exactly. Here's Toshi Asaka, the owner of one.

T: I decided to move here from Tokyo because of the internet service. I can do my work anywhere, and here the quality of life is wonderful. There are no drawbacks, no disadvantages, about living here– my employees don't feel underpaid now!

J: Kamiyama Council has managed to reinvent the local economy, moving from traditional to modern digital business.

R: Right, using modern technology to create opportunities for young people. That makes sense. What's the next idea?

J: Well, other places are using tradition rather than technology to change their future. The small fishing village of Nakanoshima has its eye on young people, too, but not young Japanese. They offer special six-month Working Holiday Visas to foreign visitors who want to experience a truly traditional Japanese lifestyle. You stay in cheap, shared accommodations, in a traditional building and do part-time agricultural work, that is, you have a job in the farming or fishing industries.

R: That sounds like a fun thing to do. But is it such a good idea? I'm not sure it really helps the village to grow. I mean, the visitors only stay six months.

J: But then, new businesses like restaurants, cafés and language schools open up, and that encourages local young people to stay and not go to the city, so the visitors are an opportunity for the locals.

R: OK, so the experience of the foreign visitors is only half the story. What else did you discover?

J: My final stop was Mishima Island. Like the other places, they provide financial help like cheap accommodations and relocation expenses, but if you are single and looking for romance, they will also pay for your dates.

R: Pay for your dates? Cute, but, that isn't a lot of money, is it?

J: Well, perhaps you've misunderstood the goal of this plan… its intention. It isn't about attracting new people; it's about keeping them. What I mean is, they want people to move to their village, and to then stay forever. What better way to do that than to help them to find love and perhaps start a family. Isn't that both sweet and smart?

R: OK, I get it now, but what about married couples? It doesn't help them, does it?

J: Not really, no, but they also give every new resident a young cow.

R: A cow? I'm not sure that will get me moo-ving there.

J: Oh, not just any cow. Mishima cows are extremely rare, and their beef is incredibly expensive, with a kilogram worth $500.

R: That's a lot of money! I can't believe it.

J: Yeah, but it really is that expensive. And the thing is, just like the village life, these cows are in danger of extinction, of disappearing completely forever, so they're another thing the new residents are helping to save.

R: The thing I love about the Mishima Island approach is that it creates emotional bonds to a place. What I mean by that is people soon make a strong connection to their new home, either through finding love or raising a cow. Definitely blue-sky thinking.

UNIT 5

Lesson 5.1, Listening, Exercise A
5.1 **F = Fiona M = Michael**

F: Hello, sorry I'm late. You must be Michael. I'm Fiona.

M: Hi, Fiona. Nice to meet you.

F: Nice to meet you, and thank you for coming, and for waiting. I hope we can help you. So, I've had a quick look at your personality test and, in today's session, I'd like you to tell me why you're thinking about changing careers, and to find out more about the kind of work that you like doing.

M: Sure.

F: OK, so you're currently working in a bank. I see you've been there for five years, since leaving college, so why do you want to leave that behind?

M: Well, it's been a good job, but um, I just feel there's something missing. I studied business and finance in college, and getting a banking job seemed like the right thing to do at that time, but I'm not so sure now.

F: I see, and what is it that's missing exactly? Your personality test showed you have good people skills. Does your work involve using those much? And your organizational skills are strong. I'm sure that's important at the bank.

M: Yeah, absolutely. You definitely need to be well organized, to both meet deadlines and manage the money carefully. Um, I work in a local branch of the bank, so I have to deal with customers face to face, and I've recently been made assistant manager, so those people skills are important, and I do more general planning now, like team planning, you know, to make sure the work gets done – that sort of thing. I think the thing is that basically every day is pretty much the same. I rarely have to think on my feet, or deal with surprises.

F: OK, you want a little more variety in your work. So, this has been your only job since college. Did you have any part-time jobs before?

M: Well, this may surprise you, but I used to be a fashion model.

F: A fashion model? Well, now that you've told me, it isn't so surprising, I mean you look very neat and well-dressed.

M: Thank you. I didn't do it for long, um, but it was really fun. I really enjoyed the photo shoots. It's good doing something creative together; the teamwork was good and important. And, well, they'd usually give us some of the clothes after the shoot, which was great for me as a student!

F: I can imagine, and also very different from working in a bank. Um, anything else?

M: The other thing was working as a waiter. I joined an agency for part-time catering work, so I used to serve food at conferences and events, or I'd work in a café or restaurant for a few days, you know, if their employees were sick or something.

F: Well, that's great experience to have. Did you like doing that?

M: Oh, yeah, for sure. You have to work hard. At busy times, you would always be under a lot of pressure, but in a good way. I liked helping the customers enjoy the event. I used to be tired but happy at the end of a day. But, you know, that was only student work for me. It did get me into food and cooking though; that's one of my hobbies now – home baking and stuff like that.

F: Well, it's certainly interesting to hear that you liked working under pressure. Um, you just mentioned hobbies. Do you have any other interests? Anything that might involve skills that you could use in a job?

M: Well, you obviously don't mean going to the movie theater. I love skiing. Um, before college, I was a member of a ski club at a local ski center. One thing then, I used to help new members, you know, I'd coach them a little, and just help them as they were learning. That was pretty rewarding. There was a nice sense of achievement, you know.

F: Is that feeling missing from your work in the bank?

M: In a way, yes. But I don't want to be a ski instructor, you know, that's just like having your own business. I want a steady job, to have a career in a good company, but, well, just not in a bank.

F: Sure, sure. Well, from what you've said, I do have an early suggestion for you to consider.

M: Already? OK, well, what are you thinking?

Lesson 5.1, Listening, Exercise D
5.2 **F = Fiona M = Michael**

F: Sure, sure. Well, from what you've said, I do have an early suggestion for you to consider.

M: Already? OK, well, what are you thinking?

F: Well, it's clear you like using your people and communication skills, and your personality test shows you're good at organization and time management.

M: That's all true, I think.

F: Yes, and you're looking for a job that has a lot of variety. And you enjoy working on a team.

M: Uh huh.

F: So, have you thought about a career in catering? Not as a waiter or chef, but as the person who organizes the catering at events. You used to work as a waiter at them, how about running them? A catering manager is a good career, and it requires all those skills.

M: Well, I don't know, um, sounds interesting, but, I mean, I don't have any training in that area.

F: But you do have experience of those events, and actually catering companies do look for people with a business studies degree.

M: Do they?

F: Uh huh. And I think that the work of planning and running an event should suit you and your skills.

M: And food and cooking is a hobby of mine.

F: Exactly.

M: OK, well, I'm interested. Let's find out more.

Lesson 5.2, Listening, Exercise B
5.5 **C = Clive E = Ella**

C: Welcome to the *Business Business* podcast. Today, we're discussing environmental business ideas, and we're starting with the retail sector. I'm talking to our retail expert Ella Stevens.

E: Hello, Clive.

C: Ella, I understand you're going to tell us about a clothing company with some very unusual marketing ideas.

E: Yes. I'm talking today about Patagonia. It's an outdoor activities clothing company based in the US. It was started by Yvon Chouinard in 1973. He used to be a rock climber, and at first, Patagonia made climbing equipment. Since then, it has changed its focus to outdoor clothing.

C: So they make and sell clothing for activities like hiking and skiing, as well as climbing?

E: That's right. Patagonia is one of the largest brands in the outdoor clothing sector, but there are lots of others, such as North Face, Berghaus and Columbia. These brands are now so popular that you see people wearing their clothes all the time, not just when they are out in the country.

C: So what's different about Patagonia?

E: Well, a few years ago, the company launched a new marketing campaign called 'Worn Wear', which encourages customers to buy second-hand Patagonia clothes like old jackets and T-shirts.

C: That is an unusual way to run a business. It's difficult for a clothing company to make a profit selling new clothes if everyone chooses to buy second-hand instead.

E: That's a good point, Clive, but Patagonia goes even further. They also actively encourage their customers to give them their old Patagonia clothes so that they can then sell them as second-hand items.

C: Really? Why are they doing this? There must be a good reason.

E: Well, Patagonia strongly believes in taking care of the environment. They've built a brand based on respecting nature, and they are trying hard to reduce the negative impact that the company has on the world we live in. They believe that by encouraging people to repair their clothes and return them so they can be bought second-hand, they are helping the environment.

C: And is this strategy working for them?

E: Yes, it is, Clive. Patagonia is doing a good job of attracting new customers. As the results show, their sales have increased because of campaigns like 'Worn Wear'. For example, they made record profits on Black Friday a few years ago, and they donated the whole amount to environmental organizations.

C: That's incredible! And I imagine this helped them to make even more money in the long term.

E: It's certainly made their brand more attractive to customers who are concerned about the environment.

C: Is 'Worn Wear' the first time Patagonia has used such an unusual marketing campaign?

E: No, it isn't. Another instance of this is when Patagonia took out a full-page ad in The New York Times that encouraged people NOT to buy one of their jackets because of the damage it would do to the environment. Consequently, they got a lot of media attention.

C: I can imagine – that seems like a fairly risky strategy. Did they sell more jackets?

E: Probably, but there's no doubt that the company has helped to increase people's knowledge about the effect the clothing industry can have on the environment.

C: And it's a very interesting approach to building a brand. Thank you for coming in to talk to us today, Ella. Next on the podcast we're looking at …

UNIT 6

Lesson 6.1, Listening, Exercise B

6.1 Soccer, // basketball, // golf, // tennis // – four of the world's most popular sports. / They are played by millions / and watched by millions more, / and all four / are in the greatest festival of sports, // the Olympic Games.

However, // there is one sport / that is just as popular as those, / but it still hasn't been accepted in the Olympics, / and indeed, // many people say / that it is not even a sport. / What sport am I talking about? // eSports. / Yes, // electronic sports, / or competitive video gaming.

Now, I guess many of you think video games are just something people play at home or on their phones. In fact, they are played in the same way as any other sport, with teams competing against each other in large venues and stadiums, in front of thousands of paying spectators, and with millions more watching online.

Even if you already know how massive eSports are, maybe many of you think gaming is not actually a sport. But I hope to persuade you that video gaming has all the features that we see in other sports.

First of all, it is clearly competitive. Players and teams compete in national and international tournaments, with a goal to win the final, lift the trophy and become the champions. The will to win is a key part of video gaming.

Also, playing video games requires incredible mental strength and skill. You need to focus for long periods of time and the games are very fast. eSports demand smart thinking, quick decision-making and great communication between team members, just like traditional team sports.

Of course, some people argue that video gaming is not a real sport because it doesn't require physical strength. Now, I accept it isn't the same as soccer or football, for example, but, because the games are long and demanding, professional gamers have to be very fit. If your fitness levels are poor, so is your ability to concentrate. This is why the managers and coaches of professional teams make sure their players spend time training in the gym and have a healthy diet. That all sounds like a sport to me.

So, have I changed your mind yet? Do you now feel that eSports should be in the Olympics? If not, remember that when they choose new sports for the games, they are looking for ones that are popular and have strong youth appeal. That sounds like eSports to me. Online eSports platforms have hundreds of millions of users every week. While the numbers of people playing and watching traditional sports are declining, they are rapidly increasing for eSports, and most of those people are young people.

So, eSports are physically and mentally demanding. They attract young people like no other sport. They are popular all over the world, and, of course, anyone can take part. They have already become a professional success story, with famous top players, great teams, and enthusiastic fans.

Video gaming is not a sport of the future; it is a sport of today, and so, eSports should, undoubtedly, be in the Olympic Games. Now, please excuse me, but I have a game to go and play. Thank you.

Lesson 6.1, Listening, Exercise D

6.2 In fact, they are played in the same way as any other sport, with teams competing against each other in large venues and stadiums, in front of thousands of spectators, and with millions more watching online.

Lesson 6.2, Listening, Exercise B

6.5 **RP = Radio Presenter S1 = Speaker 1 S2 = Speaker 2 S3 = Speaker 3 S4 = Speaker 4 S5 = Speaker 5**

RP: Hobbies. Interests. Pastimes. They're something more than watching TV, and something different from playing a sport. I'm Gavin Ross, and in this week's *Human Behavior*, we're asking you, the public, about what you like doing in your free time. What hobbies do you have? How long have you been doing them? Why do you have them? Let's hear from some of our listeners out on the streets in Boston today.

S1: I'm really into classic or vintage cars. I've been buying them since I was 18, when I first learned to drive and got my first one, a small 1960s sports car. Obviously, it isn't exactly a cheap hobby, what with buying and then repairing them. It means I don't go on expensive vacations like my friends, but I'm not going to give it up. I've just bought an old Mini, so I'll start working on that tomorrow.

S2: Arts and crafts are my thing – jewelry making, painting, woodwork. I've had this interest since I was a child. For the last six months, I've been going to pottery classes. In fact, I've been working in the studio this afternoon – that's why my hands are so dirty. As a hobby, it's relaxing and a great escape from daily stress, and, you know, it makes time fly – a sure sign I'm enjoying myself.

S3: I don't really have a hobby, but my husband is an enthusiastic cyclist. Actually, I think that cycling is an obsession for him, rather than a hobby. If he isn't out on a ride, he's cleaning the thing, or checking out the latest accessories online. He's been doing it since his teens, so I knew what I was getting when I married him. It isn't really my thing, so I leave him to it; it seems to keep him in shape and happy.

S4: I don't know if you can call this a hobby, but I spend most of my time following Danny CJ, the singer – I'm a massive fan. I've been a member of his fan club for a long time, I've been to a lot of his concerts and I collect everything I can about him: all the music, pictures, posters, calendars. It's great following him on social media, too. He even replied to one of my tweets once. Whenever he comes to Boston, my friends and I all hang out outside his hotel. He's in there now – we've been waiting here all day, but we haven't seen him yet. Hold on, is that him? Danny! Danny! Over here!

S5: Do I have a hobby? Well, you might say my hobby is having hobbies. I tend to get really into something, like, at first, I get really obsessed with it, but then I soon lose interest. I don't know why. I've always been like this. Recently, I've been getting into bird watching – I've bought all the kits and a bunch of books, and I've joined two local societies. No idea how long this will last though. I might start cooking classes soon, or take up sailing. Anything that gets me out of the house.

RP: Those are just some of the people I've met while making this show, and I'd like to hear from even more of you. Visit our show's website to see how you can take part in this series of *Human Behavior*. The address is www.radiotalk.nett/humanbehavior …

UNIT 7

Lesson 7.1, Listening, Exercise C
7.2 **V = Vicky C = Charlie T = Tina M = Markus**

V: Charlie! You're here at last!
C: Hi, Vicky. Sorry I'm a little late.
V: No problem. You're only … 20 minutes late. Welcome to pot luck night.
C: Thanks. Am I the last person here?
V: No, actually, there's only one other person so far. He arrived half an hour early!
C: Oh, that must be Felipe, right? He's always early.
V: True. But it was good because he helped me make my dish: a cheese and chilli salad.
C: Ah … I'm allergic to dairy products. Oh, well. Never mind.
V: Hmm. Wow … those look delicious, Charlie. What are they?
C: Spicy buffalo wings. They're a traditional dish from New York made with a hot sticky sauce.
V: Wow. That's … different.
C: Yes, that's what I thought. Uh … can I heat them up in the oven? They just need 15 minutes.
V: Sure, but you'll have to wait ten minutes. I'm heating up Felipe's dish right now.
C: OK, no problem.
V: Great. Let me take your dish. Go and join Felipe – he's waiting in the backyard.
C: OK, thanks.
V: Aha … Tina. Welcome to pot luck night!
T: Thanks. Is everyone else here already?
V: No, not yet. But Felipe's here, and Charlie.
T: Those look nice. What are they?
V: Buffalo wings. Charlie brought them. Hmm … I've never eaten buffalo meat before. I wonder what it tastes like.
T: Hang on … that can't be right. They can't be buffalo wings. Buffaloes don't have wings!
V: No, you're right. But they're definitely wings. They could be chicken or something like that.
T: Aha … yes. Isn't there a city called Buffalo in New York? The name must come from the city, not the animal.
V: Good thinking. Anyway, what have you brought?
T: It's my own recipe. It's called cheesy chicken pasta surprise.
V: Oh, right. What's the surprise?
T: Ah … you'll have to wait and see. Can I just heat it up in the oven?
V: Well, uh … you'll have to wait for Charlie's dish … and Felipe's dish. It's chicken curry in a creamy sauce.
T: Oh, yes, so that's what smells so good. I love hot, spicy food.
V: Great. So let me take your dish to the kitchen. Go and join the others out in the backyard.
V: Markus! Great to see you. Come on in.
M: Thanks. I'm so sorry I'm late … again! You must think I'm so disorganized!
V: No, don't worry. Most of the others have just arrived, too. So … what have you brought?
M: Cream of chicken soup. I hope that's OK.
V: Uh … yeah, I hope so, too. But I don't have any soup bowls, so it might be a little difficult. I suppose we could drink it from cups. Uh … do I need to heat it up?
M: No, don't worry. I heated it up before I left. That looks great. What is it?
V: It's Tina's cheesy chicken pasta surprise.
M: Ah. It smells great, but … what are those red things?
V: They look like they might be chilies.
M: Oh, I hope not! I hate spicy food.
V: Well, they might not be chilies. They may be red peppers or something.
M: No, they're definitely chilies. Oh, well – hopefully there are some other dishes that I can eat.
V: Uh … you may have a problem there. We also have Felipe's spicy chicken curry and Charlie's spicy chicken wings.
M: Oh, no! Well, at least I have my chicken soup. And it means there will be more food for you.
V: Uh … not really. I don't like chicken.

Lesson 7.2, Listening, Exercise B
7.5 **H = Host MT = Mrs. Taylor Mr.T = Mr. Taylor P = Philip A = Alison**

H: Hello and welcome to *The Food Fad Show*. Today, we're talking about food waste. Did you know that globally, we waste a huge amount of the food we produce. The average person, just one person, wastes $200 of food every year. Can you believe that? $200!
H: In the studio today we have the Taylor family. A year ago, they decided to reduce the amount of food they waste every year by 50 percent. Tell us more, Mrs. Taylor.
MT: Well, I've been interested in food waste for a long time. But the more I researched the topic, the more I realized that we aren't just throwing away food; we're also throwing away hundreds of dollars per year – enough to pay for a nice family vacation. That's when I decided we needed to cut our own waste dramatically.
H: OK, so what have you done to save money?
MT: Let me give you an example. Ugly carrots taste just as good as beautiful carrots, but in our local grocery store, they cost less than half as much. As far as I'm concerned, the uglier, the better! Also, my grocery store always lowers the price of meat or dairy products that are getting close to their best if used by date. So it's usually possible to buy food a lot more cheaply by checking those dates carefully. As long as you eat the food soon after buying it, it's completely safe.
H: Right. So it's all about money, then, Mr. Taylor?
Mr.T: No, not really. Food production has a massive impact on the environment: first to produce the food and distribute it, and then to get rid of any waste. I always thought the best way to save the planet was to reduce the amount of garbage we throw away and to reuse and recycle as much as possible. But in fact, the food itself has a much greater impact than the packaging it comes in. For example, throwing away a head of lettuce harms our planet 100 times more than throwing away the plastic bag.
H: Really? That's amazing. Why?
Mr.T: Well, just think of all the water needed to grow it, the electricity to keep the greenhouse at just the right temperature, and then the environmental cost of keeping it fresh all the way from the farm to your fridge. It all adds up!
H: Wow! I'd never thought of that!
Mr.T: Here's another example. It takes 100 buckets of water to bake one loaf of bread. A hundred! Think about that the next time you throw away some one-day-old bread. If we could end all food waste around the world, it would be like taking one quarter of the world's cars off the roads. As far as I'm concerned, the less food we throw away, the better.
H: OK, so what have you done to cut down on food waste? Alison?
A: Yes, well, before our experiment, Mom or Dad always served up a large plate of food for each of us, but it was usually too much for me. So half of it always went in the garbage can. These days, we all help ourselves to food from a serving dish in the middle of the

table. It's great because now we only take what we want – and we eat everything on our plates. It's much better because the less we cook, the less we waste.

H: OK, great. And what about leftovers?

A: When we started off, we had a rule that we had to eat yesterday's leftovers before any fresh food. But it was awful, so we stopped it. I mean, yesterday's leftovers are disgusting! Who wants to eat those? But now we use those leftovers to make soup or a stew. It's still a little strange, but the longer we do it, the more normal it feels.

H: Yes, I'm sure. OK, and what about Philip? Can I ask you a question or are you too busy playing on your phone?

P: Don't worry – I'm not playing. I wanted to show you a cool cell phone app. It helps us keep track of exactly what food we have in the house – and when that food will go bad.

H: Oh, OK. Sorry. So … how does it work?

P: Well, you need to type in all the numbers whenever you buy – or eat – anything. Some people might find that to be a waste of time, but I like that sort of thing. Of course, you don't need to count every single potato, for example, but the more carefully you count things, the more accurate your results will be. It's really fascinating when you study the numbers. Now, whenever we're in the grocery store, we can check what we need and what we don't. The app also sends us a notification when something is getting close to its best if used by date. That's really useful.

H: Yes, I'm sure.

P: And it even suggests delicious meal ideas to use up the ingredients we have, instead of buying new ones all the time. I never enjoyed cooking before, but thanks to the app, it's a lot more fun. And best of all, the app tells us exactly how much money we're saving every day.

H: Oh, yes. Tell us about the money, Mrs. Taylor.

MT: Well, so far, it's been a great success. According to Philip's app, we've managed to save $730 in food bills alone over the past year. And guess what? We're going on vacation next week to celebrate our excellent achievement.

H: Wow! Congratulations!

UNIT 8

Lesson 8.1, Listening, Exercise B
8.3 **C = Caroline T = Toby**

C: Hey, Toby. Do you want some coffee?

T: No, thanks. I'm in a hurry. I need to go to the library to work on my project for college.

C: Really? What's the project?

T: We have to invent 'something that will make a difference to people's lives'. But I'm terrible at coming up with ideas. They didn't teach us how to be creative in school when I was younger! But you, you're so creative. I mean, you write amazing stories; you design beautiful clothes. How do you do it?

C: Well, you can actually learn to use your imagination better. I've read a lot of books about creativity, and I've learned some great techniques from them.

T: Really? Can you give me an example?

C: Well, whenever I feel like I have too much work, I always stop working for an hour or so.

T: But I don't have time to stop. I'm really busy!

C: I always thought the same. But when I tried it, I found that a break actually boosted my creativity. When I'm relaxed, I have lots more creative ideas, and I'm much more productive after a break – I get more work done in less time. Tell me, how do you fill your time in the evenings?

T: Uh, I usually just watch TV or play games on my phone. I'm too tired to do anything else.

C: Aha. So that's what's blocking your creativity: you're filling your brain with information all the time. You need to unplug completely. Instead of watching TV, go for a run. You need to let your mind wander freely.

T: OK, I guess I can watch less TV. But I hate running!

C: Well, it doesn't have to be running. You could go dancing or swimming, or get some other type of physical exercise. They're all good for generating new ideas.

T: OK. I love swimming, so I guess I could go to the swimming pool once a week.

C: Great. Swimming's actually perfect because the water is blue.

T: Uh, sorry? What does that have to do with creativity?

C: Well, I read recently that the color blue makes us more creative. Whenever I need to think outside the box, I go to the beach and look at the sky and the ocean. It always helps.

T: OK, but it doesn't really help me with my project. I need to start work on it right now. I'm actually getting stressed about it.

C: Well, maybe that's the problem: you're letting your emotions block your creativity. You should look at a problem from the outside, to take away the emotions. Then it's much easier to find a solution. That's why it's easier to solve other people's problems than your own – because you can focus on the problems, not the emotions.

T: OK, but …

C: So another good technique is to discuss your ideas with other people – and listen to what they say. The best solutions usually come from group discussions and brainstorming sessions. And if there's nobody you can talk to, you can imagine having a conversation with a friend. Look at the problem through someone else's eyes.

T: OK, yes, I know what you mean. But what about my project? I need to come up with an invention right now. But I don't have any ideas at all. My mind's gone blank!

C: Well, there's one last trick I usually use when I really have no ideas. I call it the alphabet technique. OK, so tell me three letters of the alphabet.

T: Uh, W, G and P.

C: Perfect. So your invention needs to solve a problem, and that problem needs to start with your first letter, W.

T: Water? It isn't really a problem, is it?

C: Well, let's use your second letter to help us. What was it?

T: G for – grass. Hmm, water, grass. Aha, maybe the invention could be a better way of watering the grass in people's yards when they're away on vacation. I mean, just pouring water onto the grass all day and all night is really wasteful. But what's the solution?

C: I don't know. But it needs to start with your third letter, which was …?

T: P – for plastic bottles. Aha, I could use old plastic bottles, filled with water. Then I could make tiny holes in the bottles, so the water comes out really slowly, over a week or two.

C: Sounds good!

T: Hmm. I need to think about this carefully. OK, I'm going for a long walk along the beach to figure out the details. See you later.

C: OK. Call me if you need any help! Good luck!

Lesson 8.2, Listening, Exercises B and C
8.4 **L = Leo T = Teresa**

L: Hello, and welcome to this week's *Must-have Gadgets* podcast. I'm Leo Kovalski.

T: And I'm Teresa Martinez. Now, earlier this week I went to the International Gadget Show, where I saw some really amazing gadgets. And I've brought two along today to show you, Leo.

L: Sounds great. So what do you have for us?

T: Well, let's start with a very sensible invention: the Oombrella. What do you think, Leo?

L: Uh … it just looks like a normal umbrella. I mean, the design is gorgeous, really nice, but … it isn't exactly innovative, is it?

T: Oh! But this Oombrella is unique. It's the world's first umbrella that's connected to the internet.

L: What? Why on earth do I need an umbrella that connects to the internet?

T: Well, did you bring an umbrella to work today?

L: No, unfortunately. I forgot to check the weather forecast, so I didn't know it was going to rain.

T: Aha. Well, you can borrow my Oombrella today. It'll check the weather forecast for you. If the forecast says it's going to rain later, Oombrella will send a message to your cell phone.

L: OK, but why do I need a special umbrella just to send weather forecasts to my phone?

T: Well, the Oombrella is especially suitable for forgetful people, like you, who forget to check the weather forecast on their phones.

L: Yes, well, I am a fairly forgetful person. But what do forgetful people do all the time? They leave their umbrellas behind in cafés, or on the bus! What if I lose your Oombrella tonight?

T: Well, if you leave it behind, you'll get a message on your phone. They call it the unforgettable umbrella because you can't forget it.

L: OK, yes, that is pretty practical, I suppose.

T: Yes. And the Oombrella also has lots of sophisticated electronics: if you go for a long walk in the rain tonight, the app will send you a weather report when you get home. So you can read all about the weather during your walk.

L: Hmm … I'm not sure I need an Oombrella. I never go for a walk unless the sun's shining. The big question for me is: will it keep me dry if there's a storm tomorrow morning when I'm coming to work?

T: Absolutely! It's made of super-strong materials, so it won't break. You'll be able to use it for years.

L: Really? Well that is impressive. My umbrellas always break after five minutes in a storm. So if this Oombrella lasts for years, I'll be very happy.

T: Well, I only said you could borrow mine. I'd like to have it back tomorrow.

L: Oh, yes, of course. So … what else do you have?

T: Well, the second gadget is called CleverPet. It's a food bowl for dogs and cats.

L: Great. And don't tell me … it's connected to the internet, right?

T: Yes! How did you guess? Do you have any pets, Leo?

L: Yes, I have a dog named Henry.

T: And what does Henry do all day, while you're at work?

L: Uh … not much. He sleeps most of the day, but sometimes he chews the furniture in my apartment.

T: Well, that's because he's bored. Of course he chews your furniture if he has nothing else to do all day.

L: OK. And what does this have to do with your incredible internet-connected dog food bowl?

T: Well, it isn't just a bowl. It's a puzzle.

L: A puzzle? For dogs?

T: Yes. There are three buttons with lights. When a light flashes, the dog has to press a button. If he presses the right button, the light goes on again and he wins something to eat.

L: OK.

T: Then, over the next few days, weeks, even years, the puzzles get more and more difficult. The dog has to remember lots of information and press the buttons in the right order.

L: Oh, right. And, uh, do dogs enjoy puzzles?

T: Absolutely! They love them. It keeps them busy for hours, which means they never get bored. And if they don't get bored, they don't chew the furniture.

L: Well, I must admit, it sounds fascinating.

T: It is. And it really helps pets stay active. Scientists have shown that pets stay healthier and they live longer if they keep busy. You should definitely get one for Henry.

L: Yes, I think I might!

T: Great.

L: OK, so that's all from today's podcast. We'll be back next time with more must-have gadgets. Thanks for listening.

UNIT 9

Lesson 9.1, Listening, Exercise B

9.1 **C = Chair L = Leon V = Violet F = Florian**

C: Welcome to the final of the Warehouse Project competition. Now, we received hundreds of excellent ideas, but there can only be one winner. Today, the three finalists are here to present their proposals before the public vote later this evening. But for now, let's hear from the first finalist, Leon MacGregor.

L: Thank you. I'd like to present my proposal to turn the warehouse into a community music center, with modern recording studios, rehearsal rooms and a performance area for live concerts. If the proposal is successful, people will be able to use the center free of charge. I believe music can make a big difference to our community, especially for older people who have retired from work. If we open a community music center, it will change thousands of people's lives, by giving them opportunities to go out, meet new people and learn new skills. Won't that be wonderful for our city?

My dream is for the people of this city to join music classes with professional musicians, to learn how to sing or to play a musical instrument. They'll work together to form bands, orchestras and choirs. They'll have the space and equipment they need to rehearse and create new music. And they'll be able to perform live in front of an audience. If you share my dream, vote for my proposal to help it come true. Music … for the community.

C: Thank you, Leon. Our next finalist is Violet Spring.

V: Thank you. As an actor, I love the theater. And I'm not alone – tens of thousands of people all over the country visit the theater every day. But not in this city. Since the Grand Theater closed down ten years ago, theater-lovers have had nowhere to go. They have to travel to theaters in other cities – and spend their money there instead of here. But I'm convinced that if we had a good, modern theater in this city, it would be extremely popular. What do I mean by a modern theater? Well, I firmly believe that the future is immersive theater.

Immersive theater is where the audience becomes part of the performance. There's no stage – just one shared space for actors and spectators alike. You don't just watch a play – you experience it. Immersive theater works best in a large open area, where groups of audience members can move around to watch different scenes of the play in different parts of the theater. And I think the city's warehouse would make a wonderful immersive theater. But it isn't just about art. Immersive theater is also a great business. The best shows attract rich international tourists who are prepared to pay premium prices. If we turned the warehouse into a theater, it would make a lot of money. This money could be spent on schools, roads and other important things for the city. If you like the sound of that, please support my proposal.

C: Thank you, Violet. Very interesting. Our final finalist is Florian Quirk.

F: Thank you. Let me ask you a question. What … is the purpose … of art? To keep bored people busy? To make money from rich tourists? No, I don't think so. Art is about opening your mind to new experiences, new emotions. It's about losing yourself … and finding yourself. Great art makes you laugh; it makes you cry; it makes you think. It helps you see things you've never seen, feel things you've never felt, understand things you've never understood. In short, the purpose of art … is to give a purpose … to life. That's why I'd like to turn the warehouse into a gallery of modern art. A place where audiences can view the works of today's best artists, including exhibits by some of the talented artists from this city. And if we make it free of charge, all the people of this city can enjoy the exhibits, displays and live performances. So if you really want to use this space for the arts, then forget about business plans and community projects. Let's create a gallery that will change the way the people of this city think … forever. Thank you.

C: OK, thank you. Well, I must say, all three proposals sound excellent! If the city council had three warehouses, maybe we could do all of those wonderful things. But we only have one warehouse, unfortunately, so we need to make a choice. Erm … I'd like to call a 15-minute break now so we can …

Lesson 9.2, Listening, Exercise B

9.5 Z = Zoe J = Jacob

Z: So, Jacob, how's your creative writing class going?

J: Really well, thanks, Zoe. This week, we've been writing flash fiction. That's where you have to write stories within a word limit, usually 1,000 words. It's really difficult.

Z: Really? Why?

J: Because you have to make every word count. It makes you think hard, and that makes you more creative.

Z: Yes, I see what you mean, but 1,000 sounds very extreme.

J: Well, it isn't as extreme as micro-stories. They're stories on social media sites like Twitter. A whole story told in a 140-character message.

Z: You're joking, right?

J: No, I'm not. Do you want to hear one of my favorites? 'It was him! She sat in embarrassed silence. She wondered if he even knew she existed. He sat beside her, wondering the same. Nobody spoke.'

Z: OK. It isn't much of a story, is it? I mean, nothing happened.

J: No. But it's about creating a powerful scene, and characters with real emotions.

Z: Characters? You just said 'he' and 'she'.

J: Well, it's usually better if the writer provides less information, so that you, the reader, can create the missing information from your own imagination.

Z: Uh, OK.

J: OK, so here's another one. 'Alone, he ran nervously into the dark forest. A shadow. "Who's there?" he shouted. "Don't worry," whispered a cold voice. "You aren't alone."'

Z: Oh, that's better. I see what you mean about using your imagination. I like the twist at the end.

J: What do you mean by 'twist'?

Z: It's when something happens in the story that you didn't expect. I mean, you think he's alone, but then he isn't. It's really powerful, isn't it?!

J: Yeah, I think so. There are also some groups on social media that write collaborative stories: stories that are created by a large group of people working together. So for example, I'll write the beginning of a story, in one 140-character message, and then you'll write the next part of the story, and so on. Eventually, we'll end up with an amazing story.

Z: Ah. It reminds me of a game we played when I was a child. We called it 'Pass the paper'. You write one line of a story on a sheet of paper, fold it down and pass it to the next player, who writes the next line, and so on. We could play it now, if you like. You'll enjoy it!

J: No, thanks. It isn't my kind of thing. But there are actually websites now that do similar things. You write a sentence online, and then someone else writes the next sentence, and so on. I know some people in my class use websites like those to give them ideas. Of course, most of the stories are trash, but it's all about opening your mind to new ideas.

Z: Yes, I'm sure.

J: And there's another one where each person can just write three words. Some of the stories are really funny.

Z: Oh, yes. That reminds me of another game we frequently played when I was a student in California, 'Add a word'. Do you know it? It's when a group of you sit in a circle. The first person says the first word from a sentence, like 'My'. And then the next person says the next word. For example …

J: Favorite?

Z: OK, yes. So, my – favorite, uh, frog.

J: Lives?

Z: Uh, under.

J: My.

Z: Uh, bed?

J: OK. Uh, because.

Z: He.

J: Can't.

Z: Afford.

J: A.

Z: Hotel?

J: Yeah, why not. Hey, that's a great game for collaborative stories, Zoe. You see! When you work together, you come up with ideas that you'd never have if you were on your own.

Z: Sure. So is that how you always come up with new ideas?

J: Not always, no. I sometimes use story dice.

Z: Story dice?

J: Yes. I have a set of 12 dice, and each one has six pictures, one on each side.

Z: OK.

J: So if I'm figuring out an idea for my story, I throw six dice. Then I have to use all six pictures in my story. Let's say the pictures on my dice show a castle, the color blue, an angry face, a bag of money, a motorcycle and a fish. So I have to write my story so that it includes all those things.

Z: Wow! So how about 'My fish was angry because he crashed his expensive motorcycle into a blue castle'?

J: Well, that's very creative, but it has to sound natural and believable. The story can have up to 1,000 words, remember.

Z: Cool. OK, I'm going to try to write it.

J: Great. It won't be easy … but it should be fun!

UNIT 10

Lesson 10.1, Listening, Exercise B

10.2 R = Robert V = Vicky

R: Would you mind if I borrowed your laptop for a few minutes?

V: No, of course not. Go ahead. Just bear in mind that it's really slow and it keeps crashing all the time.

R: Sounds like you need a new one.

V: Yeah, I know. I'm trying to buy one, but … it's difficult.

R: What do you mean?

V: Well, I went to the electronics store last week. They had over 100 laptops to choose from. After about three hours in the store, looking at every single laptop, I found two that I liked, but I was of two minds and I couldn't decide which one to buy. It was horrible. In the end, I gave up! But never mind. I still have my old computer, so it isn't so bad.

R: Ah. Sounds like the Paradox of Choice.

V: What's that?

R: Well, the name comes from an American psychologist, Professor Barry Schwartz. According to Professor Schwartz, most people assume that having lots of choices is always a good thing. But he's shown that in fact too many choices is bad for us. It makes us stressed, so we can't make decisions.

V: Uh … OK. So why do stores give us so many choices? Surely they'd sell more if they reduced the number of choices?

R: Exactly. The problem is, most companies still think more is better. But a few smart companies have realized that they'll sell more if they offer fewer choices. I read recently that a shampoo company cut the number of shampoo choices from 26 to 15. Everyone thought they'd lose sales, but in fact, their sales went up by ten percent.

V: Really? Wow! So fewer choices is better.

R: Yes, in general. But of course it's better to have some choice than no choice at all – that's just common sense.

V: Right.

R: So with your laptop, you should have gone to a smaller store. If you'd done that, you'd have had fewer choices, but your decision would have been much easier. The store where I bought mine had just three laptops to choose from. One was too expensive; one was too basic; the third one was absolutely fine, so I bought it. It took me five minutes. And I'm very happy with it.

V: Wow! I could never do that. I'd be worried that I'd missed the chance to buy a better computer somewhere else.

R: That's because you're a perfectionist.

V: A perfectionist? What's that?

R: It's a person who always looks for the perfect thing to buy. You can't relax unless you're sure you've studied every option and chosen the best one. And even after you've made a decision, you still worry that you've made the wrong choice.

V: Yeah, that definitely sounds like me! For example, I went shopping for some new shoes last week. After about six hours, I finally bought a pair. But when I got them home, I regretted my decision immediately. I realized that they weren't perfect and I shouldn't have bought them. So I took them back to the store to get my money back. Then I bought a different pair of shoes, but I took them back to the store a few days later. In the end, I bought the first pair again.

R: Yes, you're definitely a perfectionist. I, on the other hand, am what I call a 'quick decider'.

V: What's that?

R: It's a person who makes quick decisions without worrying about perfection. When I'm shopping for new jeans, for instance, and I find some jeans that are good enough, I buy them and stop worrying about them. And I never take them back to the store – unless they're damaged, of course. Once I've made up my mind, I stick with my decision.

V: Wow! You're so lucky. I could never do that!

R: Well, you think it's impossible, but maybe it's all in the mind. I think you can become a quick decider – you just need to put your mind to it! It'll make life much easier.

V: Yes, you're right. I'll definitely do that! From now on, I'm going to be a quick decider. But, uh, what if I change my mind later?

Lesson 10.2, Listening, Exercise B
10.3 **D = David B = Barbara A = Alice L = Leo**

D: Hello, and welcome back to *All in the Mind*. On today's show, we're talking about habits. I'm joined by Professor Barbara Janovich, an expert in habits. Welcome to the show, Professor.

B: Thanks, David.

D: So, Barbara, why do we develop bad habits? And why are they so hard to break?

B: Well, the best way to understand habits is to break them into four parts. First, there's a cue, which might be something that you see or hear or feel. So in your example with fast food, the cue might be that you're driving in your car and you see a sign for a fast-food restaurant. Or maybe you're walking through a shopping mall and suddenly you smell the fast food.

D: Oh, yes. That smell always makes me want to eat fast food, even when I'm not hungry! I wish it didn't, but it does!

B: Exactly. So the next stage is the routine – the actions you always take. So this is where you go into the fast food restaurant, order your food and eat it. In a true habit, you can do all of this without really thinking – it kind of happens to you, and your brain almost shuts off.

D: OK.

B: And then the third part is the reward: something nice happens. In this case, the sugar and salt in the food cause your brain to produce feel-good chemicals.

D: OK, so the cycle is cue, routine, reward. But you said there are four parts. What's the fourth part?

B: Well, this is the dangerous part: the craving. Let me explain. If you repeat the cycle a few times, your brain produces those feel-good chemicals earlier and earlier in the process. So instead of being part of the reward, you get that nice feeling at the cue stage – when you see the restaurant sign, for example, or you smell the food and you know the reward is coming soon. And now you have a problem: you've had the good feeling, but you haven't had the reward yet. This creates the craving – a powerful need to get your reward. Now you can't relax until you have your reward.

D: Ah. I wish I'd known about all this a few years ago! But I guess it's too late for me now. Is there anything I can do to break the cycle?

B: Yes, but isn't easy. You can't stop the cues, and you still need the reward. So the trick is to change the routine. So for example, I always keep a package of low-fat salty snacks in my bag. That means that when I drive past a sign for a fast-food restaurant, I treat myself to a snack from the package.

D: Uh, can I try one of those?

B: Sure! Help yourself.

B: So the cue is the same, and the reward is similar – salty food – but I've changed the routine. Of course, salty snacks aren't perfect, but they're a lot cheaper and healthier than a burger and fries.

D: Sounds good. OK, so earlier we asked our listeners to call in to tell us about their bad habits. Our first caller is Leo. Leo, what's your habit?

L: Hello. Well, it's coffee. I drink about eight cups a day, but I don't even like it very much! I wish I could stop, but I can't control myself.

B: OK. Well, let's start with the first cup of coffee each day, Leo. What's your cue for drinking it?

L: It's when I arrive at work. I always make myself a cup of coffee before I check my emails.

B: How long does it take to get to work?

L: About an hour. Why?

B: Well, it sounds like the reward isn't really the coffee, but a five-minute break after your long, tiring trip.

L: Uh, yes, maybe.

B: So now we know the cue and the reward, the question is: is there a different routine that would give you the same reward after your trip to work?

L: I suppose I could get myself a glass of water and go for a quick walk around the office.

B: Sounds good.

D: OK, great. I hope your new routine works for you, Leo. I wish we had time to talk about your other seven cups of coffee, but we need to go to our next caller, Alice. What's your bad habit, Alice?

A: Well, actually, I'd like some help creating a new habit. You see, I wish I could run a marathon next year. I go running from time to time, but I want to get into the habit of running every day. I always set myself goals, but nothing seems to work. I really wish I were better organized.

D: Thanks for that, Alice. Professor?

B: Well, first of all, Alice, don't blame yourself. This is a very common problem. If you want to create a new habit, again you need to think about cues and rewards: what will make you remember to go running at the same time every day? How will you reward yourself for being good? So let's start by creating your cue, Alice. When would be a good time of day to go running?

Contents

GRAMMAR

Simple present and present progressive

A Underline the correct options to complete the sentences.

1 How many languages *do you speak* / *are you speaking*?
2 I *take* / *am taking* the Number 36 bus to work every morning.
3 Misha *learns* / *is learning* Spanish right now.
4 Ahmed *seems* / *is seeming* to like living in another country for now.
5 I *look* / *am looking* for my tablet. Have you seen it anywhere?
6 They *become* / *are becoming* increasingly depressed with the wet weather.
7 Don't worry – the movie *doesn't contain* / *isn't containing* anything unsuitable for children.
8 My husband *thinks* / *is thinking* of buying a smartphone.

B Complete the table with the verbs in the box.

believe belong bring complain cost get include know mean need own prefer relax seem show take understand want watch write

Stative	Dynamic

C Complete the blog post with the simple present or present progressive form of the verbs in parentheses.

Blog post

My Travel Adventures

2/23/2018 | 12:26pm | 3 comments

What a week we had! I [1] ________________ (*relax*) at home now because I [2] ________________ (*need*) a good rest. I [3] ________________ (*have*) a very busy life but I [4] ________________ (*not think*) it's something to complain about. I [5] ________________ (*travel*) all over the world for work and I [6] ________________ (*love*) that aspect of my job. Last week, we were in Russia. That's me in the photograph, in St. Petersburg. I [7] ________________ (*smile*) because it was a beautiful sunny day. It usually [8] ________________ (*snow*) in February!

Like | Comment | Share

VOCABULARY
Seeing and hearing

A Complete the sentences with the correct form of the verbs in the box. You will need to use some of the verbs more than once.

hear listen look see sound watch

1 Ava ______________ like she's been very sick.
2 Do you want to ______________ to the podcast about rock climbing?
3 Can you ______________ that strange noise coming from the computer?
4 Ute didn't ______________ the step in the hallway and tripped over it.
5 I can't talk now because I ______________ my favorite comedy series.
6 In today's lesson, we ______________ at the use of technology for language learning.
7 That song ______________ a lot like an old folk song my father used to sing.
8 Does this dress ______________ good on me?

B Read each sentence. Circle the correct answer, a, b or c.

1 With her bright pink hair you can always ___ Sandra in a crowd.
   a observe
   b spot
   c stare
2 Part of his job is to ___ people's behavior in group situations.
   a spot
   b recognize
   c observe
3 He edits his selfies so much that sometimes I don't ___ him!
   a recognize
   b observe
   c spot
4 It's very rude to ___ at other people like that!
   a notice
   b stare
   c observe
5 Luckily, my teacher didn't ___ when I arrived five minutes late for class.
   a recognize
   b spot
   c notice

C Complete the following sentences so that they are true for you.

1 I enjoy watching ______________ (*type of sports/movies/TV shows*).
2 I've been told I look just like ______________ (*family member or celebrity*).
3 I really hate/love the sound of ______________ (*noise*).
4 I've been listening to ______________ (*music or podcast*) a lot lately.
5 I'm good at noticing when ______________ (*thing or action*).

PRONUNCIATION
Schwa /ə/

A Underline three schwas in each sentence.

1 We speak a lot of English at home.
2 The Spanish exam was difficult, but I think I passed.
3 I don't usually listen to podcasts.
4 A photo doesn't always show the real you.
5 I met up with an old friend at the park.
6 That's me in the photograph with my family.

1.1 **B Listen. Check your answers to Exercise A.**

1.1 **C Listen again and repeat each sentence.**

GRAMMAR

Subject and object questions

A Correct the mistakes in each question.

1 What do you guys go out the other night?

2 Which do you want, an ice-cream cone?

3 What Jack want to do for his birthday next week?

4 How much did she have to wait at the bank?

5 Who shoes are these?

6 How doesn't Laura come to the party with us?

B Rewrite these sentences as questions. The underlined words are the answer to each question.

1 Kyoko speaks English with a strong Japanese accent.

Who speaks English with a strong Japanese accent?

2 Danny learned Spanish at a school in Madrid.

3 The language lab is open from 10 am to 9 pm.

4 You can improve your English by watching English movies.

5 Yes, we should ask the teacher what this word means.

6 Shakespeare is considered the greatest writer of modern English.

7 I'm studying modern American literature this semester.

8 We speak Jamaican English at home.

C Complete the conversation with one to four words in each space.

Charley: Simone, [1] *how many languages* are spoken in South Africa?

Simone: Well, officially there are 11 languages.

Charley: Wow, that's a lot. [2] ______ all of them?

Simone: Yes, I can. Well, ... a little bit of all of them, and one or two completely.

Charley: [3] ______ language is your native language?

Simone: I speak Southern Sesotho, which is also called *Sotho*. This language is also commonly spoken in Lesotho.

Charley: Ah, interesting. [4] ______ for English speakers to learn?

Simone: Yes, it's difficult to learn, unfortunately. It's very different from English.

Charley: Oh, [5] ______ different?

Simone: Well, there are 9 vowels and 35 consonants, and 3 of the consonants are clicks, written as *x*, *c* and *q*.

Charley: Oh, I've heard about that. [6] ______ that sound?

Simone: You make it by clicking your tongue against your mouth. It takes some practice to get used to it, but anyone can learn!

Charley: Cool! I'd like to try that. [7] ______ me how to do it sometime?

Simone: Of course I'll teach you! But [8] ______ so interested in languages?

Charley: I suppose because I enjoy communicating in very different ways.

VOCABULARY
Languages

A **Match the words (1–7) with the definitions (a–g).**

1 phrase	**a** the way someone pronounces words
2 bilingual	**b** able to speak only one language
3 fluently	**c** (speaking) correctly, without making mistakes
4 accent	**d** able to speak two languages
5 accurately	**e** any small group of words that form a single meaning
6 monolingual	**f** a group of words which, when used together, have a different meaning from the individual words
7 idiom	**g** (speaking) easily, without difficulty

B **Complete the sentences with the words from Exercise A.**

1 When teachers want you to use a dictionary to find out the meaning of a word, they usually use the ________________ *Look it up!*

2 His tongue wasn't literally tied; to 'have your tongue tied' is a(n) ________________ meaning that you have nothing to say.

3 I can't speak Russian ________________, but I can understand it when I hear it.

4 Many English speakers are ________________ because they don't have a major need to learn another language.

5 I can tell by her ________________ that she's from Argentina.

6 If you don't spell the words ________________, you will lose points.

7 Canadians living in Quebec are usually ________________; they can speak both French and English.

PRONUNCIATION
Pronouncing questions

1.2 **A** **Listen to the speakers and underline which question you hear.**

1 **a** What do you learn in class?
b What did you learn in class?

2 **a** What do you want for lunch?
b What did you want for lunch?

3 **a** How do you like your class?
b How did you like your class?

4 **a** How do you know Marcus?
b How did you know Marcus?

5 **a** Do you want to use my phone?
b Did you want to use my phone?

B **Practice saying the questions in Exercise A.**

1.2 **C** **Listen again and check your pronunciation.**

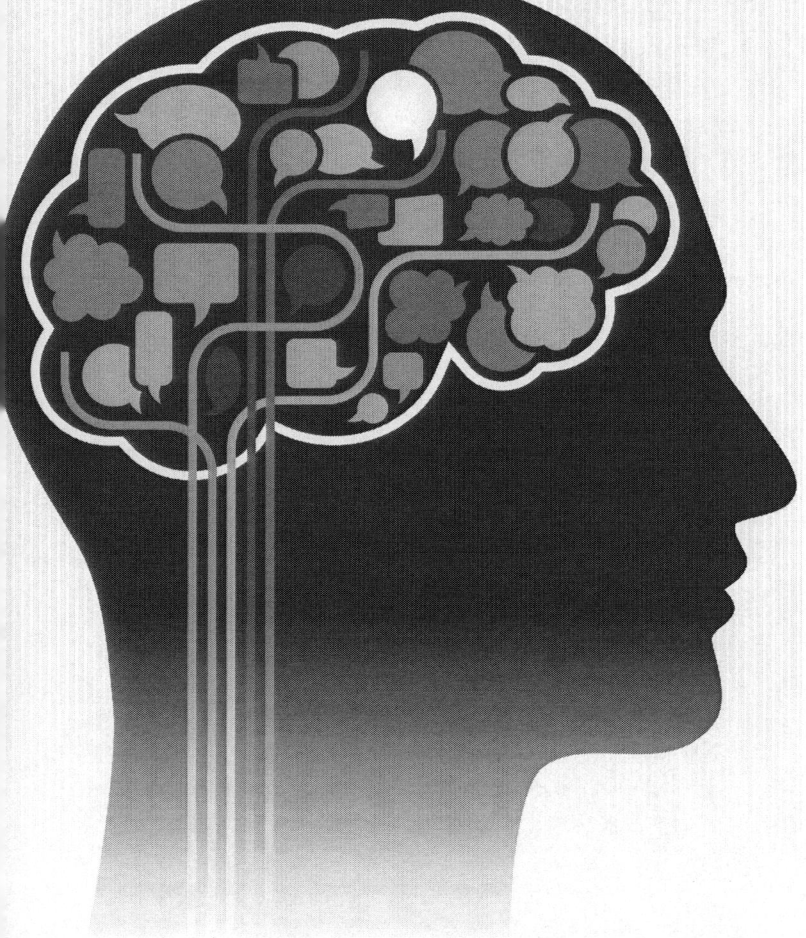

READING

A PREDICT What are some possible answers to these questions?

1 Are there countries where more than ten languages are spoken?
2 How many languages do you think it's possible for one person to learn?
3 Does learning a new language make us more intelligent?

B READ FOR GIST Read *Secrets of the super language learners* quickly to check your predictions.

C READ FOR DETAIL Match the rhetorical questions with paragraphs 1–3 of the article. There are two rhetorical questions you do not need to use.

a What are the benefits of speaking other languages?
b Do monolinguals have better memories?
c How many languages is it possible for one person to learn?
d Are hyperglots smarter than the rest of us?
e What's the record number of languages spoken?

Secrets of the super language learners

1 ___ Some European citizens may use two or three languages regularly, but the number of languages spoken in some African countries is incredible. Cameroon in Central Africa has an amazing 250! People who have learned several languages through hearing them on a daily basis are known as *multilinguals*. A different type of learner altogether is the *hyperglot* – a person who has spent their entire life learning and perfecting dozens of different languages.

2 ___ This question is difficult to answer as some of the world's most famous hyperglots lived many years ago. Emil Krebs, who was born in 1867, spoke and wrote 68 languages fluently and also studied another 120 languages. In more recent times, Kenneth Hale, an American college professor, probably holds the modern-day record with 50 languages spoken. What's more, he could pick up a new language with incredible speed and was able to have a basic conversation after just 15 minutes of listening to a native speaker.

3 ___ Studies have shown that the brain activity of both multilinguals and hyperglots is very different from that of people who speak only one language. The act of learning a new language, like any cognitive process, builds new neural pathways and actually increases the size of the brain. Other benefits include improved ability to focus and better memory.

Glossary

cognitive (adj) related to mental processes such as memory, reasoning, etc
neural pathway (n) nerve cells that receive messages from your brain
pick up (phr v) to learn a new language without effort or study

D REFLECT Think about the answers to these questions.

1 Do you think learning many languages is a good idea?
2 Which new language(s) would you like to learn? Why?

5:15 pm: In today's *TechHub*,
presenter John Grimes examines the selfie phenomenon.

LISTENING

1.3 **A PREDICT** Look at the pictures and the magazine listing and circle the best answer. Listen to the introduction and check your answers.

1. I'm going to hear *an advertisement for a selfie camera / part of a radio show.*
2. The recording will be about *selfie addiction / a new selfie app*.

1.4 **B LISTEN FOR GIST** Listen to the full interview and answer the questions.

1. The purpose of *Meitu* is to
   - **a** share your personal information.
   - **b** create the perfect selfie.
2. *Meitu* is
   - **a** the same as other similar apps.
   - **b** better and more advanced than other similar apps.

Glossary

facial recognition technology (n) computer technology used to scan and recognize human faces
launch (v) to start selling a new product or service
retouch (v) to make small changes to a photo or picture

1.4 **C LISTEN FOR DETAIL** Are the sentences true (T) or false (F)? Correct the false sentences. Then listen again and check your answers.

1. *Meitu* is a new app.
2. It is only available in Asia.
3. *Meitu* is for people who want to look perfect.
4. The user ends up looking like a different person.
5. The app is now being used by airport security companies.
6. *Meitu* is different because it has access to all your personal information.

D REFLECT Think about the answers to these questions.

1. How important is it to look good in selfies?
2. Are you worried about phone apps accessing your personal information? Why/Why not?

FUNCTIONAL LANGUAGE

Asking for, offering and responding to help

A Complete the conversation with one or two words in each space.

Jess: Would you [1] ______ me a hand with something?
Matt: I'd be happy [2] ______. What's the problem?
Jess: I'm trying to download *Meitu* onto my phone. It's a Chinese photo-editing app.
Matt: First go to your settings and click on *clear cache*.
Jess: OK. I've done that.
Matt: Now you need to restart your phone. Do you want me [3] ______ that?
Jess: That [4] ______ great. If [5] ______ mind.
Matt: No problem. There you [6] ______.
Jess: Thank you so much.

B Circle the correct words to complete the conversation.

Milo: Do you want a [1]*hand / help* with your project?
Fiona: Hi, Milo. Yes, I could use your [2]*hand / help*. I have to Photoshop this picture I drew in art class.
Milo: Hmm. That isn't going to be [3]*nice / easy* because your computer is slow. Why don't you use my laptop?
Fiona: Thanks, Milo. You're [4]*a myth / amazing*! I owe you one!
Milo: Actually, I need a [5]*help / favor*, too. My drawing is terrible. Can you help me draw it again?
Fiona: Of course I can.

WRITING

A Look at the results of a college survey and answer the questions.

Where do you get your news?

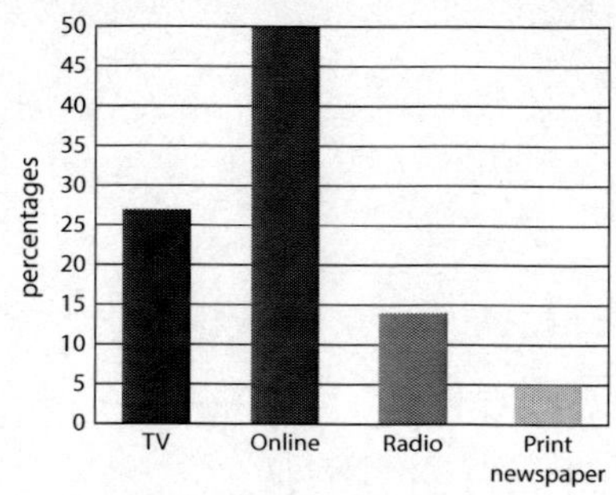

1 Are these results surprising? Why/Why not?
2 Where do you and your friends usually get your news?

B ORGANIZATION **Match the sections (a–g) from a report about trends in news media with the paragraphs in which you think they will appear. Then read the report to check your ideas.**

a Where they got their information.
b A summary of the situation.
c The purpose of the report.
d Information about TV news.
e Information about radio news.
f Information about print newspapers.
g Information about online news.

Introduction: ___, ___
Paragraph 1: ___
Paragraph 2: ___
Paragraph 3: ___, ___
Conclusion: ___

C **Match the headings (a–f) to the paragraphs (1–3) in the report. There are three headings you do not need to use.**

a Nobody watches TV these days.
b Digital is more popular than print.
c Where most students get the news.
d Newspapers are boring.
e Why television scores low.
f Online news tops the charts.

Report about trends in news media

Statistics suggest that young people today are not particularly interested in *hard news*. We [1]***conducted / did*** a survey to see how true this is. While our results might seem to confirm the statistics, they do not give the whole picture.

1 ___

Half of those surveyed got their news online. [2]***A lot of them said / Many claimed*** that they did not have time to keep up with all the news and preferred to read brief summaries. If there was a big news story, they followed it in greater detail.

2 ___

The surprisingly low figure for television news is partly explained by the fact that few of them have televisions. This does not suggest [3]***they don't like / a lack of interest in*** the news.

3 ___

The very low percentage of print newspaper readers is [4]***due to the fact that / because*** most newspapers have an online version. Those that got their news from the radio said that it was because they had the radio on most of the time anyway.

Conclusion

While it is true that few young people read print newspapers or watch television news, this is a sign of the times. [5]***I know that / It seems that*** they get the news they want online and are as well-informed as any previous generation.

D USING FORMAL LANGUAGE **Circle the more formal phrases to complete the report.**

WRITING PRACTICE

A PREPARE **You are going to write a report about trends in the use of technology for education.**

- Choose two or three points to include in your report. These will be your main paragraphs.

B WRITE **Write your report in 150–200 words. Remember:**

- to start with an introduction, stating the purpose of your report and where you got your information.
- to provide suitable headings for each paragraph.
- to use formal language.
- to end with a conclusion.

PRONUNCIATION
's and 've

2.1 **A** **Listen to eight sentences. Complete the sentences with a missing word or contraction.**

1. ________ planted a tree.
2. ________ finished my work.
3. ________ made a list.
4. ________ started an online course.
5. ________ saved a lot of money.
6. ________ climbed a mountain.
7. ________ started a new job.
8. ________ made our decision.

B **Practice saying the sentences in Exercise A.**

GRAMMAR
Present perfect and simple past

A **Complete the conversation with the present perfect or simple past form of the verbs in parentheses.**

Alex: So, [1] ________ you ever ________ (*make*) a bucket list?

Bex: Yes, I have. I [2] ________ (*write*) one about five years ago. But I [3] ________ (*not do*) many of the things yet!

Alex: How many [4] ________ you ________ (*do*) so far?

Bex: Only one, actually! On my last birthday, I [5] ________ (*go*) skydiving. That [6] ________ (*be*) wonderful. So, only 99 more things to do! How about you?

Alex: Oh, I [7] ________ never ________ (*make*) a bucket list. My brother [8] ________ (*write*) one, though. He's always doing the things on his list.

Bex: Such as?

Alex: Well, for example, already this year, he [9] ________ (*learn*) how to fly. Last December, he [10] ________ (*go*) swimming with dolphins. He loves doing new and unusual things if he has the money.

B **Underline the correct option to complete the sentences.**

1. I *still* / *yet* haven't visited Australia, but I will one day.
2. My friend *has gone* / *went* swimming with dolphins last year.
3. Where is the most memorable place you *have ever been* / *ever went*?
4. I've *still* / *just* solved a difficult problem we had at work.
5. Philippe *has been* / *was* here for three months so far.
6. I've *just* / *never* wanted to do anything daring, like climbing a mountain.
7. Marta *went* / *has gone* skydiving on her 30th birthday.
8. I've been so busy that I haven't answered that email *already* / *yet*.

C **Complete the blog so that it is true for you.**

Have you ever ...? blog

When I was younger two of my dreams were ________ and ________.

Unfortunately I haven't ________ yet, but I have ________.

I achieved my dream ________ (*when*) in ________ (*where*). I was with ________ (*who*) at time. I felt so ________ (*emotion*).

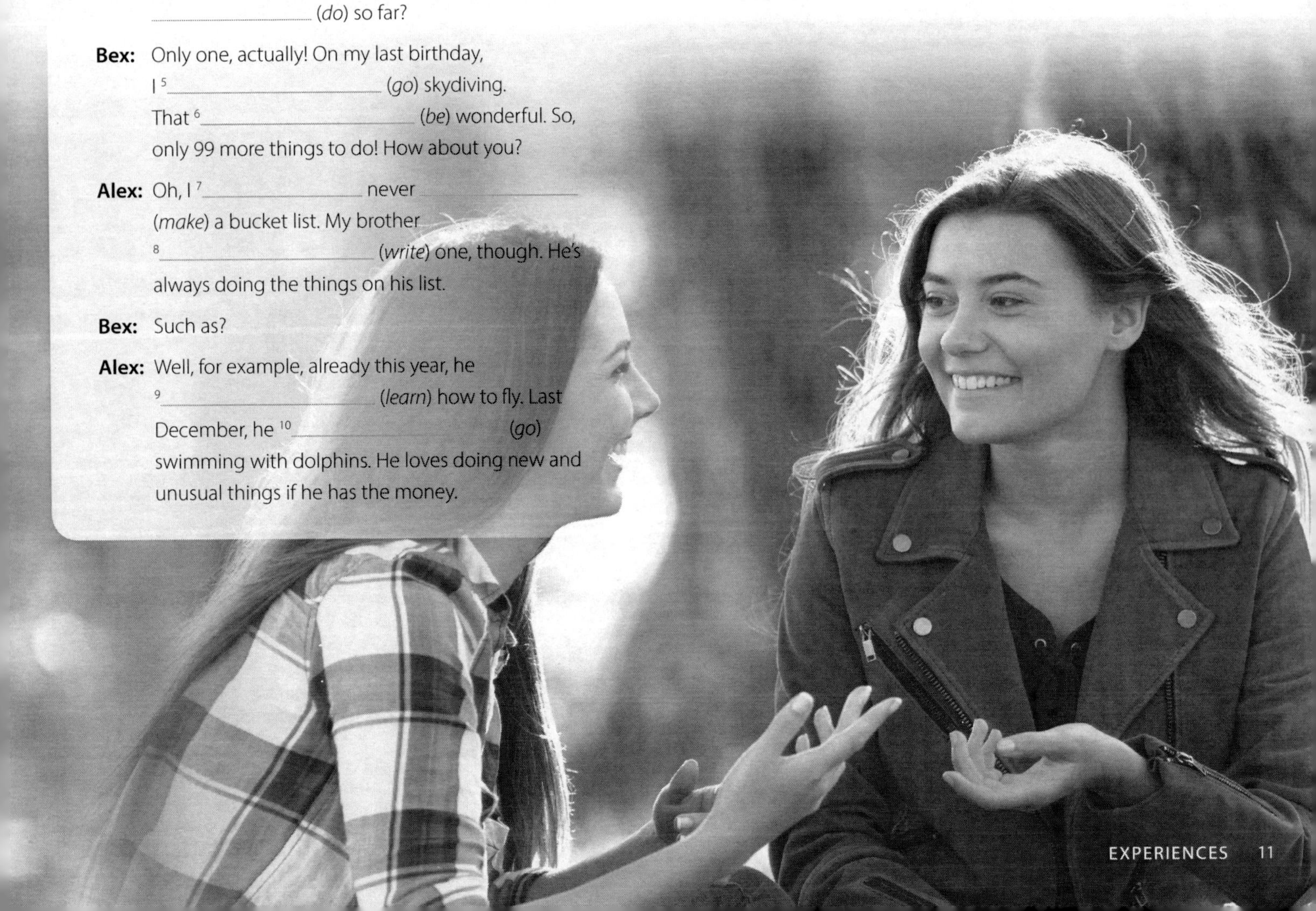

VOCABULARY
Collocations: making big decisions

A Complete the collocations with the verbs in the box.

lose make (x2) put set stay take turn work

1 ________ the next step
2 ________ a plan into action
3 ________ a dream into reality
4 ________ short-term and long-term goals
5 ________ heart
6 ________ the break
7 ________ toward a goal
8 ________ motivated
9 ________ a decision

B Complete the sentences with the collocations from Exercise A.

1 Don't ________ – we'll get to the top of the mountain in the end.
2 We have to find a way to stay ________, otherwise we'll never finish this project.
3 Making a list of your plans and ambitions is great in theory, but you won't achieve them unless you put those plans ________.
4 Leaving home is a difficult decision, Anya, but I really think you need to make ________ and learn to be independent.
5 You came first in the local talent contest, but are you ready to take ________ and audition for the national contest?
6 I have to make ________ – do I stay at this job or look for something better?
7 Giles is working toward ________ of becoming a successful businessman.
8 We all have a dream, but some of us manage to turn that dream ________.
9 I know what I want to achieve in the long term, but it's important to set ________ along the way.

VOCABULARY

Dependent prepositions (verb / adjective + *for* / *of*)

A Match the beginnings of the sentences (1–8) with the endings (a–h).

1 This job would only be suitable
2 Management doesn't seem to be aware
3 It was typical
4 Niaz has asked for
5 Sally is very proud
6 In my first job I worked
7 It can be difficult to prepare
8 Are you looking

a of Joel to try to solve the problem on his own.
b for an animal charity as a volunteer.
c for someone who speaks Japanese.
d for your first job interview.
e of herself for learning how to surf.
f permission to take the day off.
g of how big the problem is.
h for a new job now?

B Complete the sentences with the collocations from Exercise A.

1 Anyone who takes up mountaineering should be __________ the dangers involved.
2 Sandra was going to take her kids to see a new fantasy movie; luckily her sister warned her that it wasn't __________ children before she bought the tickets.
3 The dishes in the restaurant were very __________ the region – all the food was delicious!
4 Thomas spent all morning __________ his keys, but he still couldn't find them.
5 Melissa is __________ a big tech company in California. She absolutely loves it there.
6 Lara's parents were so __________ her when she graduated from college last year.
7 The couple in the café __________ their bill.
8 Claire has been __________ her first marathon for the past six months.

Problems and solutions

C Complete the letter of advice with the correct form of the verbs in the box.

agree analyze cause come deal solve suggest

Dear Carlo,

In your letter you told me that you don't know how to [1] __________ with a difficult situation at work. Well, first you need to think about what's [2] __________ the problem. You say that whenever you [3] __________ solutions for problems at work, your boss is very negative and just rejects them all. Have you tried [4] __________ up with a variety of different solutions? Do you try to look at all the different ways you can [5] __________ a work problem? Maybe your boss thinks that your ideas aren't flexible enough. And finally, get together with your colleagues to [6] __________ each issue as it occurs. Maybe if you work together and [7] __________ on a plan of action, your boss will be less likely to reject it!

PRONUNCIATION

Word stress: verbs with two syllables

A Put the verbs in the box in the correct column.

achieve focus manage regret study suggest

Verbs with stress on first syllable	Verbs with stress on second syllable
__________	__________
__________	__________
__________	__________

2.2 **B** Listen to the verbs. Check your answers to Exercise A. Listen again.

GRAMMAR
Present and past ability

A Circle the correct option to complete the interview.

Interviewer: Today, my guest is 52-year-old Lydia Maleknia. Lydia, you have completed two full marathons now, but you told me earlier that two years ago you [1]*couldn't / can't* even run 200 meters without getting tired!

Lydia: That's right! I started running a couple of years ago to get in shape and now I [2]*am able to / could* run 26 miles in under four hours.

Interviewer: Amazing. You also said that you found the motivation to train when you read about the difficulties other women marathon runners had faced in the past.

Lydia: Yes, I did. Kathrine Switzer, for example, is an inspirational athlete. She only [3]*could / managed to* get a place in the 1967 Boston Marathon because the organizers didn't realize she was a woman.

Interviewer: [4]*Could she / Was she able to* finish the race?

Lydia: Yes, she finished the race – and she proved that both women and men [5]*are able to / manage* run marathons.

Interviewer: You also [6]*managed to / could* show your friends and family that it isn't only young people who [7]*can / could* run marathons.

Lydia: Yes, that's right. My daughter was so happy when I got a medal for the fastest time in my age group that she [8]*didn't manage to / couldn't* stop crying!

B Complete the second sentence so that it has a similar meaning to the first sentence, using the word given. Use between two and five words.

1 How is Kate able to work and take care of her children?
MANAGE
How ______________ work and take care of her children?

2 Joe Bartley likes the fact that he can work part-time at the café.
ABLE
Joe Bartley enjoys ______________ part-time at the café.

3 Callum didn't manage to do much preparation for the interview.
NOT
Callum was ______________ for the interview very well.

4 Helga's low wage means that she can't spend much money on clothes.
SPEND
Helga's low wage means that she is not ______________ much money on clothes.

5 Were you able to speak French before you went to France?
COULD
______________ French before you went to France?

6 We weren't able to solve the problem.
DIDN'T
We ______________ a solution to the problem.

7 Just think what it would be like to swim with dolphins!
IMAGINE
Can you ______________ to swim with dolphins!

Walk on the Wild Side

READING

A READ FOR GIST Read *Walk on the Wild Side* quickly and circle the correct option for each sentence.

1 The article is about people who *don't want smartphones / want a simpler life.*

2 Dan Usher is *a TV announcer / somebody who lives in a remote place.*

3 According to Tessa, her lifestyle is suitable *for everyone / for some people.*

B Read the article again. Match the words and phrases in bold from the article (1–6) with their meanings (a–f). Underline the parts of the text which helped you understand the meanings.

1 off the grid ___	a easy to find or get to
2 the rat race ___	b things you need to live
3 accessible ___	c with no modern technology
4 supplies ___	d fixing
5 maintaining ___	e change ideas or behavior
6 adapt themselves ___	f modern life

C READ FOR DETAIL Read the article again. Are the sentences true (T) or false (F)?

1 The people on the TV show reject modern technology. ___

2 They sometimes have to share their homes with rats. ___

3 You cannot get to the island by helicopter. ___

4 Tessa and Jack had to transport all the things they would need. ___

5 They have to be good at fixing things. ___

6 Dan thinks the couple is good at solving problems. ___

Glossary

isolation (n) the state of being alone
lighthouse (n) a tower built next to the ocean with a flashing light to warn ships of danger
readings (n pl) measurements
remote (adj) far away from other people or places

D REFLECT Think about the answers to these questions.

1 How would you feel about living off the grid?

2 Would you like to live on Maatsuyker Island? Why/Why not?

For some people, the idea of being without their smartphone for an hour is enough to send shivers down their spine. But how about being without an internet connection, without electricity, without a car – completely **off the grid**? Who would willingly put themselves into such a situation? The answer is – a growing number of men and women who want to leave behind the security of a nine-to-five routine to explore the wild places of the Earth.

In the new series of *Walk on the Wild Side*, Dan Usher travels to the remotest corners of the Earth to meet some of the daring people who have left **the rat race** behind to find a way of life that is simpler and more satisfying.

In the first episode, Dan visited Maatsuyker Island, Australia's southernmost lighthouse station. Tasmania Parks and Wildlife Service advertized for a couple to live on the island for a period of six months. **Accessible** only by helicopter, a six-month stay on the island means total isolation and very little communication with the outside world. However, this didn't daunt Tessa and Jack Littleton who made the decision to come and live here.

'Although we have a landline, it's usually out of order and our only other means of communication is the emergency radio, explains Jack. 'Obviously there's no internet or email. At the beginning of our stay, we had to bring all the **supplies** we would need for six months – food, fuel, clothing and bedding.'

I asked Tessa what everyday life is like. 'Our jobs on the island include cutting the grass, taking weather readings, **maintaining** the buildings and the lighthouse – things are regularly broken or damaged by the wind and rain. It isn't for everyone, but we love the challenge.' Weather conditions on the island are extreme with strong winds and frequent storms which cause a variety of problems.

At the end of his visit to the island, presenter Dan told viewers, 'What was most interesting about these people was that they are able to deal with change on a daily basis. They have an amazing ability to accept new situations and **adapt themselves** to new surroundings.'

2.4 Experiences

LISTENING

A PREDICT Look at the picture and the caption. Check (✓) the things you think a guidance counselor does.

1. analyzes situations ☐
2. teaches students ☐
3. solves problems ☐
4. suggests solutions ☐
5. deals with money ☐

2.3 **B LISTEN FOR THE MAIN IDEA** Listen to an interview with a guidance counselor and check your ideas from Exercise A. Complete the job description with the words in the box.

adults dealing decisions pressure solve support

Children and young [1]________ need guidance and [2]________, especially when it comes to [3]________ with academic, personal, parental and social [4]________. A guidance counselor assists young people by listening to their concerns and uses different techniques to help them to [5]________ problems and make the right [6]________.

2.3 **C LISTEN FOR DETAIL** Listen again and complete the sentences (1–7) with one word in each space. The first letters have been given to help you.

1. The main focus of the interview is how Gareth helps young people to make l________-ch________ d________.
2. Young people have to deal with f________ t________, exams, as well as worrying about their career prospects.
3. Gareth asks young people to write down a l________ of advantages and disadvantages.
4. Sometimes parents d________ a________ with the choices their children are making.
5. Gareth believes that it's important to set l________-t________ g________ and not just to think about the near future.
6. It can be helpful to imagine that you are giving a________ to a friend.
7. It's possible to spend too much t________ and e________ thinking about a difficult situation.

Glossary

fatigue (n) tiredness
imaginary (adj) not real, only existing in the mind

D REFLECT Think about the answers to these questions.

1. Have you ever spoken to a guidance counselor? Would you like to?
2. Do you think that Gareth's suggestions for making decisions were helpful? Why/Why not?

FUNCTIONAL LANGUAGE

Asking for, giving and refusing permission

Complete the conversation with the words and phrases in the box.

can call can we start if I ask I'd like
I'm afraid I'm sorry must be would it be

Tania: Hi. Is this the right place for the skydiving club?
Jamal: Yep! Let me see. You [1]________ Tania. I saw your name on the list of new members.
Tania: Yes, that's me! But you [2]________ me 'Tan' – all my friends do.
Jamal: OK, Tan. Well, I'm going to need a few details from you. Is it alright [3]________ you a few questions?
Tania: No problem. What do you need to know?
Jamal: [4]________ with your height? How tall are you, Tan?
Tania: [5]________, but I don't understand why you need to know that.
Jamal: It's for the safety equipment. I need to have your measurements so I can provide you with the right kit.
Tania: Oh, OK. I'm one meter and 70 centimeters.
Jamal: Good – that's fine. And, how old are you?
Tania: I'm 17.
Jamal: Oh dear. You're too young; our rules say that you have to be 18 to join the club.
Tania: [6]________ OK to *say* I'm 18? It doesn't matter, does it? Just write down '18'.
Jamal: [7]________ that isn't possible. We take safety very seriously, Tania. [8]________ to help, but at the end of the day I'm responsible for you and the other club members. You'll just have to come back again next year.
Tania: What a disappointment!
Jamal: Sorry, Tania.

2.5 Experiences

Write an informal email

WRITING

A Which of these sentences or phrases are you most likely to see in an email from a friend or family member?

1 I look forward to hearing from you.
2 A friend of mine's just gotten married.
3 Yours truly
4 You'll never guess what happened!
5 Lots of love
6 I'm writing in reply to your email from July 7th .
7 Hi Mike
8 Know what I mean ☺?

B USING INFORMAL LANGUAGE Rewrite these sentences in informal language.

1 I apologize for not having written sooner.
2 I am most grateful for the advice you gave me.
3 I hope this email finds you in good health.
4 I didn't attend due to the fact that I was unwell.
5 I haven't found suitable accommodations yet.

C Read Heike's email to Adriana and circle the best answers.

1 Heike *rarely* / *regularly* writes to her friend, Adriana.
2 Heike has some *good* / *bad* news.
3 She is *sure* / *not sure* about her plans for the future.
4 She thinks Adriana *will not* / *will* be able to help her.

D USING INFORMAL LANGUAGE Find at least one example of each of these in Heike's email.

1 informal opening and closing expressions
2 sentences with incomplete grammar
3 informal punctuation
4 contractions
5 informal words and phrases
6 an emoji

To: Adriana

Subject: Hard choice

Hi Adriana,

What's up? It's been a couple of weeks since I last wrote, but a lot of stuff's been happening. Remember I told you I was applying for jobs at fashion magazines? I thought I'd made a mess of the interviews, but obviously not. Guess what? I've been accepted by two!!! Woo-hoo!

Trouble is, though, I don't know which one to go for! They're both well-paid, but the one that pays best is in London! The other one's here in New York. So what to do? I'll be far away from my friends and family if I go to the UK. Plus, I'll have to find somewhere to live, make new friends … I know it's a great opportunity, but … what do you think?

It would be so cool if we could talk about this in person. How about going out for coffee? It would really help me to talk it all through with you. Great new café has opened near me – it's called *Bean There* (like 'coffee bean' – get it? lol ☺). Let me know if you can make it.

Love to you & Dave & the baby,

Heike

WRITING PRACTICE

A PREPARE You are going to write an informal email to a friend telling him/her about some good news you've received and asking for advice. Think about the answers to these questions and write notes.

1 Who are you writing to?
2 What's your good news?
3 What advice do you need from your friend?

B WRITE Write your email in 150–200 words.

- Use your notes and ideas from Exercise A.
- Remember to use an informal writing style.

GRAMMAR
Narrative tenses

A **Circle the correct answer, a, b or c.**

1 I ___ down the street when a bus passed by and splashed water all over me!
  a was walking
  b walked
  c had walked

2 It was a typical Monday morning commute; the trains were running late and everyone ___ about it.
  a complained
  b was complaining
  c had complained

3 Elsa took her seat on the plane, but after ten minutes, the flight attendant ___ a delay.
  a had announced
  b was announcing
  c announced

4 She turned around to pay the taxi driver, but he ___ off and was nowhere to be seen.
  a already drove
  b had already driven
  c was already driving

5 Hamish saw a great travel deal online and ___ it immediately.
  a was reserving
  b had reserved
  c reserved

6 Because Hank ___ a cheap ticket, he couldn't change it without paying a penalty.
  a bought
  b had bought
  c was buying

7 Although the weather was bad, it ___ when the accident occurred.
  a was raining
  b rained
  c wasn't raining

8 She wanted to sit in the back by the window, but someone ___ the seat already.
  a had taken
  b took
  c was taking

B **Rewrite the verbs in bold in the story using the correct forms of the simple past, past progressive or past perfect.**

Chapter one: An observation

While Louis [1]**drove** ___*was driving*___ to work one day, he noticed a bike lane on his street.

He [2]**didn't see** ______ it before, so he guessed that it was new. He mentioned it to his neighbors, but they said it [3]**was** ______ there for months. 'How did I not notice that?' Louis wondered to himself.

He [4]**had decided** ______ to give the *new* bike lane a try. So, the next day, he got his bicycle out of the garage and [5]**was leaving** ______ home half an hour early, to give himself more time to get to work. As he rode down the street, he [6]**had suddenly found** ______ that he was looking at his neighborhood in a completely new way.

He [7]**had seen** ______ the children walking to school, the trees by the side of the road and his neighbors calling out greetings. He [8]**was never noticing** ______ these things before because he usually took his car to work. Now commuting to work had become the best part of his work day!

VOCABULARY
Collocations: travel information

A **Match the beginnings of the sentences (1–8) with the endings (a–h).**

1 Be careful driving here; the road	___	a	rain, so drive slowly on the way to Revi's house.
2 If I leave during rush	___	b	light is red and I have to wait for it to turn green to go!
3 Is there a subway	___	c	hour, the highways will be packed.
4 I really hate overcrowded	___	d	buses because there's never anywhere to sit!
5 We're in a terrible traffic	___	e	work up ahead, so we'll have to go by a different route.
6 Steven, the traffic	___	f	sign says there are falling rocks.
7 The forecast is for heavy		g	line that runs below this building?
8 There is road	___	h	jam – we haven't moved for 20 minutes!

Nouns ending in *-ion*

B Rewrite the following verbs as a noun using *-ion*. Other spelling changes may be necessary.

1 connect ____________
2 decide ____________
3 pollute ____________
4 act ____________
5 react ____________
6 situate ____________

C Complete the blog post with the nouns from Exercise B.

Goodbye, car! Hello, clean air!

I've finally made the [1]____________ to stop using my car and start using public transportation. Well, we all know that there is a direct [2]____________ between cars and air [3]____________.

But what was my inspiration for making this choice? The [4]____________ in my home city is particularly bad; the air quality is just terrible. One day, I noticed an ugly brown cloud hanging over the city and my [5]____________ was one of disgust. And that was it – I parked my car in the garage and that's where it's going to stay.

Now I use buses and I usually walk short distances. We simply can't have the expectation that our environment will improve if we ourselves do not take [6]____________.

PRONUNCIATION

Word stress in nouns ending in *-ion*

A 3.1 Listen to two speakers saying the same sentence. Check (✓) the speaker who pronounces the *-ion* word correctly.

1 *information*
Speaker A: ☑ Speaker B: ☐
2 *reaction*
Speaker A: ☐ Speaker B: ☐
3 *decision*
Speaker A: ☐ Speaker B: ☐
4 *destination*
Speaker A: ☐ Speaker B: ☐
5 *expression*
Speaker A: ☐ Speaker B: ☐
6 *situation*
Speaker A: ☐ Speaker B: ☐

B Practice saying the *-ion* words in Exercise A.

GRAMMAR
Articles and quantifiers

A Fill in the blanks with *a/an*, *the* or – (no article).

Bicycles are better

Everyone wants to live in [1] ________ town or city without pollution. And, naturally, we also want [2] ________ town or city where we live to be people-friendly and easy to get around. But, like all [3] ________ city-dwellers, we know there's [4] ________ issue with transportation. How do we get around without causing pollution? The city of [5] ________ Helsinki is [6] ________ European capital that has always embraced bikes and bike riding, so why not here in [7] ________ US, too? Officials in American cities throughout the country need to do more to encourage people to use [8] ________ bicycles by creating more bike lanes and safe spaces for bike riders.

B Circle the correct option to complete the sentences.

1 How *few* / *much* / *many* luggage are we allowed to take on the plane?
2 There aren't *much* / *enough* / *plenty* trains during rush hour, so they're usually very crowded.
3 I have very *enough* / *much* / *little* money so I can't afford to buy a new car.
4 There's *plenty of* / *little* / *too much* time until the train leaves – let's go and get some coffee.
5 Would you like *very few* / *a lot* / *a little* sugar in your tea?
6 The Kutsuplus service had *enough* / *a lot of* / *too many* advantages.
7 *Few* / *Little* / *A few* people use the local bus service, so it's in danger of being canceled.
8 I can't hear you – there's *plenty of* / *not enough* / *too much* noise in this train car!

C Complete the sentences with one word in each space.

1 There was ________ of traffic in the city center today.
2 We'd better buy some gas because we don't have ________ left.
3 There aren't ________ seats for everybody to sit down.
4 There's ________ chance of finding a taxi at this time of the day.
5 ________ of pollution is created by private cars.
6 Sadly ________ few people in my town use bicycles as a means of transportation.

PRONUNCIATION
Sentence stress: quantifiers

A 3.2 Listen and underline the quantifiers the speakers stress in each sentence.

1 A lot of people were angry about the delay.
2 There were a few trains operating on Sunday.
3 Were there many people on the bus?
4 There's too much traffic in the city center.
5 Do you have enough money for the tickets?
6 There's little chance of leaving early today.

B Practice saying the sentences in Exercise A with the correct intonation.

3.2 On the move

Travel smart

VOCABULARY
Gradable and ungradable adjectives

A Underline the correct answers to complete the letter to a newspaper.

Dear Sir/Madam,

Yesterday's article on reducing traffic in towns and cities was [1]***really / completely*** interesting and I wanted to add my thoughts on the issue.

Many of my friends find it [2]***absolutely / a little*** surprising that I have never learned to drive. I point out to them that since I live in a big city, it is [3]***completely / very*** easy to get around using public transportation.

Some of them are [4]***very furious / furious*** when I point out that driving cars is [5]***extremely / a little*** damaging to the environment and the number one cause of air pollution in our cities. I find it [6]***very funny / very hilarious*** how people react to unpleasant truths.

I look forward to more articles on this topic.

Sincerely,
Femi Oke

B Which adjectives collocate with *very*? Put a check mark (✓) or an ✗ in the box.

1 brilliant ☐
2 enormous ☐
3 smart ☐
4 impossible ☐
5 filthy ☐
6 excellent ☐
7 dirty ☐
8 large ☐

C Complete the sentences using an adjective from Exercise A or Exercise B.

1 The exam was almost ________. No one in the class got more than 30%!
2 Stephen Hawking was considered to be one of the most ________ physicists of his generation.
3 The skyscraper being built in the city center is going to be ________.
4 My boss was ________ with me when I accidently deleted some important files.
5 Simon's van is absolutely ________. He really should get it cleaned.
6 We knew the movie would be funny, but it was ________. I'd definitely recommend seeing it.

READING

A PREDICT Look at the title of the article and the picture and answer the questions.

1 What do you think the article is going to be about?
2 Will the tone of the article be positive or negative?

B SKIM Read the article quickly, paying particular attention to the paragraph headings. Complete each paragraph with the missing topic sentences (a–e).

a Maybe the most important, but also the most expensive, innovation will be the insertion of thousands of tiny sensors into the surface of highways and main roads.
b Smart road technology, including solar-powered road surfaces, wi-fi communication and embedded sensors, will transform road transportation as we know it.
c The term *smart road* covers a range of developing technologies which scientists believe will transform the future of road transportation.
d Modern roads have been in existence for more than a hundred years.
e While the electronic surface-to-vehicle system will help drivers, a different kind of technology is being developed to help the environment.

C READ FOR DETAIL Read the article again. Circle the correct answer, a, b or c.

1 What has changed during the last 100 years?
  a Only cars
  b Only roads
  c Cars and roads
2 The term *smart roads* refers to
  a road safety applications.
  b a range of technologies.
  c the use of solar energy.
3 Using smart road technology, drivers will be able to
  a ignore traffic lights.
  b communicate with each other.
  c make time-saving choices.
4 The vehicles of the future will
  a work better in winter.
  b be powered by the road.
  c be made of glass.

D REFLECT Think about the answers to these questions.

1 What are the advantages of smart road technology?
2 When do you think this technology will exist in your country?

Glossary

congestion (n) when a road is crowded with vehicles, so that it is difficult for them to move
fossil fuel (n) a fuel such as gas, oil or coal
relay (v) to communicate information
sensor (n) an electronic device that reacts to changes such as the amount of heat or movement

Smart roads: the transportation technology of the future?

What is the situation today?

1 ___ The smooth, solid surface allows us to drive cars, trucks and buses over short and long distances, connecting us to other people, cities and faraway places. Modern cars, with their incredibly powerful engines, GPS systems and excellent safety features, would be unrecognizable to the road user of a hundred years ago. However, the roads they drive on remain largely unchanged by time or technology.

What are *smart roads*?

2 ___ Some technological advances include the creation of road surfaces which will generate power using solar energy, and wi-fi communication between vehicles and the road surface. Another advance is the monitoring of road traffic in order to reduce congestion and improve driving times and road safety.

How can they improve traffic congestion?

3 ___ The sensors will register the number of cars passing over them. This information will be relayed to the traffic control system which will change speed limits, traffic lights and recommended routes, depending on the volume of traffic. The information could also be sent directly to drivers who can choose to change their route in order to avoid delays.

How can they help the environment?

4 ___ Solar panels embedded into glass road surfaces will power electric cars as they drive along them. Alternatively, electric cars can recharge their batteries while parked in solar-powered parking lots. In addition, the road surface will contain LED lights and road markings as well as heating elements to melt snow and ice during the winter months. Glass is renewable, environmentally friendly and as strong as traditional road surfaces. This technology will allow road transportation to become independent of fossil fuels as vehicles will no longer be using gas-driven engines.

What will the future bring?

5 ___ These emerging technologies will save time and money for drivers, leading to faster and more economic road transportation. They will improve road safety, especially in poor weather conditions, and most important of all, they will contribute to slowing down climate change by reducing greenhouse gas emissions from today's gas-driven engines. Smart road technology may still be at an experimental stage, but it won't be long before it becomes a part of our everyday lives.

3.4 On the move

Listening; Functional Language

LISTENING

A Look at the pictures and answer the questions.

1 Are car accidents a problem in your country?

2 Do young people have more accidents than older drivers?

3 What could be done to improve the situation?

3.3 **B LISTEN FOR SIGNPOSTING LANGUAGE** Listen to a talk about road safety. Check (✓) the phrases you hear the speaker use.

1 First, I want to talk about … ☐

2 Now, let's turn to … ☐

3 Moving on, I'll now discuss … ☐

4 In addition, … ☐

5 That's all I want to say … ☐

6 In conclusion, … ☐

3.3 **C LISTEN FOR DETAIL** Listen again. Underline the correct option to complete the sentences.

1 Drivers who are over 40 are *more* / *less* likely to die in a car accident.

2 *Older* / *Younger* drivers are better at seeing possible dangers on the road.

3 Young drivers want to *live dangerously* / *gain more driving experience*.

4 The speaker thinks that young people shouldn't be so *confident* / *excited* about their driving skills.

5 *Family members* / *Different groups of people* must help young people to deal with problems.

6 The speaker believes that young adults should go through *a more difficult test* / *different stages* before gaining a full license.

7 Young people should be encouraged to *wait until they are older* / *learn to ride a bicycle* before taking their driving test.

Glossary

fatal (adj) which causes death
hazard (n) danger
trial period (n) period of time during which you test somebody's abilities, skills, etc
vital (adj) very important, necessary or essential

D REFLECT Think about the answers to these questions.

1 Were your ideas about improving road safety similar to the speaker's?

2 Do you agree with the speaker's possible solutions? Why/Why not?

FUNCTIONAL LANGUAGE

Telling a story in five stages

Complete the conversation with one word in each space.

Camila: You'll never [1] ________ what happened to me when I was taking that class last week.

Matias: What?

Camila: Well, after class, we could use the campus athletic facilities. On Wednesday, I [2] ________ just had a really tough class, so I decided to go to the swimming pool.

Matias: And?

Camila: There were some other kids from the program at the pool … mostly boys and just a couple of us girls. The funny [3] ________ was that I had just gone there to relax – I didn't have any other plan in mind. Well, [4] ________ I was just floating in the water, I noticed that the boys were organizing a race among themselves.

Matias: So what did you do?

Camila: I lined up at the end of the pool along with the boys. One of them turned to me and said, 'You're a girl. Do you really want to race against us? You know you're going to lose.' I just looked at him and didn't reply. Then somebody yelled 'Ready, Set, Go!' and we were off.

Matias: So, what [5] ________?

Camila: Well – this is the [6] ________ part – I beat them all!

Matias: No way! You're [7] ________?

Camila: Nope. I've been training as a swimmer since I was little you know. In the [8] ________, the boy apologized for being so rude to me. I'm still laughing about it now!

WRITING

A ORGANIZATION Look at the points (a–d) from an email of complaint. Match the points with the main paragraphs in the email.

a the effects of the event, the problems it has caused Paragraph ___

b the result you want from your email Paragraph ___

c a description of the main complaint Paragraph ___

d the reason for writing Paragraph ___

B Complete the email with the adverbs in the box.

definitely extremely regularly seriously totally unnecessarily

Subject: Local buses

Dear Sir or Madam,

I am writing to complain about the new bus schedule for the town of Bedford, because I am [1] ____________ concerned about how this has affected the lives of residents.

Up until two years ago, the bus came [2] ____________ every half an hour. Now there is an hour and a half wait between buses. This is [3] ____________ unacceptable. It has made life for those without their own transportation [4] ____________ difficult and I know of several people who have missed important appointments – for example, with the doctor – because of it.

If, for example, you have a dentist appointment at 9:45, you must catch the 8:00 am bus because the next one is at 9:30 and you [5] ____________ risk missing the appointment. In addition, now there is only one bus during school times and it is usually packed with noisy students, with no room for older people to sit down.

In short, we in the town [6] ____________ want to see a return to the old schedule.

I hope to hear from you soon regarding this matter.

Kind regards,

Bernard Wise

WRITING PRACTICE

A PREPARE You are going to write an email of complaint about a problem you had while traveling. Choose one of these topics to write about.

- A travel agency booked you into a terrible hotel.
- Your train/plane was rerouted to a different destination.
- There was no transportation to take you from the airport to your vacation destination.
- The car you rented was badly maintained and broke down.

B PREPARE Think about the answers to these questions and write notes.

1 What happened? What are the key dates, events, etc?
2 What problems did this cause?
3 What result do you expect after writing this email?

C WRITE Write your email in 150–200 words.

- Use your notes and ideas from Exercise B.
- Remember to use adverbs to give emphasis to your writing.

GRAMMAR
Future forms

A Complete the sentences with the correct future form using the prompts.

1 *I / meet / Sarah* ______________ tomorrow at 6 pm.
2 *We / have* ______________ a test on Tuesday.
3 Petra says *she / run* ______________ her own business one day.
4 *I / try* ______________ hard to finish my classes this year.
5 I forgot to call Danny – *I / do* ______________ it now.
6 *What / you / do* ______________ tomorrow morning?
7 Carl will be in town tomorrow because *he / buy* ______________ a new coat.
8 If you don't like the music, *I / turn* ______________ it down.

B Complete the conversations with the correct future form of the verbs in parentheses.

Ben: So, have you made any resolutions for this year?
Tom: Just one. I [1] ______________ (*learn*) to drive.
Ben: Finally! Let me know when your classes are; I [2] ______________ (*make sure*) I keep off the roads then!
Tom: Very funny. What about you? You said you wanted to get in shape. What about riding your bike to work?
Ben: Yeah, but I don't have a bike.
Tom: No problem. I have a spare one. I [3] ______________ (*lend*) it to you.
Ben: Oh wow! Thanks a lot! Can I pick it up next week?
Tom: Yes, but I [4] ______________ (*start*) my first class on Monday, so I won't be at home then.

Anna: Hi Claire! What are you doing with all those Italian books? [5] ______________ (*you / learn*) Italian?
Claire: Yes, I am! We [6] ______________ (*go*) to Rome in the summer.
Anna: But you [7] ______________ (*not be*) able to learn Italian in six months!
Claire: No, I know. I just want to be able to speak a little of the language – that's all.
Anna: Oh, I see. Anyway, a few of us are meeting up later. [8] ______________ (*you / do*) anything tonight?
Claire: No, I'm free.
Anna: Great! I'll call you later and give you details.

C Choose the correct option (a, b or c) to complete the sentences.

1 Ian promised his professor that he ______________ harder in class this semester.
 a 'll try
 b 's trying
 c 's going to

2 ______________ to the party with us or with Liz?
 a Will Sarah come
 b Is Sarah coming
 c Is Sarah going to come

3 We ______________ in the ocean if it's freezing. We'll have to see how cold it is when we get there.
 a won't swim
 b aren't swimming
 c aren't going to swim

4 I think I ______________ the steak and fries please.
 a 'll have
 b 'm having
 c 'm going to have

5 William ______________ a candidate for the job tomorrow afternoon.
 a 'll interview
 b 's interviewing
 c interviews

4.1 Change

PRONUNCIATION
Intonation for attitude and mood

4.1 **A** **Listen to eight sentences. Circle the option that best describes each speaker's attitude or mood.**

1	I'll help you if you want.	*happy to help / not interested*
2	Are you going to go to that restaurant again?	*excited / bored*
3	I need to make some changes starting tomorrow.	*determined / unsure*
4	Peter's coming for lunch tomorrow.	*negative / positive*
5	Really? You do surprise me.	*surprised / sarcastic*
6	OK, OK. I understand.	*thoughtful / angry*
7	What are you going to do?	*nervous / curious*
8	Thanks a lot!	*ironic / excited*

B **Practice saying the sentences in Exercise A using the same intonation.**

4.1 **C** **Listen again to check your intonation.**

VOCABULARY
Collocations: goals and resolutions

A **Complete the collocations with the verbs in the box. Use each verb only once.**

break cut keep make quit reach

1 ____________ down on something
2 ____________ a resolution
3 ____________ a target
4 ____________ a resolution
5 ____________ a bad habit
6 ____________ a resolution

B **Match the collocations in Exercise A to the correct definition.**

1 stop doing something that isn't good for you ____________
2 not do what you promised ____________
3 set (yourself) a goal ____________
4 achieve something ____________
5 do less of something ____________
6 stick to a plan ____________

C **Complete the sentences with one word in each space. Use words from Exercise A and B.**

1 You should cut ________ on eating chocolate and candy.
2 Linda has finally managed to ________ drinking coffee.
3 I'm determined to ________ my resolution to pass my English exam by working extra hard.
4 If your target is not realistic, you'll never ________ it.
5 I've made a ________ to stop playing video games until I have finished my work.
6 You will never ________ success if you don't try.
7 I've ________ myself a goal – I want to be ready to run in the next marathon.
8 We decided to ________ to the original plan.

GRAMMAR
Making predictions

A Circle the correct option to complete the sentences.

1 The council *will* / *is going to* knock down that old building because it's dangerous.

2 She *may* / *will* take a job with a media company, but she hasn't decided yet.

3 I'm *definitely* / *probably* going to attend the climate change conference – I'm one of the speakers!

4 We *will* / *might* use less paper if we receive all our bills electronically – that's much more environmentally friendly.

5 I think we need industry to survive, but companies *are going to* / *could* try to pollute less.

6 You *will probably* / *are going to* make a huge difference in the world – I just know it!

7 They *won't* / *might not* come tonight – it depends on how tired they are after work.

8 Danielle *probably will* / *will probably* move out of the city if she can find a house she likes.

B Complete the sentences with one word in each space.

1 They ________ definitely support our program; they plan to donate $1 million!

2 She's ________ to work with her neighbors to set up a community garden.

3 I'll ________ see you later tonight, but I'll see how tired I am when I get home.

4 Lionel ________ be here tonight; he called earlier to say he can't make it.

5 You never know, English ________ not always be a global language.

6 My brother ________ become a rich man if his latest business deal succeeds.

7 You're ________ going to get the job; I heard the manager telling her assistant that she's chosen you.

8 We're ________ going to buy a hybrid car just yet; our old one still has some life in it.

C Correct the mistakes in each sentence

1 Hannah probably will get the job.

________.

2 It depends how busy Lisa and Alan are, but they definitely will come tonight.

________.

3 The weather probably might be good this weekend.

________.

4 My neighbors could to at least try to keep the noise down a little!

________.

5 The local soccer club won't definitely win the league this season.

________.

D Complete the predictions so that they are true for you.

1 This year I'll definitely ________.

2 Next month I definitely won't ________.

3 Next year I might ________.

4 In five years, I'll probably ________.

5 Next weekend, I probably won't ________.

PRONUNCIATION

'll: contraction of will

4.2 **A** Listen to five sentences and underline which phrase you hear.

1 a We work b We'll work
2 a I make b I'll make
3 a It cost b It'll cost
4 a You quit b You'll quit
5 a She let b She'll let

Linking words: final consonant sound and first vowel sound

4.3 **B** Listen and complete the sentences with a missing phrase.

1 You won't find ______ a self-help book.
2 ______ things can we do to help?
3 I think she ______.
4 ______ terrific plan!
5 You ______ what I'm saying!

C Practice saying the sentences in Exercise B. Make the links between the final consonants and the first vowel sounds.

4.3 **D** Listen again to check your pronunciation.

VOCABULARY

Prefixes: *dis-*, *mis-*, *over-*, *re-*, *under-*

A Circle the correct answer, a, b or c.

1 Oh, I thought you said you were a *lifestyle* expert. Sorry, I ___understood you.
a over b dis c mis

2 I wanted to move to the country, but I've had to ___think my plans.
a re b over c mis

3 I can't seem to find my wallet; I must have ___placed it.
a re b dis c mis

4 If ocean levels keep rising, many low-lying islands will ___ appear.
a over b dis c re

5 This town used to be a nice place to live, but it's becoming ___populated.
a under b over c re

6 Working as a teacher is very difficult, and on top of that, you're generally ___paid.
a over b dis c under

7 Is it better to fix up an old building or knock it down and ___build it?
a re b dis c over

8 If you ___agree with your boss too many times, you might find yourself out of a job!
a mis b over c dis

B Complete the text with the correct form of the words given in capital letters.

The sea is rising

Urban areas all over the world are [1] *rethinking* their city planning as a result of rising sea levels. Officials must consider whether they should [2] ______ housing to better withstand the changing environment or erect high concrete walls. Of course, wealthier cities can manage climate change much better. THINK BUILD

Experts may [3] ______ over the best approach, but they are at least able to implement a solution when they come up with one. Bangladesh, for example, is at sea level and its capital was already [4] ______ before thousands of *climate refugees* began arriving. Many came to the capital because they were already experiencing changes in the environment – leaving behind coastal towns that will probably have [5] ______ in a few years' time. AGREE POPULATE APPEAR

Ultimately, it will take a global effort to find a solution to climate change, particularly by policymakers who [6] ______ the problem and heavy polluters who don't even want to admit there is one. UNDERSTAND

Indian Summer School at 9 pm on Channel 4

Challenge and change are the keywords to describe the experience of a group of teenagers in *Indian Summer School*, broadcast on Channel 4 in three episodes. This documentary follows the progress of five working-class British boys who are preparing to retake their high school exams at the Doon School in India. Having failed their exams in the UK, they hope that the famous Indian boarding school with the world-class reputation will help them to improve their academic performance and achieve the grades that they need.

The Doon School in Uttarakhand is one of India's finest, and most expensive, private boarding schools. Set in 70 acres of beautiful gardens and open spaces, the school was founded in 1935 by Satish Ranjan Das, a lawyer from Calcutta. The school has an exam pass rate of 100 percent and a zero-tolerance approach to any kind of misbehavior. Staff at the school encourage hard work, personal development and respect for others – there's no room here for somebody who is not prepared to accept the school's ethos.

However, this communal philosophy is not one that the British boys are used to. On their arrival, they are expected to have their hair cut short and are required to hand over their smartphones and tablets. The principal, Matthew Raggett, believes that up to 80 percent of problems in the classroom are caused by the distractions of electronic devices. One of the boys, Ethan, refuses to have his hair cut and none of the boys are happy about having their smartphones taken from them.

As the show progresses, we see a clash of two cultures, as the British boys find it extremely hard to adhere to the strict rules and traditional values of the Indian school. Ethan finds it difficult to socialize with the other students and usually skips classes. Alfie and Jack do better and become interested in the Hindu religion, as well as working hard to contribute to class discussions and homework projects.

As viewers, we all want the boys to do well, but we are possibly frustrated by their refusal to make an effort and gain from their experience. Will the boys manage to complete their six-month course? Are they up for the challenge? Will this be a life-changing experience or another academic failure? Watch the full series to find out!

READING

A Look at the title of the text and read the first paragraph. Answer the questions.

1 Is this a magazine article, a review or a letter to a newspaper?
2 Is it about fictional or real people?
3 Which countries are mentioned?

B READ FOR DETAIL Read the rest of the review and check (✓) the information that is mentioned.

1 the number of classes ☐
2 where the school is ☐
3 the people in the program ☐
4 when the school started ☐
5 the idea of the TV show ☐
6 the students' hobbies ☐
7 the size of the school campus ☐
8 why the boys are there ☐
9 what kind of program it is ☐

C SUMMARIZE Which of the points you checked in Exercise B should be included in a summary? Why should the other points NOT be included?

D SUMMARIZE Complete the summary with a word or phrase from the box.

British boys | deal with the challenge | documentary | failed | India

In this TV [1] ________, five [2] ________ who have [3] ________ their exams are given a second chance when they take part in a study program at the world-famous Doon School in [4] ________. In this three-part Channel 4 series, we see how the boys [5] ________ and changes in their lives when they have to adapt to a very different way of life and learning.

E REFLECT Think about the answers to these questions.

1 Would you like to watch this documentary? Why/Why not?
2 How easy or difficult do you think it would be to adapt to life in a different country?

Glossary

boarding school (n) school that students live at
clash (n) conflict between different ideas/systems/etc
ethos (n) set of beliefs
zero-tolerance approach (n phrase) a system where no rule-breaking of any kind is accepted

LISTENING

A **What changes would you like to make in your life? Think about:**

- your health and fitness.
- your work, career or school.
- your free time.

4.4 **B** **LISTEN FOR GIST You will hear Doctor Maria Davos, a psychologist, talking about how people can achieve their personal goals. Listen and check (✓) the statements you think Doctor Davos would agree with.**

a It's easy to achieve your goals. ☐
b Changing your life takes time. ☐
c Setting smaller goals is more realistic than setting one big goal. ☐
d People are happy when they can measure the results of their efforts. ☐
e Everybody should try to improve their diet. ☐
f Make changes one step at a time. ☐

Glossary

overdo (v) do too much, do more than is possible
transform (v) change completely

C **PARAPHRASING Read the sentences and circle the answer, a or b, which has a similar meaning.**

1 She failed to stick to her resolution.
  a She made a resolution but didn't keep it.
  b She didn't make a resolution.
2 You can only achieve long-term goals.
  a Your goals must be challenging.
  b You can't change your life overnight.
3 Track your progress by taking photos.
  a Use photos to keep a visual record.
  b Use photos to improve your appearance.
4 I want to cut down on sugar in my diet.
  a I have too much sugar in my diet.
  b I don't have enough sugar in my diet.

4.4 **D** **LISTEN FOR DETAIL** Listen and circle the correct answer, a, b or c.

1 Many people
  a stick to their resolutions.
  b make resolutions but don't keep them.
  c don't make good plans.
2 You will succeed in changing your life if you
  a set difficult challenges for yourself.
  b act quickly and decisively.
  c set long-term goals.
3 A good way of achieving your goal is to
  a break it into smaller steps.
  b make a list.
  c concentrate.
4 Why does Doctor Davos suggest taking photos?
  a So you can admire your nails.
  b So that you have a visual record of your progress.
  c Because it will keep your hands busy.
5 Keeping a food diary can help you to
  a cut down on something.
  b feel more positive.
  c have more strength.
6 Doctor Davos says we should
  a try to achieve several goals.
  b achieve our goals one by one.
  c only ever make one change.

E **REFLECT Think about the answers to these questions.**

1 Are you good at achieving your goals?
2 Have you ever used any of the techniques that were suggested in the interview?

FUNCTIONAL LANGUAGE

Clarifying and asking for clarification

Complete the conversation with the words in the box.

catch going leave lost up what

Adele: Hi, Hector. What's [1] ________? How's your first day of college [2] ________?
Hector: Umm … it's OK but I'm having a little trouble with the layout.
Adele: With the … [3] ________ did you say? Sorry I didn't [4] ________ that.
Hector: With the layout … of the building.
Adele: You've [5] ________ me.
Hector: Actually, it's me that's lost! I mean I can't find my way around. The college is really big and I've been late for all my classes because I can't find the rooms!
Adele: Oh, I see. [6] ________ it to me. I have a map somewhere … of the college. Here you go. It shows the different rooms, the gym, the cafeteria. That should be a help.
Hector: Thanks, Adele.

4.5 Change Write a short essay

Win a chance to see the future @ Roboworld!

Enter our competition and win a guided tour of our laboratories where we design and build robots for top science-fiction movies *and* for use in the real world.

Here, science fiction becomes science fact!

Robotics has already changed our lives in many ways and will continue to do so. We want to know how you think robots will change everyday life in the home over the next 50 years.

Write a short essay describing two changes you think robots will make to our home lives. Explain why you think these changes will happen and any consequences they may have.

The winning entries will be published in this magazine and on our website roboworld.com.

WRITING

A Read the ad for a competition above. Would you like to visit Roboworld? Why/Why not?

B ORGANIZATION Read a competition essay entry. Put the paragraphs (a–d) in the correct order.

a ___ Second, I believe that in the future, people will demand more free time to develop their personal interests, **and so** we will want machines to do more work. Robots will take over all of the housework **because** we will be busy with more useful and creative tasks.

b ___ To sum up, it is probable that robots will play a bigger part in our lives in the future. **Consequently**, we must decide how we will deal with those changes if robots are there to do everything for us.

c ___ One way in which they will be useful is in helping older people. **Because** people are living longer, the population has more elderly people, and **as a result** they need more care and practical help. The robots of the future will do household chores as well as keeping their 'owners' company with conversation and entertainment. In addition, they will be able to call for help in an emergency.

d ___ We already have a lot of machines in our homes which could be classified as robots, for example, washing machines and dishwashers. I believe that **because of** advances in robotics, we will soon have walking, talking machines which will live and work in our homes.

C Read the essay again and answer the questions.

1 What sort of machines in the home can be considered as robots?
2 What is the consequence of people living longer?
3 Why will humans want machines to do even more household chores?

D USING LINKING WORDS Complete the sentences with the words and phrases in bold from Exercise B. In two sentences, more than one answer is possible.

1 Robots will do all of the household chores, ________ we will have more free time.
2 We all have more free time ________ all the gadgets we have in our homes.
3 Almost every home now has a washing machine; ________, we no longer waste time washing clothes by hand.
4 There was an increase in unemployment ________ more and more machines were used.
5 Older people will need more care ________ people are living longer and longer.
6 Some elderly people do not have access to the internet and ________ they cannot benefit from modern technology.

WRITING PRACTICE

A PREPARE You are going to write an essay about what effect robots and machines will have on work and jobs in the future. Think about the answers to these questions and write notes.

1 What effect have recent developments in technology had on people's jobs?
2 How will technology affect work and jobs in the future? Think of two ideas.
3 What are the reasons for these possible changes?
4 What consequences do you think these developments will have?

B WRITE Write your essay in 150–200 words.

- Use your notes and ideas from Exercise A.
- Remember to use linking words to describe reasons and consequences.

5.1 Work and business

At work

VOCABULARY

Employment skills and qualities

A Complete the text with the words and phrases in the box.

communication skills | creative | people | pressure | reliable | teamwork | time management

TIPS FOR A SUCCESSFUL INTERVIEW

I've interviewed hundreds of people over the years. So, what do I look for when I'm hiring new staff?

Well, first, I'm looking for people who can get their ideas across to others effectively; in other words, people who have good [1] ________. Of course, to be able to do this, they also need to come up with good ideas and that means having [2] ________ thinking skills as well.

Anyone with both of these qualities will probably work well with others and be good at [3] ________, which is very important. Of course, all companies want their employees to have [4] ________ skills, not only with colleagues, but with clients, too.

Finally, if people aren't [5] ________ or aren't able to work well under [6] ________, then they don't make good employees. To be good at [7] ________ is as much a skill as anything else.

Verbs of influence

B Find and correct the mistakes in the sentences.

1 I was pleased that the manager let me to use my digital technology skills.

____

2 Did you encourage him looking for a new job?

____

3 She's tired because her boss made she come to work at 7 am today!

____

4 Our company allows us work from home one day a week.

____

5 She persuaded them that they cancel the meeting at the last minute.

____

6 Mrs. Carter told to me to improve my time management skills.

____

7 I advised my colleague for speaking to our manager about the problem.

____

8 Mr. Jones doesn't want that I give the presentation today.

____

C Choose the correct verb for each sentence.

1 My parents used to ***let / allow*** me to stay up late on the weekend.

2 Fans are supposed to ***encourage / persuade*** their team not *boo* them.

3 No one is ***making / wanting*** Jonathan quit college. It's his decision.

4 You really need to stop ***advising / telling*** me what to do!

5 Natasha's sister sometimes ***lets / allows*** her borrow her clothes.

6 Bill couldn't be ***persuaded / encouraged*** to come to the party.

7 Harry's friend Charlotte ***wants / makes*** him to teach her how to speak English.

8 I ***advise / tell*** you to leave early because the traffic can be terrible.

PRONUNCIATION

Intonation and rhythm: holding your turn

5.1 **A Listen to eight sentences. Check (✓) the sentences where the speaker makes words longer or uses rising intonation to show they want to continue speaking.**

1 I think that my people skills are excellent. ☐

2 In the end, I realized that it wasn't the job I wanted. ☐

3 I left because I was overworked and underpaid. ☐

4 Job satisfaction makes employees more productive. ☐

5 The perks in my last job were really great. ☐

6 It wasn't just the pay that attracted me to the job. ☐

7 My work doesn't offer enough challenges. ☐

8 You can't imagine what kind of people work there. ☐

B Practice saying the sentences in Exercise A using rising intonation to show that you want to continue speaking.

C Practice saying the sentences from Exercise A using falling intonation to show that you have finished speaking.

GRAMMAR
Past habits and states

A Complete the article with *used to* or *would* and the correct form of the verbs in parentheses. In some sentences, more than one answer is possible.

It [1] ____________ (*be*) very difficult for women in the United States to get good jobs and be financially independent. Very few women [2] ____________ (*work*) in professions such as medicine or law. For one thing, they [3] ____________ (*not have*) access to a college education in order to be able to train for a profession.

It was even harder for working-class women. My grandmother [4] ____________ (*work*) in a factory until she got married. She [5] ____________ (*leave*) the house at dawn and return late in the evening. The workers [6] ____________ (*rarely/get*) vacations, except for once a year, when the factories all closed down for a week. Then, everyone [7] ____________ (*leave*) to spend time with family in the country.

B Complete the second sentence so that it has a similar meaning to the first sentence, using the word given. Write between two and five words.

1 Were you a career advisor?
____________ be a career advisor? (*use*)

2 We didn't go on vacation when I was young.
We ____________ go on vacation when I was young. (*never*)

3 She enjoyed their trips to the beach as a child.
She ____________ their trips to the beach as a child. (*used*)

4 The whole team used to meet to discuss the day's business.
The whole team ____________ to discuss the day's business. (*would*)

5 Darren didn't have good communication skills back then.
Darren ____________ good communication skills. (*to*)

6 Sonja worked at a vacation resort when she was a student.
Sonja ____________ at a vacation resort when she was a student. (*work*)

GRAMMAR
The passive voice

A Complete the sentences about the company *Aethaer* with the correct passive voice of the verbs in the box.

not prove usually/buy order sell set up train

1 The project ______________ by De Watts after he read an article about bottled air.
2 Since the company started, 200 jars ______________ to customers in China.
3 The jars of air ______________ as gifts for wealthy customers' friends.
4 Jars of *Aethaer* can ______________ online.
5 Right now, new 'air-gricultural' workers ______________ to collect and bottle the product.
6 So far the health benefits of *Aethaer* ______________ by scientists.

B Rewrite these sentences using the passive voice.

1 Someone robbed Christopher's house last night.
____
2 Some people can learn the correct technique.
____
3 Someone has stolen the necklace.
____
4 Usain Bolt broke the 100-meter record.
____
5 The artist's assistant had completed the painting.
____

C Rewrite these passive voice sentences so they are active.

1 The alarm had been set off by Sheila.
____
2 The building was designed by Zaha Hadid.
____
3 The championship was held in Russia.
____
4 The Oscar for Best Picture was won by *Moonlight*.
____
5 Communities are being destroyed by the government's policies.
____

D Complete the extracts from a business magazine with the active or passive form of the verbs in parentheses.

He sells seawater

This year, a Scottish businessman [1] ______________ (*start*) selling his country's cheapest natural resource – seawater. The water [2] ______________ (*collect*) from the clear northern seas, and then it [3] ______________ (*use*) in restaurants for cooking. Since the New Year, 20 orders [4] ______________ (*receive*) from all over Europe.

Plastic Revolution in Ghana

Plastic trash is a serious problem, but now, in Ghana, trash [5] ______________ (*turn into*) handbags.
The process is simple. Plastic water containers [6] ______________ (*pick up*) from the streets. After they [7] ______________ (*clean*), they [8] ______________ (*can/make*) into the bags.

The rock millionaire

Gary Dahl, the inventor of the *Pet Rock*, [9] ______________ (*die*) recently at the age of 78. He [10] ______________ (*run*) his *Pet Rock* business for one year in 1975 and he [11] ______________ (*make*) $1 million. The small rocks and stones [12] ______________ (*take*) from Mexican beaches, and they [13] ______________ (*sell*) as novelty gifts.

VOCABULARY
Business collocations

A Match words 1–5 to a–e to make collocations.

1 launch
2 run
3 make
4 build
5 attract

a a profit
b a business
c a brand
d a campaign
e new customers

B Complete the sentences with the correct form of the collocations from Exercise A.

1 A lot of people dream of ________________ their own ________________, but they don't realize how hard it is to set one up.
2 Our company has just ________________ to make more people aware of our products.
3 Some people are only in business to make money fast, but it's important to provide quality so that your satisfied customers can help you ________________.
4 Sales figures are poor; if the company's going to survive, we need to ________________ – preferably ones with spending power.
5 We lost money in the first two years of running the company, but I'm happy to say we have just started to ________________.

PRONUNCIATION
Silent consonants

A Underline the silent consonants in each sentence.

1 Who launched this campaign to protect the environment?
2 We should talk on Wednesday.
3 The sign on the door said knock, so I did, but there was no answer.
4 I can't eat a whole sandwich – do you want half?
5 He's written a lot but I doubt that he knows everything.
6 We listened for an hour but his foreign accent made it hard.
7 When they gave the design prize, it went to the wrong person.
8 To be honest, I'd say that psychology would not be a good subject for you.

5.2 **B Listen to the sentences from Exercise A and check your answers. Practice saying the words and the sentences.**

READING

A Read the first paragraph of the text and underline the best title for the article.

1 All about the money
2 Not just a job
3 Modern working conditions

B PREDICT What do you think the article will be about?

C REFERENCE LINKS Read the rest of the article quickly. Circle the correct person, place or thing that each numbered word or phrase in bold refers to.

1 company owners / employees
2 an employee's diet goals / tech firms' work environment
3 people at the recruiting agency / employees in general
4 the game developer's website / the amount of benefits
5 employees / dogs
6 at the beach / at the clothing company
7 make a difference / help the environment

D READ FOR DETAIL Read again and circle the correct answer, a or b.

1 Which of these do tech firms not offer their employees?
 a a diet plan b transportation
2 According to the article, what motivates many young people when looking for a job?
 a a high salary b job satisfaction
3 Working at the game development company mentioned in the text is unusual because you can
 a take your dog to work. b have free medical treatment.
4 What effect does the game development company's unusual policy have on its employees?
 a They work more. b They become more active.
5 How do working conditions at the clothing company reflect its products?
 a They are both related to the ocean. b They both promote fitness.

Glossary

boost (v) to help something increase
motivated (adj) enthusiastic and wanting to succeed
productive (adj) achieving good results

E REFLECT Think about the answers to these questions.

1 Which do you think is more important – a high salary or job satisfaction?
2 Which of the benefits mentioned in the text would be important for you?

Company owners and entrepreneurs all know that employee satisfaction is essential to a company's success, so it's very important that [1]**they** offer a working environment that nurtures and supports the staff. So what can a company do to keep employees motivated, loyal and productive?

Tech companies, such as Google and Apple, are now famous for their trendy office spaces with perks like free transportation to and from work, weekly massage sessions and, of course, free food and drinks. One employee at a well-known tech firm told us, 'It saves me time and money, and helps me stick to my diet goals.' But which other companies are following [2]**this** example? Hilary works for a large recruiting agency. 'We want and require the best – bright and intelligent young people who want to contribute to the development of the company they work for, and who really want to make a difference. A good salary is important, but [3]**they** are not only motivated by money. There are other ways to reward your staff.'

Take a leading developer of online games as an example. The games are played by millions of people around the world. The company website lists a large number of benefits: [4]**it** includes medical and dental care, paid parental leave, free gym membership and an on-site dry-cleaning service. But maybe the most unusual item on the list is this: 'Every day is bring your dog to work day.' Pet-friendly services include a rooftop park for dogs to play in, pet insurance and special treats for employees' pets. You probably won't be surprised to learn that in a survey carried out by *Business Options* magazine, employees who take their furry friends to work with them say that they are more satisfied with their working life than [5]**those** who can't. In addition, pets can help people to improve their physical and psychological well-being, and this in turn boosts productivity because fewer days are lost to illness.

Other types of companies which are known to care about the health and well-being of their employees are those which sell outdoor clothing and equipment for adventure sports. To help promote their brand they want their employees to stay in shape. What better example to its customers than to have an active staff? Employees are encouraged to use the company bikes, volleyball courts and on-site yoga classes. An example is a well-known American clothing company that has its offices right on the beachfront. Staff members can go surfing on their lunch breaks. In addition, the company runs campaigns to raise awareness of issues such as climate change, environmental protection and fair trade. 'The staff [6]**there** is motivated by more than just good pay', says Hilary. 'Employees believe that in their own small way they can make a difference. Working for an ethically sound company allows them to do [7]**that**.'

LISTENING

A PREDICT **What kinds of problems do you think school teachers have in the course of their work? Put the problems in order (1 = most important, 4 = least important).**

a difficult students ___
b heavy workload ___
c too much paperwork ___
d stress ___

5.3 **B LISTEN FOR EXAMPLES** **You are going to listen to a report about problems which teachers face. Check (✓) the phrases for introducing examples which you hear.**

1 To be more specific … ☐
2 For example, … ☐
3 What's most important is … ☐
4 … as the survey results show … ☐
5 That brings me to … ☐
6 For instance, … ☐
7 … such as … ☐
8 … like … ☐
9 … a more specific idea … ☐
10 Let's take a look at … ☐

Glossary

exodus (n) a situation in which a lot of people leave a place at the same time
qualify (v) earn the certificate, degree, etc which you need to do a certain job
vacancy (n) a job that is available for somebody to do
workload (n) the amount of work you have to do

5.4 **C LISTEN FOR EXAMPLES** **Listen to the report again. Complete the sentences with one word in each space.**

1 For example, toward the end of my time in the teaching profession, I was grading up to ________ notebooks every ________.
2 That's what's important to students, and teachers, not just things like … ________ and ________.
3 For instance, government figures for this year show that there are 10,000 ________ for ________ school teachers.

5.3 **D LISTEN FOR DETAIL** **Listen again and answer the questions.**

1 According to the survey, how many newly certified teachers quit their jobs after less than five years?
2 Do more language teachers or science teachers leave the profession every year?
3 What did 80% of teachers consider doing?
4 How many teachers are missing from high schools this year?
5 How many types of assessments does Amal mention?
6 What did Amal have to do every week which took up all her time?
7 What does Amal believe is *not* so important, compared to a student's personal development?
8 When did Amal's heavy workload increase even more?

E REFLECT **Think about the answers to these questions.**

1 Is a teacher's job stressful in your country?
2 Would you like to become a teacher? Why/Why not?

FUNCTIONAL LANGUAGE
Structuring a presentation

Circle the best options to complete the talk given by a speaker on the topic of 'Interview Skills'.

Good morning and thank you [1]***for coming / that you came*** to today's workshop. The [2]***purpose / reason*** of today's [3]***interaction / presentation*** is to teach you how to succeed in a job interview. So [4]***first of all / at first***, I'd like to talk about introductions. Offer the interviewer a firm handshake, stand straight and look him or her in the eye. Confidence is the key here. Let's [5]***throw a glance / take a look*** at the first slide – this diagram shows the *dos and don'ts* of personal appearance. We'll talk more about these later.

Let's [6]***continue on / move on*** now to think about what you're going to say in the interview. Give thoughtful answers but … don't talk too much! [7]***From / Within*** our research we know that a candidate who talks a lot without interacting with the interviewer can leave a negative impression.

That [8]***carries / brings*** me to the final part of this *introduction to interview skills*. Try to use language which is suitable for the occasion – you should avoid slang words and any references to sensitive topics; and avoid humor if possible, it doesn't always go over well!

So the next [9]***theme / question*** is how to put these ideas into action. In pairs, you're going to role-play an imaginary interview. Now, [10]***do you have / will you make*** any questions before we move on?

WRITING

A **Read the job ad and answer the questions.**

1 What do you think the job involves?

2 Is having previous experience in the travel business essential?

3 What are the most important skills you need for this job?

Eurojobs.com: Travel Consultant

(Ref: 2713)

An amazing opportunity has become available to work for a dynamic, award-winning travel company.

Responsibilities include: being the first point of contact with customers, both face to face and on social media; creating and planning tailor-made travel arrangements; keeping up to date with offers, promotions and new products; providing advice and solutions to travel problems; providing first-class customer service; and attracting new customers.

The skills we are looking for:

- one year's travel agent experience or sales experience or relevant degree plus work experience
- a real passion for travel and interest in other countries and cultures
- confident, polite and reliable, with a can-do approach and a good work ethic
- comfortable dealing with people at all levels
- ambitious and capable of working well under pressure in a tough sales environment

To apply, email a cover letter and résumé to Carl Dennis: C.Dennis@wdtravel.nett

B **ORGANIZATION** Read Edward Browning's cover letter. What is the main topic of each paragraph? Write brief notes.

Paragraph 1 ______

Paragraph 2 ______

Paragraph 3 ______

Paragraph 4 ______

Dear Mr. Dennis,

I am writing to apply for the position of Travel Consultant currently advertised on Eurojobs.com (Ref: 2713). I have attached my résumé. I recently graduated with a BA in Tourism Management and am interested in starting a career in the tourism industry.

[a]The course included hands-on experience as well as insight into how different countries approach tourism. [b]This required organizational ability, good communication skills and the ability to work with others. [c]As well as being an active member of student societies, I organized the annual Meeting of Minds event, which gathers tourism graduates from all over the world. [d]I believe that the skills and experience I gained in college make me the ideal candidate for this position.

Working for your company would be a great opportunity for me to share my passion for travel. I am interested in working for a company which offers such excellent customer service. A role at one of the top companies in the travel industry would fulfill my ambition to work in the tourism industry.

Thank you for considering my application. I am available for interview at any time, and look forward to hearing from you.

Sincerely yours,

Edward Browning

C **PARAGRAPH STRUCTURE** The sentences (a–d) in the second paragraph are in the wrong order. Put them in the correct order to make a better-organized paragraph. Find the topic sentence first.

1 ___

2 ___

3 ___

4 ___

WRITING PRACTICE

A **PREPARE** You are going to write a cover letter for a job. Find an advertisement online or in a newspaper for a job you would like to apply for. Think about the answers to these questions and write notes.

1 Which phrases will you use to open and close this formal letter?

2 What is the job title and where did you see it advertised?

3 Why are you interested in this company and the job opening?

4 What skills and experience do you have which make you suitable for the role? Think of examples.

B **WRITE** Write your cover letter for the advertisement you found in Exercise A. Write your letter in 150–200 words.

- Use your notes and ideas from Exercise A.
- Remember to use standard phrases suitable for a formal letter.
- Don't forget to begin each paragraph with a topic sentence and give examples where necessary.

GRAMMAR
Modals of obligation

A Circle the correct answer, a, b or c.

1 You ___ attend soccer practice today – you can come tomorrow if you like.
  a shouldn't
  b don't have to
  c must not

2 You ___ tell the coach if you can't play in Saturday's game or she'll be annoyed with you.
  a must
  b need
  c don't have to

3 Don't disturb him – he ___ concentrate on making the shot.
  a doesn't have to
  b has to
  c should

4 You ___ wear the helmet, but I strongly recommend that you do.
  a must not
  b shouldn't
  c don't have to

5 If you want to improve your performance, you ___ train every day.
  a have
  b should
  c don't need to

6 Hey! You ___ kick the ball – you can only use your hands!
  a must not
  b don't have to
  c don't need to

B Circle the modal verb which *cannot* be used in each sentence.

1 When running a marathon, you ___ drink water regularly so that you stay hydrated.

need to / must / shouldn't

2 But, you ___ drink too much liquid, or you'll get a stomachache.

don't need to / shouldn't / must not

3 Frank, you ___ yell; I'm sitting right next to you!

don't have to / don't need to / must not

4 We ___ be at the stadium until noon, so we're free until 12.

must / don't need to / don't have to

5 She ___ score any more points to win the game – she has enough already.

doesn't have to / shouldn't / doesn't need to

6 You ___ hit the other players – it isn't the right way to play.

don't have to / must not / shouldn't

7 If you're interested in volleyball, you ___ sign up for the school team.

should / must / don't need to

8 You ___ throw the ball into the net to score a point.

must / have to / don't have to

6.1 Sports and hobbies

VOCABULARY
Adjectives ending in *-ive*

A Complete the text with the correct form of the words given in capital letters.

The Olympics are considered the greatest sporting event ever known. However, it takes more than being a [1]______ athlete to win. **COMPETE**
There is a [2]______ amount of pressure from the media. **MASS**

Players are sometimes greeted by camera crews when they arrive for practice. The media can be very [3]______ at times, **AGGRESSION** and this can break a player's concentration. Without a doubt, having this added pressure is not the most [4]______ way for **EFFECT** a player to train.

Athletes have to employ [5]______ **CREATE** ways of dealing with the stress, such as meditation, taking long baths or using positive thinking to calm them. All Olympians deserve a medal for their [6]______ strength in competing **IMPRESS** under these conditions.

B Matching the nouns in the box to the meanings.

champion fan final league medal players spectator stadium tournament trophy

1 A large building, usually without a roof, where people watch sporting events such as soccer games or races. ______

2 Someone who has won an important competition, especially in a sport. ______

3 People who play a particular game or sport. ______

4 The last game, race, etc in a competition. The winner of this is the winner of the whole competition. ______

5 A large silver cup or similar object given as a prize to the winner of a competition, especially a sporting event. ______

6 Someone who likes to watch a particular sports team and wants that team to win. ______

7 A small flat piece of metal that you are given for winning a competition. ______

8 A group of teams or players who regularly compete against one another, put in order according to how many games they have won. ______

9 A series of games in which the winner of each game plays in the next game until there is one player or team left. ______

10 Someone who watches a sporting event. ______

Sports

C Circle the correct option to complete the sentences.

1 Roger is a terrific baseball *spectator / coach*; his team always wins the championship.

2 His shelves weren't tall enough for the *trophy / medal* he had just won!

3 The FIVB is the world *champion / league* of international volleyball teams.

4 The *spectator / stadium* was so packed with fans that there was nowhere to sit.

5 If you don't win this last game, you'll lose the whole *trophy / tournament*.

6 The team's *fans / spectators* arrived at the game wearing red and white scarves.

7 To win the competition, you'll have to compete against last year's *final / champion*.

8 Getting a place on the team is very difficult; they only pick the top *fans / players*.

9 I'd rather play a sport than be a *spectator / champion* – participating is more fun than watching.

10 If he wins this game, he'll be through to the *final / league*.

PRONUNCIATION
Rhythm: pausing

A Read this excerpt from a radio show. Mark (/) where you think the speaker will use a short pause and (//) for a longer pause which is used to add emphasis or drama.

Stay tuned, / folks. We have an exciting show for you today. Later on in the show, Lionel Messi – world famous athlete, considered by some to be the greatest soccer player of all time – will be joining us to talk about his life and career. We'll speak about the challenges he's faced, both on and off the field, and how he overcame them to be who he is today.

6.1 **B Listen and check whether you have placed your pauses appropriately.**

C Practice reading the excerpt aloud with the correct use of pauses.

6.2 Sports and hobbies

VOCABULARY
Hobbies and free time activities

A Circle the correct option to complete the radio interview.

Presenter: Aisha has come on to the show today to tell us about her work as a life coach. Aisha, how do you help people [1]***escape / get*** from daily stress?

Aisha: There are a lot of ways, actually. But, mainly, it's all about finding out what is [2]***relaxing / fitting*** for you, personally. I do think, though, that the best activities are ones that you both enjoy and that [3]***close / get*** you out of the house.

Presenter: I see. I've always really enjoyed [4]***keeping / collecting*** stamps, but I don't think that's a very popular hobby anymore.

Aisha: It doesn't matter what it is, as long as you really enjoy doing it. The real benefits come from having a [5]***close / near*** interest in a hobby. Whatever you [6]***have / are*** into doing is going to have positive results for you.

B Complete the sentences with the words in the box.

active fan hobby member society thing

1 Why don't you join a ______________ to be with other people who share your interest in old books?

2 I decided to take up a ______________ and I've started doing yoga once a week.

3 Going to a gym isn't really my ______________ to be honest.

4 I'm a ______________ of the Rihanna fan club.

5 Cross-training is becoming a very popular way to keep ______________.

6 I'm a huge ______________ of Drake and his music.

6.2 Sports and hobbies

GRAMMAR
Present perfect progressive

A **Complete the blog post with the present perfect or present perfect progressive form of the verbs in parentheses.**

> ### MY SPORTY SISTER AND ME
>
> My sister Samia loves sports. I [1] ______________ (*never / know*) anyone as active as her. She [2] ______________ (*play*) soccer, tennis, basketball and other sports for years. If you ask her 'How long [3] ______________ (*you / take part*) in sports competitions?' She'll tell you that she started as soon as she could walk! This month she [4] ______________ (*train*) for another marathon. She [5] ______________ (*complete*) two so far. One in New York and one in Chicago.
>
> I [6] ______________ (*not achieve*) very much all day today, apart from writing this blog post. Not like Samia. She [7] ______________ (*just / come in*) very hot and sweaty because she [8] ______________ (*work out*) at the gym all afternoon.

B **Rewrite each sentence using the present perfect progressive and the word given in capital letters. Write no more than five words.**

1 Clara moved here six years ago.

FOR

Clara ______________ six years.

2 Seth started playing tennis as a child.

SINCE

Seth ______________ he was a child.

3 I go to the gym a lot less recently.

NOT

I ______________ to the gym a lot recently.

4 They began to train last year to get ready for the marathon.

A

They ______________ year to get ready for the marathon.

had to / needed to

C **Find and correct the mistakes in the sentences.**

1 I hadn't to buy a yoga mat because my sister lent me hers.

____

2 We have to have lessons before we could jump out of the plane for the first time.

____

3 Julio need to practice a lot before he became good at fly fishing.

____

4 Kayleigh hadn't to watch the ukulele teacher because she already knew how to play the song.

____

5 She didn't had to do anything yesterday so she spent the day relaxing at home.

____

6 I had spend a lot of money to buy this stamp, but I'm pleased that I did.

____

7 The coach said we needed practice more, so we did.

____

8 I had use my friend's Ping-Pong paddle last week because I broke mine.

____

PRONUNCIATION
been: unstressed

6.2 **A** **Listen and underline the words the speaker stresses in each sentence.**

1 I've never been to India.
2 Tanya's been playing tennis for hours.
3 He's been very quiet all day.
4 How long have you been captain of the club?
5 We've been training since last year.
6 Have you been surfing before?

B **Practice saying the sentences in Exercise A. Don't forget that *been* should be unstressed.**

6.3 Sports and hobbies

READING

A Read three short texts which are all on the same topic. What is that topic?

B **IDENTIFY TONE** Where would you expect to read the three different texts? Match the texts (a–c) with the sources (1–3).

1 an encyclopedia ____
2 a blog ____
3 a magazine ____

C **READ FOR DETAIL** Which text mentions …

1 international styles of music?
2 work and free time?
3 children?
4 a life-changing experience?
5 different kinds of instrument?
6 helping others?

D **REFLECT** Think about the answers to these questions.

1 Do you play a musical instrument? If not, would you like to?
2 How can music help people to overcome a difficult experience?

a Great concert at the Memorial Hall last night – and all for charity! We raised $350 for the Hope Children's Hospital. Wonderful result! Well done everybody – the ladies of the organizing committee, Kingfisher Café who provided the refreshments … AND the band! They were just sensational … so impressive! I loved EVERY MINUTE of the concert. And a special thank you to the kids – it's great to see the young ones getting involved at such an early age. We hope we'll see you again next year, guys!

b A brass band is a musical group generally consisting entirely of brass instruments, frequently accompanied by a percussion section. Some groups include both brass and woodwind instruments, and this combination is typified by the New Orleans-style band. Variations on the make-up of the brass band vary across the world; the Balkan countries have a strong brass band tradition and have a distinctive style influenced by gypsy trumpet music, Turkish marching bands and traditional folk music. A British brass band usually consists of 28 players. The British scene is characterized by a strong competitive element, with annual contests being held to determine the best band in the country.

c Founded in 1917 to give miners something to do in their free time, the Grimethorpe Colliery Band has a long and proud history. The musicians were full-time mine workers, spending their days deep under the ground, digging out coal, and their evenings in music rehearsals. Sadly, the band is all that remains of Grimethorpe Colliery since the government closed it down in 1992. The closure of the pit came as a terrible shock and hundreds of people lost their jobs. At that time, 17 members of the band were working miners. Since then, the band has risen to fame for its part in the award-winning movie *Brassed Off*.

Glossary

colliery (n) a coal mine (place where coal is dug from the ground)
percussion (n) musical instruments which you hit or shake (e.g. drums)
woodwind (adj) musical instruments made of wood which you blow into to produce a sound

6.4 Sports and hobbies

Listening; Functional Language

LISTENING

A Look at the pictures (a–c). How could these people make money from their hobbies?

B LISTEN FOR MAIN IDEAS You will hear a talk about how to turn a hobby into a business. Read the main ideas of the talk. Listen and put them in the order (1–6) that they are mentioned.
6.3

- **a** Organize your ideas and your time. ___
- **b** Advertise your new business. ___
- **c** Make money from what you enjoy. ___
- **d** Organize the money side of your business. ___
- **e** Don't be scared – it's the right decision. ___
- **f** Use different ideas, not just one. ___

C LISTEN FOR DETAIL Listen again and circle the correct answer, a, b or c.
6.3

1. The advantage of turning your hobby into a business is that you will
   - **a** learn how to make things.
   - **b** have more free time.
   - **c** enjoy what you do to earn money.
2. Which statement best describes how people feel after making a business from a hobby?
   - **a** I'm too scared of failure to start up my own business.
   - **b** I don't regret making this life-changing decision.
   - **c** Starting my own business was a mistake.
3. New businesspeople should organize their time by
   - **a** practicing how to concentrate.
   - **b** setting detailed short-term actions.
   - **c** focusing only on positive targets.
4. Why should you use your hobby in different ways?
   - **a** To have various ways of making money.
   - **b** So you can teach others about it.
   - **c** To sell more products.
5. How can you attract customers?
   - **a** By using the internet effectively.
   - **b** By giving away free products.
   - **c** By sharing your ideas.
6. What is the speaker's advice about money?
   - **a** Enjoying your hobby is more important than money.
   - **b** You must earn more than you spend.
   - **c** It's a good idea to consult a professional.

Glossary

entrepreneur (n) person who creates a successful business
profitable (adj) which makes money

D REFLECT Think about the answers to these questions.

1. Do you have a hobby which you could turn into a business?
2. If you turned passion into profit, do you think you would still enjoy your hobby?

FUNCTIONAL LANGUAGE

Expressing your opinion

Complete the conversation with the words and phrases in the box.

another example | brutally honest | don't think | for instance | if you | my opinion | probably right

Leon: I've decided to turn my hobby into a business.

Pam: What – working out at the gym and keeping active?

Leon: Yes, [1] ______, I could set up an online fitness advice service, or, to give you [2] ______, I could become a personal trainer.

Pam: [3] ______ ask me, that's not a good idea.

Leon: Why not?

Pam: In [4] ______, if you turn your hobby into a business, you won't enjoy it. It won't be fun anymore – it will be stressful and boring.

Leon: I certainly [5] ______ that's true. I'll just be making money doing something I love, instead of sitting at a desk all day.

Pam: And to be [6] ______, Leon, I don't think you have what it takes to become a businessman. You need to know about finances and marketing and so on.

Leon: Hmm. You're [7] ______.

Your chance to win an adventure vacation with *Pursuits* magazine!

In our **'What to do'** section we're going to publish a series of readers' articles called *Try it!*

Send us your articles about a sport or hobby you think our readers should try doing. At the end of the series, readers will vote for the best article. Get writing!

WRITING

A Read the magazine ad above. Think about the answers to these questions.

1 Which sport or hobby would you choose to write about?

2 The first prize for this competition is an adventure vacation. Would you enjoy that? Why/Why not?

B ORGANIZATION Read *Try it – canoeing,* ignoring the blanks. You will see that each paragraph has a clear topic. Put the topics (a–e) in the order they are mentioned in the article.

a start in a group with others ___

b buying your own equipment ___

c risk-taking or relaxing ___

d taking safety precautions ___

e canoeing in other countries ___

Try it – canoeing

Whether it's paddling slowly along a river or racing down a white-water run, canoeing is one of the most exciting activities I've ever tried.

[1]___ about canoeing is that it can be both relaxing *and* thrilling. If you want excitement, try a white-water run. If you want a quiet day in the countryside, [2]___ and canals is that you can stop off wherever you like to rest.

If you've never done it before, it's best to join a club. [3]___ is that you get basic training and safety tips, and you make a lot of new friends. [4]___ joining a club is you don't have to provide your own canoe.

[5]___ is that you become part of a community. And you don't have to limit yourself to canoeing near home. There are clubs all over the country and … all over the world! Traveling to another country for a canoeing trip is just awesome!

Try it! It's great fun and a good way to meet new people. [6]___, though, is to put safety first and always wear a lifejacket. It isn't just a walk in the park!

C INTRODUCTORY CLAUSES Read the article again and fill in the blanks (1–6) with the introductory clauses (a–f).

a The reason for joining a club

b One thing I especially like about canoeing

c One of the nice things about exploring rivers

d Another good thing about

e The most important thing to remember

f One of the great things

WRITING PRACTICE

A PREPARE You are going to write a magazine article called *Try it!* about a sport or hobby you think other people would enjoy. Write notes about each of the points below.

1 Look back at Writing Exercise A. Which sport/hobby did you choose?

2 Think of three or four reasons why you enjoy it.

3 Think of a way to grab the reader's attention in your first paragraph.

4 Can you think of a memorable closing sentence?

B WRITE Write your article in 150–200 words.

- Use your notes and ideas from Exercise A.
- Remember to give each paragraph a clear topic.
- Don't forget to use introductory clauses.

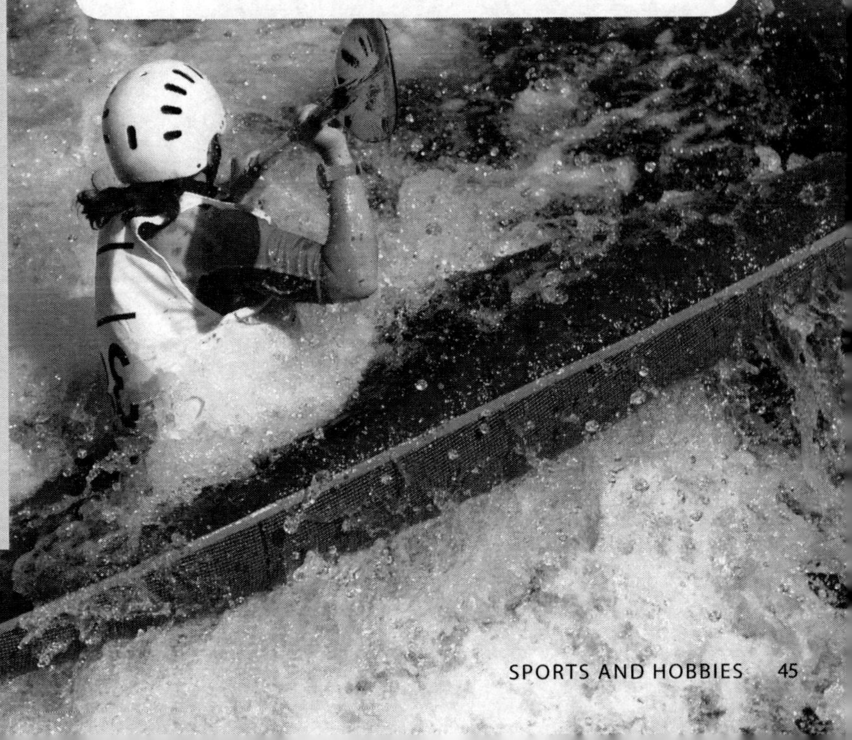

PRONUNCIATION
Word stress with modals

A Complete the conversation with the missing modal verbs. Use one to three words in each space. Then practice the conversation.

Woman: What do you think of the food?

Man: It's very nice. I'm glad you brought me here … Wait a minute; what's this in my soup?

Woman: I don't know – it [1] ______ a piece of meat.

Man: That [2] ______ right – this is a vegetarian restaurant, remember?

Woman: Right, yeah. It [3] ______ some kind of vegetable. Of course. It [4] ______ a potato. Do you want to ask the waiter?

Man: No, it [5] ______ meat and then I'll look stupid! I'm sure it [6] ______ anyway. It [7] ______ a vegetable, like you said, but I don't recognize the taste. I [8] ______ a look at the menu and see if it says anything there.

Diphthongs

B Match words (1–7) with words (a–h) which have the same diphthong sounds.

1 human ___	a phone
2 boy ___	b choice
3 cry ___	c say
4 straight ___	d computer
5 no ___	e choose
6 brown ___	f doubt
7 fruit ___	g light

7.1 **C Listen and check your answers. Then practice saying the words in Exercise B.**

VOCABULARY
Phrasal verbs

A Complete the sentences with the correct form of the phrasal verbs in the box.

give up serve up set up show up start off take off try out

1 Stay for dinner! I've found a new recipe online that I want to ______.

2 I don't mind ______ my place at tonight's meal – I'll go another time.

3 My dad hates it if anyone ______ late for a family meal.

4 Can you call everyone to the table? I'm ready to ______ the food.

5 I know Chinese food is popular here, but it never really ______ in my country.

6 This restaurant ______ as a fast food place but it was sold to a young chef last year.

7 It takes a lot of time and money to ______ a new restaurant.

Adjectives to describe food

B Complete the restaurant reviews with the missing words. The first letter has been given to help you.

To be honest, the meat was [1]d__________ because it was clearly not cooked properly and was [2]r__________ in the middle. The soup was very [3]w__________, too – there was very little in it. We won't be going back there!

They have a great selection of sweet and [4]s__________ snacks, which are so [5]f__________ that you really won't be hungry afterward. We've now tried most things on the menu and have to say that the food is delicious – really [6]t__________!
A word of warning, though – the home-made ice cream is so [7]r__________ and chocolatey that you won't want to move for an hour!

I had a pizza, which was very [8]c__________ (you can never have enough cheese!) and well-cooked with fresh ingredients. My friend had a [9]f__________ chicken dish with apple and banana in it – very unusual! It was [10]s__________ but not too hot. We were very impressed!

C Look at the table below. Put the adjectives from Exercise B in the correct column based on the context of the reviews.

Positive	Neutral	Negative

GRAMMAR
Modals of speculation and deduction

A Find and correct the mistakes in the sentences.

1 That must not be our bill – we only had a snack!
____

2 We should call and make a reservation – there might don't be a table.
____

3 You must to think I'm very rude eating with my fingers!
____

4 You maybe are right about this food – it doesn't taste good.
____

5 Let's try this new restaurant – it could maybe good.
____

6 This place might have not the best food, but it's good enough and very cheap.
____

B Rewrite these sentences using modals of speculation and deduction.

1 I've never tried buffalo wings, but I love all the ingredients so I'm sure they're delicious.

I've never tried buffalo wings, but I love all the ingredients so they *must be* delicious.

2 Allergy warning! It is possible that this snack contains nuts.

Allergy warning! This snack __________ nuts.

3 You've just eaten two whole meals! It's impossible that you want more food!

You've just eaten two whole meals! You __________ more food!

4 That salad looks strange, but maybe it doesn't taste too bad.

That salad looks strange, but it __________ too bad.

5 This sauce is OK, but I'm sure it isn't homemade – surely it's from a store.

This sauce is OK, but it __________ homemade – it __________ from a store.

6 I'm sure you think it's strange that I don't eat meat, but I just don't like it.

You __________ it's strange that I don't eat meat, but I just don't like it.

GRAMMAR

Comparatives and superlatives; *the …, the …*

A Complete the second sentence so that it has a similar meaning to the first sentence, using the word given. Write between two and five words.

1 Buy these chips – they don't have as much salt as the others.
Buy these chips – they have ________ of all the bags. (*the*)

2 David doesn't cook as well as Mark.
Mark ________ David (*than*)

3 If you add more pepper, the sauce will be spicier.
The more pepper you add, ________ sauce will be. (*the*)

4 The juice in a carton isn't as fruity as the homemade kind.
The homemade juice ________ the carton kind. (*tastes*)

5 Does a carrot have as many calories as a potato?
Which has ________ – a carrot or a potato? (*calories*)

6 I didn't do as badly as Kate on the cooking exam.
Kate did ________ on the cooking exam. (*me*)

B Circle the correct answer, a, b or c.

1 I find that the longer you leave a fruit on the tree, the ___ it tastes.
a juicy **b** as juicy **c** more juicy

2 That was ___ pizza ever! It was delicious!
a tastiest **b** the tastiest **c** more tasty

3 I think that curry will be too spicy for me. Do you have anything ___?
a milder **b** mild **c** more mild

4 Hank wants to eat ___ than he does now, but he simply doesn't know how.
a more healthy **b** most healthily **c** more healthily

5 Goji berries are ___ than strawberries, but they contain fewer calories.
a more expensive
b the most expensive
c expensive

6 I felt full after one bowl. That was one of ___ soups I've ever eaten!
a most filling **b** the more filling **c** the most filling

7 Açaí berries became popular ___ than anyone expected.
a quickly **b** quicker **c** more quickly

8 I've noticed that the more I eat at lunch, the ___ I want to work in the afternoon!
a little **b** less **c** least

PRONUNCIATION

Vowel + *w*

A Circle the word, a or b, which has the same vowel sound as the word in bold.

1 She **knew** her grandma would make her favorite recipe!
a now **b** you

2 Tell me again **how** you made your famous apple pie.
a about **b** go

3 Don't **throw** that potato peel in the trash can – we can use it in the garden.
a toe **b** wow

4 I ate too much for dinner – now I feel **awful**.
a owe **b** for

5 Are we **allowed** to bring drinks into the museum?
a throw **b** now

6 You can't smoke in here – it's against the **law**.
a view **b** draw

7 It didn't rain much this spring, so the plants **grew** very slowly.
a flew **b** so

8 How much do I **owe** you for this sandwich?
a flower **b** go

7.2 **B Listen and check your answers. Then practice saying the sentences in Exercise A.**

VOCABULARY
Waste

A Circle the correct option to complete the sentences.

1 If we ***recycled*** / ***reduced*** more, we wouldn't have to produce more plastic or glass.

2 I can't believe you ***threw*** / ***wasted*** so much money on that silly diet that didn't even work!

3 Once these glass bottles are empty, we can ***reduce*** / ***reuse*** them for storing water.

4 There's so much ***trash can*** / ***garbage*** in the streets, and it really looks awful!

5 We're trying to ***get rid*** / ***reduce*** expenses, so we're buying cheap brands of products.

6 You should ***use up*** / ***throw away*** all of the sauce in that jar – don't waste it!

B Complete the conversation with the words in the box.

away can down of garbage up

Gregory: What do you do about recycling in your house, Sasha?

Sasha: Well, my mom had this great idea. She put a small recycling bin next to every trash 1__________ in the house.

Gregory: That sounds handy.

Sasha: It works very well in the bathroom. Instead of throwing 2__________ the packaging of a tube of toothpaste, for example, it gets recycled.

Gregory: I see what you mean. In my house, we only have one place to get rid 3__________ our plastic, paper and glass. And that container fills up really quickly!

Sasha: That's right. I have to say, my mom's system works well. It really cuts 4__________ on the amount of 5__________ we throw away every week. The only disadvantage is that we use 6__________ a lot of plastic garbage bags.

C Complete the crossword using the clues.

Across

2 a container for putting garbage in

4 to make something smaller or less in size, amount, importance etc

6 to get rid of something that you no longer want, for example by putting it in a trash can

7 to use something again, sometimes for a different purpose

Down

1 things that are no longer useful, such as old food, paper or plastic used for wrapping things, and empty containers

3 to change waste materials such as newspapers and bottles so that they can be used again

5 the failure to use something valuable in an effective way

Angela: Recipe tester

I love cooking and I buy a lot of cooking magazines. One week, I saw an ad: 'Wanted: Recipe Tester – must love cooking.' Well I *do* love cooking and all my free time was spent in the kitchen anyway, so I applied and … that's what I do now. I test recipes for popular food magazines and publishers. There are also jobs available for big manufacturers like Kraft or Nestle but personally, I prefer to work for a smaller company. When you buy a fancy new cookbook, it's me, or someone like me, who has practiced every recipe in that book – once, twice, maybe even three or four times. Some recipe testers have a background in food science or nutrition and some, like me, have taught themselves instead. I've worked on recipes for all kinds of people, even celebrity chefs – it's my job to translate the chef's ideas into practical instructions which are suitable for a home kitchen. I don't earn much but to be honest, I don't mind – I'm just happy doing a job I love!

Jason: Food stylist

I started out in catering. I used to work as a chef and then I moved into writing for magazines and cookbooks. Apart from anything else, I now earn a lot more! Then, for one of my books, I had to create the recipes *and* photograph the dishes. That's when I learned that it's really an art to make food *look* as good as it tastes. Some people in the profession have graduated from a catering school but I'm self-taught. And you can't just show up and take some pretty pictures – you have to make all the dishes yourself, so you have to be a good cook as well as a good photographer! My friends ask me how they can make their Insta pictures look good – well, probably the most important thing is lighting. Use white or light-colored plates to serve the food – it will show off the colors of the food better. If a food is brown-colored, use green herbs or brightly colored vegetables to brighten it up.

Yoko: Food taster

In ancient times, powerful kings and emperors were frequently murdered with poison. That's the origin of a food taster's job – powerful men and women hired servants to taste their food and drink. Not so good for the food taster if it *was* poisoned! But don't worry, the modern-day job doesn't involve getting poisoned! No, my job is to taste new products created by a large international food manufacturer. I have to assess how the food looks and smells, as well as how it tastes. The product must always be exactly the same – customers don't want a product which looks or tastes different every time they buy it. I graduated from college with a degree in nutrition and a lot of my day is spent in the food laboratory where we test products for their nutritional content. I'm well-paid for what I do – in fact, I earn more than most of my friends. The worst thing about my job? I have to watch my weight and I regularly go without lunch or dinner.

READING

A PREDICT What do you think each of these jobs involves?

B READ FOR SPECIFIC INFORMATION Read again. Which person or people …

1. don't have any formal qualifications? ____ ____
2. mentions a negative aspect of his/her work? ____ ____
3. doesn't get a lot of money for the job? ____
4. are concerned with the appearance of food? ____ ____
5. works for a big company? ____
6. has a job which does not include cooking? ____
7. has to understand other people's ideas? ____
8. offers tips on how to do what he/she does? ____

Glossary

assess (v) look at something or test it carefully
manufacturer (n) a company which makes a product

C REFLECT Think about the answers to these questions.

1. In your opinion, which of the three jobs sounds the most interesting?
2. Which job would you like to do? Why?

LISTENING

A In your opinion, which of these are food fads and which are sensible guidelines for a healthy diet?

1 Only eat one kind of food for a week.
2 Eat a balanced diet from all the food groups (proteins, dairy, etc).
3 Eat the same food as prehistoric people.
4 Never cook your food – eat everything raw.
5 Eat five portions of fruits and vegetables a day.

B IDENTIFYING OPINIONS Read these sentences. Are the people describing a fact or expressing an opinion? Write F (fact) or O (opinion).

1 It sounds crazy. ___
2 They only eat food which has been found in the wild. ___
3 Fresh ingredients have more nutrients than processed food. ___
4 They're interesting ways of exploring new ideas. ___
5 I feel more energetic and less tired. ___
6 Olive oil is better for you than butter. ___
7 It prevents heart disease. ___
8 I don't think that's such a big deal. ___

7.3 **C LISTEN FOR SPECIFIC INFORMATION You will hear three people talking about food fads. Listen and match the sentences (1–6) to the speakers.**

1 A varied diet of different foods can prevent serious illness.
2 These foods can't be bought in a grocery store.
3 This diet has been in existence for a very long time.
4 It's OK if you don't stick strictly to a healthy eating plan.
5 Food fads can help people to be more aware of what they eat.
6 This food fad makes me feel sick.

César ___ ___
Olivia ___ ___
Wing Shan ___ ___

Glossary

forage (v) search for food out in the country

D REFLECT Think about the answers to these questions.

1 Have you ever heard of any of these food fads and diets?
2 Would you like to try any of the ideas from the listening exercise? Why/Why not?

FUNCTIONAL LANGUAGE

Complete the conversation with one word in each space.

Ellie: 1 ___ up, Jude?
Jude: I haven't been feeling very well. I'm always tired and I usually feel sick after I've eaten.
Ellie: 2 ___ you tried talking to your doctor?
Jude: No, I haven't.
Ellie: What 3 ___ changing your diet?
Jude: What do you mean?
Ellie: Well, maybe you're eating the wrong foods. If I 4 ___ you, I would go and see a nutritionist. It could be a real help.
Jude: That wouldn't be a good 5 ___. I don't think it would help.
Ellie: It's worth a 6 ___ though, isn't it? 7 ___ don't we go together?
Jude: That's a good 8 ___. OK.

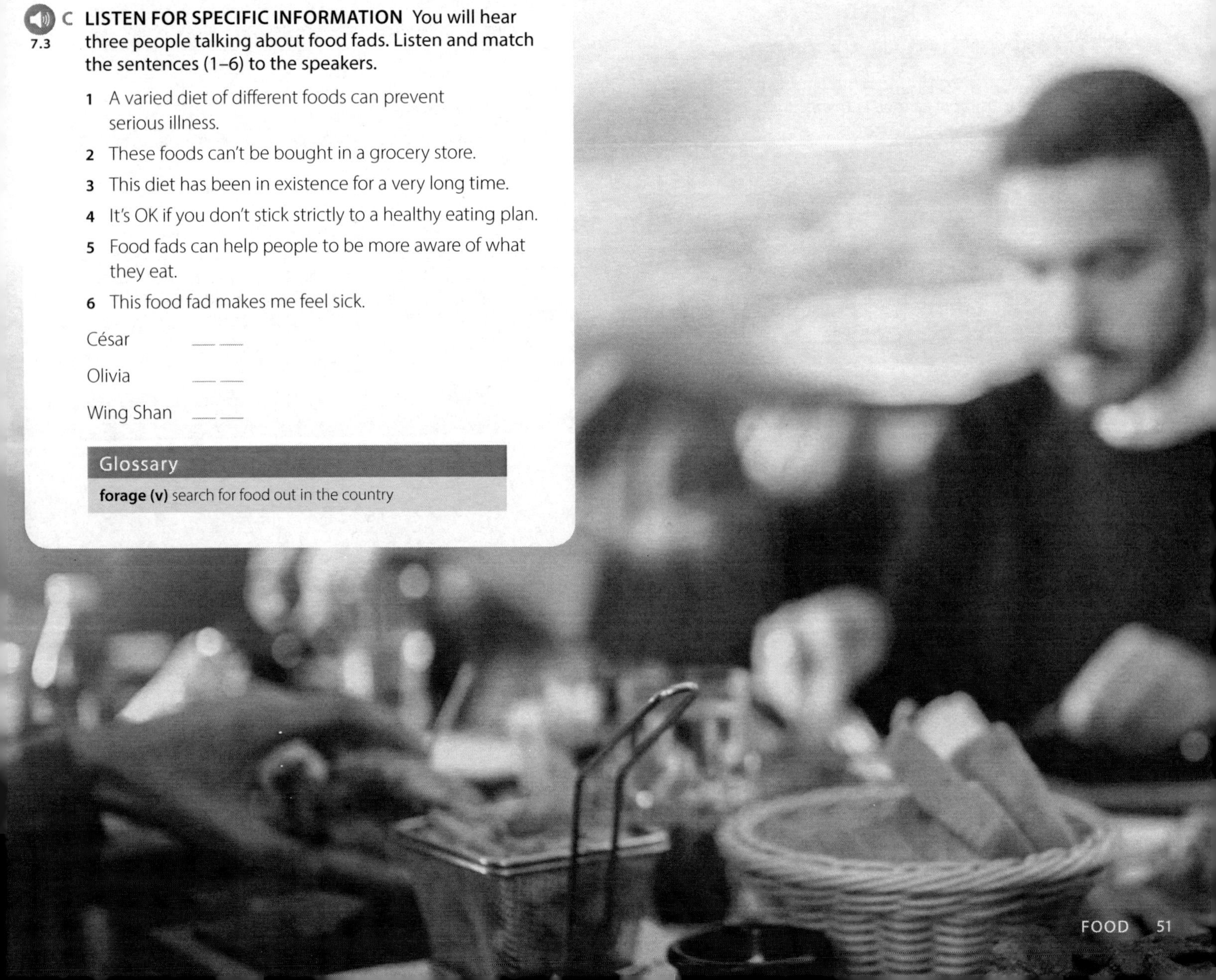

WRITING

A Think about the answers to these questions.

1 How often do you eat out?

2 Would you go to a restaurant because of a friend's recommendation?

3 Have you ever recommended a restaurant to a friend? Why?

B RECOMMENDING Read the forum post and the three replies. Which person (or people) make(s) these mistakes? Write *Gourmand*, *SloppyJoe* or *Sylvya*. Then say whose recommendation you think Betty should follow and why.

1 Doesn't start with a clear recommendation. ______

2 Says the decision '… depends …'. ______

3 Only talks about his/her personal preferences. ______

4 Doesn't mention the wishes of the friend. ______

5 Doesn't end with a clear recommendation. ______

C COMPARING AND RECOMMENDING Read again and circle the correct option to complete the posts.

Message from Betty

Hi everyone. Has anyone been to *Bamu* yet, the new restaurant in town? I've heard good things about it from people at work, but the review in the paper wasn't so good. Says it isn't as good as *Yukio's* if you want authentic Japanese – which I do. I'm thinking of taking a friend there for a birthday treat – she's never tried sushi before. What do you recommend?

Reply from Gourmand:

Are you asking us to choose between the two? I've been to both and I prefer *Bamu*. For a start it's [1]***more quieter / quieter***. OK, *Yukio's* is one of [2]***popular / the most popular*** restaurants in town, but, in my opinion the reviewer got it wrong; *Bamu* is just as authentic. It depends on what you and your friend want. *Yukio's* is [3]***most casual / more casual*** – at *Bamu* I always feel that I have to dress and behave kind of formally, but the food's tastier. [4]***I'd recommend / I like*** Yukio's if you want a fun time and *Bamu* if you want a dining out 'experience'.

Reply from SloppyJoe:

You do realize there's a perfectly good sushi bar in the mall, don't you? Just kidding. Remember, *Bamu* is new and fancy, as my friend calls it – and much more expensive [5]***than / as*** Yukio's. Is your heart set on Japanese food? It may be a small town, but there are other and, in my opinion, [6]***more nice / nicer*** restaurants around here. You can go somewhere just as nice as those two, but cheaper, and then go to a show afterward.

Reply from Sylvya:

I recommend that you put your friend first. What's important is how she feels and what she wants, not which is the best restaurant. [7]***I think you / You should*** try to find out if your friend wants to go to a Japanese restaurant on her birthday. Maybe she'd prefer to eat somewhere else, or even do something else. Not easy to do without spoiling the surprise, I know. [8]***Why don't you / It's better if you*** ask her family and other friends what she'd really like to do?

WRITING PRACTICE

A PREPARE You are going to write a reply to a forum post. Read the forum post below. Think about the answers to these questions and write notes.

1 What are the two options?

2 Can you think of some points for and against each option?

3 Whose wishes should you focus on?

I want to invite some friends who are coming down from New York for dinner. My first thought was that we could have a barbecue in the backyard. I'm really good at grilling food, and barbecues are such fun. But the weather forecast for the weekend is bad. The alternative is to reserve a table at a nice restaurant – less fun, I think, but possibly the safer option. What do you recommend?

B WRITE Write your reply to the forum post in approximately 100 words.

- Use your notes and ideas from Exercise A.
- Remember to start and end with a clear recommendation, giving reasons.
- Don't forget to use comparatives to show why your recommendation is better.

VOCABULARY
Word families

A Complete the text with the correct form of the words given in capital letters.

WHAT WILL YOU DISCOVER?

Is your ambition to become a ¹__________ and make the next great discovery? Or maybe you would like to go into the field of ²__________ and help build the machines of the future? Whatever your dreams are, to ³__________ in these fields you need more than just knowledge and a college degree. What will make the difference is your ability to be ⁴__________ and to come up with original ideas. For instance, creating a ⁵__________ that can be turned into a ⁶__________ that everyone needs and wants. The more ⁷__________ you are, the better your chances of becoming the next Steve Jobs!

SCIENCE
ENGINEER
SUCCESS
INNOVATE
DESIGNER
PRODUCE
INVENT

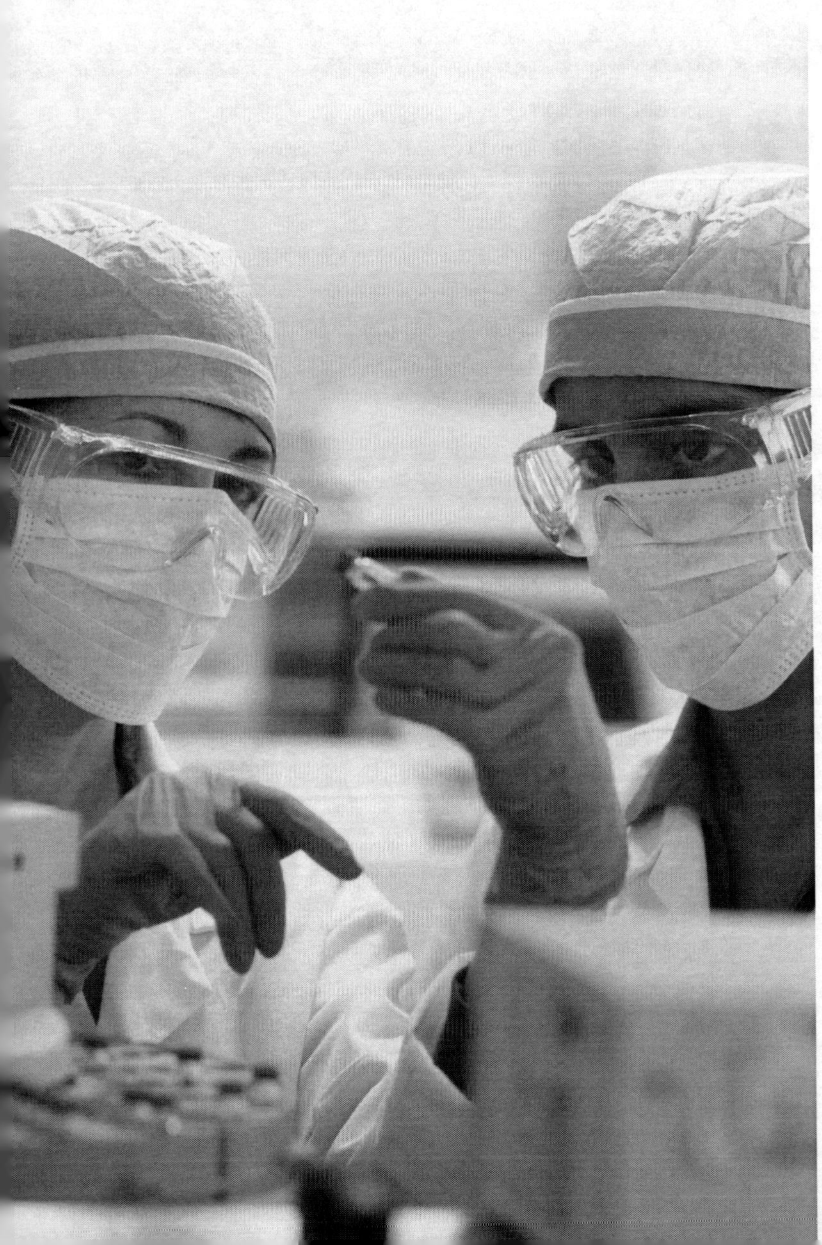

'Creative thinking' phrases

B Circle the correct answer, a, b or c.

1 I need new ideas for the spring fashion show, but my mind's gone ___.
- a empty
- b blank
- c out

2 At today's meeting, we want to come up ___ fresh ideas for the advertising campaign.
- a with
- b to
- c for

3 Try ___ unplug completely for a couple of hours – you'll feel less stressed.
- a to
- b on
- c out

4 A good way to generate new ideas is to ___ your mind wander freely.
- a give
- b go
- c let

5 They say that eating certain kinds of food can ___ your creativity.
- a grow
- b boost
- c switch

6 One characteristic of brilliant inventors is that they can think outside the ___.
- a block
- b square
- c box

7 A lack of confidence can ___ your creativity.
- a close
- b shut
- c block

8 ___ your imagination to picture life in the future.
- a Use
- b Try
- c Feel

9 Yoga and other forms of gentle exercise can help you to ___ new ideas.
- a design
- b generate
- c engineer

10 Why don't you try looking at the problem from the ___?
- a outside
- b upside
- c inside

PRONUNCIATION
Adjective clauses

8.1 Listen and check (✓) the sentences that contain non-essential adjective clauses.

1 ☐ 4 ☐

2 ☐ 5 ☐

3 ☐ 6 ☐

GRAMMAR
Adjective clauses

A Circle the correct option to complete the sentences.

1 It was Afua ***who / whose*** came up with the idea.

2 The college, ***that / which*** was established in 1840, is famous for its science department.

3 The invention ***who / that*** made him famous was the clockwork radio.

4 She visited the Science Museum ***where / when*** she was in New York last year.

5 I don't know ***which / whose*** idea it was to use a laser beam.

6 The town ***which / where*** her parents live is on the northern coast of the island.

7 Cyrus, ***which / who*** is wearing a black jacket, is an astronomer.

8 It was a decade ago, ***when / where*** I was still a teenager, that I first became interested in computers.

B Complete the short biography with the words in the box.

when where which which who whose

The amazing Ms. Jackson

Shirley Ann Jackson is a scientist [1] ________ achievements and research have helped the development of modern communications technology.

Shirley Ann, [2] ________ was the first African-American woman to get a PhD in Physics in the United States, started her studies in the mid-1960s.

The college [3] ________ she studied, the Massachusetts Institute of Technology (MIT), [4] ________ is near the city of Boston, is one of the most famous colleges in the country.

After graduating from college, she worked for the communications company AT&T Bell Laboratories. The 1970s was a time [5] ________ there were a great many developments in communications technology.

The research for [6] ________ she is most famous contributed to the development of *call waiting*, portable fax machines and fiber optic cables.

VOCABULARY
Positive adjectives

A Unscramble the words in parentheses to complete the sentences.

1. Nobody is the same as anyone else – we are all __________. (*quinue*)
2. I think you will look __________ in that jacket – try it on. (*soorgeug*)
3. We spent a __________ afternoon at the museum. (*gnifacsniat*)
4. I don't think it's very __________ to spend all your money on gadgets. (*blessien*)
5. Meeting and talking to an inventor was an __________ experience. (*blettanforgeu*)
6. My laptop is old and it isn't really __________ for what I need to do on it. (*blesatui*)
7. His ability to find solutions to problems is very __________. (*vemispresi*)
8. Those shoes look very nice but they're not very __________ for walking long distances. (*lactiparc*)
9. The picture on my new TV is __________ – I can see so much more detail than on the old one. (*bledcreini*)
10. The electrical gadgets in my home are very __________ and I can control them using my cell phone. (*catphosistied*)

B Complete the text with the missing positive adjectives from Exercise A. The beginning of each word has been given to help you.

Are gadgets a good thing?

Electronic gadgets are getting more and more [1]**s**__________, and we can do an amazing number of [2]**p**__________ things using them – a lot of the work is now done by machines. In home entertainment, technology used to have one [3]**u**__________ job, like playing music or showing videos. Now, the emphasis is on doing many different tasks from a central control point. How much more [4]**im**__________ will our gadgets become? We don't know, but the future promises to be [5]**in**__________.

However, many people worry about the effect that all this technology will have on us. Will we become lazy, or will we be [6]**s**__________ and limit our use of technology so that we can enjoy nature and get healthy exercise? For example, will we still choose to sit and admire a [7]**g**__________ sunset or enjoy the [8]**un**__________ experience of climbing to the top of a mountain? Or will we lose all our creativity because we get all our experiences digitally?

GRAMMAR
Zero and first conditional

A Complete the sentences with the correct form of the verbs in parentheses.

1 The computer gets really slow if you ________ (*keep*) too much on the desktop.

2 I'll buy some new batteries if you ________ (*tell*) me what size you need.

3 Unless we can fix this problem, we ________ (*have to*) change the design.

4 The phone can last about 24 hours if you ________ (*not charge*) it.

5 I ________ (*not buy*) this product again – it's awful!

6 He'll help you tomorrow if it still ________ (*not work*).

B Find and correct the mistakes in four of the sentences.

1 If you'll listen to next week's podcast, you'll hear about some more amazing gadgets.
____

2 Are you angry if I cancel our plans for tonight?
____

3 If the puzzles are too difficult, I usually get bored.
____

4 I won't go out tomorrow unless the weather will be good.
____

5 It's easy to share photos on social media if you want to.
____

6 What happens if you press this button?
____

7 I never buy gadgets unless I don't really need them.
____

8 Will you buy a new tablet if the price is right?
____

Conditionals with modals and imperatives

C Complete the sentences with the words and phrases in the box.

can always borrow can go can wait come and see don't try might help must be prepared should we still

1 The price will go down if you ________ for a few months.

2 If you stop using electronic gadgets in the evening, it ________ you sleep at night.

3 You can't succeed if you ________.

4 If it rains, ________ go to the beach?

5 If you're free tonight, ________ my band playing live.

6 You ________ to work hard if you decide to take this exam.

7 If you need a laptop, you ________ mine for a day or two.

8 Many restaurants seem to have the attitude: if you don't like it here, you ________ somewhere else.

PRONUNCIATION
'll and *won't*

8.2 **A Listen to the conversation and underline the phrases you hear the speakers say.**

1 *if you want to / if you won't*
2 *you'll really like it / you really like it*
3 *I want to go / I won't go*
4 *I lend / I'll lend*
5 *I'll enjoy / I enjoy*
6 *we'll have a nice time / we have a nice time*
7 *I won't miss it / I want to miss it*
8 *I call them / I'll call them*

B Practice saying the pairs of phrases in Exercise A.

READING

A **How long do you spend every day doing the following household tasks? Make a list of the electrical appliances you use to do them.**

- washing the dishes
- cooking food
- doing the laundry

B **TOPIC SENTENCES** **Read the article about household gadgets in the Victorian kitchen. Match the topic sentences (A–D) with the main paragraphs (1–4).**

A The task of washing, ironing and folding clothes may seem never-ending, but that's nothing compared to how tiring and time-consuming it was in Victorian times.

B The Industrial Revolution was marked by the invention of steam power and the use of mass production, but was this technological progress also reflected in the home?

C Maybe the most important task in any household, old or modern, is cooking, which today we do on a gas or electric stove.

D Another modern invention which we take for granted is the fridge-freezer.

C **READ FOR GIST** **In which main paragraph (1–4) would you expect to read about the following items?**

a soap
b food
c different kitchen gadgets
d coal

D **READ FOR DETAIL** **Read again. Are the sentences true (T) or false (F)? Correct the false sentences.**

1. According to the writer, people today appreciate the household appliances which they use every day. ___
2. Only the rich benefited from advances in technology in the Victorian era. ___
3. Some of the Victorians' appliances were similar to those we use today. ___
4. Servants had to take coal out of the kitchen range to keep it burning. ___
5. It was possible to preserve food by covering it with salt. ___
6. Rich Victorians could only keep their food cold in the winter. ___
7. Water was available in every Victorian household. ___
8. The 'dolly' was a kind of simple washing machine. ___

E **REFLECT** **Think about the answers to these questions.**

1. Which modern household appliance could you *not* live without? Why?
2. Do you think we still spend too long doing housework?

Must-have gadgets – Victorian style!

For most of us, an ordinary day will probably include starting the coffee maker for a cup of coffee, preparing a meal on the stove or in the microwave (using fresh ingredients from the fridge) and maybe loading the washing machine with the family's dirty clothes. These are all household gadgets that we take for granted and wouldn't dream of doing without. But how did people manage in the not-so-distant past?

1 ___ For poor families, the answer is 'no', but for the aristocracy and for well-off middle-class homes, then the answer is a definite 'yes'. Although the gadgets which were used in the Victorian kitchen relied on hand power rather than electricity, they were sophisticated machines which could accomplish many of the jobs that we do today with modern appliances. They had food processors to chop food, machines to slice bread and even a gadget to make ice cream!

2 ___ The Victorian kitchen used an iron *range* which consisted of a kind of iron box with a coal fire – this heated the oven and the hotplates and also boiled water. Although this style of kitchen stove was efficient, it certainly wasn't convenient. Coal had to be carried in regularly and ashes removed throughout the day. A servant would have to light the stove in the early hours of the morning and keep it burning all day.

3 ___ But without electricity, how did the Victorians keep things cold? Traditionally, both rich and poor used other food preservation techniques, such as keeping food in salt or vinegar, or smoking it, in order to make it last longer. However, the very rich had ice houses. The ice house was built underground, near a water source such as a lake, so that during the winter, ice could be taken from it into the ice house. The ice blocks, packed together underground, stayed frozen, even during the warm summer months. Here, the Victorians were able to keep food throughout the year.

4 ___ Since there was no running water, it usually had to be carried some distance, before being boiled in a huge pot over a wood or coal fire. And then just add soap? No, because the soap had to be made by hand, using a mixture of fat and ashes! In wealthier households, the clothes would be put into a *dolly*, a kind of bucket with a long wooden pole which was used to hit and move the clothes around. The whole process would take an entire day!

So, next time you take a carton of cold milk out of the fridge, press a button on your electric oven or complain about having to load the washing machine, spare a thought for the women of the Victorian era, who spent most of their lives doing what electricity and modern gadgets do for us in a few minutes!

Glossary

accomplish (v) to succeed in doing something
dolly (n) a kind of bucket with a long wooden pole
preservation (n) the process of stopping food from going bad
time-consuming (adj) taking a long time

LISTENING

A What advice could you offer a friend in each of these situations?

1 'I have to go to work every day and take care of my children, too.'

2 'There's so much housework that I don't know where to start.'

3 'My teenage children never help around the house.'

8.3 **B LISTEN FOR GIST** Listen to a conversation between two friends, Adam and Lucy. Check (✓) the problems which Adam mentions.

1 pressure at work ☐

2 studying for his exams ☐

3 preparing for a business trip ☐

4 juggling work and family ☐

5 ironing the clothes ☐

6 not having enough time ☐

8.3 **C LISTEN FOR DETAIL** Listen again and circle the correct answer, a, b or c.

1 Adam is worried because …
 a his wife has to work.
 b he can't cope with doing so many things.
 c his children are badly behaved.

2 Lucy thinks that it's important to …
 a dress your children in clean clothes.
 b have a family and a career.
 c accept that you can't be perfect.

3 Lucy advises Adam to …
 a achieve the most important tasks.
 b forget about cooking meals.
 c focus only on one goal.

4 Adam will have fewer jobs to do if he …
 a sets a better example to his children.
 b makes his own sandwiches.
 c asks his children to help.

5 What should Adam do to avoid heaps of dirty clothes or dishes?
 a Always do jobs right away.
 b Do everything at the end of the week.
 c Make the children do the dishes.

6 The best kind of checklist includes …
 a a list of the day's meals.
 b who will do a task and when.
 c only a few items.

Glossary

chore (n) a difficult or boring household job
delegate (v) give part of your work or responsibilities to somebody else
juggle (v) try to do several important things at the same time
prioritize (v) decide which order to do a number of different tasks

D REFLECT Think about the answers to these questions.

1 Do you agree with Lucy's advice to Adam?

2 Should men and women share the household chores and childcare? Why/Why not?

FUNCTIONAL LANGUAGE

Circle the correct option to complete the conversation between a woman and her granddaughter.

Rhoda: Amber – your mother bought me this new gadget. It's called a tablet, but I don't know how to use it.
Amber: Well, the [1]***first / start*** thing to do is press this little button here – to turn it on.
Rhoda: This one?
Amber: Yes, that's right. [2]***When / As*** you've done that, the screen comes on. See? Now, let's say you want to google something …
Rhoda: Sorry, can you [3]***tell / say*** that again?
Amber: Yes, 'google' something. Google is a search engine. It helps you to find information. So, you touch this little icon – the picture – with the letter *g*. Here – [4]***leave / let*** me show you.
Rhoda: Is this [5]***what / how*** you do it?
Amber: Yes, that's it. Well done, Grandma! [6]***After / Later*** that, you'll see a long white box. Use the letter keys to write what you want to know.
Rhoda: I'm not sure what you [7]***mean / say***.
Amber: Look – can you see the letters of the alphabet? Tap each letter that you want with your finger. [8]***Do / Make*** sure you don't press too hard.
Rhoda: Like this?
Amber: Yes, Grandma. That's it. Finally, you tap this key, and you'll see a list of all the different websites with the information you want.
Rhoda: That's wonderful. Thank you, Amber.

WRITING

A **Read the short biography of Ada Lovelace and answer the questions.**

1 Who was Ada Lovelace?

2 What was the turning point in her life?

3 What important contribution did she make to the field of computing?

B **ORGANIZATION** **Read the biography again. Match the headings (a–e) with the paragraphs (1–5).**

a Her early life. ___

b Introduction. ___

c Conclusion. ___

d A turning point. ___

e Her most important work. ___

C **USING LINKING WORDS TO SHOW CONTRAST** **Complete the sentences with the linking words in bold from the text.**

1 ________ she didn't have a college degree, she was treated as an equal by fellow scientists.

2 The design looked good on paper. ________, it proved impossible to build.

3 He managed to complete the project, ________ not having financial support.

Glossary

insist on (phr v) to say that you must have something

pioneer (n) one of the first people to do something important that is later continued and developed by other people

WRITING PRACTICE

A **PREPARE** **You are going to write a short biography of an innovative person. It can be someone famous or someone you know personally. Think about the answers to these questions and write notes.**

1 Which person are you going to write about?

2 What do you know about his/her early life?

3 Was there a turning point in his/her life? What was it?

4 How did he/she make an impact?

5 What can we learn from his/her life?

B **WRITE** **Write your biography in 150–200 words.**

- Use your notes and ideas from Exercise A.
- Divide your writing into five clear paragraphs.
- Remember to use linking words and phrases to show contrast.

C **REVIEW** **Check and edit your biography.**

BIOGRAPHY

Ada Lovelace: the first computer programmer?

1 Ada Lovelace is known as one of the pioneers of computer science. Her methods led her to see the possibilities of what were, at the time, simply *calculating* machines. She realized they could do much more than just calculate.

2 Born in 1815, her father, the poet Lord Byron, abandoned her as a baby, and her mother, Annabella Milbanke, left her to be brought up by her grandmother. **However**, she did insist on Ada getting a good education, especially in science and mathematics.

3 **Despite** her difficult childhood, she proved to be a good student. **Although** women could not enter college in those days, she was educated to a high level by private tutors. One of them introduced her to Charles Babbage, a professor of mathematics at Cambridge University – a meeting that changed her life.

4 Babbage wanted to build a machine that could do calculations and Ada asked to see his plans. She wrote and published notes on the machine including how to give it instructions. That is why she is often called the world's first computer programmer.

5 Ideas matter, and she realized that anything could be operated by computer programs. Her work changed the way the world worked.

9.1 The arts Art for everybody

VOCABULARY The arts

A Complete the sentences with the words in the box.

choir	concert	exhibit	instrument	musician
orchestra	performed	rehearsed	stage	studio

1 Maya had never sung better and she left the recording __________ with a big smile on her face.

2 She was the only __________ in her family; her father was an actor and her mother a dancer.

3 Most singers will tell you that it's a great joy to sing at a live __________.

4 They __________ the play every afternoon until the day of the performance.

5 The __________ consisted of violinists, trumpeters and drummers from Eastern Europe.

6 He was really nervous because he had never __________ live before in front of such a large audience.

7 Jose spent hours setting up an __________ of his latest work at the famous art gallery.

8 At what age did you first learn how to play a musical __________?

9 Thirty people sing in our __________ and we perform at festivals all over the country.

10 She stepped out onto the __________ and froze – she couldn't remember her lines!

Verbal idioms

B Circle the correct option to complete the sentences.

1 I'm going to be taking ***note of*** / ***part in*** a community theater project this summer.

2 The audience didn't find the play funny – all the jokes ***fell*** / ***dropped*** flat.

3 Can you ***make*** / ***tell*** the difference between a 3D-printed sculpture and a hand-carved one?

4 Don't do the work for free; your employer might take ***place*** / ***advantage*** of you later on.

5 Isaac made ***fun of*** / ***friends with*** the other members of the cast during rehearsals; they still like him to this day.

6 Even famous artists who are wealthy have to ***keep*** / ***make*** track of their finances like everyone else.

7 When she got the lead role in the movie, she felt as if her wildest dreams had ***come*** / ***gone*** true.

8 If you want to be a famous director like your uncle, you should ***draw*** / ***pay*** attention to his advice.

9 The director wants us to ***take*** / ***make*** use of the whole stage – not just the front part.

10 We're ready for the live concert – the choir is ready and the sound system is working. I hope nothing goes ***wrong*** / ***off***!

GRAMMAR
Second conditional

A Circle the correct answer, a, b or c.

1 Yiannis would study art in another country if he ___ enough money.
 a has
 b had
 c would have

2 If we all ___ Katrina's work, she'd make a lot of money.
 a would buy
 b will buy
 c bought

3 The actors ___ more if they had time.
 a would rehearse
 b rehearsed
 c can rehearse

4 Do you think more people would visit the museum if they ___ charge an entrance fee?
 a doesn't
 b didn't
 c wouldn't

5 If I ___ you, I'd try to sell my art on the street.
 a were
 b am
 c be

6 He'd give away his art for free if he ___ afford to do so.
 a will
 b would
 c could

7 Would you perform at the Grand Theater even if the job ___ well?
 a won't pay
 b didn't pay
 c doesn't pay

8 If you ___ a gallery, what type of art would you display?
 a would own
 b owned
 c own

B Complete the second conditional sentences with the correct form of the verbs in parentheses.

1 Tony is a talented artist, but he's also lazy! If he ______ (*work*) harder, he ______ (*become*) really successful.

2 If I ______ (*have*) more time, I ______ (*learn*) to play a musical instrument.

3 I ______ (*go*) to the exhibit if it ______ (*be*) free, but I'm not going to pay $20 for a ticket!

4 I love dancing. If I ______ (*cannot*) dance, my life ______ (*be*) so empty!

5 You have a good voice, but you need to practice more. If I ______ (*be*) you, I ______ (*take*) singing lessons.

6 They ______ (*have*) a lot more money if they ______ (*not spend*) it all on paintings!

PRONUNCIATION
/tʃ/, /ʃ/ and /k/

A Read the sentences and underline the *ch* words. Then match the sequence of three phonemes to the order of the *ch* sounds as they appear in each sentence.

1 Her character on the TV show is a young, talented chef from China.
 a /ʃ/, /k/, /tʃ/ ☐
 b /k/, /ʃ/, /tʃ/ ☑

2 Malek is doing research for his role as a chemist, and he's learning a lot about science and technology.
 a /tʃ/, /k/, /k/ ☐
 b /ʃ/, /tʃ/, /k/ ☐

3 When Danny was a child, he wanted to become a mechanic, just like his dad, Charley.
 a /tʃ/, /k/, /ʃ/ ☐
 b /tʃ/, /k/, /tʃ/ ☐

4 She had two choices; she could sing in a choir or play in an orchestra.
 a /tʃ/, /k/, /ʃ/ ☐
 b /tʃ/, /k/, /k/ ☐

5 It's a challenge to learn new singing techniques; in some ways, your voice is like a machine.
 a /ʃ/, /k/, /ʃ/ ☐
 b /tʃ/, /k/, /ʃ/ ☐

6 Standing outside the church, Matthew noticed a strange chemical smell.
 a /tʃ/, /tʃ/, /k/ ☐
 b /tʃ/, /k/, /k/ ☐

9.1 **B Listen and check your answers. Then practice saying the sentences in Exercise A.**

GRAMMAR

Reported speech

A Complete the second sentence so that it has a similar meaning to the first sentence, using the word given. Write between two and five words.

1 'What time are you leaving?'
She asked ________________ leaving. (*him*)

2 'We've never read any of J.K. Rowling's books.'
They said ________________ any of J.K. Rowling's books. (*read*)

3 'I'm sorry I made a mistake.'
She said she was sorry ________________ a mistake. (*she*)

4 'I can't understand why you changed your mind.'
She said she ________________ I had changed my mind. (*why*)

5 'Where is the manager?'
They wanted to know ________________. (*where*)

6 'Do you want to go to the movie theater?'
They asked me ________________ to the movie theater. (*go*)

7 'I won't come tomorrow.'
Susan said that she ________________ day. (*come*)

8 'Is Aisha here yet?'
I asked ________________ yet. (*there*)

B Complete the dialogue with one to three words in each space. Use the reported conversation to find the information you need.

Dialogue

George: I'm reading a great book right now. It's called *Saturday* and it's by a writer named Ian McEwan. [1] ________________ a few of his books. Have you heard of him?

Caroline: No, I haven't. What's it about?

George: I don't want to tell you because I will spoil it for you. I'll probably finish it tomorrow. You [2] ________________ it if you want.

Caroline: Thanks. Let me know when you finish it. I [3] ________________ a report I'm writing this week so I don't have a lot of time for reading. I read a book on vacation – that was the last time I read a novel.

George: What was it called?

Caroline: *The Rosie Project.*

George: I've heard of that. [4] ________________?

Caroline: Yes, [5] ________________. Do you want to borrow it?

George: Yeah sure. We can swap!

C Now complete the reported conversation using the information from the dialogue.

Reported conversation

George said that he was reading a great book called *Saturday* by Ian McEwan. He said he'd read a few books by the same writer. Caroline, however, said she hadn't heard of him and she asked what the book [6] ________________. George said he didn't want to tell Caroline because he [7] ________________ it for her, but he said she could borrow it if she wanted. He said he would probably finish it the [8] ________________ day. Caroline told him to let her know when he had finished it but she said that she had to finish a report she was writing that week so she didn't have much time for reading. She said the last time she [9] ________________ a novel was on vacation and that it was called *The Rosie Project*. George asked her if it was good. Caroline said it was and she asked George [10] ________________ to borrow it.

VOCABULARY

Reporting verbs

A Circle the correct answer, a, b or c.

1 Smith ___ that he had taken the money.
  a told b admitted c wondered

2 The woman ___ that she had been in front of me in the line.
  a reminded b refused c argued

3 Penelope ___ Tom to fix the garden gate.
  a explained b persuaded c replied

4 Giles ___ me he was tired.
  a told b insisted c mentioned

5 I ___ that the store was closed and she would have to come back the following day.
  a explained b asked c told

6 David ___ that he was right, even though it was obvious he had made a mistake.
  a persuaded b insisted c advised

7 Why are you ___? Is the baby asleep?
  a repeating b yelling c whispering

8 Did Farid ___ his sickness during your conversation?
  a mention b advise c remind

B Circle the correct option to complete the sentences.

1 Julia said she was tired and *added that* / *added me that* she had a headache.

2 They warned *us* / *to us* that the test would be hard.

3 I wondered *where* / *that* Rosemary was and why she was so late.

4 Harriet agreed *to come* / *come* with me to the doctor's.

5 He asked *me to go* / *that I go* to the movie theater with him.

6 My boss advised *to me* / *me* to say nothing about our conversation.

7 Frank predicted *to snow* / *that it would snow* the next day and he was right!

8 We reminded *them to leave* / *that they leave* home early.

9 The children refused *them to go* / *to go* outside in the rain.

10 I finally persuaded the police *that* / *to* take action.

PRONUNCIATION

Using your voice to make a story more interesting

A Read the extract aloud.

'Don't worry, my friend,' said the voice, 'I'm not going to hurt you,' the voice died to a whisper. 'But I might kill you! Ha, ha, ha!' 'You'll never get away with it,' Jim warned. 'The police will be here any minute.' Jim was, in fact, just keeping him talking because, unknown to his captor, Jim had almost untied the rope. Suddenly, without a word of warning, Jim leaped free, and using the rope that had held him firmly tied to the chair, he grabbed the man around the neck. 'Don't worry,' whispered Jim as he tightened the rope, 'I might wait for the police ... but I might not.'

9.2 **B** Look at the extract, this time with instructions in brackets. Listen to someone reading the extract while following the instructions. Does it sound different from when you read the extract in Exercise A?

[**spoken in an evil way, like a bad guy from a James Bond movie**] 'Don't worry, my friend,' said the voice. [**said in a sarcastic tone**] 'I'm not going to hurt you,' the voice died to a whisper. [**with more enthusiasm, as if the speaker finds it amusing, followed by an evil laugh**] 'But I might kill you! Ha, ha, ha!' [**frightened but trying to sound brave**] 'You'll never get away with it,' Jim warned. [**hopeful more than realistic**] 'The police will be here any minute.' Jim was, in fact, just keeping him talking because, unknown to his captor, Jim had almost untied the rope. [**dramatically on the word *Suddenly*, speaking fast**] Suddenly, without a word of warning, Jim leaped free, and using the rope that had held him firmly tied to the chair, he [**stress *grabbed* and *neck***] grabbed the man around the neck. [**mimicking the earlier comment from the other man, this time sarcastically**] 'Don't worry,' whispered Jim as he tightened the rope, 'I [**stress *might***] might wait for the police [**dramatic pause; evil, threatening**] but I might not.'

Glossary

mimic (v) to copy someone's voice or behavior, especially in order to make people laugh or to make someone feel annoyed

C Now practice reading the text while following the instructions.

READING

A Look at the pictures and answer the questions.

1 What do the two events have in common?

2 What is different about the two events?

3 How do you think the people at each event feel?

B **READ FOR GIST** Read *Europe's most unusual (and less well-known) music festivals*. Match the headings (a–e) with the paragraphs (1–5).

a New styles and genres

b More than just music

c Taking part

d See the world

e Unusual venues

C **UNDERSTANDING THE WRITER'S OPINION** Read again. Check (✓) the statements you think the writer would agree with.

1 I love being with thousands of other people. ☐

2 Things are too expensive at big festivals. ☐

3 I like places which are far away. ☐

4 The most popular styles of music are the best. ☐

5 Music is just one of my interests. ☐

D **READ FOR DETAIL** Are the sentences true (T) or false (F)? Correct the false sentences.

1 The writer enjoys the feeling of being in a big crowd. ____

2 The Saristra venue was once inhabited by local people. ____

3 Both Saristra and Gottwood Festivals take place in remote locations. ____

4 The writer finds rock and pop music uninteresting. ____

5 You can hear a single style of brass band music in Guca. ____

6 Traveling is a more important experience than music. ____

7 The writer recommends taking part in music contests. ____

8 Some events include large groups of musicians. ____

Europe's most unusual (and less well-known) music festivals

There won't be many readers who haven't heard of the Glastonbury Festival in the UK, Rock in Roma in Italy's capital or Coachella in the US. However, while thousands of festival-goers descend on these venues every year, there are some music-lovers who feel that these mega-events have gotten a little out of control: the huge crowds, the miserable cold and mud (in the UK at least!), not to mention the overpriced food, drinks and accommodations.

1 ____

More and more young people want a festival experience which is less mainstream and more unusual. Sometimes the venue itself is part of the experience. A good example is the Saristra Festival in Greece which takes place in an abandoned village on the island of Kefalonia. The half-ruined houses form a spectacular background to the music events and art installations which are staged there. Similarly, the Gottwood Festival takes place in the depths of a forest in the Welsh countryside and is an absolutely unforgettable experience.

2 ____

In the same way that some festival-goers want to go to more unusual venues, they may also want to listen to a different kind of music. Pop and rock music have dominated the festival scene for decades now, but isn't it time that we started exploring some different styles? It can get so dull listening to the same style of music year after year. And it's for this reason that a lot of young people are seeking out new genres. For example, a festival which has been going on for 50 years, but which has become increasingly popular in recent years, is Guca in central Serbia. And what kind of music can you listen to here? Brass band music! Musicians from all over the Balkans bring their own magical touch to brass instruments with gypsy music, funk and jazz.

3 ____

You will have understood by now that another very important element of this new wave of festivals is travel. Why stay in your home country which you probably know really well already? Where's the fun in that? People are ready and willing to travel all over Europe, to experience something new. It means that they can combine a once-in-a-lifetime vacation to a little-known European country, with a whole new world of music. Traveling by train or by bus to these remote locations gives an added excitement to the whole experience.

4 ____

And it's not just a love of travel and music which motivates these festival-goers. If you travel to a different country to listen to music, then of course you're going to experience a different culture, too. If the nighttime is for partying, then the daytime is for visiting incredible archaeological sites, listening to the words of a new language or sampling delicious local specialities.

5 ____

Maybe the most exciting music experience of all is actually performing yourself! More and more venues are setting up platforms for young people to showcase their talents in a friendly, noncompetitive atmosphere. Like-minded instrumentalists and vocalists come together to share their knowledge and their skills. Sometimes a whole choir or orchestra travels far from home to share their passion for music with others.

So what's stopping you? Pack your bags and leave the crowds behind. A whole new world of musical and cultural experiences is out there waiting for you!

Glossary

abandoned (adj) which is no longer used or lived in
mainstream (adj) considered ordinary or normal and accepted or used by most people
seek out (v) look for
vocalist (n) singer

E **REFLECT** Think about the answers to these questions.

1 Have you ever been to a music festival? If not, would you like to?

2 Would you prefer to go to a big, well-known event or a smaller, less popular event? Why?

LISTENING

A Look at the picture and answer the questions.

1 Do you think it's a good idea to study art? Why/Why not?
2 Do you enjoy painting and drawing?
3 What other kinds of art do you think you can study at art college?

9.3 **B LISTEN FOR GIST Listen to a conversation between Agata and Ethan about studying art. Answer the questions.**

1 Have Agata and Ethan seen each other recently?
2 Did she enjoy the course?
3 Did Agata study one or many areas of art?
4 What is her view of the project called *Pathways*?
5 Is she enjoying her current course of study?

9.3 **C LISTEN FOR DEFINITIONS OF NEW WORDS Listen again and complete the definitions with the words in the box.**

attractive bridge examples idea pressing subject wool

1 art foundation course: course of study in art and design which is a ________ between school and college
2 portfolio: a collection of artwork which you use as ________ of your work
3 discipline: a ________ that people study, especially at a college or university
4 conceptual art: kind of art where the ________ the artist wishes to express is more important than the end product
5 fleece: the ________ on a sheep
6 printmaking: the process of making images by ________ paper against a surface
7 illustration: a picture in a book used for explaining something or to look ________

9.3 **D LISTEN FOR DETAIL Complete the sentences with one or two words in each space.**

1 Agata explains her year-long course was a ________ between high school and college.
2 A good portfolio should demonstrate a ________ of different styles.
3 Agata enjoyed learning about ________ kinds of art.
4 Conceptual art first appeared during ________.
5 The project which Agata's fellow student did involved dressing up as ________.
6 She made ________ of her experience using 14 cameras.
7 Agata thinks that the word '________' does not describe the other student's project well.
8 According to Agata, you can use wood, ________ or ________ to create a print.
9 Agata is now learning how to create ________ for books.

E REFLECT Think about the answers to these questions.

1 Which of these disciplines on Agata's foundation course would you be most interested in: drawing, painting, fashion and textiles, printmaking or 3D design? Why?
2 What do you think about the idea of 'conceptual art'? Can you think of any examples of conceptual artworks?

FUNCTIONAL LANGUAGE

Complete the conversation with the words and phrases in the box.

actor ending follow like scene tearjerker worth

Kate: I watched an excellent movie on TV last night. It was called *Message in a Bottle*. I cried so much at the end!

Eleni: Oh, I love movies that make me cry!

Kate: Well, if you [1] ________ sad movies, then this is the movie for you. It's about this woman who finds a tragic love letter in a bottle on the beach and she tries to find the person who wrote it.

Eleni: And of course she finds him and he's incredibly good-looking and they fall in love!

Kate: Exactly! It has Kevin Costner in it, and he's a wonderful [2] ________. And then at the end, …

Eleni: No – don't tell me!

Kate: Well, just let me say that there's a sad [3] ________ – a real [4] ________.

Eleni: It sounds like it's really [5] ________ watching.

Kate: It is. The plot was a little difficult to [6] ________ but I loved the [7] ________ where he writes the letter to his dead wife.

Eleni: OK. Don't say anymore because I'm definitely going to watch it!

WRITING

A Think about the answers to these questions.

1 What is the purpose of a book review?
2 Where would you find a book review?
3 Have you ever been influenced by a review to buy a book?
4 What other art forms can you read reviews of?

B Read the book review and answer the questions.

1 Is the review mainly positive or negative?
2 Is the book a novel or a collection of short stories?
3 Are the nine sections of the book related in any way?
4 What negative point does the reviewer make about the book?

David Szalay: *All That Man Is*

1 I greatly enjoyed David Szalay's first novel, *London and the South-East*, a darkly comic novel about a young man dissatisfied with life in London. This new book, *All That Man Is*, his fourth, is similar in its themes but has several protagonists and explores new territory.

2 For a start, is it a novel? It is made up of nine sections each about a different male character: they range from the 17-year-old Simon to 73-year-old Mr. Parson. So, there is no plot, although the sections are thematically linked: let's call them short stories.

3 These men are trying to make sense of life and are mostly disappointed by it. They are lonely and their main concerns seem to be love and money. If this makes it sound depressing, it isn't: Szalay's prose is lively throughout. And while he exposes their faults, he does so sympathetically and without mocking them.

4 If there is a fault – remember it is a book about men – it is the lack of any fully rounded female characters. But, that aside, I urge you to read him because his is a rare talent and he is one of the most interesting fiction writers we have.

C ORGANIZATION Read again. Match the topics (a–d) with the paragraphs (1–4).

a plot and characters ___
b title, themes, main characters ___
c overall assessment, reasons for recommendation ___
d more detailed analysis, writing style ___

D Find three colons in the review. Note how they are used to introduce explanations. Then match the beginnings of the sentences (1–3) with the endings (a–c).

1 I stopped reading after 20 pages: ___
2 There's a lesson to be learned from this: ___
3 You need a strong stomach to read this: ___

a there are some disturbing scenes.
b don't believe everything the reviewers say.
c the writing was awful and the plot unbelievable.

WRITING PRACTICE

A PREPARE You are going to write a review of a book which you have read recently and particularly enjoyed. Write notes about each of the points below.

- Write down the title, genre, theme and main characters.
- Think about the main points of the plot.
- Think about the writing style. Write down one or two adjectives.
- Take note of anything you didn't like about the book.
- Think about your overall impression of the book and why somebody else should read it.

B WRITE Write your review in 150–200 words.

- Use your notes and ideas from Exercise A.
- Divide your writing into clear paragraphs.
- Remember to use colons to introduce explanations.

VOCABULARY
Psychology verbs

A Complete the sentences with the words in the box. The first two sentences have two possible answers.

affects assume attract avoid encourage influences persuade regret tempted tricking

1 Store owners want to ________ / ________ you to spend as much money as possible.
2 The thing that most ________ / ________ my decision to buy something is the price.
3 I was ________ by that flat screen TV, but I thought I'd wait until the prices fall a little.
4 Reducing the prices of things is just a way of ________ you into buying something you don't need.
5 I ________ spending so much money on a computer – it was a big mistake.
6 A store window is designed to ________ customers as they pass by.
7 If you buy something second-hand, you shouldn't ________ that it's in good condition.
8 Try to ________ buying things on impulse (in other words, don't buy anything without thinking it through beforehand).

Expressions with *mind*

B Complete the sentences with one word in each space.

1 I've ________ up my mind – I'm getting that new car!
2 If you're tempted to buy more than you can afford, just walk away – it's all ________ the mind.
3 I lost some data on my computer, but ________ mind – I had backed it up.
4 I'd love to see you next week. Just ________ in mind that I will be away on Wednesday.
5 I was of ________ minds about whether to buy this tablet, but I bought it anyway.
6 If you ________ your mind to it, I'm sure you'll make the right decision.
7 Paul used to hate smartphones, but he's ________ his mind now!
8 ________ you mind if I copied some music from you sometime?

PRONUNCIATION
Third conditional

A Listen to two speakers saying the same sentence. Check (✓) the speaker who pronounces the sentence correctly. 10.1

1 If I'd had all the information, I'd have made a better decision.
Speaker A: ☐ Speaker B: ☐
2 You'd have done better if you'd bought it online.
Speaker A: ☐ Speaker B: ☐
3 If I'd been of two minds, I would never have bought anything!
Speaker A: ☐ Speaker B: ☐
4 What would you have done if I'd been late?
Speaker A: ☐ Speaker B: ☐
5 I wouldn't have minded if you'd decided to cancel.
Speaker A: ☐ Speaker B: ☐
6 I could have made other arrangements if they'd told me sooner.
Speaker A: ☐ Speaker B: ☐

B Practice saying the sentences in Exercise A with the correct pronunciation.

GRAMMAR
Third conditional

A **Complete the third conditional sentences with the correct form of the verbs in parentheses. Use short forms where possible.**

1 You ____________ (*get*) better from your sickness much sooner if you ____________ (*not go*) away for the weekend.

2 If I ____________ (*know*) the watch was made of plastic, I ____________ (*not pay*) so much for it!

3 If the teacher ____________ (*tell*) us about the test a little earlier, we ____________ (*can / spend*) more time preparing for it.

4 I ____________ (*not choose*) that language school if I ____________ (*think*) about the number of students who failed the exam.

5 If you ____________ (*not assume*) the saleswoman was trying to help you, you ____________ (*might / make*) a better decision.

6 Sam ____________ (*might / not / be / tempted*) to spend all that money if he ____________ (*not go*) shopping.

7 The poor man ____________ (*can / avoid*) a lot of trouble if he ____________ (*read*) the details on the contract.

8 If I ____________ (*realize*) how much the ink costs, I ____________ (*not buy*) this make of printer.

should have + past participle

B **Read the conversation and rewrite the underlined sections with *should/shouldn't have* + past participle.**

Margarita: I wouldn't have bought this laptop if I'd realized I'd have to pay for all these extras.

Angela: Oh dear. And I knew that. [1]<u>I wish you'd asked me</u> before you made up your mind to buy it.

Margarita: Then I found exactly the same laptop for 50 dollars cheaper in the store closest to my house!

Angela: Sometimes the bigger stores are more expensive, not less. [2]<u>It would've been better if you'd checked</u> the prices.

Margarita: I was in too much of a hurry to buy it. [3]<u>It would've been better if I'd waited</u>.

Angela: Yes – [4]<u>it was a mistake to buy</u> it at the first store you went to.

Margarita: Do you know what [5]<u>it would've been better to do?</u>

Angela: What's that?

Margarita: [6]<u>It would've been better to take</u> you with me!

Angela: Next time!

1 ____________
2 ____________
3 ____________
4 ____________
5 ____________
6 ____________

VOCABULARY
Reflexive verbs

A Complete the sentences with the correct reflexive pronouns.

1 Even though it wasn't our fault, we couldn't help but blame ________.

2 There's ham and cheese in the fridge and bread on the counter; if you want a sandwich, you can make it ________.

3 That silly dog of mine; he's always getting ________ into trouble.

4 Children! If you can't control ________, we're going home right now!

5 Do you mind if I help ________ to one of these snacks?

6 After she got the promotion, Lucy treated ________ to an expensive meal in a fancy restaurant.

7 What goals have you set ________ for the next six months?

8 The team decided to reward ________ for doing a great job on the project and turning it in on time.

Staying organized

B Circle the correct option to complete the sentences.

1 After I finish ***cleaning / sorting*** up my desk, I'm going to write a long to-do list.

2 If you ***focus / keep*** a record of your finances, you'll improve your spending habits.

3 Her life was a mess, so she ***sorted / scheduled*** an appointment with a lifestyle guru.

4 Martin got so involved in the details that he completely forgot the main ***action point / objective***.

5 Where can we ***store / sort*** all these old files and papers?

6 So we've done the first task; what's the next ***objective / action point*** on the list?

7 Once you have your plans ***sorted / tidied***, let me know what you're doing.

8 I have a simple ***task / objective*** for you – fold the invitations and put them into the envelopes.

PRONUNCIATION
Emphasis and reflexive pronouns

A Read the sentences, paying particular attention to the reflexive verbs. Underline either the main verb or the reflexive pronoun which should be stressed in each sentence.

1 Mary brought a cake into work and I helped myself to a slice at lunchtime.

2 You're good at praising others when they do well, but how do you reward yourself?

3 You'll have to prepare John's lunch today, because he can't make it himself.

4 When something goes wrong, my Aunt Tilda tends to blame herself.

5 I believe that it's a good idea to set yourself goals in life.

6 They treated themselves to pizza after winning the game.

10.2 **B Listen and check your answers. Practice saying the sentences in Exercise A.**

GRAMMAR
Hopes and wishes

A Circle the correct answer, a, b or c.

1 I hope you ___ Leon to change his mind about leaving.
  a would persuade
  b persuade
  c persuaded
2 He wishes he ___ keep his desk neat.
  a had
  b can
  c could
3 Good luck! I hope your mom ___ yell at you for being late!
  a couldn't
  b doesn't
  c didn't
4 Tomas wishes he ___ his mind to passing the exam; he regrets not studying.
  a puts
  b had put
  c put
5 Look at these beautiful gold earrings – I wish I ___ rich enough to afford them!
  a am
  b would be
  c were
6 It sounds like you had fun on your trip. I wish I ___ with you!
  a could have come
  b can come
  c could come
7 I can't remember what we decided at the meeting – I wish I ___ a record of what we said.
  a kept
  b have kept
  c had kept
8 Dylan is responsible for the project for the next month; I hope he ___ the action points.
  a wouldn't forget
  b didn't forget
  c doesn't forget

B Circle the correct option. Then complete the short conversation with the correct form of the verbs in parentheses.

1 **Natalie:** I (hope) / *wish* we ___are___ (*be*) able to cover all the material before the exam.
Devin: Me, too. I ***hope*** / ***wish*** we ___________ (*plan*) it better. We could have finished already!

2 **Isaiah:** Beth wants me to pick up some things we need for moving to a new house. I ***wish*** / ***hope*** I ___________ (*can / remember*) everything she told me!
Ben: Moving is difficult. I ***wish*** / ***hope*** it ___________ (*go*) well for you.

3 **Rosana:** My sister has a terrible social anxiety; she always tells me that she ***hopes*** / ***wishes*** she ___________ (*no be*) so shy.
Pravat: I know the feeling. I ***hope*** / ***wish*** everyone ___________ (*can / have*) confidence, but for some, it takes a lot of effort.

4 **Josey:** I talked to Margie the other day. She ***wishes*** / ***hopes*** you and she ___________ (*can / meet*) soon.
Ivan: Oh, how nice! I think next Friday could be good. I asked my boss for that day off. I ***wish*** / ***hope*** he ___________ (*give*) it to me.

READING

A Read the statements. Do they surprise you? Why/Why not?

1 Most adults will suffer from anxiety and depression at some point in their lives.

2 Millions of people suffer from anxiety or depression worldwide.

B READ FOR GIST Read the article about anxiety. According to the article, are these statements true (T) or false (F)?

1 Anxiety has both psychological and physical symptoms. ___

2 People who suffer from anxiety usually face serious work, family or health issues. ___

3 The origins of anxiety as a human problem are very old. ___

4 It's a good idea for sufferers to avoid situations which upset them. ___

5 Sufferers can be helped by using a variety of different treatments. ___

6 Calming activities and exercises can help sufferers to cope better. ___

Glossary

dread (n) fear of what might happen in the future

overcompensate (v) do more than is necessary in order to correct a problem

C READ FOR KEY INFORMATION Read again and look carefully at the underlined parts. Complete the article with the missing sentences (1–5).

1 A longer-term and more effective strategy is to use a combination of psychotherapy, behavioral therapy and, in extreme cases, medication.

2 Implementing a stress management plan could include keeping an eye on deadlines, creating lists to organize different aspects of work and home life and allocating time off from school or work.

3 Back then, humans had an internal alarm system which was there to protect them from the very real dangers which they had to face in the wild.

4 Fear of such ordinary people and places may lead the sufferer to avoid seeing certain people or going to certain places.

5 Psychologists believe that this primitive alert system, in a world where we are no longer in danger from wild animals or aggressive attackers, is what prompts the feelings which we know today as *anxiety*.

D REFLECT Think about the answers to these questions.

1 What common social or work situations could cause anxiety?

2 How could family members help somebody who is suffering from anxiety?

Anxiety:

what it is and what can be done about it

We frequently hear people talking about *anxiety* but what is it exactly? Anxiety is a normal but unpleasant part of our everyday lives which can affect different people in different ways. Sufferers describe it as a feeling of unease, nervousness or dread. It may produce symptoms such as nausea, trembling or increased heart rate. Anxiety isn't necessarily triggered by a situation which is genuinely dangerous or difficult – it can be an everyday event, such as going into the grocery store or having to talk with colleagues, which brings on symptoms.

a ___ They might start shopping in a different grocery store, or pretending to be overworked in the office so that they don't have to interact with colleagues. Some people start working late because they are anxious about completing tasks, or waking up in the middle of the night to check their to-do lists in case they have forgotten something.

Anxiety can make a person believe that things in their life are worse than they really are. Some people even reach the stage of thinking they are losing their sanity or *going crazy*. However, what is important to remember is that anxiety is normal and exists due to physical reactions that have existed since prehistoric times.

b ___ It caused individuals to be on the alert for possible attack and produced a boost of adrenaline that increased the heart rate and the amount of oxygen in the blood. This response is commonly known as the *fight or flight* reaction.

c ___ However, instead of our system reacting to a real danger, it is overcompensating by reacting to perfectly normal problems and difficulties which everybody faces in their everyday lives.

So what can sufferers do to reduce the symptoms of anxiety and cope better with their lives? What they usually do is to simply avoid the anxiety-provoking situation, as we saw earlier. However, although such a strategy does provide short-term relief, it does not solve the overall problem. There will no doubt be another situation to replace the one you've managed to avoid.

d ___ Many people successfully treat their anxiety by implementing a number of self-help techniques, without resorting to a medical practitioner. These may include any or all of the following: stress management, relaxation techniques and physical exercise.

e ___ Relaxation techniques vary from person to person but could include breathing exercises, a long bath or yoga and meditation sessions. Physical exercise is also known to increase serotonin levels which in turn trigger positive emotions.

10.4 Psychology

LISTENING

A Which of these statements do you agree with? Why?

1 If you have a mental health disorder, it's better not to say anything about it.

2 Most people think that mental health problems are related to violence.

3 People shouldn't feel embarrassed to talk about mental health problems.

10.3 **B LISTEN FOR KEY PHRASES** **Listen to an extract from a radio show about mental health. Check (✓) the phrases you hear.**

1 According to research ☐
2 … statistics … have shown that … ☐
3 But surely … ☐
4 As you can imagine, … ☐
5 For example, … ☐
6 Obviously, … ☐
7 In fact, … ☐

Glossary

bipolar disorder (n) a serious mental illness where people experience extreme mood changes
discrimination (n) unfair treatment because of race, religion, illness, etc
stigma (n) a feeling that something is wrong or embarrassing

10.4 **C LISTEN FOR DETAIL** **Now listen to the complete recording and underline the correct option to complete the sentences.**

1 According to Doctor Patel, over 615 million people suffer from anxiety or depression *in the UK / all over the world*.

2 In the UK, *a quarter of the population / one or two people* suffer from mental health problems.

3 Doctor Patel has shown that a majority of people with mental health problems have to deal with *discrimination / aggression*.

4 People with mental health problems are *more likely / less likely* to be able to find work.

5 Most patients are *violent / not violent* or aggressive.

6 Publicity campaigns organized by *charities / research groups* have a positive effect.

7 Employers are *not allowed / allowed* to refuse somebody a job because of their mental health problems.

D REFLECT **Think about the answers to these questions.**

1 Do you think that there is a stigma attached to mental illness in your country?

2 What could be done to improve the situation?

FUNCTIONAL LANGUAGE

Complete two short conversations with one word in each space.

Steve: It's [1] ________ for me to go. I have to work on my psychology project. Sorry.
Inge: There's no [2] ________ to apologize.
Steve: I'm a little stressed about it, to be honest.
Inge: Don't [3] ________; you'll be fine.

Carla: Hi, Zoe. Did you buy the tickets for the concert?
Zoe: Oh no! I completely forgot! I'm really [4] ________!
Carla: Don't worry [5] ________ it.
Zoe: Now you're going to miss your favorite singer. And it's all my [6] ________!
Carla: It isn't your fault; it's my fault. I should have bought them a long time ago.
Zoe: I'm [7] ________ an idiot!
Carla: Never mind. It's just one of those [8] ________.

WRITING

A Read *Report on Downey Town Fair* and answer the questions.

1 What is the main purpose of the report?
2 To what extent was the fair a success?
3 What was/were the main problem(s)?
4 What measures do you think they will adopt next year?

B **ORGANIZATION** Read the report again. Match the headings (a–f) with the paragraphs (1–6) in the report.

a Poor planning
b Summary
c Analysis
d Wrong predictions
e Recommendations
f Background

Report on Downey Town Fair

1 ___
On June 14th, we held our Town Fair to raise money for local projects. Although we met our financial targets, we received complaints about poor organization. This report explores what we did wrong.

2 ___
The fair has become increasingly popular, attracting visitors from all over the country. This year more people came than we had planned for, and lack of parking areas caused chaos both in town and in the surrounding area.

3 ___
I believe we should have foreseen the larger number of visitors because this has been increasing annually. In fact, the matter was raised at one meeting, and the offer by Mr. Orton, a farmer, of one of his fields for parking was refused.

4 ___
Lack of parking spaces led to traffic jams extending five to ten miles out of town, and at the end of the day, it took hours for the traffic to return to normal.

5 ___
Obviously, we need more parking spaces and better signs and directions. In the future, we should take up the offers of landowners such as Mr. Orton.

6 ___
We should have more people employed to direct cars to available parking spaces and, if possible, get the police involved in regulating traffic in and out of town.

WRITING PRACTICE

A **PREPARE** You are going to write a short report about an event you helped to organize where there were some problems. Think about the answers to these questions and write notes.

1 Which event are you going to write about? When did it take place?
2 What happened? What was/were the problem(s)?
3 What was the cause of the problem(s)?
4 What are your recommendations for future events?

B **WRITE** Write your report in 150–200 words.

- Use your notes and ideas from Exercise A.
- Divide your writing into clear sections.
- Remember to use headings, bullet points and numbered lists.
- Include some facts and figures and examples of the problems.

Audio scripts

UNIT 1

Lesson 1.4, Listening, Exercise A
1.3 **J = John K = Karen**

J: Coming up on today's show, a discussion on selfie addiction and an interview with an expert on the history of selfies. But first of all, we're going to talk to Karen Harris about the Chinese phenomenon of *Meitu*. Karen, what exactly is *Meitu*?

K: Well, John, it's a new Chinese photo-editing and sharing app. I say it's new, but in fact, it was launched in 2014 and is super-popular in China and throughout Asia.

Lesson 1.4, Listening, Exercise B
1.4 **J = John K = Karen**

J: Coming up on today's show, a discussion on selfie addiction and an interview with an expert on the history of selfies. But first of all, we're going to talk to Karen Harris about the Chinese phenomenon of *Meitu*. Karen, what exactly is *Meitu*?

K: Well, John, it's a new Chinese photo-editing and sharing app. I say it's new, but in fact, it was launched in 2014 and is super-popular in China and throughout Asia. It was only recently launched here in the US though. Just to give you an idea of its popularity … the app has been installed more than a billion times and has more than 450 million unique users throughout the world.

J: That's incredible! OK. So tell us a little more about it, Karen.

K: Well, *Meitu* means *beautiful picture* in Chinese and it's an app available on iOS and Android platforms which helps you to look more beautiful in selfies. For example, you can retouch your skin to make it appear smoother and younger, or remove spots or dark circles from under your eyes. You end up with an idealized version of yourself.

J: But don't most photo apps allow you to do that kind of thing anyway?

K: Yes, they do, but *Meitu* goes much further. After you've chosen one of seven filters …

J: What kind of filters?

K: Well, they have names like *Angelic*, *Blossoms*, *Mermaid* … so you can probably imagine the style. It creates a soft focus for your picture and makes you look kind of dreamy as well as giving you the option of adding effects like stars, flowers and tears.

J: And then?

K: And then … well, the best part … the most unusual aspect of this app is that it has an incredible hand-drawn mode that allows you to change your eye color, whiten your teeth, make your nose smaller, change the shape of your face …

J: Umm … a little like plastic surgery without the surgery!

K: Yes, exactly!

J: So how does it work?

K: *Meitu* uses facial recognition technology – you know – the kind of thing they use at airport security – to map your face using 171 different points. Then it puts make-up, effects and so on over the top of the image.

J: So have you tried it yourself, Karen?

K: Yes, I have. It took me about forty minutes to create the perfect me. The problem is …

J: Yes, …?

K: Well, some tech experts have warned that the app is collecting people's personal information. Every time you use it to create the perfect selfie, it accesses your phone's location, your app history, your photos, wi-fi connection information …

J: OK … that's a little scary.

K: Well, it is, but so many phone apps do that these days. I think the threat has been exaggerated a little.

J: Thanks, Karen, for sharing all that with us. Now, moving on to other aspects of selfies …

UNIT 2

Lesson 2.4, Listening, Exercise B
2.3 **M = Megan G = Gareth**

M: One difficult aspect of growing up is decision-making. You learn, as you get older, that there are tough choices to be made – life-changing decisions. Now, Gareth, you're a guidance counselor – what kind of support can you offer young people?

G: Well, it's important to note that there are a range of problems affecting young adults today – family troubles for one thing, exam stress, career choices. And, as you say, they need to make tough choices. And that can be hard. To give you an example – a lot of young people who come to see me have just left school and they don't know how to go on from there. They ask me things like, *Should I go to college, or should I get a job?* or they tell me that they're worried about living on their own for the first time in their lives.

M: So how do you help the young people who come to you?

G: The first thing we do in a counseling session is a classic technique. *Write it down*, is what I tell them. I get them to write a list of advantages and disadvantages. This seems like an obvious thing to do, but a lot of people don't actually think of it, and it's amazing how just seeing something written down in black and white can help to clear your thoughts.

M: Can't family members help with difficult decisions like these, Gareth? Why do young people feel they need to talk to a stranger – to you?

G: Family can be an issue. Even if the young person's problem isn't related to their family specifically, their families don't always support them in the way that, maybe, they would like. There's usually a lot of pressure.

Parents don't always agree with their children's choices. I regularly talk to people who know what they want to do, but their parents don't agree. And then you have issues of family loyalty, you know – not wanting to disappoint your parents, and so on. It's difficult to put a plan into action if you don't have support from your family.

M: So what do you tell them, Gareth?

G: Well I always stress the importance of thinking long term. *Think in years, not days*, is what I tell them. Consider the consequences of your decision. Set long-term goals. Think – will there be a positive outcome for me in five years, ten years?

M: How else can you help somebody to make a decision?

G: Something which a lot of people find very useful is the idea of having 'an imaginary friend'.

M: What do you mean?

G: Well, it's very easy to get absorbed in your own problem, to only see a very narrow, personal view. I tell them to imagine that it's somebody else's problem. If this was your friend, what advice would you give them?

M: I see – it's easier to come up with a solution when you're on the outside?

G: Exactly. And finally, just stop thinking for a while! Experts talk about 'decision fatigue' where you spend so much time and energy worrying about the problem that you just can't deal with it any more. Take some time off. Do something else. Get away for a few hours or days.

UNIT 3

Lesson 3.4, Listening, Exercise B

3.3 Good morning and welcome to today's lecture about young drivers and road safety. I want to start by giving you a few facts. You are probably aware that young drivers, that is to say, young adults between the ages of 17 and 24, are at a much higher risk of being involved in a fatal traffic accident than older drivers. Numbers from the National Highway Traffic Safety Administration show that young drivers are a third more likely to die in a crash than drivers who are over the age of 40. That's a pretty terrifying number and it's extremely important that we do something to change that.

First, I want to talk about some of the causes of the problem. Younger drivers have less experience, and this means that they're not as good at spotting hazards as older drivers. But more important is the fact that they are risk-takers. They are far more likely to drive without a seat belt, pass dangerously or drive too fast. Speeding is a real killer.

Many young people feel very proud that they have mastered how to drive a car – and … I'm sure you know the feeling yourselves … it's so exciting … sitting at the wheel for the first time – they feel very confident. Too confident. And this is another problem. They think they're in control, but in fact, they're actually driving too fast and dangerously.

It's absolutely vital that we see a combined effort on the part of schools, healthcare professionals, social workers and the police, of course, to deal with this problem.

Now, let's turn to the solutions to some of these problems. The first thing we need to do is to improve driver training and testing. One suggestion is for us to introduce 'graduated' driver learning and licensing. What does that mean? Well, I'll explain this idea in more detail. We want to see a driving test which is divided into stages – smaller steps if you like. This offers a more structured approach and would include a minimum number of driving lessons followed by a trial period before young adults are actually issued with full licenses. For example, during the trial period, they wouldn't be allowed to drive at night, or to carry passengers.

In addition, studies have shown that raising the age at which young people can take their driving test would have a major impact on road fatalities. Parents especially should discourage the idea of learning to drive as soon as possible. If local authorities provide realistic transportation alternatives for young people – for example, regular buses and better bike paths, free train travel – then they might be more likely to delay getting their first car.

Now, that's all I want to say on the subject of solutions to this problem. Do we have any questions from …

UNIT 4

Lesson 4.4, Listening, Exercise B

4.4 **H = Henry M = Maria**

H: How many times have you said to yourself, *I'm going to exercise more* or *I want to stop wasting time and organize my life*? You make a plan and then … you fail to stick to it! Today, I've asked psychologist, Doctor Maria Davos, to come onto the show and talk to us about how we can not only set goals, but actually achieve them. Good morning, Doctor Davos.

M: Good morning. Thank you for inviting me onto the show.

H: Why do we find it so difficult to keep our resolutions?

M: I think the main reason is that we try to do too much, too soon. People think that they're going to transform their lives overnight. But it doesn't work like that. Making a lifestyle change is challenging, and it's part of a process that takes time and a lot of patience.

H: So how do you suggest we go about making changes that will stick?

M: A lot of people make a list of their goals, but these are usually fairly general. If you write down, 'Exercise more', that's not very specific, is it? Yes, you want to exercise more, but how and when? Be more focused in your goals. Write a note about which days you're going to exercise and for how long. You need to be realistic.

H: Yes, but, those kinds of goals are achievable because you can measure them. You can exercise for ten minutes every day, for example. But what if you want to quit a bad habit? For example, I bite my nails. I hate it, but I just can't stop doing it.

M: Again, you need to measure the progress you're making so try this idea – use your phone to take a photo of your nails every day and then you'll be able to track your progress as your nails grow back. Each time you reach your fingers to your mouth, take out your phone and look at the 'before and after' pictures. You'll be really happy when you see how good they look now!

H: That certainly sounds like very good advice.

M: Another idea is to keep a food diary. If you eat too much chocolate, for example, or drink too much coffee – write down how much you have each day. Then you can actually see, in your diary, the progress that you're making. It can be a really positive process and will keep you strong – help you to stick to your resolution. And remember – this is so important – don't try to do everything at once. Don't overdo it. Focus on one goal or change at a time. When you have succeeded in making one change in your life, you can move on to another goal.

H: How can our family and friends help us, Maria?

M: That's a good question, Henry. I believe that the support of family and friends is …

UNIT 5

Lesson 5.4, Listening, Exercise B

5.3 **J = John T = Tony A = Amal**

J: Today on *Education Matters*, we have a report from Tony Mills, our education correspondent. Tony – you're going to be telling us about a crisis in our high schools, is that right?

T: Yes, that's right, John. New statistics from a recent survey show that an increasing number of teachers are leaving schools. To be more specific, of all the young people who were certified as teachers in 2011, 30% had left the profession within five years. A different study found that this figure was even worse for teachers of core subjects. For example, 10.4% of science teachers and 10.2% of those teaching languages leave each year.

And maybe even more revealing is the fact that, as the survey results show, an astonishing 80% of teachers have actually thought about leaving their jobs over the last 12 months. Now of course, many young graduates qualify to become teachers every year, but the trend is definitely for declining teacher numbers – more people are leaving than entering. For instance, government figures for this year show that there are 10,000 vacancies for high school teachers. In college, the numbers are even worse, with a shortage of 20,000.

So what's the reason for this mass exodus? When asked, almost all teachers talk about the increase in their workload and the stress this brings with it. I asked Amal Hussain, a math teacher from New York about her experience.

Amal, you quit your job several months ago. How long had you been teaching?

A: I got my certification 11 years ago and, well, to be honest with you, I'd just had enough. I resigned in June last year and now I'm retraining as a career advisor.

T: So why did you leave the job?

A: My workload was just … well … it was overwhelming. The new government standards mean that the students are constantly being tested … assessed … through means such as coursework, oral exams, written exams, and we have to create those exams, grade them and complete endless paperwork … data collection they call it. For example, toward the end of my time in the teaching profession, I was grading up to 200 notebooks every week – I didn't have time for anything else! It's not teaching you know … it's just … well … it's not how I imagined the job when I first started.

T: And how does all of this affect the students?

A: Well, that's just it. Because the only important thing is getting good grades – teachers are forced to focus only on preparing students for exams. That's not why I became a teacher. I believe education is an ongoing process which is about learning, developing. I wanted to make a difference in students' lives – and I wasn't. That's what's important to students, and teachers, not just things like … exams and grades.

T: How many hours were you working on average? Can you give us a more specific idea of your workload?

A: Umm … about 60 hours most weeks, maybe more if we had end-of-year exams. The workload is what most of my colleagues complain about. I loved my job. I loved working with young people, helping them to grow. But … well, it was just too much.

T: So … an insider's view from Amal there. So what exactly, is the government planning to do …

UNIT 6

Lesson 6.4, Listening, Exercise B

6.3

Good morning and thank you for coming. Today's presentation is called *Passion into Profit* and it's all about how you can achieve the dream of turning what you love into a profitable business. No doubt everybody in this room has a hobby which they're passionate about – whether it's baking beautiful cupcakes, making jewelry or collecting vintage cars. Now, many people think that their hobbies are just that – something to do in your free time. But what if you could make a living from something you actually like doing instead of earning money in a boring or unsatisfying job?

Turning your hobby into a successful business can seem like a scary idea, but you must not let that discourage you. Many people are afraid to take action and leave their job or career because they are afraid they might fail. Well, I'm here to tell you that an amazing 37% of entrepreneurs have created their businesses from what was originally a hobby! And the results of a recent survey show that 86% of people who started a hobby-based business said they were happier now than before they gave up their traditional nine-to-five jobs.

My first piece of advice is focus on your goal. Like everyone starting a business for the first time, you will have your ups and downs, but the important thing is to set a target and stick to it. Make a plan of what exactly you want to achieve and by when; a detailed week-by-week schedule of actions and results will help to keep you on target.

That brings me to the subject of flexibility; you may need to do more than one thing in order to actually make money from your hobby. For example, if you make jewelry, you might sell your jewelry online, but you could also teach other people to make jewelry, or have a stand at a flea market and sell jewelry-making supplies.

The next point I would like to explore is marketing. You may create beautiful objects or be extremely skilled, but if nobody knows it, then you'll never get any customers. Use social media to advertise your product or service and develop your sales. Some online platforms allow you to list your products for free. Join online forums and chat groups so you can attract customers who have the same interests as you.

Finally, learn to think like a businessperson – after all, this isn't just a hobby anymore. Learn how to manage your finances by balancing your income and your expenses. Set up a bank account and don't be afraid to ask for advice from the experts – your bank manager or a professional accountant will be able to advise you on the best way to keep your new business financially healthy!

So, the next question is when do I …

UNIT 7

Lesson 7.4, Listening, Exercise C

7.3 **M = Mark C = César O = Olivia W = Wing Shan**

M: On today's edition of *Food for Thought*, we're here in the center of Birmingham to find out what people think about the latest food fads. Here we go …. excuse me … good morning …

C: Um … hi …

M: Hi, I'm Mark from *Food for Thought* on Radio 7. What's your name? Can we talk to you?

C: Yes, sure. I'm César.

M: OK. Thanks for talking to us, César. So … I'd like to ask you a question. What do you think about food fads? Do you believe they're a good thing or do you think they're just nonsense?

C: Food fads? Well, um … some food fads are good, like, you know, the five-a-day thing. It's a really good idea to encourage people to eat plenty of fruits and vegetables, you know, but … some others … like oh yes … foraging. I've read about that and it sounds crazy. It's this new fad where they only eat food which has been found in the wild. Stuff like mushrooms, green leaves, wild garlic, nuts. I mean, like I said, I think it's a good idea to eat fresh ingredients. There are more nutrients than in processed foods, but I mean, come on! I heard of one restaurant where they put these special ants – yes, the insects – into their salads. Makes the salad taste lemony or something. I think it sounds disgusting.

M: OK. Thanks César. Good to talk to you. Excuse me. Can we ask you a question? What do you think about food fads?

O: Hiya. I'm Olivia. Oh, I think any kind of food fad can help people to eat more healthily. Whatever it is, it gets you thinking about what you eat, doesn't it? To be honest, I wouldn't really call them fads. I think they're interesting ways of exploring new ideas. For example, I've been on the Paleo Diet for six months and I feel great – more energetic, less tired. It's a kind of eating plan where you only eat foods that existed millions of years ago – from Paleolithic times … paleo – get it? So that means lots of seeds and nuts, heaps of fruits and vegetables and, of course, no sugar, wheat or dairy. It's like if a caveman – or cavewoman – didn't eat it, then neither do I.

M: I see. Well thanks, Olivia. That's fascinating. And, this lady, … um … excuse me. Hi … what's your name? Can I ask you a question?

W: My name's Wing Shan. Sure, go ahead.

M: What do you think about food fads?

W: I don't really believe that food fads can help us. I think that what's important is to stick to a balanced diet. I just think that if you eat a little of everything then it's the best way. Having said that, I do believe that the Mediterranean diet is a good way of eating. But that's not really a fad, is it? It just means cooking and eating plenty of fresh food – a lot of fish, of course, and not so much meat. Lots of olive oil – it's much better for you than butter or animal fat. A lot of fresh fruits and vegetables. They say that it helps to prevent heart disease and cancer. Keeps your blood pressure down, too. I'll be brutally honest, though – I do sometimes have a burger. But honestly, if you eat … fast food … unhealthy food … now and then, I don't think that's such a big deal, do you?

M: And that was Wing Shan with her view on food fads. So, back to studio where we're going to discuss the latest trends with Doctor …

UNIT 8

Lesson 8.1, Pronunciation

8.1
1 The internet, which is a relatively new invention, is now a vital part of people's lives across the world.
2 It was Edison who first used publicity to promote a new invention.
3 The Cloud is where many people store photos and other files.
4 In the 1980s, when I was in school, no one had a cell phone.
5 Coco Chanel, who invented the little black dress, was a very influential fashion designer.
6 The physicist whose theories have influenced generations of scientists is Einstein.

Lesson 8.2, Pronunciation, Exercise A
8.2 **W = Woman M = Man**

W: You know … I've been thinking … if you want to go to the theater on Saturday night, it's OK with me.

M: To be honest, I was surprised you weren't more interested. I think you'll really like it.

W: I know. I'm sorry. I want to go – it's just that I don't have a lot of money.

M: I'll lend you the money if you want. Or we can do something cheaper.

W: That's very sweet of you! No, it's OK. I enjoy the theater. I'm sure we'll have a nice time.

M: Great. I'm really happy that I won't miss it. I think they still have some seats left. I'll call them now.

Lesson 8.4, Listening, Exercise B
8.3 **L = Lucy A = Adam**

L: What's the matter, Adam? You look a little stressed.

A: Yes, I am a little. It's exam time at school, and I have to grade all my students' exam papers and be at school to help with the organization of the exams. The thing is that my wife's away on a work trip right now. I mean, we normally share all the household chores, and childcare of course, but this week, I have to manage the house, the kids and work, … well … it's a lot of pressure.

L: My kids are grown-up now, but I have a lot of experience juggling a family and a job. I can give you plenty of tips. And my first piece of advice is – don't be such a perfectionist! I mean, did your children have breakfast and get to school on time?

A: Well, yes of course they did. But their school shirts were wrinkled because I hadn't had time to iron them.

L: Now, you see. That's exactly what I mean. Don't be so hard on yourself. I mean, we all want our lives to be reasonably organized, but sometimes it's just not possible. Well, I'm here to tell you that it isn't the end of the world, you know? Have you achieved what you wanted, but not as well as normal? Well, that's OK.

A: Yes, I suppose you're right. So what else do you suggest?

L: When you have a lot of different tasks to achieve and not enough time, you have to prioritize. Think about what is absolutely essential, what you have to do, and focus only on that. It sounds to me as if you're doing that already. I mean, the important thing is that your children are at school and that they had a good breakfast before they left.

A: Yes, but I forgot to make sandwiches for them – you know, to have at lunchtime.

L: OK, well that's the next thing. You simply must delegate.

A: Delegate? Can you give me an example?

L: Your example is right there! Your children aren't so little anymore. I mean, your daughter's fifteen, isn't she? Well, delegate the task of making sandwiches to her. She's old enough. She can make her own sandwiches and her little brother's. That's one less thing for you to worry about – and it will teach them to be more responsible.

A: Yes, you're right. That's a really good idea. But what about the rest of the housework? There's just more and more – heaps of dirty dishes, dirty laundry, recyclables …

L: It's true that if you don't keep on top of the housework, it can get out of control. So – my advice? Clean as you go. Do the dishes right after dinner. Same with the dirty clothes. Put them straight into the washing machine. And get the kids to do the same. That way, you won't end up with a huge pile of dirty laundry or dishes at the end of the week.

A: Sounds good. To be honest, I sometimes forget what I need to do. There are so many things to remember that my mind just goes blank.

L: Then make a list. Write down those essential tasks that we talked about, but make a note of when you're going to do them and, of course, who is going to do them. For example, 'sandwiches – Josie, early morning.' You'll find that it really focuses your mind.

A: Lucy – I feel better already. Thanks. You've been a big help.

L: You're welcome. Let me know how it goes.

UNIT 9

Lesson 9.4, Listening, Exercise B
9.3 **E = Ethan A = Agata**

E: Hi Agata. I haven't seen you in a long time. How are you? What have you been doing since we left high school?

A: Hello, Ethan. Good to see you. Well, I took a year-long art foundation course.

E: What's that exactly?

A: Well, it's supposed to be a transition period between high school and the study of specialist art and design courses in college.

E: Oh, right. So where did you go to do that?

A: At Kingston College of Art and Design. The course is designed to help you … unlock your creative abilities. That's the idea anyway! And of course, it gives you the chance to build your portfolio. That's a collection of all your work – drawings, paintings, sketches. It should be fairly … um … diverse. So people can see that you have a range of styles and ideas. Anyway, it was really fun because I tried all kinds of different disciplines as well as straightforward drawing and painting – fashion and textiles, printmaking, 3D design.

E: But …?

A: Yes, there was a but! A lot of the projects we did were conceptual art and that was, well, it just isn't me.

E: You've lost me.

A: It's very popular at most art schools, and galleries and so on. It was a movement which emerged in the 60s, and the theory is that the concept behind the art is more important than the finished artwork itself. To give you an example, one of my fellow students did a project entitled *Pathways*. She did this thing where she wore a fleece.

E: Sorry, I didn't catch that.

A: A fleece – a … like a sheepskin … a big woolly sheepskin that you wear like a coat …

E: OK …

A: Anyway, she wore this sheep … coat and she attached fourteen little cameras all over her and crawled along the paths on a mountain. I mean, can you believe it? The idea was that she would experience and understand the mountain, the life of the sheep, the landscape … or something. And the video was displayed at a gallery afterwards.

E: Well, that sounds interesting.

A: Interesting? Anyway, that's the kind of thing that we were expected to do, well not that exactly, but something similar. Well … to be brutally honest, I just find it all … let's just say, it's not my kind of thing.

E: So, what are you doing now?

A: Well, after I finished the course … I specialized in printmaking, by the way. That's where you create an image on a block of wood or metal, could be a stone, too – you carve the image into the material – and then you cover the block in ink and press paper onto it. The image is transferred to the paper. Well, that's a very simplistic explanation, but that's basically it. So, anyway, I got my diploma and now I'm at a different college studying illustration.

E: Illustration? You mean like for books?

A: Yes, basically. An illustration is any drawing that accompanies a written text – it might help to explain what's in the text, or maybe it's just there for decoration. For instance, children's books are full of illustrations because children are more responsive to visual images than to the written word. Anyway, that's what I'm studying now, and guess what? I love it!

E: Well, that's good news!

A: But enough about me, what about you. Did you go traveling like you told me …

UNIT 10

Lesson 10.4, Listening, Exercise B
10.3 **D = Dr. Patel J = John Ingrams**

D: Well, we're talking about a huge variety of conditions, ranging from social anxiety and mild depression to very serious illnesses such as bipolar disorder. In fact, statistics from the World Health Organization have shown that more than 615 million people suffer from anxiety or depression on a worldwide scale. And in the UK, for example, one in four people will suffer from some kind of mental health problem at some point in their lives. So we're not talking about just one or two people.

J: Those are pretty scary numbers, Doctor Patel. But surely that must mean that there's more understanding in society about these conditions?

D: Well John, there certainly should be. But even though so many people suffer from mental health problems, there is still a stigma attached to them. According to research carried out by my team at the college, nearly nine out of ten people with mental health problems say that they've experienced discrimination.

Lesson 10.4, Listening, Exercise C
10.4 **J = John Ingrams D = Dr. Patel**

J: Good morning and welcome to *Mind Matters* with me, John Ingrams. Today, I'm going to be talking to Doctor Patel about mental illness and the stigma of mental illness. So tell me, Doctor Patel, is it really possible that in the 21st century there is still a certain amount of … well, let's say shame related to mental illness?

D: Unfortunately, yes. That's very much the case.

J: First of all, what do we mean by mental illness?

D: Well, we're talking about a huge variety of conditions, ranging from social anxiety and mild depression to very serious illnesses such as bipolar disorder. In fact, statistics from the World Health Organization have shown that more than 615 million people suffer from anxiety or depression on a worldwide scale. And in the UK, for example, one in four people will suffer from some kind of mental health problem at some point in their lives. So we're not talking about just one or two people.

J: Those are pretty scary numbers, Doctor Patel. But surely that must mean that there's more understanding in society about these conditions?

D: Well John, there certainly should be. But even though so many people suffer from mental health problems, there is still a stigma attached to them. According to research carried out by my team at the college, nearly nine out of ten people with mental health problems say that they've experienced discrimination.

J: So what does that mean for them in practical terms?

D: Well, it can affect many aspects of their lives. For instance, they are more likely to be unemployed. This comes about because many employers believe that people with mental illness are violent or dangerous, but that just isn't true. A tiny percentage of patients display aggressive or antisocial behavior. As you can imagine, this has a negative impact on a person's feelings of self-worth and confidence.

J: Clearly something has to be done to overcome these kinds of negative impressions, but what?

D: Well, John, a lot of good work is being done by mental health charities which run publicity campaigns and workshops. Research has shown that those kinds of actions are really helpful in changing the negative views which are associated with mental health conditions.

J: What are the authorities trying to do about this problem?

D: A lot has been done already. Actually, here in the UK, the 2010 Equality Act makes it illegal to discriminate against somebody in the workplace because they have a mental health disorder, and that has helped a great deal. In addition, official organizations, such as our college, for example, are creating blogs, newsletters and so on, where we raise awareness of the problem. And to tell you the truth John …

Answer key

1.1 Communication today

GRAMMAR

A

1 do you speak
2 take
3 is learning
4 seems
5 am looking
6 are becoming
7 doesn't contain
8 is thinking

B

Stative	Dynamic
believe, belong, cost, include, know, mean, need, own, prefer, seem, understand, want	bring, complain, get, relax, show, take, watch, write

C

1 am/'m relaxing
2 need
3 have
4 don't think
5 travel
6 love
7 am/'m smiling
8 snows

VOCABULARY

A

1 looks
2 listen
3 hear
4 see
5 am/'m watching
6 are/'re looking
7 sounds
8 look

B

1 b 2 c 3 a 4 b 5 c

PRONUNCIATION

A

1 We speak a lot of English at home.
2 The Spanish exam was difficult, but I think I passed.
3 I don't usually listen to podcasts.
4 A photo doesn't always show the real you.
5 I met up with an old friend at the park.
6 That's me in the photograph with my family.

1.2 Who owns English?

GRAMMAR

A

1 ~~What do~~ **Did** you guys go out the other night?
2 ~~Which~~ **What** do you want, an ice-cream cone?
3 ~~What Jack~~ **What does Jack** want to do for his birthday next week?
4 ~~How much~~ **How long** did she have to wait at the bank?
5 ~~Who~~ **Whose** shoes are these?
6 ~~How~~ **Why** doesn't Laura come to the party with us?

B

2 Where did Danny learn Spanish?
3 When is the language lab open?
4 How can I improve my English?
5 Should we ask the teacher what this word means?
6 Who is considered the greatest writer of modern English?
7 What are you studying this semester?
8 What language do you speak at home?

C

2 Can you understand
3 Which/What
4 Is it difficult
5 how is it
6 How do you make
7 Will you teach
8 why are you

VOCABULARY

A

1 e 2 d 3 g 4 a 5 c 6 b 7 f

B

1 phrase
2 idiom
3 fluently
4 monolingual
5 accent
6 accurately
7 bilingual

PRONUNCIATION

A

1 b 2 a 3 b 4 a 5 a

1.3 Reading

READING

A

1 In many African countries, hundreds of languages are spoken.
2 Some people, known as *hyperglots*, are capable of learning 50 or 60 languages.
3 Learning new languages increases the size of the brain.

C

1 c 2 e 3 a

1.4 Listening; Functional Language

LISTENING

A

1 part of a radio show
2 a new selfie app

B

1 b 2 b

C

1 F (It's new in the US, but it was originally launched in 2014.)
2 F (It's available throughout the world.)
3 T
4 T
5 F (The technology is similar to that used by airport security companies.)
6 F (Many apps access and collect personal information.)

FUNCTIONAL LANGUAGE

A

1 mind giving
2 to (help)
3 to do
4 would be
5 you wouldn't/don't
6 go

B
1 hand **2** help **3** easy **4** amazing **5** favor

1.5 Write a report about trends

WRITING

B
Introduction: a and c
Paragraph 1: g
Paragraph 2: d
Paragraph 3: e and f
Conclusion: b

C
1 f **2** e **3** b

D
1 conducted
2 Many claimed
3 a lack of interest in
4 due to the fact that
5 It seems that

WRITING PRACTICE

B
Model answer
Report about trends in the use of technology for education
This report examines how people are using technology as part of the educational process. We asked one hundred young people about their experiences of technology in education and what they believe its advantages are.

Individual learning
Not everybody is successful at learning using traditional methods of study, and digital tools such as computers, iPads and digital whiteboards. This means that both teaching and learning can be adapted to suit individual students' various styles of learning.

Distance learning
Access to online learning allows teachers to reach students in different places at the same time. It also allows people who work to pursue educational goals in their free time. In this way, learning has become available to anyone and everyone.

Motivation
Most of the people we asked said that with computer-based courses they felt more in control of their learning. Digital methods make learning more fun, and students are less afraid of making mistakes.

Conclusion
No one suggested that technology should replace teachers, but it seems that the trend toward computer-based and distance learning has made educational opportunities available to more people and students can learn more by engaging in motivating educational activities.

2.1 Important decisions

PRONUNCIATION

A
1 We
2 I've
3 They've
4 I
5 He's
6 They
7 She
8 We've

GRAMMAR

A
1 have (you ever) made
2 wrote
3 haven't done
4 have (you) done
5 went
6 was
7 have/'ve (never) made
8 has/'s written
9 has/'s learned
10 went

B
1 still
2 went
3 have ever been
4 just
5 has been
6 never
7 went
8 yet

VOCABULARY

A
1 take
2 put
3 turn
4 set
5 lose
6 make
7 work
8 stay
9 make

B
1 lose heart
2 motivated
3 into action
4 the break
5 the next step
6 a decision
7 his/a goal
8 into reality
9 short-term goals

2.2 You can do it!

VOCABULARY

A
1 c
2 g
3 a
4 f
5 e
6 b
7 d
8 h

B
1 aware of
2 suitable for
3 typical of
4 looking for
5 working for
6 proud of
7 asked for
8 preparing for

C
1 deal
2 causing
3 suggest
4 coming
5 solve
6 analyze
7 agree

PRONUNCIATION

A

Verbs with stress on first syllable: focus, manage, study
Verbs with stress on second syllable: achieve, regret, suggest

GRAMMAR

A

1 couldn't
2 am able to
3 managed to
4 Was she able to
5 are able to
6 managed to
7 can
8 couldn't

B

1 does Kate manage to
2 being able to work
3 not able to prepare
4 able to spend
5 Could you speak
6 didn't manage to find
7 imagine being able

2.3 Reading

READING

A

1 want a simpler life
2 a TV announcer
3 for some people

B

1 c (without an internet connection, without electricity, without a car)
2 f (the security of a nine-to-five routine, left … behind in order to find a way of life that is simpler)
3 a (by helicopter)
4 b (food, fuel, clothing and bedding)
5 d (Things are regularly broken or damaged by the wind and rain.)
6 e (They are able to deal with change on a daily basis, ability to accept new situations.)

C

1 T
2 F (They have left the 'rat race' behind.)
3 F (The island is only accessible by helicopter.)
4 T
5 T
6 T

2.4 Listening; Functional Language

LISTENING

A

Answers will vary, but 1, 3 and 4 are the most likely.

B

1 adults
2 support
3 dealing
4 pressure
5 solve
6 decisions

C

1 life-changing decisions
2 family troubles
3 list
4 don't agree
5 long-term goals
6 advice
7 time, energy

FUNCTIONAL LANGUAGE

1 must be
2 can call
3 if I ask
4 Can we start
5 I'm sorry
6 Would it be
7 I'm afraid
8 I'd like

2.5 Write an informal email

WRITING

A

Sentences 2, 4, 5, 7 and 8

B

1 Sorry I haven't written / didn't write sooner.
2 Thanks for the advice.
3 I hope you're well. / How are you?
4 I didn't go because I was sick.
5 I haven't found anywhere (nice/cheap/etc) to live yet.

C

1 regularly 2 good 3 not sure 4 will

D

1 Hi Adriana; Love to you & Dave & the baby
2 So what to do?; Great new café near me
3 !!!; –; …
4 What's; It's been; a lot of stuff's been happening; I'd made; I've been; don't know; They're both; The other one's; I'll be far away; I'll have to find; it's a great opportunity
5 What's up?; stuff; magazines; Woo-hoo; cool; get it?; lol
6 ☺

WRITING PRACTICE

B

Model answer

Hiya Lottie,

Thanks for the birthday present. *The Necks*! You know me so well! It's their best so far. Thanks again ☺!! The card was great, too. Really funny!

Guess what? You know how you're always trying to persuade me to go skydiving? Well, … ta-da … Pete got me a ride in a hot-air balloon for my birthday! Trouble is, I have a thing about heights – really scared of them actually! I *so* want to go but at the same time I'm really frightened – terrified! I know that it will be an amazing experience but … will I have the courage to do it? Plus, I don't want to hurt Pete's feelings by refusing his gift. What should I do? Help!

BTW, when do you next get a break? Maybe I can come to Germany for a visit, or you can come over here – you know you're always welcome. Anyway … give me a call if you get the chance. Tell me what I should do about the whole hot-air balloon thing!

That's all for now, but write and tell me all your news.

Hugs and kisses,
Tonia

3.1 Travel experiences

GRAMMAR

A

1 a
2 b
3 c
4 b
5 c
6 b
7 c
8 a

B

2 hadn't seen
3 had been
4 decided
5 left
6 suddenly found
7 saw
8 had never noticed

VOCABULARY

A

1 f
2 c
3 g
4 d
5 h
6 b
7 a
8 e

B

1 connection
2 decision
3 pollution
4 action
5 reaction
6 situation

C

1 decision
2 connection
3 pollution
4 situation
5 reaction
6 action

PRONUNCIATION

A

2 Speaker B
3 Speaker B
4 Speaker A
5 Speaker B
6 Speaker B

3.2 Travel smart

GRAMMAR

A

1 a
2 the
3 –
4 an
5 –
6 a
7 the
8 –

B

1 much
2 enough
3 little
4 plenty of
5 a little
6 a lot of
7 Few
8 too much

C

1 a lot
2 much
3 enough
4 little/no
5 A lot
6 very

PRONUNCIATION

A

Students underline these phrases:
1 a lot of
2 a few
3 many
4 too much
5 enough
6 little

VOCABULARY

A

1 really
2 a little
3 very
4 furious
5 extremely
6 very funny

B

1 ✗ 2 ✗ 3 ✓ 4 ✗ 5 ✗ 6 ✗ 7 ✓ 8 ✓

C

1 impossible
2 brilliant
3 enormous
4 furious
5 filthy
6 hilarious

3.3 Reading

READING

A

Suggested answers

1 Maybe it will be about the use of technological advances in road transportation.
2 Probably positive.

B

1 d 2 c 3 a 4 e 5 b

C

1 a 2 b 3 c 4 b

3.4 Listening; Functional Language

LISTENING

B

1, 2, 4 and 5.

C

1 less
2 Older
3 live dangerously
4 confident
5 Different groups of people
6 different stages
7 wait until they are older

FUNCTIONAL LANGUAGE

1 guess 2 had/'d 3 thing 4 while 5 happened
6 best 7 kidding 8 end

3.5 Write an email of complaint

WRITING

A

a 3 **b** 4 **c** 2 **d** 1

B

1 extremely
2 regularly
3 totally
4 unnecessarily
5 seriously
6 definitely

WRITING PRACTICE

C

Model answer

Dear Sir or Madam,

I am writing to complain about the disastrous vacation package to Majorca we booked with your company. It is the worst vacation we have ever had.

First of all, there was no bus to meet us at the airport to take us to the hotel. We had to wait five hours for one to arrive, and when we arrived at the hotel, the kitchen was closed so we went to bed without having dinner.

The extremely loud noise of building work woke us up very early since the hotel is having an extension built. This went on for our whole stay, making it totally impossible to relax by the hotel pool or beach.

The service was completely unacceptable, too – beds not made or changed, rooms not cleaned – and the staff was very rude. Also, the planned trips to sites of interest either didn't happen or we had to pay extra for them.

This is to inform you that I am seeking compensation for a ruined vacation, because what was promised by your representative at the travel agency was nothing like the reality.

I hope to hear from you soon regarding this matter.
Harold Purly

PRONUNCIATION

A

1 not interested
2 excited
3 determined
4 positive
5 sarcastic
6 thoughtful
7 curious
8 ironic

VOCABULARY

A

1 cut
2 make/break/keep
3 reach
4 keep/make/break
5 quit
6 break/make/keep

B

1 quit a bad habit
2 break a resolution
3 make a resolution
4 reach a target
5 cut down on something
6 keep a resolution

C

1 down
2 quit/stop
3 keep
4 reach
5 resolution
6 achieve
7 set
8 stick

4.1 Personal change

GRAMMAR

A

1 I am / I'm meeting Sarah
2 We are / We're having or We are / We're going to have
3 she is / she's going to run
4 I am / I'm going to try or I will / I'll try
5 I will / I'll do
6 What are you doing
7 he is / he's going to buy
8 I will / I'll turn

B

1 am/'m going to learn
2 will/'ll make sure
3 will/'ll lend
4 am/'m starting
5 Are you going to learn / Are you learning
6 are going
7 will not / won't be
8 Are you doing

C

1 a **2** b **3** a **4** a **5** b

4.2 Social change

GRAMMAR

A

1 is going to
2 may
3 definitely
4 will
5 could
6 are going to
7 might not
8 will probably

B

1 will
2 going
3 probably
4 won't
5 might/may
6 could/will
7 definitely
8 not

C

1 Hannah ~~probably~~ will **probably** get the job.
2 It depends how busy Lisa and Alan are, but they ~~definitely~~ will **probably** come tonight.
3 The weather ~~probably~~ might be good this weekend.
4 My neighbors could ~~to~~ at least try to keep the noise down a little!
5 The local soccer club ~~won't~~ definitely **won't** win the league this season.

PRONUNCIATION

A

1 b **2** a **3** a **4** b **5** b

B

1 that in **2** What other **3** is overpaid **4** That's a
5 don't understand

VOCABULARY

A

1 c
2 a
3 c
4 b
5 b
6 c
7 a
8 c

B

2 rebuild
3 disagree
4 overpopulated
5 disappeared
6 misunderstand

4.3 Reading

READING

A

1 a review 2 real people 3 India and the UK

B

2, 3, 4, 5, 7, 8 and 9.

C

Suggested answers

2, 3, 5, 8 and 9 should be included.
4 and 7 are not relevant to the main idea of the program.

D

1 documentary
2 British boys
3 failed
4 India
5 deal with the challenge

4.4 Listening; Functional Language

LISTENING

B

b, c, d and f.

C

1 a 2 b 3 a 4 a

D

1 b
2 c
3 a
4 b
5 a
6 b

FUNCTIONAL LANGUAGE

1 up
2 going
3 what
4 catch
5 lost
6 Leave

4.5 Write a short essay

WRITING

B

a 3 b 4 c 2 d 1

C

1 Washing machines and dishwashers.
2 The elderly will need more help in the home.
3 Because we will want more free time to develop personal interests.

D

1 and so
2 because of
3 as a result / consequently
4 because
5 because
6 as a result / consequently

WRITING PRACTICE

B

Model answer

For some time now, robots have been used to build products such as cars and medical equipment, but how long will it be before they do the jobs we think only humans can do? Computers are becoming more intelligent, and as a result they regularly beat humans at chess. What else could they be taught to do?

Medicine is one area in which robots will be used much more. You can already see a doctor online, which is an important development, because people in remote areas can easily speak to a doctor. Consequently, healthcare will improve greatly. Robots can even be used to perform difficult operations, which will allow a surgeon in Germany to operate on a patient in Japan.

Another area where robots will change traditional ways of working is farming. Farm workers will not be needed any more because driverless tractors, GPS devices and robotic fruit pickers will do their jobs. However, some people worry that this kind of development will cause unemployment.

To sum up, because of new developments in robotics and technology, there will be both positive and negative consequences, and we humans will have to find new ways to live in the new world of machines.

5.1 At work

VOCABULARY

A

1 communication skills
2 creative
3 teamwork
4 people
5 reliable
6 pressure
7 time management

B

1 I was pleased that the manager let me ~~to~~ use my digital technology skills.
2 Did you encourage him **to look** ~~looking~~ for a new job?
3 She's tired because her boss made **her** ~~she~~ come to work at 7 am today!
4 Our company allows us **to** work from home one day a week.
5 She persuaded them **to** ~~that they~~ cancel the meeting at the last minute.
6 Mrs. Carter told ~~to~~ me to improve my time management skills.
7 I advised my colleague **to speak** ~~for speaking~~ to our manager about the problem.
8 Mr. Jones doesn't want **me to** ~~that I~~ give the presentation today.

C

1 allow
2 encourage
3 making
4 telling
5 lets
6 persuaded
7 wants
8 advise

PRONUNCIATION

A

1 ✓
2 –
3 –
4 ✓
5 ✓
6 ✓
7 –
8 ✓

GRAMMAR

A

1 used to be
2 used to work
3 didn't use to have
4 used to work
5 would leave / used to leave
6 would rarely get
7 would leave / used to leave

B

1 Did you use to
2 never used to
3 used to enjoy
4 would meet
5 didn't use to have
6 used to work

5.2 In business

GRAMMAR

A

1 was set up
2 have been sold
3 are usually bought
4 be ordered
5 are being trained
6 have not been proven

B

1 Christopher's house was robbed last night.
2 The correct technique can be learned.
3 The necklace has been stolen.
4 The 100-meter record was broken by Usain Bolt.
5 The painting had been completed by the artist's assistant.

C

1 Sheila had set off the alarm.
2 Zaha Hadid designed the building.
3 Russia held the championship.
4 *Moonlight* won the Oscar for Best Picture.
5 The government's policies are destroying communities.

D

1 started
2 is collected
3 is used
4 have been received
5 is being turned into
6 are picked up
7 are cleaned / have been cleaned
8 can be made
9 died
10 ran
11 made
12 were taken
13 were sold

VOCABULARY

A

1 d 2 b 3 a 4 c 5 e

B

1 running, business
2 launched a campaign
3 build a brand
4 attract new customers
5 make a profit

PRONUNCIATION

B

1 Who launched this campaign to protect the environment?
2 We should talk on Wednesday.
3 The sign on the door said knock, so I did, but there was no answer.
4 I can't eat a whole sandwich – do you want half?
5 He's written a lot but I doubt that he knows everything.
6 We listened for an hour but his foreign accent made it hard.
7 When they gave the design prize, it went to the wrong person.
8 To be honest, I'd say that psychology would not be a good subject for you.

5.3 Reading

READING

A

Not just a job

B

Suggested answers

Perks and benefits of working for a modern firm and how these affect employees' well-being and productivity.

C

1 company owners
2 tech firms' work environment
3 employees in general
4 the game developer's website
5 employees
6 at the clothing company
7 make a difference

D

1 a 2 b 3 a 4 a 5 b

5.4 Listening; Functional Language

LISTENING

B

1, 2, 4, 6, 7, 8 and 9.

C

1 200, week
2 exams, grades
3 vacancies, high

D

1 30% / thirty percent
2 science teachers
3 leaving their jobs
4 10,000 / ten thousand
5 3/three (coursework, oral exams, written exams)
6 grade 200 notebooks every week
7 exams and grades
8 when there were end-of-year exams

FUNCTIONAL LANGUAGE

1 for coming
2 purpose
3 presentation
4 first of all
5 take a look
6 move on
7 From
8 brings
9 question
10 do you have

5.5 Write a cover letter for a job application

WRITING

A

Suggested answers

1 Customer service, dealing with people, selling vacations, working in an office.
2 No – a degree and some work experience is enough.
3 Good people skills, being persuasive, knowledge of the travel business.

B

Suggested answers

Paragraph 1: Which job he is applying for and why (including where he saw the job ad and its reference number)
Paragraph 2: His suitability for the role
Paragraph 3: Why he is applying for this job in particular
Paragraph 4: When he is available for an interview

C

1 d
2 a
3 c
4 b

WRITING PRACTICE

B

Model answer

Dear Ms. McMahon,

I am writing to apply for the position of Assistant Manager which is currently advertised on jobsforu.com (Ref: 273A). I have attached my résumé. I recently graduated with a degree in Sports Marketing and Management and wish to start a career in the health and fitness industry.

I believe my experience and skills, gained both in college and working at health clubs during the vacations, make me an ideal candidate for the job. While in college I was chairman of the Athletics Committee and oversaw inter-university sports competitions, which required great organizational and leadership skills. Working at health clubs gave me an insight into how they were run.

Working for your company would be a great opportunity for me to share my passion for health and fitness and to put my skills and knowledge in sales and marketing into practice in an industry I have always had an ambition to work in.

Thank you for considering my application. I am available for interview at any time and look forward to hearing from you.

Sincerely yours,
Philip Stevens

6.1 Take part!

GRAMMAR

A

1 b
2 a
3 b
4 c
5 b
6 a

B

1 shouldn't
2 don't need to
3 must not
4 must
5 shouldn't
6 don't have to
7 don't need to
8 don't have to

VOCABULARY

A

1 competitive
2 massive
3 aggressive
4 effective
5 creative
6 impressive

B

1 stadium
2 champion
3 players
4 final
5 trophy
6 fan
7 medal
8 league
9 tournament
10 spectator

C

1 coach
2 trophy
3 league
4 stadium
5 tournament
6 fans
7 champion
8 players
9 spectator
10 final

PRONUNCIATION

A

Stay tuned, (/) folks. (/) We have an exciting show for you today. (/) Later on in the show, (/) Lionel Messi (//) – world famous athlete, (/) considered by some to be the greatest soccer player of all time – (/) will be joining us to talk about his life and career. (/) We'll speak about the challenges he's faced, (//) both on and off the field, (/) and how he overcame them to be who he is today.

6.2 Hobbies

VOCABULARY

A

1 escape
2 relaxing
3 get
4 collecting
5 close
6 are

B

1 society
2 hobby
3 thing
4 member
5 active
6 fan

GRAMMAR

A

1 have/'ve never known
2 has/'s been playing
3 have you been taking part
4 has/'s been training
5 has/'s completed
6 have not / haven't achieved
7 has/'s just come in
8 has/'s been working out

B

1 's/has been living here for
2 's/has been playing tennis since
3 have not been going
4 've/have been training for a

C

1 I didn't need to buy a yoga mat because my sister lent me hers.
2 We **had** ~~have~~ to have lessons before we could jump out of the plane for the first time.
3 Julio need**ed** to practice a lot before he became good at fly fishing.
4 Kayleigh **didn't have** ~~hadn't~~ to watch the ukulele teacher because she already knew how to play the song.
5 She didn't **have** ~~had~~ to do anything yesterday so she spent the day relaxing at home.
6 I had **to** spend a lot of money to buy this stamp, but I'm pleased that I did.
7 The coach said we needed **to** practice more, so we did.
8 I had **to** use my friend's Ping-Pong paddle last week because I broke mine.

PRONUNCIATION

A

1 I've never been to India.
2 Tanya's been playing tennis for hours.
3 He's been very quiet all day.
4 How long have you been captain of the club?
5 We've been training since last year.
6 Have you been surfing before?

6.3 Reading

READING

A

brass bands

B

1 b 2 a 3 c

C

1 b
2 c
3 a
4 c
5 b
6 a

6.4 Listening; Functional Language

LISTENING

B

a 3
b 5
c 1
d 6
e 2
f 4

C

1 c
2 b
3 b
4 a
5 a
6 c

FUNCTIONAL LANGUAGE

1 for instance
2 another example
3 If you
4 my opinion
5 don't think
6 brutally honest
7 probably right

6.5 Write an article for a magazine

WRITING

B

a 2 **b** 3 **c** 1 **d** 5 **e** 4

C

1 f
2 c
3 a
4 d
5 b
6 e

WRITING PRACTICE

B

Model answer

Fishing may not sound exciting, but I can tell you that there's nothing like the thrill you get when you feel the pull on your line as a fish takes the bait.

One of the great things about fishing is that you spend time outdoors – either in the peace and quiet of the country or by the ocean. You can relax and think and leave the worries of everyday life behind.

Another thing I like about fishing is how it helps the environment. One good thing about our hobby is that we keep rivers and waterways clean and trash-free. As for the fish, most of us usually throw them back into the water. Although, and this is another great thing about it, you may go home with a delicious fish for supper!

Another good reason to take up fishing is that you don't need any expensive gear to enjoy it, just a simple rod and some bait and a little stool to sit on.

Everyone wants to escape from the stress of their busy lives, and fishing is an inexpensive and peaceful way to do it. I'm hooked – and I think you will be, too, once you try it!

7.1 Eating out

PRONUNCIATION

A

1 could be
2 can't be
3 must be
4 might be/could be
5 might not be
6 can't be
7 must be
8 might take/could take

B

1 d **2** b **3** g **4** c **5** a **6** f **7** e

VOCABULARY

A

1 try out
2 giving up
3 shows up
4 serve up
5 took off
6 started off
7 set up

B

1 disgusting
2 raw
3 watery
4 salty/savory
5 filling
6 tasty
7 rich
8 cheesy
9 fruity
10 spicy

C

Positive	Neutral	Negative
rich	cheesy	disgusting
tasty	fruity	raw
	raw	rich
	salty/savory	salty
	spicy	watery

GRAMMAR

A

1 That **can't** ~~must not~~ be our bill – we only had a snack!
2 We should call and make a reservation – there might **not** ~~don't~~ be a table.
3 You must ~~to~~ think I'm very rude eating with my fingers!
4 You **may/might/could** ~~maybe~~ be right about this food – it doesn't taste good.
5 Let's try this new restaurant – it **may/might/could** ~~could maybe~~ **be** good.
6 This place might **not** have ~~not~~ the best food, but it's good enough and very cheap.

B

2 may/might/could contain
3 can't (possibly) want
4 might not taste
5 can't/couldn't be; must be
6 must/may/might think

7.2 Food fads

GRAMMAR

A

1 the least salt
2 cooks better than
3 the spicier the
4 tastes fruitier than
5 more / the most calories
6 worse than me

B

1 c **2** b **3** a **4** c **5** a **6** c **7** c **8** b

PRONUNCIATION

A

1 b **2** a **3** a **4** b **5** b **6** b **7** a **8** b

VOCABULARY

A

1 recycled
2 wasted
3 reuse
4 garbage
5 reduce
6 use up

B

1 can
2 away
3 of
4 down
5 garbage
6 up

C

Across: 2 wastebasket **4** reduce **6** throw away **7** reuse
Down: 1 trash **3** recycle **5** waste

7.3 Reading

READING

B

1 Angela, Jason
2 Yoko, Angela
3 Angela
4 Jason, Yoko
5 Yoko
6 Yoko
7 Angela
8 Jason

7.4 Listening; Functional Language

LISTENING

B

1 O **2** F **3** F **4** O **5** F **6** F **7** F **8** O

C

César 2, 6 Olivia 3, 5 Wing Shan 1, 4

FUNCTIONAL LANGUAGE

1 What's
2 Have
3 about
4 were
5 plan/idea
6 try/shot
7 Why
8 suggestion/idea

7.5 Write a reply in an online discussion forum

WRITING

B

1 SloppyJoe
2 Gourmand
3 Gourmand
4 SloppyJoe
5 SloppyJoe, Sylvya

C

1 quieter
2 the most popular
3 more casual
4 I'd recommend
5 than
6 nicer
7 You should
8 Why don't you

WRITING PRACTICE

B

Model answer

I think you should go for the restaurant option. So many things can go wrong with a barbecue – not just the weather. Your guests might be tired after a long trip, and it's more comfortable and relaxing to be seated at a table and waited on than it is to stand around trying to balance a paper plate in one hand and a drink in the other. Besides, in my experience it's just as expensive and time-consuming to have a barbecue as it is to dress up and go out to a restaurant. You can relax and talk rather than attend to the cooking. So, I'd recommend going to a nice restaurant. Better to be safe than sorry!

8.1 Making a difference

VOCABULARY

A

1 scientist
2 engineering
3 succeed
4 innovative
5 design
6 product
7 inventive

B

1 b **2** a **3** a **4** c **5** b **6** c **7** c **8** a **9** b **10** a

PRONUNCIATION

1 ✓ **2** – **3** – **4** ✓ **5** ✓ **6** –

GRAMMAR

A

1 who
2 which
3 that
4 when
5 whose
6 where
7 who
8 when

B

1 whose
2 who
3 where
4 which
5 when
6 which

8.2 Must-have gadgets

VOCABULARY

A

1 unique
2 gorgeous
3 fascinating
4 sensible
5 unforgettable
6 suitable
7 impressive
8 practical
9 incredible
10 sophisticated

B

1 sophisticated
2 practical
3 unique
4 impressive
5 incredible
6 sensible
7 gorgeous
8 unforgettable

GRAMMAR

A

1 keep
2 tell
3 will have to
4 don't charge
5 won't buy
6 doesn't work/isn't working

B

1 If you~~'ll~~ listen to next week's podcast, you'll hear about some more amazing gadgets.
2 **Will** ~~Are~~ you **be** angry if I cancel our plans for tonight?
3 correct
4 I won't go out tomorrow unless the weather **is** ~~will~~ good.
5 correct
6 correct
7 I never buy gadgets unless I ~~don't~~ really need them.
8 correct

C

1 can wait
2 might help
3 don't try
4 should we still
5 come and see
6 must be prepared
7 can always borrow
8 can go

PRONUNCIATION

A

1 if you want to
2 you'll really like it
3 I want to go
4 I'll lend
5 I enjoy
6 we'll have a nice time
7 I won't miss it
8 I'll call them

8.3 Reading

READING

B

1 B **2** C **3** D **4** A

C

Suggested answers

a 4 **b** 3 **c** 1 **d** 2

D

1 F (We take them for granted today.)
2 T
3 T
4 F (They had to take out the ashes, not the coal.)
5 T
6 F (The ice blocks stayed frozen, even in the summer.)
7 F (There was no running water. / They had to carry the water some distance.)
8 T

8.4 Listening; Functional Language

LISTENING

B

1, 4, 5 and 6.

C

1 b **2** c **3** a **4** c **5** a **6** b

FUNCTIONAL LANGUAGE

1 first
2 When
3 say
4 let
5 how
6 After
7 mean
8 Make

8.5 Write a short biography

WRITING

A

1 A pioneer in the field of computer science.
2 Meeting Charles Babbage.
3 She wrote and published notes about the first calculating machine (computer) including how to give it instructions. It was the first-ever computer program.

B

a 2 **b** 1 **c** 5 **d** 3 **e** 4

C

1 Although
2 However
3 despite

WRITING PRACTICE

B

Model answer

Trevor Baylis

Trevor Baylis is best known for his invention of the wind-up radio, which brought information, education and entertainment to millions of poor people around the world.

He was born in 1937 and raised in London. From a very young age, Baylis enjoyed making things. However, his education was disrupted by the Second World War, and he failed his school exams. Despite this setback, he was able to study mechanical and structural engineering at the local technical college.

The idea for his most famous invention came to him in a flash when he was watching a TV show about the poor in Africa. He realized that communication and education would help them enormously. Radio was the answer – but in many parts of Africa, there was no electricity. So, he decided to invent a wind-up radio.

His invention has brought information, communication and education to millions of people around the world who most needed them.

He once said, 'Anyone can have a good idea and turn it into something that works. If you find yourself trying to solve a problem, you are halfway to inventing something'. That's something for us to think about.

9.1 Art for everybody

VOCABULARY

A

1 studio
2 musician
3 concert
4 rehearsed
5 orchestra
6 performed
7 exhibit
8 instrument
9 choir
10 stage

B

1 part in
2 fell
3 tell
4 advantage
5 friends with
6 keep
7 come
8 pay
9 make
10 wrong

GRAMMAR

A

1 b 2 c 3 a 4 b 5 a 6 c 7 b 8 b

B

1 worked, would/'d become
2 had, would/'d learn
3 would/'d go, were/was
4 couldn't, would be
5 were, would/'d take
6 would/'d have, didn't spend

PRONUNCIATION

A

2 research, chemist, technology; a
3 child, mechanic, Charley; b
4 choices, choir, orchestra; b
5 challenge, techniques, machine; b
6 church, chemical; a

9.2 Tell me a story

GRAMMAR

A

1 him what time he was
2 they had never read / they had not read / they hadn't read / they hadn't ever read
3 (that) she had/'d made
4 couldn't understand why
5 where the manager was
6 if / whether I wanted to go
7 wouldn't come the next/following
8 if / whether Aisha was there

B

1 I have/'ve read
2 can borrow
3 have to finish
4 Is it good
5 it is

C

6 was about
7 would spoil
8 following/next
9 had read
10 if / whether he wanted

VOCABULARY

A

1 b 2 c 3 b 4 a 5 a 6 b 7 c 8 a

B

1 added that
2 us
3 where
4 to come
5 me to go
6 me
7 that it would snow
8 them to leave
9 to go
10 to

9.3 Reading

READING

B

1 e **2** a **3** d **4** b **5** c

C

Students check 2, 3 and 5.

D

1 F (The writer says that mega-events have gotten out of control, especially the huge crowds.)
2 T
3 T
4 T
5 F (There's gypsy music, funk and jazz.)
6 F (The writer believes that the two experiences complement each other.)
7 F (These events are friendly and noncompetitive.)
8 T

9.4 Listening; Functional Language

LISTENING

B

1 No, they haven't seen each other *in a long time.*
2 Not really. She liked learning about different kinds of art, but didn't enjoy doing *conceptual art.*
3 She studied many.
4 She thought it was silly.
5 Yes, she is.

C

1 bridge
2 examples
3 subject
4 idea
5 wool
6 pressing
7 attractive

D

1 transition period
2 range
3 different
4 the 60s (1960s)
5 a sheep
6 a video
7 interesting
8 metal, stone
9 drawings/illustrations

FUNCTIONAL LANGUAGE

1 like
2 actor
3 ending
4 tearjerker
5 worth
6 follow
7 scene

9.5 Write a short review

WRITING

A

Suggested answers

1 To describe a book for others in order to persuade them to read it, or possibly to discourage them from reading it.
2 In a newspaper, a magazine or a website about books.
3 Students' own answers.
4 Movies, plays, concerts, exhibits, etc.

B

1 Mainly positive.
2 The reviewer thinks it's like a collection of short stories.
3 They have a similar theme.
4 There are no fully rounded female characters.

C

a 2 **b** 1 **c** 4 **d** 3

D

1 c **2** b **3** a

WRITING PRACTICE

B

Model answer

Val McDermid's new psychological thriller, *Insidious Intent*, will be a big hit with fans of crime-busting duo, DCI Carol Jordan and profiler Tony Hill. Once again, they are on the hunt for a bright and terrifying criminal.

It all starts on a quiet country road with a car engulfed in flames and a body in the driver's seat. They realize that this is no ordinary accident and discover a series of similar cases. More lives are at risk, and Tony and Carol must go to extreme lengths to catch the evil genius behind the crimes. They are forced to question the very idea of justice.

As you would expect from this writer, the plot is complex and intriguing and will grip you from start to finish. But it's not all about plot with Val McDermid – her books are as character-driven as many so-called literary novels. The difficult relationship between Tony and Carol is beautifully done, and her writing displays her descriptive powers and psychological insight.

I needed no persuading: this is a first-class thriller by a master of the genre. If you haven't read her yet, go out and buy this book: you're in for a treat.

10.1 Making up your mind

VOCABULARY

A

1 encourage/persuade
2 affects/influences
3 tempted
4 tricking
5 regret
6 attract
7 assume
8 avoid

B

1 made
2 in
3 never
4 bear
5 two
6 put
7 changed
8 Would

PRONUNCIATION

A

1 Speaker A
2 Speaker B
3 Speaker B
4 Speaker B
5 Speaker A
6 Speaker A

GRAMMAR

A

1 'd have gotten, hadn't gone
2 'd known, wouldn't have paid
3 had told, could have/'ve spent
4 wouldn't have chosen, 'd thought
5 hadn't assumed, might have/'ve made
6 might not have been tempted, hadn't gone
7 could have/'ve avoided, 'd read
8 'd realized, wouldn't have bought

B

1 You should have/'ve asked me
2 You should have/'ve checked
3 I should have/'ve waited
4 you shouldn't have bought
5 I should have/'ve done
6 I should have taken

10.2 Wish lists

VOCABULARY

A

1 ourselves
2 yourself
3 himself
4 yourselves
5 myself
6 herself
7 yourself
8 themselves

B

1 cleaning
2 keep
3 scheduled
4 objective
5 store
6 action point
7 sorted
8 task

PRONUNCIATION

A

Students underline
1 helped
2 yourself
3 himself
4 herself
5 set
6 treated

GRAMMAR

A

1 b 2 c 3 b 4 b 5 c 6 a 7 c 8 c

B

1 wish, had planned
2 hope, can remember; hope, goes
3 wishes, weren't/wasn't; wish, could have
4 hopes, can meet; hope, gives

10.3 Reading

READING

B

1 T
2 F (Anxiety can be triggered by everyday events.)
3 T
4 F (This strategy does not solve the overall problem.)
5 T
6 T

C

1 d 2 e 3 b 4 a 5 c

10.4 Listening; Functional Language

LISTENING

B

1, 2, 3, 5 and 7.

C

1 all over the world
2 a quarter of the population
3 discrimination
4 less likely
5 not violent
6 charities
7 not allowed

FUNCTIONAL LANGUAGE

1 time
2 need
3 worry
4 sorry
5 about
6 fault
7 such
8 things

10.5 Write a report

WRITING

A

1 To discuss problems which occurred at Downey Town Fair.
2 It was financially a success, but not in terms of organization.
3 Not enough parking space and problems with traffic on the roads.
4 Larger number of parking spaces, more areas (e.g. fields) allocated for parking, volunteers to direct traffic and parking.

B

1 b **2** f **3** c **4** d **5** a **6** e

WRITING PRACTICE

B

Model answer

Report on The Huffington and District Mobile Library

Summary

The mobile library was set up to satisfy a demand to provide books to rural areas in the county. It is a subscription service, yet despite the initial demand, we can barely afford to pay running costs. This report explores the problem.

Background

We provide a library service to areas where there is no easy access to books, magazines, DVDs and music CDs. A survey suggested that the service was much needed, yet the actual number of subscribers is far short of what we expected.

Analysis

1 **Lack of information:** Not enough people are paying the subscription, usually because they did not realize that they had to. Also, many did not know that such a service existed.
2 **Reading habits:** Some have complained about the limited choice of reading matter available. While it is difficult to please everybody, we should stock a wider variety of books and magazines.

Recommendations

- An advertising campaign to publicize the service. Send out flyers through the mail and hold a town hall meeting to explain.
- Conduct a survey in the area to establish reading habits and tastes to provide a better service.

Macmillan Education Limited
4 Crinan Street
London N1 9XW

Companies and representatives throughout the world

American Language Hub Level 3 Student's Book ISBN 978-0-230-49714-6
American Language Hub Level 3 Student's Book with Student's App
ISBN 978-0-230-49718-4

Written by Jeremy Day and Gareth Rees.

With thanks to Signature Manuscripts for the Grammar Hub pages.

First published 2020

Designed by emc design ltd
Illustrated by Rasmus Juul represented by Lemonade Illustration Agency, Daniel Limon (Beehive Illustration)
Cover design by Restless
Cover photograph by Peathegee Inc/Getty Images
Picture research by Emily Taylor and Victoria Gaunt
Café Hub videos produced by Creative Listening
Café Hub video scripts written by James and Luke Vyner

The authors and publishers would like to thank the following for permission to reproduce their photographs:

www.AETHAER.com p54(jar); **Alamy Stock Photo** Samuel Bay p62(tl,tr), Cultura Creative (RF) p17(bl), Chris Howes/Wild Places Photography p68(cl), JTB MEDIA CREATION, Inc. p44, EVREN KALINBACAK p51, Maskot p100(tr), Iain Masterton p20(tmr), Mladen Mitrinovic p147(tr), David L. Moore – JPN p56, roibu p98(t), Kurt De Leon Wulf p104(r); **Ages** scyther5 p22(camera); **Bridgeman Images** Passengers in the dining room aboard the airship LZ 127 'Graf Zeppelin' during the trip from Germany to America, 1928 (b/w photo)/© SZ Photo/Scherl p116(b); **Corbis** 94–95 (background); DIGITALVISION pp82(b), 118(background), Uwe Krejci p114(tl); **Eden Full Goh** p86(r); **Flickr RF** Martin Pickard p151(m); **Getty Alija** p26(b), p68(bl), 71(background); **Getty Images** 97 p112(a), Getty Images p62(bl), Alija pp100(br), 101, al_irfan78 p154(bl), AMe Photo p112(c), andresr p143, Arterra/Contributor p80(3), Jose A. Bernat Bacete p86(l), Ezra Bailey p163, Thomas Barwick p112(d), Caspar Benson p154(br), Howard Berman p52(tr), Blend Images – KidStock p65, Bloomberg/Contributor p91(b), Warren Bolster 61, Phil Boorman p156, Marco Bottigelli p152(l), Paul Bradbury pp29, 28(tr), 67(r), brunorbs p78(tcr), Peter Cade p21, Helmut Meyer zur Capellen p11(b), cristianoalessandro p164(t), Ian Cumming p14(bl), Daisy-Daisy p80(1), Peter Dazeley p67(l), Steve Debenport p98(bc), Nick Dolding p64(br), Blasius Erlinger p109, Robert DalyThomas_EyeDesign p26(tr), DrAfter123 p88(t), JackF p112(b), Marlene Ford p68(cr), franckreporter p104(l), Stephen Frink p15(bl), Photo By Gabriel@@ p35, Alena Gamm/EyeEm p76(c), JGI/Jamie Grill p117, Bert Hardy Advertising Archive p52(cr), p52(tl), Mike Harrington p161(tl), Creativ Studio Heinemann p55(red leaf), Hinterhaus Productions p28(cr), Hero Images pp17(tl), 52(cl), 69, 85, 161(cl), Hoffmann Photography p100(tl), Mohammad Hossain/ EyeEm p158, iStockphoto pp110–111, iStockphoto/97 p113, iStockphoto/ DaniloAndjus p151(l), iStockphoto/ laurence123 p47(background), iStockphoto/ LUHUANFENG p79br), iStockphoto/ miflippo p59(br), Thinkstock Images/Monkey Business Images Ltd p145(br), iStockphoto/pilipphoto p115((tl), iStockphoto Thinkstock Images/photoncatcher pp106(b)–107(b), iStockphoto/Stevo24 p103(bl), iStockphoto Thinkstock Images/ Gary Blakeley p144(b), iStockphoto Thinkstock Images/Gabrielle Morehead p83(background), iStockphoto Thinkstock Images pp59(bl), iStockphoto Thinkstock Images/Vladimir Arndt p159, iStockphoto Thinkstock Images/fleurdrz p145(bl), iStockphoto Thinkstock Images/kasto80 p154(tl), iStockphoto/Thinkstock Images/tolokonov p105 iStockphoto Thinkstock Images/XiXinXing p151(r), Johner Images p40, George W Johnson p16(l), jgroup pp22–23(Background), thejokerstrick pp70(background, t), Chaithanya Krishna Photography p74(c), LeoPatrizi p45(t), Mads Perch p97, PictureIndia RF/Asia Images Group p114(tr), David Madison p62(br), maxchu p161(tr), Joe McBride p13, Mediaphotos p20(tr), Betsie Van der Meer p157, Anik Messier p66(r), Helmut Meyer zur Capellen pp8(t), 9, Dean Mitchel pp98, 99(b), moisseyev p80(2), Morsa Images p148(t), Kelvin Murray p78(tcl), Naga Film pp30–31(b), Richard Newstead pp92–93, Dimitri Otis p27(br), oversnap p153(l), PeopleImages p39(t), PhotoDisc pp34(background), 63(br), 58–59(background), Sergey Podvarsky/EyeEm p26(tl), Quiet Noise Creative p154(tr), Monty Rakusen p50(tr), Photo-Lyn Randle p14(br), Ingrid Rasmussen/ Design Pics p80(4), Lew Robertson pp79(cl),(t) Douglas Sacha p78(bcl), VisitBritain/ Ben Selway p16(r), shironosov p66(m), stefaniedesign p55, Cultura RM Exclusive/ BRETT STEVENS p76(t), Hulton Archive/Stringer 102(tr), SuperStock p68(br), Tetra Images p152(r), Hindustan Times/Contributor p74; **Gilaxia** 164(b); **Hemera Thinkstock Images** p43; **Hero Images** pp98(tc), 153(r); **Imagesource** pp45(b), 10–11(background), 145(tl); **iStockphoto** alexsl p59(bml), taratata p59(bmr), yang5i p147(bl); **Helsinki Region Transport** p30(tl); **Macmillan Education Limited** Paul Bricknell p145(tr); **MEC Batch 2** pp105–106(background); **PhotoDisc** pp94(br), 95(cl,b), Getty Images p147(br), Getty Images/Anthony Saint James p71(background-Tennis); REX/Shutterstock Oombrella/Bournemouth News p90(r), Bazmark Films/Warner Bros./Kobal p103(br), Flyte/Solent News p90(l), Solent News p52(bcr); **123RF/anyka** p54(background), belchonock p165, delcreations p8(b), handmadepictures p78(bl), Somchai Jongmeesuk p115(tm), Kzenon p4, Vitalii Nesterchuk p17(tr), Nadezda Murmakova p147(tl), raptorcaptor p78(br), Cathy Yeulet p50(tl); **Science Photo Library** SPUTNIK p116(t); **Shutterstock** Matveev Aleksandr p55(yellow leaf), Chesky p80(6), Alfazet Chronicles p19(H/S Avatar), Olga Danylenko p66(l), goodluz p3(b), Mila Supinskaya Glashchenko p2(t), Gorodenkoff p64(bl), maxuser p42, Yulia Mayorova p3(b), Pressmaster p50(tmr), SpeedKingz p80(5), thodonal88 p114(tm), wavebreakmedia p50(tml), Wedding Stock Photo p20(tml); **SWNS.com** pp18(t,b); **Thinkstock Images** pidjoe p52(br), Purestock p148(b), Rana Faure/Corbis/VCG p19(br), Klaus Vedfelt p144(t), vchal p81, vichie81 p100(bc), vladislavnosick p76(b), Volhah pp14(H/S Avatar), Andrew Watson p38, Westend61 pp20(tl), 52(bcl), 62(bl), 73, Dong Wenjie, Wenjie Dong p142, Oscar Wong p1, Ross Woodhal p68(tl), Kathrin Ziegler p89, zodebala p74(b), p75: **Westend61** p115(b).

Commissioned photographs in the Café Hubs by Creative Listening.

The authors and publishers are grateful for permission to reprint the following copyright material:

p8 Extract from 'Why being bilingual helps keep your brain fit' by Gaia Vince. Originally published in Mosaic Science, August 6, 2016. © The Wellcome Trust Limited 2018. Republished under a Creative Commons licence. https://mosaicscience.com/bilingual-brains/

p18 Extract from 'War veteran, 89, posts ad for job to stop him 'dying of boredom'' by Alexandra Topping. Originally published in The Guardian, November 29, 2016. Copyright © Guardian News & Media Ltd 2018. Reprinted with permission of The Guardian.

p18 Extract from 'Eager 89-year-old seeks job: café snaps him up' by Alexandra Topping. Originally published in The Guardian, December 1, 2016. Copyright © Guardian News & Media Ltd 2018. Reprinted with permission of The Guardian.

p28 Epley, N., & Schroeder, J. (2014). Mistakenly seeking solitude. Journal of Experimental Psychology: General, 143(5), 1980–1999.

Printed and bound in Argentina

2022

7